United States Public Policy

United States
Public Policy
A Geographical View

EDITED BY

JOHN W. HOUSE

Halford Mackinder Professor of Geography,
University of Oxford

CLARENDON PRESS · OXFORD
1983

Oxford University Press, Walton Street, Oxford OX2 6DP

London Glasgow New York Toronto
Delhi Bombay Calcutta Madras Karachi
Kuala Lumpur Singapore Hong Kong Tokyo
Nairobi Dar es Salaam Cape Town
Melbourne Auckland

and associated companies in
Beirut Berlin Ibadan Mexico City Nicosia

Oxford is a trade mark of Oxford University Press

Published in the United States
by Oxford University Press, New York

British Library Cataloguing in Publication Data

United States public policy.
   1. Policy sciences   2. United States—
   Politics and government—1977–
   I. House, John W.
   353'.072   HG1
   ISBN 0-19-874116-2
   ISBN 0-19-874117-0 Pbk

Library of Congress Cataloging in Publication Data
Main entry under title:
United States public policy.
   Bibliography: p.
   Includes index.
   Contents: The policy arena; Regional and area
   development; Energy problems and policies/John W.
   House—Government policy and industrial location/
   John Rees and Bernard L. Weinstein—The imprint of
   federal policy on evolving urban form/Christopher S.
   Davies—[etc.]
   1. United States—Economic policy—1981–
   2. United States—Social policy—1980–   3. Urban
   policy—United States.   4. Regional planning—Government
   policy—United States.   5. Environmental policy—United
   States.   6. Energy policy—United States.   7. Policy
   sciences.   I. House, John William.
   HC106.8.U55 1983 361.6'1'0973 83-8071
   ISBN 0-19-874116-2
   ISBN 0-19-874117-0 (pbk.)

Typeset by Oxprint Ltd, Oxford
and printed in Great Britain by
Redwood Burn Ltd, Trowbridge

Preface

In the western world during the early 1980s there seems to be a growing sense of governmental, if not yet widespread public, uncertainty about social sciences. The misgivings stem from fears of partiality, even partisanship, in research findings, to a suspicion about the relevance and utility of their contribution to the pressing needs of the environment, economy, society, or polity. The attitudes and actions of governments, in both the United States and the United Kingdom, discriminating against funding for the social sciences, is a disturbing expression of such a seeming loss of confidence in their research potentials.

Yet the most profound, intractable, if not insoluble, problems of our times are less those of science or technology than those of the human condition, of Man in his global environment. Problems of poverty, human rights, race, ideology, deprivation, rootlessness, or anomie need to be tackled by material means, but will not yield to those means alone. As moral issues they demand political concern and commitment to remedial action. It is towards helping in that task, both material and moral, that all applied social sciences, including human geography, ought logically to be targeted.

Media presentations keep the problems constantly as front-page news in a democratic society. Even those vehemently opposed to public policy intervention in the environmental, economic, or social marketplaces admit a need to be better informed on the origins of problems, their characteristics, trends, or variations in space and time, and the likely future prospects for bettering the human condition. Through techniques of survey, analysis, and synthesis the social scientist is trained to supply this need for information and advice, on issues far too dangerous to be left to unbridled politics.

Since it is through political action that policies are made and implemented, there is an urgent need for social scientists, policy-makers, and governments to understand each others' concerns more fully, to harness social science endeavors for the benefit of environment, economy, and society. At present the two communities, government and social science, seem as far apart as ever were C. P. Snow's Two Cultures. Each community possesses its own values, is based on a distinctive but different reward system, and communicates only through particular usages of language. Social scientists need to understand policy needs and the policy process better, including its inevitable political constraints, and this carries implications for training in all social science disciplines. Policy-makers need no less to appreciate the potentials as well as the limitations of social science, if a dialogue of the deaf is to be avoided.

This book offers a modest contribution to develop the dialogue between the human geographer, as one kind of social scientist, and some of those involved in policy-making and its implementation. First, for a selection of the major spatial problems of environment, economy, and society in the United States there is a critical geographical commentary on the nature and trends of change. The range and characteristics of public policies devoted to these problems are evaluated, their geographical impact and degree of effectiveness assessed. Critique stops short of prescription but there is some attempt to look ahead and also, in some cases, to set the problems within a theoretical, as well as an operational, framework.

Though written by geographers, it is hoped that the book will also appeal to non-geographical academic or lay audiences, reflecting a particular set of perspectives on some urgent problems which face policy-makers in our very critical times. To geographers in training, the relevance of applications of the discipline should be a major concern, whether to add practical purpose to their studies, or to point in the direction of possible professional careers outside the education field.

Thanks are due to all who have collaborated in this study, contributing its chapters, drafting the line-drawings, typing, or proof-reading the text. The authors are drawn from Great Britain, the US Snowbelt and Sunbelt, from the Northeast, the Southwest, and the Pacific Northwest. The editor, a British applied geographer, freely acknowledges his debt to experience gained whilst teaching in the Universities of Nebraska, Southern Illinois, and Texas. It was indeed in Austin, Texas, that the ideas behind this book came to fruition, in pursuit of Brian Berry's exhortation to geographers to 'perform in policy-relevant terms, lest we should cease to be called upon to perform at all'.

University of Oxford   J. W. HOUSE
October 1982

Contents

List of Figures

List of Tables

1. The Policy Arena

JOHN W. HOUSE
(*University of Oxford*)

1.1 INTRODUCTION

1.1.1 *The United States at the crossroads*

Overseeing the process of a post-industrial society requires an accurate grasp not only of where we are but also of where we need to be and the merits of alternative ways of getting there. (Advisory Committee on National Growth Policy Processes, 1978)

As Americans move through the 1980s, there are many different views on the present turbulent situation and considerable uncertainties on what may lie ahead, even in the short-term. On the remarkable economic growth in the US since World War II there is little room for debate. Within the 25 years to 1970 GNP more than doubled, and real income per family increased by 90 per cent. Only one-fifth of Americans were in the middle class in the 1950s, by 1970 no fewer than one of every two. A birthright to the good life seemed assured, with more mobility, leisure, consumer choice, and job opportunity. This American dream was sustained by abundant cheap energy, a rich pool of technology and innovation, pent-up demand, and triumphant marketing, with public attitudes ever favorable to growth and the pursuit of material values (Allvine and Tarpley 1977). The traumas of the poor and the deprived, the racial and ethnic minorities in city ghettos and the countryside, were increasingly evident, to be sure. The Vietnam War too scarred American society and divided the nation, but until the early 1970s there was abundant confidence that all might be set to rights through the onward march of the most powerful economy in the world. The New Frontier gave place to the Great Society and the postindustrial age was heralded with fanfares. To some the postindustrial age was an advance on the mass-consumption society; to others (Bell 1973, 13) it was only a limited change in social structure and not a transformation of the entire face of the nation. The service economy spearheaded growth, the professional and technological class formed a new elite, theoretical knowledge became the central source of innovation and policy formulation, technology bid fair to be the key to the future, and the quaternary sector of employment offered administration and control by information exchange. Even in its limited form, to enhance economic markets, planning prospered and government intervention, at all levels in economy and society, reached a high-water mark.

Then in the early 1970s there was an abrupt change. The oil crisis precipitated by supplier cartels hit the US particularly hard, the dollar system was threatened, and some sensed national economic mismanagement in addition. Slow growth became stagnation in several economic sectors, unemployment and inflation escalated. America was not alone among industrial nations struggling to recapture the lost momentum of the 1960s in order to seek balanced noninflationary growth (Greenspan 1980, 46), but her adjustments to unfavorable trends in the international marketplace were larger in scale and less controlled by government. To some this was but a temporary stumble on the path to further growth. It would be only a matter of time and good management for the inevitable sixth long-term Kondratieff upswing to set in (Rostow 1977, 88). The majority view, though for conflicting reasons, was quite otherwise. The Golden Economic Age was gone forever (Allvine and Tarpley 1977, xi), the Age of Austerity (Clavel *et al.* 1980) had arrived, and with it, according to radical thinkers (Magdoff and Sweezy 1977) capitalism had passed into a late maturity from which it would scarcely recover. Other seers and prophets (Friedman and Friedman 1980) felt that the tide was turning, but it was a tide away from government intervention in the economy and society: 'the time towards Fabian socialism or New Deal liberalism has crested, after fifty years'. Not only had the economy been overmanaged by government, it had also been mismanaged. Economic policy had been excessively dependent on the theory and tools of Keynes, combatting Depression by stimulating demand, whereas today's problems were on the supply side and many not due to economic forces at all (Hamrin 1978, 36). Easier money, lower taxes, and increased government spending would not cure 'stagflation' (economic stagnation combined with inflation). Indeed, the powers of government on economic and social issues would need to be curbed, new public policy initiatives strictly limited, and market forces liberated (Duignan and Rabushka 1980).

Others focussed quite differently on the important part Federal policy, in particular, had to play in assisting the difficult adjustments to an emerging post-industrial era (President's Commission 1980, 9). A fitting role would be to cushion the impact on people (primarily) and on places (only secondarily) of the transformations in the national settlement pattern, employment structure, and ways of life. New and better-coordinated policies would be needed, fuller partnership developed between the Federal, State, and local levels of government, to replace the incoherence of previous policies, their internal contradictions, and the traditional inertia of the past. The complexities of longer-range interrelated trends would need to be better understood: approaching zero population growth, with its implications for capital requirements and demand on resources; the increasing cost of natural resources, notably fuels, and the rise of substitution by new materials; the implications of technological maturity for resource recovery and rising unemployment; and the withering of the growth ethic (Hamrin 1978, 37).

Public opinion too had become a more powerful political force (Edwards and Sharkansky 1978, 19–60; Ladd and Lipset 1980). Consumerism and environmentalism erupted as 'social tornadoes' of the late 1960s (Allvine and Tarpley 1977, xi), constraining American business practice. For a short time and in limited areas conservation bid fair to replace the pro-growth lobby. Furthermore, policies for economic growth should no longer treat conditions within society as stable (Hamrin 1978, 38). Indeed, social concerns were expanding at a dizzying pace (Crane 1981, 1), with claims to decentralize government, safeguard minorities, solve the energy crisis, protect resources, and to get more involved in the democratic political process. Not only would a new legitimacy in government at all levels be required, there should also be an expanded social marketplace, for social goods and services, like the highly successful marketplace for their material equivalent. Within society the relations of the individual to the private and public sectors would need to be redefined and enhanced in the spirit of the spreading conservatism of the 1980s. Not only should executive, legislative, and judicial controls be reviewed, but also the powers of advertising, propaganda, lobbying, and coercion. In short, the entire field of public and private policy-making should come under closer scrutiny, at a critical time when social tensions no longer offer governments much room to maneuver or much margin for error.

After an initial consideration of the policy arena (ch. 1) the succeeding chapters are intended to contribute to this review, in certain salient fields of policy: regional and area development (ch. 2); social problems (ch. 3); the environment (ch. 4); energy (ch. 5); industry (ch. 6); and urban issues (ch. 7). Chapter 8 offers a brief summing up and considers possible social science contributions to policy-making. The perspective adopted is geographical, focussing upon space, place, and people, in their interactions over time, the influence they have had on policy-making, and the way in which in their turn they have been affected by policy outcomes. Prescriptions and recommendations on policy are less centrally-addressed. The focus is rather upon description and explanation of the causes and consequences of government activity set within a geographical framework.

1.1.2 Policies and politics

Policies are as inescapable for individual success as they are for business firms or for government at all levels. Nevertheless, because public policies are the outcome of a political process they may seem more than usually disordered, ambiguous, complex, or conflicting. Even the term 'policy' is more a generic symbol than a precise scientific concept (Nagel 1975, 61), at times fragmented in character, with uncertain boundaries and often no clearly defined beginning or end. Moreover, problems of public policy are likely to be elusive, lacking in clear-cut formulation, and with no stopping rule to tell the would-be problem-solver if and when he had a solution (Quade 1975, 8). Yet the all-pervasive nature of public policies and their cumulative intrusion into the economic and social marketplace cannot be gainsaid. Nor can their collective significance be denied, consuming no less than 40 per cent of GNP and employing 18 per cent of the US national workforce in the later 1970s (Edwards and Sharkansky 1978, 288).

In pursuit of one or more commendable, if at times conflicting, goals for efficiency, equity, environmental integrity, quality of life, or balanced growth and development, public policy-makers would defend their efforts as hoping, indeed expecting, that they could alter the human situation in some predictable and desirable direction. The potentials for public policy involvement may thus be infinitely great, but in practice are severely constrained by the political framework within which decisions on policy implementation are taken. To some there is already far too much public policy, to others too little to meet the needs of a complex urban, industrial economy at a critical stage in readjustment to the international marketplace, to an uneven space-economy, or to an unjust structure of society.

Scarce resources for public policy-making are a further important constraint, enforcing choices in the definition of priority agenda items, priorities which are likely to be defined in political terms and changeable over time for that reason. Furthermore, in the decentralized system of US policy-making the priorities may well vary also spatially, by region, State, or locality, in addition to the structural impact of changing circumstances. Quite apart from the political will to restrain or stimulate government policy-making there is a perennial risk of overvaluing what public intervention can or will achieve. Some problems of economy or society may be incapable of solution, most notably those defined in relative terms, as for example the relief of poverty, or of racial and regional inequalities. Furthermore, as conditions are improved by policy enactment, renewed expectations may outdistance the capacity of government to perform at an enhanced scale (Dye 1981, 390–2). Policies that solve problems for one group in society or a particular area of the nation may, moreover, create problems for others. This is the classic 'zero-sum' game of winners and losers, likely to be more prevalent in a slow-growth economy, though masked in times of prosperity and rising affluence. Some changes in society or economy may prove incapable of being harnessed by government, witness the limited success in influencing major entrepreneurial location decisions (ch. 6) or the great tides of migration across the face of the US (ch. 3). Then again many problems have multiple causes which cannot be effectively addressed by any single policy, however well designed and implemented, a truth to which Federal aid to the inner cities has borne eloquent witness. Finally, no political system is capable of responding to problems in an entirely rational or comprehensive manner. The interaction of executive, legislative, and judicial branches of government, political parties, pressure groups, and citizens (Quade 1975, 28) ensures checks and balances, built-in compromises, and political manipulation of any technocratic policy proposals, however elegant or wellcrafted. In the ultimate, all policies must be, and be seen to be, politically feasible, all are equally constrained in some measure by antecedents from past experience, and all must in time meet the tests of popular satisfaction and cost-effectiveness, if they are to persist unchanged or even to persist at all.

1.2 THE POLICY PROCESS

Though policy-making is thus an imperfect process, operating in an at times turbulent political arena, it is nevertheless capable of being logically and rationally analyzed. Indeed, such a task should surely be among the major objectives of any applied social science, at all stages of policy preparation, formulation, implementation, monitoring, and evaluation. Inevitably, there is a risk of seeking a rationale where none may exist, or where any existing rationale may be diffused as the result of political or interest-group pressures. Likewise, in his analysis the social scientist, equipped with sophisticated tools and methodologies, may introduce more order than the realities will bear. To relate the contribution of social science to policy-making and its analysis the first step is to look at the process of policy formulation and implementation, before considering the modest achievements of social scientists in that field to date.

Figure 1.1 illustrates diagrammatically in perhaps an oversimplified form, certainly in too rational and sequential a manner, the general course of the policy process. In considering the process it is important to distinguish what

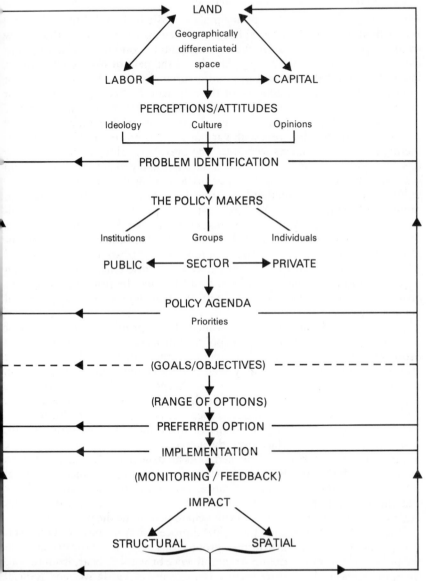

1.1   The policy process: an outline

actually happens in the real world from what ideally should or could be the case. The operational stance of the policy-maker is inevitably in contrast to that of any academic analyst, who may wish to inhabit a more perfect world and usually hopes to contribute to an improvement in the ways in which effective policies are made, without perhaps sufficiently appreciating the multitudinous political impediments along the road.

1.2.1 Stances: operational and analytical

An *operational* stance for policy-makers (Mitchell and Mitchell 1971; Edwards and Sharkansky 1978; Leach and Stewart 1982) starts with a review of the relevant transactions in the environmental, economic, social, or political marketplaces. To the geographer this is the field of man–environment, land–labor–capital relationships in differentiated space. The nature, lack, or intensity of certain transactions, or their evident ill effects (from growth or decline) upon groups of people or particular localities may or may not give rise to identifiable problems. However, a so-called problem may be viewed very differently by observers with various responsibilities, political commitments, or special interests to foster. The prevalent value system, including ideology, culture, and conventional wisdom, is likely to act as a background scanning-device, consciously or subconsciously, in the minds of those involved. Implicit rules, whether legislative, legal, or bureaucratic, are likely to mingle with remembered traditions, customary practises, and norms of politically inspired behavior in conditioning response; nor should the possibilities of non-normative or maverick behavior ever be discounted. Even the symptoms of a problem may give rise to altogether contrasting definitions, and what is seen as a problem by some may be of little consequence, or even represent an opportunity, to others. Problems may be primarily related to groups of people or to localities, both of equal interest in a geographical perspective.

Once identified, measured, and evaluated as a problem, an issue may or may not engage the interests of the political process; if not, it continues as a problem in the marketplace. Who identifies the problem and the extent of mobilized opinion about it may well condition the degree of success in reaching a place, if not a priority, on the policy-making agenda. Some problems are identified by those within the political system, in the executive, legislative, or judicial arms of government, at Federal, State, or local levels. Others come to light through the work of governmental agencies or officials, whilst yet others may surface from the activities of political parties, pressure or interest groups, citizens or the media. As an issue of public importance, an identified problem must be ranked on the policy agenda, for which the tests of scarce means (time, personnel, finance, resources), political preference or expediency, and the extent of effective pressure from concerned parties (against the efforts of opponents) will help to determine the priorities.

Once on the policy agenda the political process may or may not take over. The policy-makers are institutions, groups, or key individuals, primarily in the public sector, but with important influence brought to bear, from time to time, by peers in the private sector. The executive, legislative, and judicial arms of government at all levels, the political parties (constituents, representatives, caucuses), and public servants (Departments, agencies, officials) are the prime initiators of policy. Elite groups, in both the public and private sector, interest or pressure groups (Wilson 1981), lobbies, the media, and organized citizens are the supporting cast, intent on occasion to overthrow the intentions of the principals. Within the government apparatus and its interaction with those concerned outside there may well be advocacy, bargaining, compromise, competition, use of power, conflict or cooperation in searching for progress, equilibrium, or restraint in policy-making. From which, if the matter is to proceed further, there must be a net operational outcome of policy proposals, either people-related or place-related, or both.

The policy process which may then commence is unlikely to follow the logic, the sequence, the clarity, or the end-product of the ideal scheme shown in Figure 1.1. This is a truth which analysts would do well to bear in mind when policies are criticized with that valuable attribute, hindsight. Many, indeed in some fields most, policies are incremental, strongly identified with past experience and practice, rather than striking out in an entirely new direction. Occasionally, however, crises require fresh policies, or shifts in public opinion may require changed policies. International events, such as the oil crisis of the early 1970s, imposed their own constraints, whilst Presidents, and even bureaucrats, have not been unknown to chart entirely different courses from those of the past. Other policies may be populist, to identify with the tides of opinion, though these have rarely been decisive; yet others are intuitive, or in qualitative terms judgmental. It is, however, to the rational process of policy-making that the analyst can contribute most effectively within the stages seen on Figure 1.1. The formulation of goals or objectives is a logical prelude to any policy. Given the complicated, uncertain definition of many problems, allied with the general will of politicians to diffuse issues in order to preserve freedom to maneuver and the need to placate diverse interested parties or places, it is not surprising that goals are either usually not formulated or, if they are then in the most general, unexceptionable terms. All of which necessarily makes the next stages of the process more problematical.

The most characteristic objectives of policy pursue popular acceptability, efficiency in some form, equity (preferably to all, certainly safeguarding minorities), environmental integrity, or, fashionably nowadays, the quality of life. Efficiency and equity are not infrequently at cross-purposes, quality of life may defy a universally acceptable definition, and environmental integrity always risks being sacrificed. Trade-offs of principle, or obscuring of the issues, are not unusual as a result, while the identity of beneficiaries, whether people or places, is not uncommonly left vague, or purposely expanded to include virtually all, thus nullifying the policy in the interests of political expediency.

The range of options for fulfilling the objectives comes next on the list. There may well be many different kinds of solution to a problem and with each a diversity of choices. Since few, if any, problems admit of a single solution, the options are likely to be grouped into packages. In many cases it is the constraints on action which limit the range and nature of the available options. Scarce time is a constraint on its own account, the legacy from the past another limiting factor, whilst availability of resources and political feasibility will figure somewhere in the equation of choice. The range of options is characteristically first formulated from within the relevant part of the government bureaucracy. At this stage outside interests may begin to voice their preferences or concerns, usually through political representatives, but also by mobilization through the media, pressure groups, or public opinion.

The testing of alternative courses of action and the choice of a preferred option should logically follow in any rational decision-taking process. In practice few alternatives may be considered and in the end all may be rejected, ending the policy initiative. Furthermore, the testing of options is likely to be rudimentary, falling far short of any sophisticated cost-benefit calculation. Desirably, too, there should be an evaluation of the potential consequences of enacting each option, in terms of the impact on particular groups, localities, or the economic structure. Conflicts among objectives are likely to surface and questions of equity in the outcome of policy brought face to face with considerations of efficiency. Once the preferred course of action is determined, policy passes into the often tortuous legislative stage. Here political considerations, rational and otherwise, may greatly modify, or even arbitrarily cancel, the intended policy enactment. If approved, the policy passes through for executive implementation. This will be by policy directives, to be carried out or monitored by agencies and officials, leading possibly to further modifications enforced by the realities and diversities of the marketplace.

The impact and progress of policy enactment should, logically, be carefully monitored and feedback evaluated, with the intention of recommending policy adjustments to realize the goals and objectives more expeditiously and effectively. This final stage of policy consideration is rarely carried to a successful conclusion, since the feedback from those affected may well be politically highly charged. Furthermore, politicians may feel that in measuring the effects of policy they could lose in some measure that precious asset, freedom to maneuver. In any case, it is virtually impossible to conduct a value-free assessment of the extent to which a policy has or has not fulfilled its original, often none-too-clear, even ambivalent, purposes in pursuit of a problem which may or may not have been correctly identified. Yet any policy inevitably has structural and spatial impacts (Figure 1.1) and these add in their turn to the further differentiation of habitat, economy, and society in geographical space.

From beginning to end in policy-making there are thus constraints, uncertainties, manipulations, and distortions, perhaps an inevitable outcome of the political process in a complex, mature economy and society. Nevertheless, it would be wrong to assume that policy-making is altogether wayward, or that 'political' grounds invariably overrule the findings of skilled and objective analysts in decision-taking at the highest level (Lindblom 1965, 11). Just as it would be equally false not to admit that citizens and political leaders in the US are very apt to mistrust policy analysis as an academic science, and, even more, the analysts themselves.

At its simplest, an *analytical* stance to policy generates and presents information, in as objective and intellectually rigorous a manner as possible, to improve the basis for policy-makers and decision-takers to exercise their judgment. It may be argued that, given the complexity of policy-making, analytical inputs may be expected to have at best a very marginal effect, but even small marginal adjustments to policy can have a considerable impact on the outcomes (Quade 1975, 242).

In the US, social scientists have hitherto had limited involvement with policy-makers (Horowitz 1971), but there has been increasing interest in the potential of their contribution (OECD 1980). For the relationship to become more effective, there must be a fuller understanding between social scientists and those concerned with policy-making, if a 'dialogue of the deaf' is to be avoided. Presently, the two 'communities' are differently structured, in terms of values, rewards, and the language of communication. What is needed is a better rapprochement between the scientific skills and policy interests of the social scientist and the political skills and scientific interests of the policy-maker (OECD 1980, 8). This is no simple task. On the one hand social science research, as at present organized, may or may not be of value, either directly or marginally, to the policy-maker, even when the topic or problem under consideration is clearly of public interest. Academics may seek to answer questions the real world is not asking, and may equally prefer to pursue problems for their greater theoretical rather than their practical significance. The detached researcher is also more likely to be a prisoner to some fashionable disciplinary paradigm, constrained therein by the limitations of 'hard' knowledge, the product of quantitative analysis presented in scientific language (Caplan 1980, 184). In policy-making there is no less need for 'soft' knowledge, more qualitative in character, more subtle and difficult to define in its contribution to the policy process. Though the academic analyst may be limited because his focus is upon scholarship rather than action-orientated, there are faults too on the policy-makers' side. Social scientists cannot succeed when the political requirements of policy-makers lead them to define problems in ways which exclude possible social science contributions (OECD 1980, 8). The question may be asked in a manner which discounts the research possibilities of relevant social science disciplines. In US regional policy,

once the question became what to do about pockets of economic difficulty social scientists were virtually unable to bring professional literature and expertise to bear on the problem. The difficulties of problem areas were directly linked to general relations of the national economy, whilst regional planning focusses on *inter-relationships* between segments of the national economy. The political and legislative debate focussed on local symptoms of national relationships. Therefore the literature on regional growth or the spatial arrangements of the economy did not have an impact on the formulation or implementation of policy, though it occasionally affected the rhetoric. (Zysman 1980, 138)

Since policy-making concerns politics, social science inputs are subject, like any other, to manipulation, even distortion. 'The knowledge that gets used is that which either supports contemporary political positions or appears to have insignificant political applications' (OECD 1980, 23). The academic research contributor, too, may not be wholly detached, and his scientific input devoid of advocacy, partisanship, or some value-bias, implicit or otherwise. Rarely does he or she deal solely with an individual bureaucratic decision-taker; equally rarely does the research input find its way unmodified to the point of decision. Lipsky's *paprika* role all too often comes into play 'spicing [political] activities with social science findings and wisdom, an ingredient contributing color but little substance to the preparations' (Lipsky 1971). Alternatively, in potentially controversial policy fields the contending groups are likely to maintain close links with different sets of outside advisers, for intellectual justification in support of the desired political stance.

Then too there is often a third-party influence. Because social scientists alone are impotent to promote the use of their findings, conditions must be right for their consideration. Though social scientists may underline the seriousness of a problem, the general political climate must be sensitive to a potential crisis. If there is no great sense of urgency in government, then the dialogue with social scientists may well diminish (OECD 1980, 20). It is often third parties who generate the great concerns to be forced upon the attentions of the political arena: A Rachel Carson with her *Silent Spring* or a Ralph Nader in defense of the consumer.

On a much more modest scale are the research and analytical contributions to each stage of the policy process. Policy-related research differs from normal disciplinary research, whether conducted by academics or from within the political system. In the first place it is deliberately oriented to action and needs to produce findings of value in an operational sense. The problem is defined by the issue facing the decision-taker and not by the requirements or nature of a discipline. The findings are required within a given time-scale and the research must proceed at a speed dictated by the urgency of decision-taking, not that of the disinterested pursuit of truth. There is inevitably a disciplined concern for the future, for scenarios or predictions, an unfamiliar perspective for many social scientists. Such applied work may rank lower in the intellectual estimation of peers and may not be subject to the usual self-correcting critique from within the discipline. Finally, in the US, policy-related research needs 'to contend with differing and changing goals of competing interest groups in a society that values democratic pluralism as an end in itself' (Berry 1978, 205). The analyst may find himself working either inside or outside the political system, wherever and whenever a contribution might change the course of influence or power in the policy process. Outside as well as inside the political system the same battery of analytical skills may be needed, but outside 'they are put to another use, the identification, creation and realization of opportunities' (Berry 1978, 208), an important catalyst or corrective in any democratic structure.

Table 1.1 shows the context of academic contributions to the policy process. Again the process is not as clear-cut as it may appear. Social science inputs merge with others and their impact may be difficult to evaluate beyond the factual analysis of material presented. Knowledge as such is never likely to dictate policy and may be of only marginal instrumental importance (Caplan 1980, 184). The development of policy may indeed often be incremental, without any clear step-by-step evolution, to which the social scientist might contribute. 'Problems of air pollution, urban renewal, vocational rehabilita-

TABLE 1.1   *Contributors to policy-making*

	← POLICY →					
	problem identification/ evaluation	formulation	options	approval	implemen tation	impact evaluation/ critique
Third parties						
writers/advocates	*					*
pressure/interest groups	*					*
media	*					*
Academic						
pure research	*					
applied research	*					*
commissioned research	*					*
consultants/experts	*	*				
In-house bureaucratic						
researchers—'think tank'	*	*				*
—agency	*	*				*
—departmental	*	*				
administrators } committees		*	*			
decision-takers } committees		*	*			
Political process						
executive } all levels of government				*		
legislative }				*	*	
judicial				*	*	
politicians	*		*			
committees			*			
Policy implementation						
agencies					*	
other government bodies					*	

tion, or criminal justice involve investigating a system which has grown without conscious design, the goals of which may be obscure and conflicting ... in a situation in which authority may be diffuse, overlapping, and have different sets of goals' (Quade 1975, 157). Likewise, the elaborate quantitative analyses of social scientists may founder on the nature of politics and the environment for public decision-taking in the fields of welfare, urban development, or education (Quade 1975, 181).

It is rather 'the coincidence of public concerns and disciplinary skills and concepts which largely determines the influence which any profession can have on policy' (Coppock and Sewell 1976, 259). The impact may be primary, if, say, social science findings bear directly on a policy issue, result in the adoption of a new policy, or are of value in rethinking an entire issue; subsidiary, if the issues are political, regulatory or legal but with social science implications; or merely technical, if only routine testing is involved (Caplan 1980, 185). To improve the relevance and significance of social science inputs to policy the social scientist may become much more familiar with the policy-making process, sharpen his analytical findings, work more fully with 'in-house' researchers and third parties, as well as, which would be novel, with the decision-takers and policy-makers. 'Why should there not be fuller relations between social scientists and Congressmen, as the latter had with physical scientists on ABMs or on Soviet military evaluations?' (OECD 1980, 21.)

Though evidence on the social science contributions to policy-making in the USA is presently meager and partial (OECD 1980) it illustrates the potentials as well as demonstrating what some may see as limited achievements to date. Of 575 instances of the use of social science research reported by Federal government agencies (Caplan 1980, 171) the following were fields covered (percentages): organization and management 11; education 8; health 8; crime 7; communications 7; public opinion management 7; welfare 7; military 6; employment 6; others 6; civil rights 5; environment 4; housing 4; transport 4; international relations 3; research methods 3; consumer affairs 2; and recreation 2. The absence of energy issues is striking, though the Federal energy office came into being only in 1973. Of these instances 51 per cent were commissioned 'in house' by the using agency, 35 were extramural (academic-related) to the using agency, 8 were commissioned by another government agency, and 6 per cent by a nongovernment agency. Excluding economics, and seemingly without any reference to geography, the disciplines involved were (Caplan 1980, 176): sociology 20 per cent; psychology 15; interdisciplinary 14; social psychology 11; behavioral studies 11; organization development and management 10; political science 7; education and training 6; and anthropology 6. The research methodologies used were: program evaluation 20 per cent; survey 18; demography 13; social statistics 10; field experience 9; cost-benefit analysis 8; organization 6; labor experience 4; participant observation 4; clinical cases 4; psychological testing 3; games and simulation 1. Forty per cent of all uses were deemed of primary importance for policy, particularly by HEW, HUD, Labor, and Justice; 40 per cent were seen as of subsidiary value, including Transportation, NASA, AEC, and the regulatory agencies; the remaining 20 per cent of uses were regarded as technical, including psychological testing or selection procedures (Caplan 1980, 185). Thirteen per cent of instances concerned issues of nationwide significance, 50 per cent related to segments of the population, and 37 per cent were administrative questions on government personnel. In order of value in terms of the impact on policy were ranked: sensitization of policy-makers to social needs; the evaluation of ongoing programs; the structuring of alternative policies; implementation of programs; justification of policy decisions; and the choice among policy alternatives (Caplan 1980, 187). The most valid and reliable contributions made by social sciences, on a 10-point scale (high means less reliable) ranked the contributory disciplines as follows: economics 5.0; anthropology 5.6; history 5.7; psychology 6.4; sociology 6.6; political science 7.0; and psychiatry 7.6 (Caplan 1980, 195). Where should geography stand, given these potentials?

1.2.2 A geographical perspective

There is a fundamental difference between a decision-taking framework in which locational factors are considered along with others and a framework in which geographical balance is the dominant factor in policy and program choice. (White House Conference 1978)

Geography is nowhere directly mentioned in the 1980 OECD report on the utilization of the social sciences in policy-making in the USA. Yet of the extensive and varied policy agenda items, research methodologies used, and impacts on policy mentioned above there are few which do not have profound spatial origins, implications, interactions, and potential impacts. If geographers are to further a contribution to policy-making it is important to outline what they may effectively offer. If they do not contribute, the outlook for the discipline may be pessimistic—'if we geographers do not perform in policy-relevant terms, we will cease to be called upon to perform at all' (Berry 1970, 22). As is well known, there is a tremendous, wide, and expanding geographical literature on the environment, society, and economy of the US. There has been correspondingly a much lesser, though a growing, preoccupation with the application of geographical research to the problems of the times (Frazier 1982). Applied geography is rarely taught or practised on the campuses and geographers have made limited inroads into the public service, either as specialists or as generalists.

There are of course illustrious exceptions to the generalization on the low esteem of applied geography. The widespread and substantive work of Brian Berry (e.g. 1973, 1977, 1980) in city and regional planning; Kevin Cox on location and public problems (1979) and the geography of the city; David Harvey (1972) or Richard Morrill (1965) on urban social problems; David Smith (1973) on social well-being; or Gilbert White (1974) on environmental hazards are but a few indicators of the range and quality of achievement. Most recently (e.g. Agnew 1980) geographers have turned their attention to process research in policy-making, concerned, for example, with innovation diffusion, technology transfer, and public-policy impacts. That these achievements have not been more widely emulated may have as much to do with public attitudes to resource management or urban and regional planning as with the nature of geography as a taught discipline or the preferences and predilections among its research-workers.

Geographers in the US are working in Federal, State, and local governments, though rarely with the title of geographer. A geographical training is widely recognized as useful (Taaffe 1970), but when compared with economists, few geographers hold key policy-positions (Anderson 1979, 265). Several past presidents of the AAAG have held important posts in the Federal service and, in recent years, senior bureaucratic positions have been occupied by geographers in: specialized branches of the National Science Foundation, the Library of Congress, the CIA, US Geological Survey, Department of State, Defense Intelligence Agency, or the National Oceanic and Atmospheric Administration. In the Federal service the employment base for geographers has indeed broadened, with geographers engaged in the following activities: water policy formulations, land-use inventory, monitoring of environmental quality, urban renewal, health-care planning, international relations, energy development, transportation planning, the Law of the Sea, study of geologic hazards, remote sensing, information systems, computer cartography, and preparation of the National Atlas (Anderson 1979, 266).

A great diversity of State agencies employ geographers (Stutz 1980), notably departments of transportation, natural resource or environmental regulation, land-use planning, agriculture, and forestry. The writing of Environmental Impact Statements has offered particular opportunities to geographers, trained in comprehensive understanding of the environment. Another group of State agencies employing geographers covers social and welfare issues, health care, redevelopment of urban areas, and crime control. Local government is less likely to employ geographers as professionals, though offices concerned with land-use planning, community-services management, zoning, and environmental regulations may well be the most relevant fields for involvement (Anderson 1979, 269).

If geographers are to enlarge their professional bridgehead in the US government service at all levels, they must be rigorously trained, particularly in 'remote sensing, cartography, computer-science aspects of spatial analysis, field observation and survey techniques, statistical analysis, and the mastering of a foreign language' (Anderson 1979, 269). Furthermore, there must then be a more effective dialogue with the public service and, in particular, a 'more comprehensive understanding of the various missions' (and agencies), which will enable geographers to match their career goals more realistically with the requirements of public decision-takers and policy-makers.

In some contrast, applied geography has been developed more fully in Britain and Canada (House 1973; Coppock and Sewell 1976), in teaching, research, professional employment in resource management, urban and regional planning, and in advice to government. The hallmarks of an applied geography, whether taught or practised are: a disciplined and rigorous approach to problems; a deliberate concern for the future, as more than an extrapolation from the past; a commitment to action rather than only the disinterested pursuit of truth; an openness to inter- and multi-disciplinary work, and to a fuller understanding of the processes and needs of policy-making and public decision-taking. Both generalist and specialist geographical skills and expertise are required. In this sense, applied geography has developed in harmony with the general advance of the discipline and the concurrent shifts in the requirements of planners. In earlier days, to the 1950s, the traditional methods of resource inventory and evaluation, regional identification and interpretation, and the use of maps as a prime analytical tool were paramount. Spatial inequalities were a focus of research interest and the management of resources, in both declining and growing regions, was a major preoccupation.

During the past three decades geography, in common with other social science disciplines, has changed structurally and dramatically, passing through positivist (quantitative-theoretical) and behavioral phases to the new humanism and even the radical stance now fashionable among some practitioners. In the course of this evolution there has been some convergence in theories, methodologies, and techniques with other social sciences, and a sustained period of fertilization of human geography by transplants of ideas and methods from cognate disciplines. At the same time the systematic branches of geography have developed and deepened, becoming more specialized and with an increasing range of interdisciplinary contacts. The 'hard' knowledge content of the subject (Caplan 1980, 184) has thus been well established, with quantitative analyses and techniques today probably far ahead of what decision-takers or policy-makers either immediately require or can effectively incorporate and use (House 1973, 299).

The more generalist field of geography, the 'soft' knowledge required in policy-making, must in no way be underestimated. The technocratic skills which all specialists contribute must be complemented by disciplined ability to see the relationships between the elements of a complex problem. The regional, ecological, or geometrical (space-analytical) frameworks are means to an end of synthesis, within a wider context of man–environment relationships. Neglect of this generalist skill will ultimately deny the geographer a birthright in his contribution to the highest levels of policy-making, whether in government service, commerce, or the company boardroom. At these levels, such 'soft' knowledge is the modal type of social science used by policy-makers (Caplan 1980, 184), subtle and difficult in its interpretation and application.

Nevertheless, the verdict on achievements by geographers outside the US in the fields of decision-taking and policy-making must be double-edged, and this should be clearly understood if their utility in the US context is to be considered. For example, during the years 1945–70 geographers had virtually an unchallenged monopoly as social scientists contributing to British planning and resource management. By the mid-1960s no fewer than 40 per cent of entrants to the planning profession there had first degrees in geography. From this high-water mark there has been some recession. Regional economists have since claimed their entitlement whilst sociologists too have come more fully into planning. Moreover, though the utility of geographical findings has proven remarkably widespread at the level of problem identification and evaluation, there has been limited penetration to the greater depth of policy formulation. Individual geographers have acted in a policy role in regional and other planning organizations and 'in-house' researchers have participated through to the implementation, monitoring, and evaluation of the feedback from particular regional policies and plans.

Limiting to all geographical involvement, whether in the US or in Britain, is the poor governmental appreciation hitherto of the significance of spatial variables in the determination, enactment, and impact of public policies. Though geographers may characteristically err in overvaluing space and place, the undervaluing of these variable ingredients of social and economic reality is even more pronounced and carries its own consequences. During the past two decades the rising voice of regionalism in most mature western economies has added political expediency to the forces for considering spatial variables more understandingly. It is a central purpose of the chapters that follow to set out a geographical commentary and critique of the major US government policies in which space and place have had a significant, if not a determining, part to play.

1.3 PROBLEMS AND POLICIES

In the continental-scale, complex, metropolitan-industrial United States, with its vast differentiated terrain and variegated, highly developed resource base there is, not surprisingly, a uniquely wide spectrum of problems. Not only is the range of problems of the environment, society, economy, and polity extremely varied, but the sensitivity and articulateness of people to those problems, in groups or at particular places, is no less diverse. The roll call of problems and the priority each is accorded shifts from time to time, but some are enduring, and even on occasion regarded as insoluble. The economic health of the nation sets a framework for what can be done, political culture determines what it is appropriate to attempt by public action. For 25 years after World War II the momentum of economic growth in the US permitted many-sided attacks on the majority of perceived problems, though it led to not a few on its own account. The slowdown of the 1970s put a less favorable complexion on the 'post-industrial' society, constraining problem-solving at a time when problems were escalating. Thus was ushered in the politically sensitive 'zero-sum' game to replace that of the qualified public distribution of an ever-increasing largesse.

Few problems exist in isolation, most are interrelated in a complex way. Priorities for the policy agenda often relate to the degree of a sense of crisis, or to the net political pressures for change. The response of policy-makers, even to a perceived crisis, may well be to contain the situation at the macroeconomic level, without any specifically relevant policy measure. General fiscal or monetary policies may adjust the overall condition of the economy, contain unemployment, or influence the level of prices or interest rates. Transfer payments to individuals or families in need, or development assistance to aid States, local government, business, or individuals may supplement such prime macroeconomic policy. Though such an overall approach to the orderly management of natural and human resources is an important framework for public action, macroeconomic policy, plus short-term use of transfer payments to people or places, has not succeeded in the past in alleviating the spectrum of localized economic distress (President's Commn. 1980, 89). At issue is the extent to which, given the geographical differentiation and the political plurality of the United States, any major nationwide problem can or should be tackled by an overarching national policy, federally administered. The general political consensus in the 1980s appears to be negative, on both counts (Table 1.2).

A further general issue, perhaps of particular interest to geographers, is the extent to which policies, however and by whomsoever administered, should be place-related or primarily people-orientated. On this there is some ambivalence. On the one hand, there is a widespread feeling that nationwide policies are inappropriate if unmodified by local circumstance, and that, if administered, such policies are generally ineffective. On the other, there is nevertheless a general tendency to lay the blame on government, and to seek compensation or redress, for the imbalances and differences in growth prospects which are, in reality, mainly the result of market forces. Since World War II there have been shifts in the balance between place-related and people-related policies. During the 1960s social sensitivity was paramount. During the 1970s, though still to a limited extent, spatial sensitivity in Federal policy grew in importance, perhaps because aiding places is both more straightforward and seen to have more political payoffs than aiding people who have problems, whilst the economic and social multiplier effects may be expected to be greater (President's Commn. 1980, 98). It would, of course, be presumptuous and indicative of narrow disciplinary imperialism to assume that spatial policies are to be given priority over structural, and, that being so, the geographer has any preferential mandate to practise in the policy arena. Nevertheless, the geographical differentiation of space, place, and people is a logical starting-point from which to review environmental social, economic, or political problems, and in many public policies this reality has been inadequately recognized or catered for. Likewise, the impact of policies, whether direct or indirect, intended or inadvertent, may equally with advantage be differentiated geographically. Spatial monitoring of this impact is one of the important feedbacks for policy-makers to which geographers may also usefully contribute.

Such a contribution must be more than simply being wise after the event. It must add to the understanding of environmental, social, and economic realities and their problems, from which policies emerge, as well as offering in critique some potential improvements for future policy-making.

A mix among policy and program results of frequent failures and serendipitous successes may have less to do with depleted public coffers than with depleted imagination, less to do with a deficiency of will and good intentions than with a distinct policy orientation which is not acknowledged. That traditional orientation is characterized by the tilting of a relatively inadequate federal policy presence against a sweep of developments whose potency and scope are underestimated, whose substance is not fully understood, and whose significance is too quickly appreciated in negative terms. (President's Commn. 1980, 84)

This quotation then defines the task and underlines the challenge. Though spatial tilts are embedded in several Federal policies, in the spirit of the 1980s (op. cit. 100) some would seek to weed them out, in order to discriminate deliberately in favor of deprived groups rather than deprived places. Yet even overtly aspatial policies have implications for place and for geographical differentiation, and thus the challenge remains universal and inescapable.

In the following chapters only a selection of the many problems and policies of the contemporary US is addressed. The bundle of policy problems was chosen to embrace the major policy domains in which spatial considerations have had a relevant part to play. Within each chapter the treatment is indicative rather than exhaustive, focussing on a geographical critique of some of the salient policy problems and relevant legislation in each field. Interrelatedness of problems and yet the dissociated nature of many policies shows through strongly. Regional and area development (ch. 2) offers a varied spatial synthesis of all systematic problems and their particular mixes over the national space. The contrast of region and area with the alternative metropolitan framework (ch. 7) is inescapable, whilst inter- and intra-governmental relations (units, powers, functions) within the political system

TABLE 1.2 *Planning Assistance Programs, 1962–1982*

1962	1972	1977	1982
URBAN			
1. Urban Planning Assistance (Section 701)	1. Comprehensive Planning Assistance (Section 701)	1. Comprehensive Planning Assistance (Section 701)	1. Fy 82-0 Program cut after 1981
2. Community Renewal Program	2. Neighborhood Development Program	2. Community Development Grant	2. Community Development Block Grant expanded by: Entitlement Grants; Small Cities Programs
3. Advances for Public Works Planning	3. Model Cities		
	4. Advances for Public Works Planning		
TRANSPORT			
4. Highways	5. Highways	3. Highways	3. Highways
	6. Urban Mass Transportation	4. Urban Mass Transportation	4. Urban Mass Transportation
	7. Airport Systems	5. Airport Systems	5. Airport Systems (uncertain)
REGIONAL/AREA DEVELOPMENT			
	8. Area Economic Development	6. Area Economic Development	6. Area Economic Development expanded by: Business development assistance;
	9. Appalachian Development	7. Appalachian Development	7. Appalachian Development
	10. Rural Development	8. Rural Development	8. Rural Development
		9. Multistate Economic Development	9. Multistate Economic Development

TABLE 1.2 *(Continued)*

1962	1972	1977	1982
ENVIRONMENT			
		10. Coastal Zone Management	10. Coastal Zone Management (cut) replaced by Coastal Plains regulation of economic development
	11. Air Quality	11. Air Quality	11. Air Quality
	12. Water Quality	12. Water Quality	12. Water Quality (cut by 50 per cent)
	13. Solid Waste	13. Solid Waste	13. Solid Waste
HEALTH/WELFARE			
	14. Comprehensive Health	14. Health Systems	14. Health Systems
		15. Aging	15. Aging (uncertain funding)
		16. Social Services	16. Social Services
		17. Manpower	17. Manpower
CITIZEN RIGHTS			
	15. Community Action	18. Community Action	18. Community Action (cut)
	16. Law Enforcement	19. Law Enforcement	19. Law Enforcement

Sources: ACIR (1964) *Impact of Federal Urban Development Programs on Local Government Organization and Planning* (Washington, DC: USGPO); ACIR (1973) *Regional Decision Making: New Strategies for Substate Districts* (Washington, DC: USGPO); ACIR (1977) *Regionalism Revisited: Recent Areawide and Local Responses* (Washington, DC: USGPO); EXECUTIVE OFFICE OF THE PRESIDENT, Office of Management and Budget (1982) *1981 Catalog of Federal Domestic Assistance* (Washington, DC: USGPO); WISE, H.F. (1977) *Federal Planning Assistance Programs*, US, HUD, Contract No. H-4088.

are the driving force behind all policy-making. Social problems and policies are the most polygamous (ch. 3), interlinking closely with regional and area change (ch. 2), urbanization (ch. 7), industrialization (ch. 6), energy issues (ch. 5), and the environmental questions (ch. 4). Environmental problems (ch. 4) in a mature metropolitan-industrial society, traditionally intent on maximizing the returns from the land and the subsoil, are inevitably in potential conflict with demands for more energy (ch. 5), greater industrialization of the periphery (ch. 6), revival of the inner city (ch. 7), or the reestablishment of fast national economic growth. Energy priorities (ch. 5) relate to the restructured world marketplace and decisions on the role of domestic fuels in meeting future energy demands, but they have inescapable environmental, transportation, employment, and economic-growth policy implications. Even in a so-called postindustrial age industrialization (ch. 6) underlies many regional problems and critically affects future prospects (ch. 2), apart from its bearing on energy (ch. 5) and environmental (ch. 4) issues. Urban problems and policies (ch. 6) lie at the heart of the debate on national efficiency versus social equity. They concern too some of the most dramatic recent changes: metropolitan and, more recently, nonmetropolitan growth (chs. 2 and 3) as the crucial elements in population flows and regional shifts of balance; or the inner-city problem rivalling urban renewal as the most dramatic of all contemporary social-justice questions. Indeed, in the interrelationships between the distinctive policy-problem bundles may be detected the wider trade-offs in policy goals and objectives, involving efficiency, equity, environmental integrity, and, that most elusive of all realizations, an enhanced quality of life.

1.3.1   Policies covered

Regional and area development (ch. 2) is the most directly concerned with the spatial variables in decision-taking and policy-making. Such spatially designed policies have been rarer in the USA than in Europe, though both continents have had some major regional economic adjustment problems in common. The case for and against a deliberate regional dimension in policy needs to be made on theoretical and practical, as well as political, grounds. A taxonomy of regional problems is an essential groundwork to understanding the diversities and complexity of the regional system and the significance of major present-day structural and spatial trends of change within it. Regional politics and the administrative network of power, functions, and units at Federal, State, and local levels underlie the realities and interaction of power and influence which in their turn breed policies. The regional-policy spectrum has shown a remarkable diversity since the New Deal years of the 1930s, but without ever aiming at the strength of legislation or the plurality of institutions which have fertilized regional policy over several decades in Western Europe. Apart from the diverse Federal and federally sponsored agencies and commissions, the States and local government have become more involved in recent times, with major issues of congestion, political tension, and the need to reassign intergovernmental functions as a result.

Social problems and policies (ch. 3) sets the stage, through the settling and differentiation of the national territory, for an assessment of recent trends in migration and population change. During the process a richly variegated national system of sociocultural interaction has been established. Public and private policies have both had nationwide impacts. Some issues, such as welfare needs, inaccessibility, the demand for recreation and improved environmental conditions encouraged government intervention. The government also played other roles, first as an entrepreneur in its own right, with spatial impacts, in the creation, for example, of military bases, atomic energy research, and space exploration. Secondly, civil and human rights legislation had profound effects on people and places. Changes in the private sector also had nationwide impacts, through the influence of the media or the transformation of business, professional, and union organizations. The growth of State and local government also has had sizeable effects upon the infrastructure and services regionally available.

The spectrum of policies applicable to growing areas is to be differentiated from that relating to decline or stagnation. Planning and control are seen as the key to well-being in growing areas, whilst even in declining or stagnant areas problems cannot be solved entirely at local levels or by private efforts.

With few exceptions (Smith 1973), geographers have rarely treated the nationwide aspects of social deprivation or well-being. Most studies of the key questions of poverty and welfare, crime, health, education, or civil rights have been undertaken by other social scientists (Dye 1981; Duignan and Rabushka 1980).

Environmental policy questions (ch. 4) are no less controversial. In a continent with abundant natural resources, thought by many until recently to be virtually unlimited, the market exchange system has failed overall to respect the environment in the public interest (Kneese 1980). Materials and energy concentrated in the natural setting have been dispersed and misused with adverse effects throughout the habitat. Though preservationist movements early struggled to constrain exploiters, and even among exploiters there was a utilitarian self-interest view to regulate the use of a finite set of resources (Fitzsimmons 1980) the issue of environmental protection for long lay dormant in the public mind or among would-be legislators. Pollution of all kinds was more deadly in the 1940s and 1950s than in the 'environmental decade' of the 1970s, but it was not a visible issue around which public opinion could coalesce (ACIR 1981, 3). For 20 years before 1969 the Federal government gradually assumed the little-used environmental responsibilities of States and localities. Incrementalism and a pluralist approach typified the interaction of Congressional entrepreneurs and a wide variety of environmental groups. Water and air pollution, the control of water resources and land use, solid waste disposal, noise abatement, and chemical pollution were all addressed in piecemeal legislation, often amounting merely to small adjustments to existing rules.

The National Environmental Policy Act (1969) created the Council on Environmental Quality (CEQ). In the following year two further environmental agencies, the Environmental Protection Agency (EPA) and the National Oceanic and Atmospheric Administration (NOAA) were set up. An almost unheard-of proliferation of Federal regulations took place, in response to mass public demands which preceded policy formulation. Since the range of legislation passed lay 'admittedly beyond the immediate capacities to apply' (ACIR 1981, 41) there was a regulatory quagmire, with stalemate over policy directives and paralysis of government action characterizing many problems (Dye 1981, 208). The many environmental achievements of the decade could not disguise the growing conflicts with energy producers, manufacturers, inner-city revitalizers and, indeed, also State and local interests. Under the Reagan presidency economic development and energy security will more clearly rank before environmental protection. In an unstable economy lacking in adequate domestic energy resources, environmental policy risks being more than overshadowed. With a fuller understanding of the economic costs of environmental protection, it is no longer a case of clean air and clean water at any price. The stage is indeed set for a return to the gradualism, incrementalism, and pluralism of earlier, less heady days in environmental legislation.

The *energy* crises of the 1970s have produced perhaps the most dramatic, certainly the most confusing set of policy problems (ch. 5): disagreement or ignorance on the facts; uncertainty on the potential results of many suggested policies; an awareness of painful choices between short- and long-term policies; and, above all, no clear consensus on national energy goals (Schurr *et al.* 1979, 1). The magnitude of the problem is not in question, in a nation consuming one-third of the world's energy, one-half of that from oil, of which one-half is domestically produced. What is to be done finds a division between the diminishing-return pessimists, painfully aware of a finite wasting set of fuel and power assets, and the technology optimists, confident that more economic use, substitution, and discoveries will get economic growth back on course (Goodwin 1981, 682). That something needs to be done, some more considered policy formulated, is ever more apparent. Not without reason at the time, President Carter in 1977 spoke of the energy crisis as 'the moral equivalent of war', others of 'a threat to the American political system' (Dye 1981, 184).

Energy policies of a kind had existed for 50 years or more, but inadequate to cover a shift from abundant energy with a concern for falling prices to a desperate shortage with sharply rising prices for consumers (Goodwin 1981, xvii). There were powerful political forces in the energy marketplace: the southwestern and western oil, natural gas and coal producers, and the northeastern and midwestern consumers of energy. As energy allocations became a 'zero-sum' game agreements among producers, consumers, bureaucrats, legislators, and environmentalists became more difficult to achieve and public policies were eroded. Regulation, subsidies, penalties, and a measure of public ownership had all been tried, but not without distortion of market forces. Policies were generally protectionist and Federal regulation of oil and natural gas pricing had prevented prices rising to true marginal replacement costs, encouraged waste, and discouraged exploration and production (Dye 1981, 186). Imports were not reduced, the nation did not become more self-sufficient, and other sources of energy did not receive adequate public support. Regulation of electric power supplies by State commissions had hampered development and improvement, whilst Federal environmental and nuclear safety regulations acted as further constraints. Moreover energy issues were bound up with other policy questions: States' rights to oil and natural gas in the offshore tidelands; 'pork-barrel' costs in the siting of utility plants; regional tensions over natural gas; international trade questions on oil; and the ideology of public intervention in energy markets (Goodwin 1981, 679).

Looking ahead, energy pricing and the degree of dependence of the US on foreign energy supplies are the overarching issues (Schurr *et al.* 1979, 46). Policy needs to ensure an adequate energy supply, with a proper use of domestic resources, to permit adequate future economic growth. Domestic energy prices need to rise to international levels, environmental questions will need to be taken into account, and conservation promoted even though it be no more than the collateral against which more energy-adjustment time is borrowed' (Prast 1981, vii).

In a mature metropolitan-industrial society government policies on *manufacturing* and *industrial location* (ch. 6) may be critically significant for the economic health of localities, regions, and the nation. Great structural and locational changes have taken place in American industry in the past two decades (Rees 1979), even during a time of decreasing growth in the US economy. In the post-industrial era the service sector has grown differentially faster than manufacturing, and there has been a major interregional reallocation of industrial resources. The South and West (the Sunbelt) have grown faster than the traditional industrial heartland of the Northeastern Manufacturing Belt (the Snowbelt), whilst nonmetropolitan areas have grown at an unprecedented rate.

The *degree* to which government policies have been the catalyst in such changes is disputed. Though the media and the popular mind may believe that such policies have been formative, academic evidence (Rees 1979) concludes otherwise. An examination of four areas of direct policy: taxation, economic development assistance, defense procurement, and environmental protection, concludes that these policies have had very little direct impact on industrial location trends in the US. The implications of indirect policies, on transportation or energy for example, are more difficult to evaluate, and should be a priority research task.

Compared with many countries in Western Europe there has been a distinct lack of deliberate industrial location policy in the US. The view is advanced (Rees 1979, 97) that this absence has not been detrimental to the economic health of the various regions, given the extent of convergence in regional prosperity that has taken place without such a policy.

Urban policy problems (ch. 7) are an inescapable consequence of the dramatic shifts in US economy, society, and the metropolitan system since World War II (Burns and Van Ness 1981). Such problems are so deep-seated and widespread as to constitute the well-known 'urban crisis', a crisis born of poverty, poor housing, racial discrimination, crime, delinquency, social deprivation, poor health, overcrowding, joblessness, ignorance, the flight of whites to the suburbs, and the fiscal imbalance of city finances (Dye 1981, 11). These may be symptoms of national disorders, but their impact is on the city, particularly on the inner city (Kirwan 1980), where economic and fiscal distress of the community is compounded by the social distress of its residents. Problems exist at all scales, in the metropolis, nonmetropolitan

centers, the inner city, and the small town alike (Johnston 1982). Some take
the view (President's Commn. 1980, 99) that there are 'no national urban
problems, only an endless variety of local ones', and thus a nationwide urban
policy would be as misconceived as it would be ineffective (Kasarda 1980).
    Individual cities need to identify their own brand of problems and act
accordingly (Rand Corpn. 1977). Others (Wingo 1972) see an urgent need
for a comprehensive, overarching urban strategy to make the subnational
economy perform better. Yet others focus on the most virulent problems in
the inner city (Berry 1980, 28), prophesying that only crisis measures of
massive scale will suffice to tackle the issues effectively.
    In no other policy field have there been so many public interventions, such
legislation, such a plethora of agencies and programs, stretching back over 50
years. In none can the outcome have been so incoherent and fraught with
contradictions, with such a range of unintended, unwanted consequences. To
some this proves the failure of governmental, or at least of Federal intervention in the city (President's Commn. 1980); to others it indicates the need
for a more coherent, coordinated set of policies through partnership of all
levels of government, Federal, State, metropolitan, and local.
    The impact of Federal policies, direct and indirect, has been variously
evaluated. Although Federal policies were not the root cause of urban decentralization, they have overwhelmingly supported it (Rand Corpn. 1977,
40). Overall, Federal policies have been remarkably pervasive, but usually
with no prior knowledge of the likely geographical outcome of their implementation. Their general thrust has been 'targetted on the physical aspects of
urban life, though the urban crisis is one of human conflict' (Dye 1981, 224),
whilst the objectives and implementation of a mass (500) of uncoordinated
programs has all too often been at cross-purposes, and no meaningful priorities have been set. The delivery system of Federal policies to local authorities
has been questioned, grants to metro-regions or to the States being preferred
by some. Though the Federal budget is on balance 'pro-city', with 36 per cent
of Federal outlays going to cities of more than 50,000 (31 per cent of the
urban population), the effects of indirect policies must also be taken into
account (Clark 1980, 83). The total impact of government intervention is
still open to question. The government may (Clark 1980, 82) or may not
(President's Commn. 1980, 77) be the dominant force in urban change, but
its relationship to the market trends in the city, to technological change, rising
affluence, the changing size or composition of household, or competing
claims to a better quality of life remains an important field for social science
enquiry. The major research fields outlined by HUD as recently as 1980
(Lentz 1980) indicate some immediate priorities: urban economic development and public finance; neighborhood revitalization; site selection; the
elderly and handicapped; housing cost and alternative housing cost mechanisms. To these and other aspects of urban public policy geographers (Adams
1979) have their contribution to make.
    As a counterpart to urban-policy problems those affecting *rural America*
should be touched on, though there is no full chapter treatment. In the 30
years from 1940 a massive urbanized migration took place, millions left rural
employment, and the US farm population fell from 30 millions in 1940 to

only 9 millions in 1970. During the 1970s, however, a reverse trend of migrants to nonmetro areas was clearly apparent, but it was selective in its geographical impact (Lamb 1975). Many small towns and remoter rural areas have continued to suffer traditional problems, whereas along highway corridors and in the hinterland of metropolitan areas diffusion of jobs and residence has usually conferred benefits (US Dept. Agric. 1977).

Rural poverty continues to be endemic and widespread (Fitchen 1981), about the same in volume in nonmetropolitan areas as in the central cities, but concentrated in the South (60 per cent), and affecting minority groups most severely. The problems of the smaller communities in remote marginal farming areas on poor-quality land are the most acute, throughout the South, in the Appalachians, or in parts of the arid West. Most rural areas, even in prosperous farmlands, suffer from inadequate job opportunity off the land, underemployment, low wages, limited and dispersed social provision (since not all Americans are freely mobile over long distances), and problems of keeping the most able young people in an often unprogressive rural social environment.

Public policy faces particularly difficult problems in delivery to small, dispersed populations scattered over vast areas. Furthermore, rural development policy-making has been as fragmented as the rural people are dispersed. Three objectives are proposed for a rural development strategy (USDA 1977, 8): to expand economic opportunity for farm and nonfarm rural people through increased productivity and improved access to better jobs and higher income; to provide access to a minimum acceptable level of essential public facilities and social services; and to strengthen public and private planning and policy management. The Rural Development Act (1972) directed the Secretary for Agriculture to provide leadership and coordination in rural development. In this effort, an enhanced role for State and local government is an essential ingredient, whilst, as in all American public life, there is an imperative need for closer interagency cooperation.

Fortunately, not all the problems of rural communities are those of adjustment to decline. Population and economic growth in some areas have permitted a new division of labor. New 'growth' industries have moved into smaller towns, though often in search of cheap, nonunionized female labor. Rural areas have proved to be attractive to returning natives, but also to a growing number of folk moving on retirement. The amenities of land, water, forest, and climate have led to selective tourist and recreational developments. Such tendencies for economic growth, even locally for 'boom' conditions, bring different kinds of problems in their train, but at least they permit that flexibility in adjustment that rising revenues and an improved tax base confer.

These then are the policy-problem bundles to be considered in succeeding chapters. Each is complex, spatially differentiated, and inescapably intertwined with others. All have provoked some public-policy response, direct or indirect, for good or ill. None is without its geographical implications for the health, harmony, and progress of society and economy in the US national space.

1.4 THE POLITICAL SETTING

1.4.1 Political culture

Any appraisal of public policy must take account of the necessary content and context of political culture, and the nature of institutions through which policies are enacted and delivered. In the cosmopolitan, continental US there is, of course, great variation in the blends and shades of political culture, in both structural as well as in spatial terms (ch. 2). Furthermore, attitudes and the conventional political wisdom change through time. Yet certain enduring traits have characterized US political culture, and as such form a background to all policies at all times. The social commitments to individualism, egalitarianism, and achievement go far back in American history (Ladd and Lipset 1980, 49), however illusory or impractical such values have often proved to be in the marketplace. The belief in equality has persisted in the face of enormous inequalities, in individual liberty, though this continues to be constrained for many citizens, and in the liberal tradition, though this has eclipsed neither racism nor reaction in the past (Lees 1975, 100). Given the strong commitment to achievement, market forces are widely seen as the best basis for efficient resource allocation. Individuals, groups, and localities competed for economic advantage, in the firm belief that this led to the greater general good. Until the recent past this ethos was expressed through the unquestioned right of man to conquer nature, and a limitless faith was for long reposed in the efficacy of science and technology (Cumberland 1971) and in the triumph at the same time of both the work and the growth ethic. During the past two decades such attitudes have increasingly, though variably, been tempered by concern for equity, or for social justice, whether for minorities or for places.

Yet traditional political culture has colored the outlook on government and its role in public life. Though Jefferson's dictum of two centuries ago still has its advocates, 'That government governs best which governs least', there would today be sizeable, if not majority, support for a more positive government role in sustaining and promoting the values of a democratic pluralist society. With the increasing complexity of modern life, government functions have inevitably proliferated, but in the US under an ever more watchful eye (Berry 1980, 1). The functions of government are to be limited to the regulation and facilitation of orderly economic and social life, by means of occasional social engineering, and only when and where it is clear that the marketplace is not operating freely or fairly or is producing results which are contrary to any reasonable definition of the public interest.

At this point the two great streams in American political thought divide: the liberals and the conservatives. Left or liberal forces have given priority to the breaking down of inequalities and waging war on injustices, on 'racism', 'sexism', and 'poverty'. Conservative philosophy, on the other hand, has stressed the values of achievement, with a commitment to free enterprise, individualistic or competitive values, and an opposition to government power (Ladd and Lipset 1980, 49). Through the twentieth century there has been fluctuating sway between liberal and conservative forces in American political life, reflected in the nature and quality of the policy spectrum at any period of time. Discounting the war years, which colored the 1940s, there has been a loosely construed alternation: in the 1920s, the 1950s (eight years of Eisenhower's presidency), and the 1970s (the New Federalism of Richard Nixon and the Ford presidency) the Republican Party was dominant, responding to conservative sentiments for self-help, enrichment, and the flowering of the work and growth ethics. In the 1930s and the 1960s the Democrats for the most part held political sway and more liberal attitudes prevailed. In the 1930s Roosevelt's New Deal legislation combatted Depression by classical Keynesian methods, committing the Federal government to substantial intervention in national economic and social problems. John Kennedy and Lyndon Johnson presided over most of the 1960s, with the New Frontier and the Great Society programs to attack poverty and want, accompanied by mass movements on human rights and minority injustices (Ladd and Lipset 1980, 50). On present evidence the 1980s bid fair to continue in, even to enhance, the conservative traditions of the 1970s (Archer 1982).

1.4.2 The governmental system

Political culture transmits policy through the constitutional structure of government, in a Federal system, including 50 States and 78,000 multifarious local government entities. Opinions on the system are divided: that 'there are too many governments for effective policy-making' (Grant 1979, 262); that 'it appears that virtually all governments are involved in virtually all functions' and 'to put the matter bluntly, government in the US is chaotic' (Grodzins 1963, 1); or 'the system is fundamentally disorganized, over-regulated, and a twisted mass of good ideas and missed opportunities' (Snelling 1980, 168). On the more positive side—'the system provides for most of the competing interests in the US, and is amenable to political influence on every plane' (Elazar 1972, 213).

Federalism concerns a coordinate division of powers among the different tiers of the US government. Under the evolving Constitution the Federal government and the States have equal status and distinct areas of authority: local government is subordinate to its State. The Federal government has powers: enumerated, as in defense, currency, the Post Office, and the naturalization of citizens; inherent, in foreign relations and wage-bargaining; implied, in 'the making of all necessary and proper laws', as in interstate commerce; and concurrent, with the States, in taxation; but it is denied the power to tax exports or to favor ports in any one State. The States are denied the right to make treaties or to levy import or export duties. All nondesignated powers are reserved and residual and may be apportioned to different levels of the system (Grant 1979, 245–6).

In such a diffused and decentralized system of government it would be erroneous to think of a pyramidal structure, 'with a neat hierarchical chain of command, in which policy is made at the top and executed lower down with less and less discretion the lower one goes' (Elazar 1972, 223). A more realistic assessment needs to balance centripetal or centralizing tendencies of power at the Federal level, with centrifugal, decentralizing flows of greater authority to the States. This balance continues to shift through time, as it always has.

'The question of the relation of the States to the Federal government is the cardinal question of our constitutional system. It cannot be settled by the opinion of any one generation, because it is a question of growth, and every successive stage of our political and economic development gives it a new aspect, makes it a new question'. (President Woodrow Wilson)

In any case, political power is not a fixed, inviolate quantity, but is capable of expansion so that 'the growth of federal power is not necessarily at the expense of the authority of States or localities' (President Johnson).

Nevertheless, the policy-making role of the Federal government has escalated in volume and complexity, with progressive impact upon the States. In 1913, when the 16th Amendment first permitted the Federal government to levy taxes on income, Federal spending was one-third of total State and local government outlays; by 1973–4 it had become two-thirds. From the 1930s Federal categorical grants-in-aid grew steadily, with strings attached and subject to central authorization and supervision. Conservatives opposed such growth as unnecessarily limiting to States' rights and leading often to schemes which were unwanted, an overall process to be justified only in times of severe national economic depression or crisis. Liberals, on the other hand, saw in the grants the basis of a new creative federalism, as an alternative to direct Federal control. Backward States would be stimulated to improve standards of living and of government. Thereby would come redistributive social justice and greater equalization of wealth and opportunity (Grant 1979, 250–1).

The tension between States and the Federal government, whether creative or otherwise, has continued to wax and wane. At issue is the complexion of federalism, as either a dual mandate with division of responsibilities, competition, subject to Supreme Court arbitration, and an increasing transfer from the center to the States, or as a cooperative partnership, with increased sharing of functions and a programmed interdependence. As the US economy has developed, with complex free flows of people, goods, capital, and services across the national space, the partnership concept has gained adherents. States should not be subordinate or have their functions preempted. The Federal government should 'supplement, stimulate and assist' States, who should have spending discretion in administering jointly financed projects (Grant 1979, 253). In short, 'the geographic distribution of national growth should not be determined through a centralized policy process. Complete geographic balance as a Federal goal could not be objectively constructed or effectively carried out. If overall economic health is sustained, inter-regional adjustments are possible' (White House Conf. 1978, 8). Thus may the roles of States, metropolitan cities, and localities be vindicated.

During the 1960s, under President Johnson in particular, Federal initiatives were widespread, State accountability was increased, and there were many direct Federal financial aid policy links to the cities and localities. In the Nixon years the New Federalism led to more decentralization of spending powers to the States, on ideological grounds certainly, but also in order that the worsening problems of the cities and society could be tackled more effectively at a more local level. The principle of General Revenue Sharing

(Acts of 1972 and 1976) was developed and block grants were introduced, on a limited scale, to permit discretionary spending by States in the defined areas of communications, manpower, law enforcement, social services, or health provision (Grant 1979, 256). By the late 1970s there was some return to the earlier status quo in the Federal–States balance. Congress reverted to categorical grants, 'trussed up' with conditions and the State share of revenue sharing died (Snelling 1980, 169). Such grants-in-aid during 1979 totalled 83 billion dollars, 17 per cent of the entire US budget. With 4 of every 10 State and local employees said to be 'federals in disguise, marching to Washington guidelines' (Snelling 1980, 168), some saw the States once more as but subnational units in a centralizing Federal system. This trend has been set in reverse under the Reagan administration.

The role of the Federal government, the States, and localities in regional and area development is discussed in chapter 2. It remains here to point up, in general terms, a further difficult and growing issue in government and administration, the significance and status of metropolitan areas in the Federal system (Martin 1965). In 1969 metropolitan areas (SMSAs) generated 80 per cent of national income and housed nearly 75 per cent of the population (Burns and Van Ness 1981, 169). Metropolitan boundaries transgressed both State as well as local government jurisdictions, in itself a serious problem when political power and financing resides in a jealously guarded three-tier Federal system (Florestano and Marando 1981). 'Cities are not mentioned in the US Constitution and their powers continued to be determined by the States, yet it is in these great municipalities that the future success or failure of federalism is likely to be judged' (Grant 1979, 262). The larger cities are virtually civil societies in their own right, with a strong political voice in Washington. Some have 'home-rule' charters conferring a limited exercise of powers not prohibited by the State Constitution. Though there had been some direct Federal aid to city programs under the New Deal the major metropolitan problems date from the end of World War II (ch. 7). During the 1960s, the proliferation of Federal aid programs to the cities, to counter poverty, racial discrimination, and slum housing, or to improve education, strengthened the direct links. Increasingly, Federal bureaucrats came to prefer these direct links, bypassing 'the obstructionist attitude of some State governments and breaking through the established power structure to reach excluded groups' (Elazar 1972, 81). Though it might be asked 'if a Federal structure based on 18th century territorial and functional divisions can respond constructively and deal adequately with the *malaise* of the American cities' (Grant 1979), the truth remains that, even after all direct Federal interventions have been taken into account, the traditional role of the State in the city continues to be highly significant.

Given the coordinate division of powers in a three-tier Federal system and the constitutional checks and balances built into that system, the policy delivery process in the US is necessarily diffuse and complex (Griffith 1976). Any major shift in policy at Federal level must have widespread support, involving the President, members of the White House staff, and the Cabinet, influential Congressmen and their committees, and the senior bureaucrats in the relevant agency. Policy situations tend to be highly fluid, with strong tendencies to dispersiveness in decision-taking, and a marked degree of responsiveness to the electorate. No important center of power can persist for long without convincing its constituents that its proposals are justified. Within Congress, the creation of coalitions within and between the two major parties attempts to mobilize support from the greatest percentage of the most varied range of groups. Pressures on Congressmen from the outside seek to mandate representatives to act for special interests, whilst bureaucrats act directly on policy through agency pressure or a support role to Congressional committees. Localism is a strong political force in the policy process, both from the geographically sited pressure groups and also in the 'pork-barrel' character of claims by particular States or localities for Federal funds. To Congressmen the avowed support of local interests is 'a matter of political survival' (Griffith 1976, 115). The Senate tends to have an overrepresentation of the smaller agriculturally based States, biassed towards agricultural support and the problems of the rural area or the small town. The House of Representatives too has a flavor of strong representation of the suburbs as well as of the smaller towns and the countryside. There is thus some mismatch between the nature of the major national problems and the special interests of many Senators and Congressmen. This needs to be borne well in mind, as a constraining political reality, in the discussion of policy problems which follows. Perhaps the most realistic image is of a flexible political system, in which the search for equilibrium and consensus is a major policy objective. Political partnership in the Federal structure emphasizes the need for a balance between Federal initiatives, guidelines, or directives and the desirability of enhancing and giving fuller expression to the growing vitality of States, metropolitan governments, and localities. 'In a volatile political society there are many built-in restraints against too rapid change' (Griffith 1976, 188). Pluralism is as endemic in US government as it is in American geography, economy, and society, an ever-present constraint on the policymaker and posing problems to any analyst seeking a rational path through the political labyrinth.

References

ADAMS, A. (1979) 'A geographical basis for urban public policy', *Prof. Geogr.* 31 2, 135–45.
ADVISORY CO. INTERGOVTAL. RELNS. (1981) *Protecting the environment: politics, pollution and Federal policy*, A-83 (Washington, DC).
AGNEW, J.A. (ed.) (1980) 'Innovation research and public policy', *Syracuse Geogr. Ser.* 5.
ALLVINE, F. C. and TARPLEY, F. A. (1977) *The new state of the economy* (Cambridge, Mass.: Winthrop).
ANDERSON, J. R. (1979) 'Geographers in government' *Prof. Geogr.* 31 3, 265–70.
ARCHER, J. C. (1982) 'Some geographical aspects of the American Presidential election of 1980', *Pol. Geogr. Q.* 1 2, 123–36.
BELL, D. (1973) *The coming of post-industrial society* (New York: Basic Books).
BERRY B. J. L. (1970) 'The geography of the US in the year 2000'. *Trans. Inst. Brit. Geogr.* 51 21–53.

—— (1973) *Growth centers in the American urban system 1960–70* (Cambridge, Mass.: Ballinger).

—— (1977) *Urbanization and counterurbanization* (Beverly Hills, Cal.: Sage).

—— (1978) 'Notes on an expedition to Planland', in BURCHELL, R. W. and STERNLIEB, G. (eds.) *Planning theory in the 1980s* (New Brunswick, NJ: Center for Urb. Pol. Res.), 201–8.

—— (1980) 'Inner city futures: an American dilemma revisited', *Trans. Inst. Brit. Geogr.* NS 5 2, 174–84.

BURNS L. S. and VAN NESS K. (1981) 'The decline of the metropolitan economy', *Urb. Stud.* 18 2, 169–80.

CAPLAN, N. (1980) 'The use of social science knowledge in political decisions at national level', ch. 5 in OECD *The utilisation of the social sciences in policy-making in the USA* (Paris: OECD), 161–209.

CLARK, G. L. (1980) 'Urban impact analysis: a new tool for monitoring the geographical effects of Federal policies', *Prof. Geogr.* 32 1, 82–5.

CLAVEL, P., FORESTER, J., and GOLDSMITH W. W. (1980) *Urban and regional planning in an age of austerity* (New York: Pergamon).

COPPOCK, J. T. and SEWELL, W. R. D. (eds.) (1976) *Spatial dimensions in public policy* (Oxford: Pergamon).

COX K. R. (1979) *Location and public problems* (Oxford: Basil Blackwell).

CRANE H. D. (1981) *The new social market place: notes on effecting social change in America's third century* (Norwood, NJ: Ablex).

CUMBERLAND, J. H. (1971) *Regional development: Experiences and prospects in the USA* (Paris and The Hague: Mouton).

DUIGNAN, P. and RABUSHKA, A. (eds.) (1980) *The United States in the 1980s* (Stanford, Cal.: Hoover Instn.), 'Introduction', xix–xxxix.

DYE, T. R. (1981) *Understanding public policy* (Englewood Cliffs, NJ: Prentice-Hall).

EDWARDS, G. C. III and SHARKANSKY, I. (1978) *The policy predicament* (San Francisco, Cal.: Freeman).

ELAZAR, D. J. (1972) *American federalism: a view from the States* (New York: Crowell).

FITCHEN, J. M. (1981) *Poverty in rural America, a case study* (Boulder, Col.: Westview).

FITZSIMMONS, A. K. (1980) 'Environmental quality as a theme in Federal legislation', *Geogrl. Rev.* 70 3, 314–27.

FLORESTANO, P. S. and MARANDO, V. L. (1981) *The States and the metropolis* (New York: Dekker).

FRAZIER, J. W. (ed.) (1982) *Applied Geography: selected perspectives* (Englewood Cliffs, NJ: Prentice-Hall)

FRIEDMAN, M. and FRIEDMAN, R. (1980) 'The tide is turning', in DUIGNAN and RABUSHKA, I (I), 3–30.

GOODWIN, C. D. (ed.) (1981) *Energy policy in perspective: Today's problems, yesterday's solutions* (Washington, DC: Brookings Instn.).

GRANT, A. R. (1979) *The American political process* (London: Heinemann).

GREENSPAN, A. (1980) 'Economic policy', in DUIGNAN and RABUSHKA, I (II), 31–48.

GRIFFITH, E. S. (1976) *The American system of government* (London: Methuen).

GRODZINS, M. (1963) 'Centralization and decentralization in the American federal system' in R. G. GOLDWIN (ed.) *Nation of States: Essays on the American Federal system* (Chicago, Ill.: Rand McNally), 1–23.

HAMRIN, R. D. (1978) 'Ten major long-run forces shaping growth prospects', *White House Conference on Balanced National Growth and Economic Development* (Washington, DC).

HARVEY, D. (1972) 'Society, the city and the space-economy of urbanism', Assn. Am. Geogr. Commission on College Geogr., Res. Pap. 18 (Washington, DC).

HOROWITZ, I. L. (1971) The use and abuse of social science; behavioural science and national policy-making (New Brunswick, NJ: Transaction Books).

HOUSE, J. W. (1973) 'Geographers, decision-takers and policy-makers', ch. 8 in M. D. I. CHISHOLM and H. B. RODGERS (eds.) Studies in human geography (London: Heinemann), 272–305.

JOHNSTON, R. J. (1982) The American urban system: a geographical perspective (London: Longman).

KASARDA, J. D. (1980) 'The implications of contemporary distribution trends for national urban policy', Soc. Sci. Q. 61 373–400.

KIRWAN, R. M. (1980) The inner city in the United States (London: SSRC).

KNEESE, A. V. (1980) 'Environmental policy', in DUIGNAN and RABUSHKA, I (X), 253–84.

LADD, E. C. and LIPSET, S. M. (1980) 'Public opinion and public policy' in DUIGNAN and RABUSHKA, I (III), 49–84.

LAMB, R. (1957) 'Metropolitan impacts on rural America', Univ. Chicago, Dept. Geogr., Res. Pap. 162.

LEACH, S. and STEWART, J. (1982) Approaches in public policy (London: Allen & Unwin).

LEES, J. D. (1975) The political system of the United States (London: Faber & Faber).

LENTZ, P. (1980) 'High priority research areas in HUD's Office of policy development and research', Prof. Geogr. 322, 205–8.

LINDBLOM, C. (1965) The policy-making process (New York: Macmillan).

LIPSKY, M. (1971) 'Social scientists and the Riot Commission', Ann. Am. Acad. Pol. and Soc. Sci. 394 72–83.

MAGDOFF, H. and SWEEZY, P. M. (1977) The end of prosperity: the American economy in the 1970s (New York: Monthly Review Press).

MARTIN, R. C. (1965) The cities and the federal system (New York: Atherton).

MITCHELL, J. M. and MITCHELL, W. C. (1971) Policy-making and human welfare (Chicago, Ill.: Rand McNally).

MORRILL, R. L. (1965) 'The negro ghetto: problems and alternatives', Geogrl. Rev. 55, 339–61.

NAGEL, S. S. (1975) Policy studies in America and elsewhere (Lexington, Mass.: D. C. Heath).

OECD (1980) The utilisation of the social sciences in policy making in the USA (Paris: OECD).

PRAST, W. G. (1981) Securing US energy supplies: the private sector as an instrument of public policy (Lexington, Mass.: D. C. Heath).

PRESIDENT'S COMMISSION (1980) Urban America in the Eighties (Washington, DC: USGPO).

QUADE E.S. (1975) Analysis for public decisions (New York: American Elsevier).

REES, J. (1979) 'Government policy and industrial location in the US', SW Center for Econ. and Community Devel. (Dallas, Tx.: Univ. Texas).

ROSTOW, W. W. (1977) 'Regional change in the Fifth Kondratieff upswing', Ch. 3 in PERRY, D. C. and WATKINS, A. J. (eds.) The rise of the Sunbelt cities (Beverly Hills, Cal.: Sage).

SCHURR, S. H., DARMSTADTER, J., PERRY, H., RAMSAY, W. and RUSSELL, M. (1979) Energy in America's future: The choices before us (Baltimore, Md.: Johns Hopkins Univ. Press).

SMITH, D. M. (1973) The geography of social well-being in the US (New York: McGraw-Hill).

SNELLING, R.A. (1980) 'American federalism in the Eighties', *State Govt.*, 168–70.
STUTZ, F. P. (1980) 'Applied geographic research for State and local government: problems and prospects', *Prof. Geogr.* **32** 4, 393–9.
TAAFE, E. J. (ed.) (1970) 'Geography' *The behavioral and social sciences survey* (Englewood Cliffs, NJ.: Prentice-Hall).
US DEPT. AGRIC. (1977) *Rural America, poverty and progress, Rural development policy issues*, mimeographed.
WHITE, G. F. (ed.) (1974) *Natural Hazards* (Oxford: Clarendon Press).
WHITE HOUSE CONF. ON BALANCED NATIONAL GROWTH AND ECONOMIC DEVELOPMENT (1978) *The States' views* (Washington, DC).
WILSON, G. K. (1981) *Interest groups in the United States* (Oxford: Clarendon Press).
WINGO, L. (1975) 'Issues in a national urban development strategy in the United States', *Urb. Stud.* **9** 1, 3–28.
ZYSMAN, J. (1980) 'Research, politics and policy: regional planning in America', ch. 4 in OECD *The utilisation of the social sciences in policy-making in the USA* (Paris: OECD), 121–58.

2. Regional and Area Development

JOHN W. HOUSE

(*University of Oxford*)

Between one country and another, one province and another and even one locality and another there will always exist a certain inequality in the conditions of life. (Friedrich ENGELS 1875)

Each region of the country cannot possibly become a duplicate in microcosm of the national economy. Diversity, migration and change are all elements of growth and development. (Comm. on Science and Technology 1969)

It is a paradox that in the richest country in the world, even at peaks of prosperity, there is everywhere a deep concern about *local* economic conditions. (PERLOFF and DODDS 1963, 11)

Geographic distribution cannot be the unifying theme of all national policies. What seems possible is to improve the level of awareness by the public and policy-makers of the geographic consequences of actions which are not primarily geographic in intent. (FRIEDMANN and ALONSO 1975, 648)

2.1 SPATIAL DEVELOPMENT AS A POLICY ISSUE

The distinctiveness of the United States lies in its continent-wide Federal system, geographically highly differentiated, under largely free-market conditions within a single currency area. Though increasingly beset by economic and social problems common in other mature urban industrial countries, it has really never had a sustained, comprehensive, integrated, or effective regional or area-based set of policies. Differential spatial economic growth has been regarded as inescapable in an open, highly dynamic economy, even though the outcome may have been tragic at times for certain places and some human groups. Like economic specialization according to comparative advantage, or the basis of any division of labor, spatial diversity is seen by many as an integral element of the economic system, subject to continual change and, for that reason, in need of constant adjustments. Space is then but a negotiating variable in national policy, the region a subsystem element in the national network. Regions interact within the system through exchange and competition, but the focus is rather upon the interrelationship of parts than upon the discrete characteristics of place or space.

Any consideration of regional or area-based policies must start from the central theme of inequality or, as some prefer it, imbalance. Such potential adversities exist, and have always existed, at differing spatial scale levels and in many contrasting problem mixes. That such problems exist is generally accepted, that government intervention may be necessary is more controversial and that, if undertaken, it should be deliberately spatial, regional, or area-based even more problematical. Even though the pursuit of balance in the overall US national economy has recently been a fashionable policy objective (White House Conf. 1978), it is a concept like Victorian virtue to which many subscribe but few hope, or intend to, achieve.

The nature and policy implications of inequalities are explored throughout the succeeding chapters and are also touched upon in spatial terms in section 2.3. Geographers have traditionally used territorial social indicators (Morrill and Wohlenberg 1971; Smith 1973) to highlight 'the extent to which groups of people, defined by area of residence', have different experiences in 'levels of well-being or quality of individual life'. Territorial indicators show that 'levels of income, environmental quality, health, education, social disorganization, alienation and participation' (Smith 1973, 140) are varied between States, among or within cities, and in contrasting urban areas with the countryside. Policy initiatives to combat revealed problems have generally been fragmentary, pragmatic, partial, and short-term, with some priority, in western market economies, given to indicators of low per capita income, levels of unemployment, or rate of net migration loss (Brown and Burrows 1977, 18). Which adverse indicators merit public-policy intervention, when, for how long, and in what manner, continues to be debated, in terms of conflicting objectives in the pursuit of efficiency, equity, environmental integrity, or the quality of life. Are the inequalities inevitable, are they likely to be permanent, do disparities always imply distress for some, does it matter, and, if so, to whom? According to the answers, so will policies be formulated or the opportunity ignored.

To some, but for different reasons, the inequalities are inevitable. Diversity, migration and change are all elements of growth and development, according to liberal capitalist views. Yet to others (Holland 1976) the underlying cause of regional imbalance is capitalism itself, and in that sense it reflects the permanent economic and social malaise endemic in that system. To others (Vanhove and Klaassen 1980, 1), regional disequilibrium (from a theoretical point of view) was thought to be only a temporary problem in a general automatic system of economic equilibrium. A counterview to this (Clavel *et al.* 1980, 23) wryly observed that, if so, the 'mechanisms for equilibrium are rusty, and need both oil and applied force'. Whilst some (Holland 1976) saw inequalities primarily in spatial terms, others (Brown 1972, 83, 232) emphasized that 'the benefits of interregional equalization are small in comparison with the benefits of complete equalization of incomes [at the personal level]'.

What underlies spatial differences and what do spatial theories contribute to an understanding of the basic processes at work? Geographically differentiated space arises from a varied natural and human resource endowment, the interpretation and exploitation of position, the course of development (particularly in the context of economic and technological progress), and the stage reached in that process. The resultant economic structure contains seeds of both growth and decline, whilst capital and labor alike remain imperfectly mobile. Institutional factors and the nature of culture, both social and political, add further to the differentiation of space and place, whilst the course of change and adjustment is also inevitably conditioned by externalities. These include both the export-oriented links to varied and changeable external markets and the reverse impact of external market forces, for good and ill, upon the indigenous economy.

2.1.1 Theory and models

Theoretical models from the social sciences imperfectly explain the spatial development process and are inconclusive on the desirability or efficacy of deliberate spatial intervention policies. Classical economic equilibrium theory largely ignored spatial considerations, whilst the neo-classical model of price determination assumed an efficient self-adjusting, self-balancing system under market forces in an idealized capitalist society. Yet 'even an elementary understanding of the spatial aspects of the price system reveals a systematic tendency towards the non-optimal distribution of resources' (Stilwell 1972, 6). With an added spatial dimension, equilibrium theory postulates a set of regions, each with buyers and sellers, commodities and a price structure, operating within an interregional exchange network. The relationships between the supply and demand variables, as in the general theory, are predicted on the assumption of regional balance, consistent with rational behavior and market rules. These theoretical options have been strongly attacked (Holland 1976, 20) on grounds of lack of realism in the face of the economic, social, and political marketplaces, to say nothing of the imperatives of social or spatial justice.

Theory on spatial organization is similarly not without its critics or short-comings. Such theory attempts to connect micro- with macroeconomic per-spectives, the theory of the firm or the household, partial or sectoral equi-librium, to those concerned with the general locational equilibrium (Hermansen 1971) resulting from growth in differentiated space. Theory of spatial organiztion is, however, poorly developed, stronger in descriptive terms in the analysis of patterns, less so on positive analysis of why the patterns are as they are. Normative theory, on what ought to be, as in an optimum pattern of settlement or the location of economic activity, is still weaker and excessively dependent on static ahistorical models such as those of Christaller, Lösch, or Von Thünen. Control theory which should be the basis for policy-making and evaluation, on goals and how they are to be reached, thus rests upon rather insecure foundations.

The processes by which growth takes place, or stability is achieved, are more amply chronicled, though their linkage with changes in space are more speculative. In microeconomic theory (Stilwell 1972) entrepreneurs act as satisficers, content to achieve minimum rather than maximum objectives, whilst in the operational decisions taken by householders there is even less likelihood of optimality being attempted. No boundaries in space are postu-lated for the operations of either firms or households, but in macroeconomics a regional framework must be assumed. Models for the evaluation of macro-economic growth or stability may be formulated in broad conceptual terms, for sequential phases of development (Friedmann, Rostow) or more precisely calibrated. Resource-allocation models, for interregional or intraregional development analysis, evaluate growth towards an equilibrium position. Under neoclassical economic theory free-factor flows work towards greater spatial equalities, disturbed only by frictional short-term irregularities. In analyzing differential regional growth rates the export base model (North 1975) has had considerable currency, with exports seen as the major propulsive force on regional incomes. The model has been criticized for neglecting interindustry and interregional connections, the influence of internal technical progress, and the power of externalities on regional success (Tiebout 1975). Yet the differentiation of industries within the export base, by separate analysis of those oriented to natural resources, those complementary in character, and those oriented to urban markets, would powerfully reinforce the model. It would be strengthened even further by being harnessed to efficient input–output analysis.

Counter to the equalizing-convergent trends of the neoclassical economic models are those postulating and emphasizing divergences from the equilibrium growth paths. Concentrating on supply variables the Harrod–Domar model analyzes regional growth as resulting from capital accumulation, the increase in labor supply (including migratory flows), and technical progress. Divergence from equilibrium growth paths results in regionally divergent trends, if uncorrected by public policy. The best-known theory of divergent growth is that of cumulative causation (Myrdal 1957). Growth centers which crystallize out from a diverse resource endowment, differentially exploited through time, develop cumulative advantages over rivals and especially over remoter areas of the periphery. Such a core–periphery contrast (Gottmann 1980) in prosperity and potentials is steadily increased, with both beneficial and adverse effects upon the periphery. The beneficial or 'spread' effects are the centrifugal diffusion of growth, stimulating production, exchange, and technical progress at the periphery. 'Backwash' effects are the continued polarizing impact of core growth, draining both labor and capital resources from the periphery. It is these 'backwash' effects that have traditionally been dominant, predicting that differences will increase unless corrective action is taken.

Faced with such a range of conflicting theories and models, it is not hard to agree that 'regional theory is itself a regional problem' (Holland 1976, 20). Before summing up a case for and against deliberate area-based policies, the changing perceptions of 'regional problems' in the US need briefly to be taken into account. During the 1930s there was a great deal of 'regional rhetoric' (Levin 1969, 249) in the New Deal era of economic depression and reconstruction. National efforts were concentrated on natural-resource development and conservation, agricultural and forest improvement, and the generation of electric power. National and regional planning fleetingly enjoyed a false dawn. By the mid-1960s problems and priorities were altogether different (OECD 1980, 23). Substantial population growth was casting its longer-term shadow; strong internal migration currents were flowing from the country to the cities and from the South northwards and westwards; the need to attract new industry to lagging regions was readily apparent, and many narrowly based resource regions had proved vulnerable to distress. Public-policy expenditures were intended to help the South and West to reach parity with the rest of the nation. The principal means of public intervention to stimulate lagging regions and areas were through public works, tax incentives, and subsidies.

By 1980 the net migration from the rural areas had virtually ceased and indeed enhanced counterflow from the metropolitan regions had set in. The most acute economic and social problems were then identified as being in the inner city, among minority communities, especially those living in the older industrial regions. Manufacturing had given place to the services sector and advanced technology as the major source of employment growth, but everywhere machines were replacing human labor. Many resource-based regions had recovered and, indeed, energy supply and marketing problems had become dominant in defining the relative advantages of different regions. The Northeast and the Midwest had replaced the South and West as lagging regions. Public works were no longer seen as the key to aiding regions in distress and both incentives and subsidies were seen as of only marginal, even of dubious, value as an ingredient of policy.

There is thus no single or fixed view on the nature of regional problems, their spatial incidence or degree of severity. Correspondingly, there is a wide spectrum of political views, from radical liberal to ultraconservative, on what part, if any, public intervention should play. Only on an affirmative assumption is it then possible to consider the nature of spatial policies, universal or territorially discriminant, nationwide, regional, or local that might be appropriate for meeting acknowledged problems.

2.1.2 Spatial public policies: the case for and against

The case for or against deliberate spatial public policies can be argued on theoretical or political grounds, equally in terms of equity or efficiency. Underlying all aspects is the belief in greater spatial equality on the one hand and on national growth optimization on the other, for which spatial considerations would be an impediment, if not a blockage. The theoretical arguments have already been outlined. In favor of policies it can be argued that the combination of neoclassical economic theory and idealized geographical models of the spatial distribution of economic activity (Holland 1976, 20) have both failed to explain reality and to prescribe effectively for a better future. Market forces have certainly not produced the postulated equilibrium, since the factors of production have proved very imperfectly mobile. Such immobility has affected both capital and labor and, furthermore, factor prices do not fairly reflect relative scarcities. Though some form of equilibrium, certainly not an optimum, might emerge in the longer term the adjustment in the short and medium term would be painful and might well be politically unacceptable. In particular, the inbuilt social costs incurred have to be borne by the community and not by the market which created them. Against these theoretical arguments for public intervention is the counter that the neoclassical model of price determination is the most efficient and leads to a self-adjusting and self-balancing economy. It is then said to be false to criticize the factor-flow mobility assumptions since these are in fact tempered by reality. For example, instead of perfect mobility of labor there is need only for an adequate margin of individuals ready and able to move (West 1973, 111). Even if market forces do work imperfectly at times the risk aversion costs are likely to be less for entrepreneurs and individuals than for governments. In any case, why should perfect markets be attacked and yet perfect public government be accepted (West 1973, 110), with politicians acting as impartial servants of the public good?

Evidence on these conflicting views comes from the extent of convergence or divergence in regional economic or social trends in the US. During the past four decades regional disparities have been reduced and, in the absence of substantive regional policies during that period, market forces must have played a dominant role. This accords with Williamson's findings (1965) that, though increasing regional inequality is generated during the early development stages, mature growth has produced greater regional convergence or a reduction in differentials. In 1930 per capita incomes in the Mideast States were more than twice those in the Southeast; by 1977 they were less than 25 per cent greater (ACIR 1980, 5). Overall, during the same period the rich regions—Mideast, Far West, New England and Great Lakes have become relatively less rich and the poor regions—Southeast, Plains, and Rocky Mountains have become less poor. Cost-of-living adjustments might change the relative regional rankings, as well as absolute differences among them, but do not disturb general validity of the comparison. The major regional convergence was achieved between 1930 and 1950, for, with exception of the Far West and Rocky Mountain States, the relative gap in incomes among regions had changed very little between 1900 and 1930. Since 1950 there has been a decrease in convergence rates and, during the economic depression of the 1970s, there was some indication of a slight widening of per capita income differentials between the regions. With continuing slow economic growth, it is calculated (ACIR 1980, 90) that, despite continued faster growth in per capita incomes in the Southeast and Southwest, these two regions would still have the lowest regional levels of per capita incomes in 1990, with the Mideast, New England, and the Far West still at the top of the range. On this evidence 'the most important regional policy, both in terms of national acceptance and regional efficiency, may well be the maintenence of a rapidly growing national economy' (ACIR 1980, 91).

The case is not, however, so simply made out for indirect macroeconomic solutions to the problems of spatial diversity or regional imbalance. As Friedmann and Alonso (1975, 109) put it—'The arithmetic of macro-economics has need of and is made more powerful by the geometry of spatial considerations'. Though skeptical of the 'utilitarian calculus' of regional science, Holland (1976, 16, 20) fears that policies on balance of payments, inflation, the promotion of *national* industrial development without proper concern for regional considerations may in fact intensify rather than diminish national policy problems.

Some would see the spatial question as one between place-related and people-related policies (Winnick 1966). In this sense place-related is a proxy for aid to people in a particular locality, State, or region. The arguments in favor of place-related policies, in the first instance, may be social and cultural, but above all are ultimately political in character. In a pluralist democracy 'the richness and variety of unique regional experience' (Cumberland 1971) needs to be accommodated. The safeguarding of cultural diversity, preferred lifestyles, rurality, concepts of community, or the preservation of social capital have their appeal for the design of spatially sensitive policies. The wish for a more local control over economic destiny focusses a political ambition for policies at regional scale or less. Such objectives fitted well with the New Regionalism of the 1970s (section 2.4), but coincide equally closely with the sensitivities of Congressmen to local or State constituencies (ch. 1.4.2). Though conceding that in certain traumatic circumstances a single region or community might legitimately have a claim for spatial discrimination, the general case for such policies is described by some (quoted by Hallett 1973, 8) as 'an economically nonsensical capitulation to political blackmail'. Perhaps this may be more colloquially termed, for an American audience, the triumph of the 'pork-barrel' over economic better judgment. In more theoretical terms, traditional welfare economics does not recognize the prosperity of a *region* as a valid objective (West 1973, 107). Furthermore, it is argued that 'neither communities, regions, nor nations have an interest collectively' (Rondinelli 1975). Some would also contend (Romans 1965, 5) that 'to insulate regions from adverse economic change must compromise aggregate national output and efficiency, lead to "beggar my neighbor" policies, and will at the same time breed provincialism.'

People-related policies are sectoral and only indirectly, if at all, place-discriminant. Intended to benefit members of statutorily defined categories, such as the poor, ethnic minorities, the unemployed, the elderly, or inner-city residents, the spatial impact falls wherever the appropriate beneficiaries are located. In many instances there is no clearly detectable spatial outcome since members of the group may be dispersed throughout a wider community. Politically, such policies are meritorious in general Congressional terms, but no politician can be sure that any additional votes may accrue to him as a result. Nor do such policies earn a politician dividends among constituents pleading special needs or pressure groups espousing a particular local cause.

2.1.3   Alternative bases of spatial policy

Amid such contending and contentious argument the validity of overt spatial policies is threatened, but not to be dismissed out of hand. In any event, the spectrum of spatial policies which have been enacted in the US merits critique and consideration. The first issue must be the relationship and relative significance between policies for the metrourban system and those for some scale of regional network. The two sets of policy are inevitably closely intertwined in any mature industrial urban society, but the primacy or priority accorded to the city or to the region controls the kind of spatial policies implemented. Urban and regional problems are linked through inter-city and interregional labor migrations and by the ever-expanding commuter hinterland of metropolitan areas. The level of development in a region is to be closely correlated with the extent and the structure of urbanization, whilst in an opposite sense interregional capital flows may undermine urban viability (Clavel *et al.* 1980, 35). For these reasons urban and regional development problems and policies have been described as 'two sides of the same economic and social coin' (Rothblatt 1974) and urban problems, in particular, cannot be dealt with in isolation from regional and interregional forces. In France policies for spatial management of the urban system and the regional network have been worked in tandem (House 1978), though the sophistication of spatial policies has rarely been matched by the sometimes piecemeal, politically distorted outcomes. In Britain both regional policy and urban policy have been more fragmentary, pragmatic, and variable through almost five decades (House 1982A). In the US there are important differences in political controls over the cities and regions (pp. 29–30). Metropolitan policies and plans (ACIR 1978A) are Federally sponsored in the first instance, as a prerequisite for public transport grants, sewerage schemes, or water-system financing (Levin 1969, 127). Yet metropolitan areas (SMSAs) often span State boundaries and one or more States thus continue to be influential in city affairs as a result (Florestano and Marando 1981). On balance, metro authorities lean more towards Federal policy-makers, but with a generally weak political backing outside Washington. Regional policies, on the other hand (section 2.5) are a product of Federal–State partnership, and in that sense politicized from the outset by the shifting balance of power within the US governmental system.

Metropolitan-urban problems and policies are the theme of chapter 7. Focus here is on spatial policies at all scale levels from Federal, through multistate, State, and substate to local levels.

2.2 SPATIAL TRENDS

During the 1970s dramatic changes in spatial trends became apparent (Wheaton 1979), in both the regional and the metropolitan/nonmetropolitan systems. The significance of these changes is still debated. Are they short-term fluctuations linked to economic depression or shifts in spatial preferences, or are they indicative of longer-term structural reversals in American economy and society? In particular, do the changes carry implications for government intervention in the space-economy, or may they be explained by the working out of yet another phase of market equilibrium? To these questions the answers must remain somewhat speculative for the present.

The nature of the changing spatial trends is not in dispute. The slowing down of national population growth has been accompanied by signs of stagnation, even 'zero growth' in parts of the metropolitan system (Burns and Van Ness 1981, 169). The older and larger industrial metropolises of the Manufacturing Belt have been the most seriously affected. Of the 39 largest US cities 7 actually lost population 1970–80 and all were located in the so-called Frost or Snowbelt. Redistribution of people within, and movement to and from metropolitan centers was accelerated and new trends became apparent (Phillips and Brunn 1980, 2). Except in parts of the South, central-city populations declined, suburbanization proliferated, but decentralization of residence also passed to the exurban zone (Morrill 1979, 65). Rural migration to the cities fell away and movement from metro to nonmetro areas became the dominant trend; some indeed wrote of a 'rural renaissance' (Phillips and Brunn 1980, 2). Nationally, there was also an overall redistribution of people between the regions (Berry and Dahmann 1977), emphasizing differentially more rapid growth in the South and West (the Sunbelt) at the expense, according to some, of the North and Midwest (the Snowbelt). The sociocultural elements of these spatial changes are considered in chapter

3, the urban and metropolitan changes in chapter 7, and the manufacturing role in change in chapter 6. Attention here is focussed on the implications of the trends for regional and area development policies.

The spatial trends have been characteristically interpreted by geographers within a core–periphery (fringe or rimland) framework (Ullmann 1958; Beyers 1979). The core is identified as the Northeast–Midwest (the traditional Manufacturing Belt), though some add California (Weinstein and Firestine 1978, 61) as a second core in a bipolar economic system. The periphery of the national space-economy is most commonly seen as the South, rather than the West, with a subdivision either side of the Mississippi valley. More specifically, core–periphery relationships may be identified at all scale levels: inner-city (or CBD) core–suburban periphery; urban (metropolitan) core–rural periphery; growth point (market center)–hinterland; prosperous, accessible farmland core–remote, poor rural perimeter; industrial core–industrial margin; regional (interregional) core–regional (interregional) periphery. Differential growth in core and periphery is interpreted through the forces of polarization, favoring the core, decentralization diffusing growth towards the periphery, and convergence making growth either more uniform or tending to reduce growth differentials.

Core and periphery are in reality extremes within a complex and highly interdependent intermetropolitan and interregional economy and society (Jusenius and Ledebur 1976, 35). According to the theoretical stance adopted, the flows within the system will be seen as equilibrating or self-balancing, or as creating disparities, possibly in need of public intervention. Borts and Stein (1964, 19) saw US interregional and interindustrial growth patterns tending towards 'intertemporal competitive equilibrium and hence towards intertemporal efficiency'. Van-Weesep (1980, 188), on the other hand, interpreted divergent development within the sytem, refuting theories of convergence and, in particular, W. W. Rostow's (1977) Kondratieff cycle of capitalist development as an autonomous process favoring regions alternately.

A recent novel approach (Casetti 1981) explores the role of 'capital formation and technological progress' in current dislocations of the 'spatial-economic system'. Supply-side catastrophe theory is used to explain the dynamics of regional product, in the expansion or contraction of regional economies. Though the same issues of 'unbounded' growth or decline are again set alongside the alternative hypothesis of a trend to stable regional equilibrium, the novelty of the explanation lies in the finding that changes in the comparative values of the marginal productivity of capital in a region or the gross regional product can produce a 'catastrophic' switch, as from growth to decline.

Major regional shifts in the traditionally mobile US economy and society are certainly not new. For example, Everett Lee (Weinstein and Firestine 1978, 68) distinguish three great migrations: westwards, and still continuing; from southern agricultural areas to northern cities, initially mostly white but increasingly black after World War II; and, most recently, in dramatic reversal a net counterflow southwards.

Nevertheless, from 1870 to 1957, in spite of the remarkable growth of the western half of the nation, the eastern core remained cumulatively and economically dominant (Pack 1978, 14). During this lengthy period there was an irregular overall convergence in incomes between the regions: before 1930, confined to the Far West and Rocky Mountain States; at its strongest 1930–50; and slowing down in equalization since 1950. Polarization of people and activities into the towns and cities was characteristic of economic-demographic development, with a countertrend towards decentralization only after the peak level of growth. Within the Continental US some regions have been growing, with urban concentrations, others have been declining and decentralizing at the mature stage (Morrill 1979, 55).

The effectiveness of deliberate spatial policy-making in changing the dynamics of the US regional system remains in question (Kasarda 1980). The turbulence of trends is massive and complex. Public intervention to accelerate regional growth or mitigate regional decline encounters powerful market forces at work. On occasion, the outcome may be self-defeating, if both intervention and the market are at cross-purposes. At other times the coincidence of both may cause an enhanced surge in the system. Perhaps more characteristically in the US over recent decades, policy interventions 'attempting to alter very stable dynamics by inadequate means are bound to change nothing and to waste resources in the process' (Casetti 1981, 579).

2.2.1 The Sunbelt–Snowbelt controversy

During the 1970s the most pronounced and politically sensitive major regional shift has been from the Northeast–Midwest to the South and West, the core to the rimland, the so-called Snow (Frost) belt to the Sunbelt (Sale 1972; Estall 1980; O'Rourke 1981). The term 'Sunbelt' was coined as late as 1976, by a GOP presidential campaign strategist, to cover the southern 'pivotal' area for the Republican Party, a land of conservative politics. Political rhetoric continues to confuse the issue, with talk of a 'myth in the making' (Jusenius and Ledebur 1976) or 'a second war between the States' (Petersen 1977, 3). Definition of the Sunbelt is no less cloudy (Browning and Gesler 1979) and in view of inter- and intrastate variation, certainly the term itself is too simplistic. Initially seen as stretching from Florida through to California, it has been narrowed, by conventional use, to a Sunbelt east of the Mississippi and one westward from that river, to include Texas, but not beyond. Cruickshank (1980) focusses attention on the Southeast Metropolitan Sunshine Crescent, a notion of the Deep South, stretching from Richmond, Va., to New Orleans.

The magnitudes of the southward interregional shifts are clearly established, their explanation and significance much more controversial. (For industrial aspects see ch. 6.3.1; for urban aspects see ch. 7.2.5.) Whereas the northern core (Northeast, North Central) attracted 2 million net migrants, 1940–60, the census South lost 3.5 million net migrants over the same period, 86 per cent of whom were blacks. From 1970 to 1977 the trends were reversed: the North lost 2.4 million net migrants, the South gained 3.4 millions (43 per cent in Florida, 23 per cent in Texas). Moreover, during the same critical seven years the South had 54 per cent of the total natural increase in population, the North only 8 per cent (Estall 1980, 370–2).

The 1980 census showed that California, Florida, and Texas had gained

9.6 million people in a decade, more than 40 per cent of the total national population increase. By contrast, rates of population growth in the Northeast and Midwest tended towards zero or were even negative. Cruickshank (1981, 178) wrote of a revived image of the 'doughnut', to replace the simplicity of the Sunbelt–Snowbelt distinction. The Northeast and Midwest were the hole in the doughnut whilst the South and West, the peripheral arc of increment, had expanded both in coverage and intensity. The simile of the doughnut, he found, could not be sustained in a preliminary examination of the more variegated detail of the county data.

In terms of new investment in manufacturing (ch. 6, pp. 217–24), 38 per cent was located in the South in 1976, 42 per cent in the North, but that mostly for replacement. In 1970–7 the North lost 1 million manufacturing jobs, the South gained 200,000. The secular shift in manufacturing saw the northern percentage of jobs fall from 66 per cent in 1950 to 50 per cent by 1977; the proportions in the South increased from 20 to 30 per cent over the same period (Estall 1980, 373). Furthermore, from 1960 to 1977 more than 70 per cent of all new nonagricultural jobs were in the services sector. From being an employer of last resort, services have now become an integral and growing part of the interregional economy (Clark 1980, 114). During 1970–7 growth in the South and West was further reinforced by a higher than national average growth in service jobs. Although the North still retains higher gross per capita income levels than the South, when adjustment is made for Federal taxes and differences in the cost of living, the mean differentials were minimal in 1975: North 102.3 per cent of the US average, South 98.9 per cent (Petersen 1977, 6).

The gross interregional differences are reflected also in the metropolitan structure (Table 2.1), but the relationship between economic and demographic shifts is more complex (Burns and Van Ness 1981, 170). In a

TABLE 2.1   *Metropolitan areas classified by rates of income, population growth, and region, 1970–1977*

| Region | Distribution Growth Rates, 1970–7 | | | |
| | population | | per capita income | |
Percentage	high	low	high	low
Total US	48.1	51.9	51.5	48.5
Northeast	3.1	96.9	12.1	87.9
North Central	22.2	77.9	44.4	55.6
South	67.0	33.0	68.0	32.0
West	78.0	22.0	53.7	46.3

Source: Adapted from Burns and Van Ness (1981), 170, Table 1.

metropolitan system showing signs of stagnation, income has grown more uniformly over the four major census regions, but demographic decline (or growth) is imperfectly related to economic decline (or growth). Decline (or growth) must be categorized and the nature of economic decline clearly differentiated from population decline. Structural differences among metropolitan areas must also be taken into account (see also chs. 3, pp. 82–5, 99–103; 6, pp. 222–4; and 7, pp. 266–70).

The rationale behind the rise of the Sunbelt usually emphasizes the loss of comparative advantage by the North and its gain by the South. The North had the cumulative advantages of an early economic and industrial start, with aggregate self-perpetuating momentum, through urbanization, metropolitan growth, and industrial maturity. The concentration of innovation, techno-logical advance, and national centers of private and public decision-taking progressively reinforced the dominant competitive status of the region, by contrast to the periphery 'remote from the centre and from self-generating momentum' (Estall 1980, 367). At the peak of economic growth 90 per cent of the production by value of the 500 largest US industrial corporations was located within the Northern Manufacturing Belt. Changes in the structure of manufacturing, shifts in locational advantages, and, in particular, freedom from natural resource ties, the obsolescence of plant and equipment in congested, rundown industrial cities, the rationalization of labor-intensive industry in low-wage areas elsewhere, and the evening up of spatial differ-ences in other regions all counted against the North. Technological innova-tion permitted more diffused migrations, migrants realized preferences for more desirable environments, whilst 'the complex infrastructure of the aging industrial metropoli of the Snowbelt had become one of their principal liabilities' (Sternlieb and Hughes 1977, 235).

The flight to the suburbs in the North had given place to regional shifts of population. The Sunbelt South had a more congenial climate, though air-conditioning costs were higher, with cheaper land, lower building and main-tenance costs (Estall 1980, 374), and cheaper, though scarcely less pro-ductive, labor. The lower costs of abundant energy at source could be realized only after deregulation of prices but in an energy-conscious age represented a major asset. The industrial growth of the South was largely by expansion of indigenous firms, with migration of firms from the North only of minor significance (Weinstein and Firestine 1978, 143; Jesenius and Ledebur 1976, 24); in 1976 only 554 of 140,000 manufacturing plants had changed location by State since 1969 (ACIR 1981, 6). Manufacturing decline in the North was due rather to the 'death' or closure of existing enterprises. Southern expan-sion was in national 'growth' industries, especially those related to high technology or to locally available natural resources or fuels. Promotional business climates and lesser State-local tax burdens proved powerful induce-ments to industrial expansion, at least at 'particular jurisdictions within a general region' (ACIR 1967, 78). Service industries grew in relation to the rising regional market, whilst the improved accessibility along the interstate highway system since the mid-1950s benefitted industrial and commercial entrepreneurs alike. The cyclical trend in terms of trade favorable to primary producers in both agriculture, minerals, and fuel buttressed the southward shift in the balance of economic power.

The mechanisms behind the shift were entrepreneurial, but, some alleged, also governmental and, to that extent, possibly 'unfair' to the North. Invest-ment strategies of the major business corporations, the multinational firms, and the principal finance and banking houses were prime movers behind the differential shifts in the space-economy (Clark 1980, 111). The low taxes, limited services, and minimal regulation of business and environment in the Sunbelt, 'the limited State', contrasted favorably with the 'expansive State' of the Snowbelt, a much more constrained setting for both entrepreneurs and citizens (O'Rourke 1981, 2). The significance of the shifts is debated. On one view (Sternlieb and Hughes 1977, 228), they are but an accelerated evolution of long-established trends, trends beginning as far back as the New Deal years (Estall 1980, 366). On another (Jusenius and Ledebur 1976, 3), there is doubt if the new trend will be long-term rather than simply a short-term reaction to the cyclical downturn in the industrialized North. Indeed, simulations in a multiregion econometric model (Milne *et al.* 1980, 188) indicate that 'the slow growth Northern regions will improve their relative positions during the 1980s, though their absolute growth will continue to lag behind that of the Southern States. Stimulative fiscal policy and an energy bill which makes energy prices more equal across regions will tend to encourage the convergence of growth rates.' Since interregional competition is not a 'zero-sum' game, long-term convergence is regarded as beneficial to the entire national system (Weinstein and Firestine 1978, 145), particularly when regions are closely interlocked by trade based on comparative advantage (Klausen 1973). The challenge to the South is to complete the transformation of the economy, develop energy resources, nurture the agricultural base, deal with the social problems arising from rapid population increase and class/ethnic polarization, whilst avoiding environmental degradation (Rostow 1977, 98). The North must bring to bear full potentials of technology, financing, and entrepreneurship, since there is little evidence of the commanding heights of the national economy passing South. Energy resources must be conserved and used more efficiently in a new price environment, the decaying transport system rehabilitated in a cost-effective manner, and potential growth industries implanted or existing plant modified. The outcome and the timing are unpredictable, but on any economic rationale the needs of the South must be matched with the means of the North (ACIR 1980, 91).

Political considerations disturb economic rationale and cultural problems too enter into the equation, though market and institutional forces may be expected to have stronger effects on the redistribution of people and economic activity (Weinstein and Firestine 1978, 65). Under the proposed 1982 political reapportionment the Sunbelt and the West will gain 16 House Congressional seats. The great cities of Megalopolis and the Midwest will lose some political power in Congress through redistricting; it is estimated (Cruickshank 1981, 181) that New York alone will lose four seats. The Northeast and Midwest, dominant in politics for 200 years, will be represented by a minority bloc of 210–15 seats (Rifkin and Barber 1978; Murray 1981). In the 1984 presidential election, for the first time, 'a candidate will be able to concede the entire Northeast to an opponent and still reach the White House' (Archer 1982, 133).

Adverse economic or social trends provoke vigorous political responses. Northern political spokesmen allege 'unfair' competition by the South (Estall 1980, 376), with claims of industrial piracy and biassed Federal aid. There is no clear evidence on the piracy charge and on Federal favoritism the verdict is double-edged. Since Federal policies are dealt with later (section 2.6), suffice it to say here that Federal expenditure–revenue patterns have differential and not necessarily intended regional effects. Since the mid-1950s the Southern States have generally received substantially more in federal expenditure than they have paid to the Federal government, but by the mid-1970s the inter-regional differences from the Northeast and Midwest had narrowed considerably, at least on the revenue side (ACIR 1980, 6). Federal policies have tended to favor poor and rural areas, much to the benefit of the Sunbelt, but as policy has shifted to greater preoccupation with metropolitan and inner-city problems, the Frostbelt should be correspondingly advantaged (Petersen 1977, 9). Indeed, 'the analogy of the aging northern industrial crescent with the long-term transformation of the older central cities is increasingly- and uncomfortably-apt' (Sternlieb and Hughes 1977, 228). Likewise, 'the discussion of regional disparities is, in fact, a discussion of other deep-rooted national problems that concern race and poverty, and their growing concentration in certain older cities' (ACIR 1980, 90). Unfortunately for the older cities, in their hour of greatest need, a diminished political strength in Congress will weaken prospects for enhanced, or even sustained, level funding.

The Reagan administration (1981) claimed its economic program to be neutral as between the regions. It argued that while its social service cutbacks hit the Northeast and Midwest hardest, its planned income tax cuts would benefit these same regions since their incomes are highest. Yet the deregulation of oil prices increases tensions between energy-rich and energy-consuming regions, whilst the Reagan 'New Federalism', in its vesting of greater financial responsibility in the States, albeit with reduced resources, may again act to the detriment of the Frostbelt with its severe urban/industrial economic and social problems (*Financial Times* 15 June 1981). Meanwhile, the political forces are strengthening on both sides of the argument. The Coalition of Northeast governors (CONEG) 1976 and the Midwest Governors' Conference were buttressed by the Northeast–Midwest Economic Advancement Coalition (NMEAC) with 200 Congressional members from 16 states, and the Northeast–Midwest Senate coalition (1978) (O'Rourke 1981, 2). The Southern Growth Policies Board (SGPB) was established in 1971 to plan for growth and change in the South, whilst in a neutral camp a western coalition of States met in 1977, primarily to combat energy-related policies favored by the Northeastern States (ACIR 1980, 3).

2.3 A TAXONOMY OF PROBLEM REGIONS

The diverse and complex patterns of spatial trends may be consolidated into a taxonomy of problem regions (Table 2.2). The core–transition–periphery framework is used (modified from Friedmann 1966), to provide a functional context for sets of growth/decline trends, at different scale-levels within an interacting spatial system. Locations are identified, though these are usually indicative rather than in any way comprehensive and the problem indicators are highlighted. The political jurisdictions affected and with prime responsibility for remedial or monitoring policies are listed in the final column of the table.

TABLE 2.2   A taxonomy of problem regions

Function	Category	Location and Character	Problem Indicators	Political Jurisdictions
CORE	distressed mature	*Complex metropolitan economies of the NE and Midwest and older, outworn, mainly single industry towns (N. Manuf. Belt). Significant historical development, capital and social investment. Parts of regional economies, e.g. Appalachia, Ozarks, Upper Great Lakes*	Adjustment to long-term downward economic and social change: Declining jobs/population ratio; static/eroding tax base, rising tax effort; persistent and high unemployment; disturbing levels of outmigration of young and able; loss of political power	Cities Counties (SMSAs, Labor Areas) States Multistate organizations Regional Commissions
	fast growth	*Major metropolises in California, the West, and the Sunbelt*	Congestion; high and rising living costs; social polarization; environmental degradation; deteriorating public welfare and social services; racial and ethnic minority problems	Cities Counties (SMSAs) and over-spill areas
TRANSITIONAL	downward	*Majority of larger and medium-sized cities in NE and Midwest*	Slow growth or stagnation; vulnerability to cyclical economic trends; unemployment and net outmigration, or trend to 'zero population growth'	Cities Counties
		Parts of the Northern Rockies and the Great Plains; much of New England; Pacific NW lumbering areas	Narrow unstable resource base; rural outmigration; small town and market center underemployment	Counties States Regional Commissions
		Social disorganization (Smith 1973, 88) California, Nevada, New York, Florida	Incidence of social pathologies; high crime, alcoholism, venereal disease, suicide	Cities Counties Multicounty organizations
	upward	*Sunbelt cities, especially medium-scale metropolises; West Coast, and NW regional economies; Four Corners region. Nonmetropolitan margins of growth metropolises. Settled regions with strong commercial relations to core markets*	Increasing tempo economic development; inflow of migrants and capital from core areas; less concentrated urbanization; attraction to mobile manufacturing; fast growth symptoms appearing; income polarization socially disturbing	Cities Counties States Regional Commissions
PERIPHERY (margins)	distressed resource base	*Areas of mining decline in the Appalachians or the West; small single industry towns in the NE and Midwest; small market towns; remote, poorer rural fringe areas*	Worked out/abandoned resources; decline, decay, dereliction, un- and underemployment; inability; under market forces to diversify or attract new jobs; persistent outmigration of young and able; serious residual welfare prob-	Townships (New England) Counties EDDs States

TABLE 2.2 (*Continued*)

Function	Category	Location and Character	Problem Indicators	Political Jurisdictions
	low social well-being	*Alabama, Arkansas, Louisiana, Mississippi, N. and S. Carolinas, Tennessee (Smith 1973, 86)*	Low per capita incomes; low median family incomes; poor housing; substandard health, education; high scores on alienation and nonparticipation	Counties EDDs States
		Black inner-city neighborhoods; Indian reservations	Chronic subarea economic and social dislocations. 'Locked-in' poverty, deprivation, and social pathologies	Neighborhood institutions Federal government agencies
	under-development	*Areas lacking natural, physical, or human resources on a scale sufficient to trigger growth and development, and lying outside influence of major growth areas, e.g. Coastal Plains, Mississippi delta, marginal mountain, or arid lands*	Inadequate communications; small-scale markets; poor capital resources; low-density population and substandard social provision; high marginal costs of production; inefficiency; lack of progress; diseconomies of scale; administrative leadership poor	Counties States Regional Commissions
	fast growth ('resource frontier')	*Rapid development based on: new or more intensive use of resources, particularly minerals, fuels, e.g. Alaskan oil, Mtn. coalfields (Wyoming, Montana)*	'Boom town' conditions: Unstable and often temporary economic base; rapid local inflation; vulnerable to market shifts, cyclical downturns in the economy; critical natural resource shortages, especially water; high living costs; lack of any economic multiplier effects; lagging services, environmental damage (ACIR 1978, 18–19)	Counties
		retirement migration, Florida, Southwest communities		
		recreational developments and vacation areas (coastal, mountain—winter and summer)		
	political frontiers	*US–Mexican Border (House 1982B) US–Canadian Border shows only distortions in land-use patterns or marketing hinterlands*	Marked economic and social asymmetry; US depressed areas; complex transactional flows across the Border; multiple problems (labor markets, illegal immigrants, drugs, tourism, vice, use of scarce common natural resources)	Counties EDDs States SW Border Commission Federal interaction

It is possible to argue that the dynamics of long-run regional change are such (see ch. 6.2) that any taxonomy highlights only a particular phase in regional life cycles, in the same sense that Kondratieff cycles characterize long-term shifts in regional and national economies. The conditions of problem regions in the core, the transition zone and the margins are, however, in many cases remarkably enduring, even cumulative. Because they generate social tensions and economic discontents these adverse conditions demand political consideration and the sustained attention of policy-makers.

2.4   REGIONALISM AND REGIONAL POLITICAL CULTURE

The mixture of social and economic problems is thus highly differentiated across the US national space, occurring with varying incidence and severity under different levels of jurisdiction. Before considering the nature, impact, and degree of success or failure of government policies upon the national space, it is appropriate to consider and evaluate the spatial patterning of political forces and their geographical diversity. The powers and functions of local, State, and Federal governments have already been sketched in (ch. 1). It remains to review the nature and reasons for the variegated geographical patterns of political life and, in particular, the basis for political regions.

The concepts of regionalism and sectionalism are endemic in any study of American history or evaluation of the contemporary political scene. Both terms refer to prime subdivisions of the national space, but with different meanings. Sectionalism is the more divisive concept, with both positive and negative aspects. The section has traditionally been regarded as more deep-seated than any region, a political identity based on the long-standing bonds of a shared interest (Elazar 1972, 84), resulting in a sharply defined politico-economic culture (Sharkansky 1970, 165), even though internally often very diverse, and a sense of opposition to other sections or the Federal authority. Some interpret the section as a segment of the hinterland within a core–periphery framework of the nation (Elazar 1972, 148). Most sectional problems through history have been forced into the network of States, but in many respects the State lines are unsatisfactory boundaries in social, cultural, or economic terms. Though indicative of a deep-seated, cultural underlying continuity, the section has frequently changed character through time, with successive waves of frontier diffusion. New England is one of the clearest sections, based on historic and social ties with a distinctive economic base and set of problems. The South too is often cited as a section, whilst intersectional conflict over water resources in the arid West is to be contrasted with unifying effects of the waves of western political populism late in the last century. Sectionalism is said to have declined as a political force during this century (Vile 1970, 33), with nationwide forces creating a more homogeneous political community. Others contest that view (Elazar 1972, 142), seeing new forms of sectionalism, even within the seeming uniformity of metropolitan or urban society.

To geographers regionalism and the region are much more elusive, multi-facetted concepts, subjective and transient in many cases, capable of definition at many scale-levels and on greatly differing bases. Natural resources, economic characteristics and links, social or cultural traits, or administrative requirements may contribute to regional definition, with very complex patterns in the city-region or metropolitan life. The mismatch of such regions with the political building-blocks of the US Federal system is wellknown, for 'most States contain more than one region, most regions contain more than one State' (Odum and Moore 1938, 383).

The search for valid political regions is the most difficult of all, both in the definition of segments of political space and in the explanation of their corporate identity. Socioeconomic characteristics are important, but so too are group iconography, a sense of heritage, and the totality of regional political culture, even within the metropolitan or urban systems. The balance among such diverse formative elements is hard to discern and changes somewhat unpredictably through time. Some cultural traits are enduring, some economic or social trends fleeting, though dominant whilst they last. In explaining regional political differences economists have laid stress on per capita personal incomes, levels of urbanization, and per capita State and local government expenditure. So too, many political scientists have identified the strongest positive correlations between policy outputs and socioeconomic characteristics (quoted in Sharkansky 1970, 180), with the nature of a particular State political system adjudged to have little independent influence. Sharkansky (1970, 121) admits the significance of economic elements, especially if the criteria are widened to include well-being and a totality of economic resources. Yet in three covariance analyses he identifies among the strongest noneconomic attributes: level of voter turnout, party competition, the size (and nature) of the State legislature, and political influences on education. Brunn (1974, 245) balances the importance of political symbols and images with the growing policy-forming forces of voluntary organizations, lobbies, pressure groups, and the media. He further indicates the volatility in the US political system in recent years, instancing the impact of population shifts, the gains by minority groups, the rise of class distinctions over ethnic awareness, and the focus on polarizing issues such as civil rights, the environment, or Vietnam (p. 251).

Regional political culture is an amalgam of elements of continuity and change, but the elements of continuity are often surprisingly enduring. The cultural character of the political system (Patterson 1966) is built up cumulatively, within the history of settlement and the evolution of society and economy, to which successive waves of settlers contributed (Brunn 1974, 261). This heritage is compounded of both indigenous and implanted mores, often reflecting those of a dominant elite. Traditional views of society, economy, and the body politic are thus brought into being and transmitted down the generations. Though modified through time, and particularly by the spread of urban-based cultural homogeneity and the mobility patterns of migrant Americans, there remain important differences in such cumulative historical experience feeding into regional political culture. In every State there are sets of perceptions, held by politicians and by the general public, about what political life should mean and what the role of governments should cover. Accordingly, there are differences in the kinds of people active in government and politics and, equally, in the actual practice of government (Elazar 1972, 90).

Elazar (1972, 90–1) analyzed the American cultural matrix in terms of marketplace, in which primary public relations are the product of bargaining by individuals and groups acting out of self-interest, and commonwealth, in which the whole people have an undivided interest in the cooperative implementation of shared principles. From this matrix, embodying both power and justice, he defined his now well-known three political cultures: individualistic, moralistic, and traditionalistic. Under the individualistic culture government is seen as utilitarian only and politics as a business for controlling the distribution of favors and rewards. Politicians respond to public pressures, ideology does not figure, and bureaucracy serves the public needs. Moralistic culture seeks the good society, with private acts to promote the public good. Governments exist to promote the general welfare and every citizen has an obligation to participate. Traditionalistic culture is ambivalent towards the marketplace, with paternalistic/elitist concepts of power in an hierarchical society. Politicians have a conservative and custodial role and government is to be focussed upon continuation of the social order. From these three contrasting cultural founts the intricate geographical patterning of political cultures has emerged, been spread by diffusion, modified in turn by local conditions, and today is represented by a variegated patchwork quilt of politico-cultural characteristics. Given the complexity and lengthy period of evolution and the massive mobility which has typified American society, few generalizations on the pattern are possible. Individualistic culture is still strong throughout the Northeastern Manufacturing Belt, traditionalistic in the Old South, and moralistic from New England through to the Upper Great Lakes. West of the Mississippi political cultures moved in with the migrant streams, each implanting its own traditions. In California, for example, the south is predominantly moralistic, from immigrant Yankees and Mid-westerners, the north individualistic, colonized from the Middle States, and the center traditionalistic, from the southern immigrants (Elazer 1972, 114). Although cultural continuity and the political attitudes which go with it may be thought stronger in the rural areas there are significant differences too in the form of political status of urban and metropolitan centers under different regional political cultures. In New York and Pennsylvania the State government is active in urban transportation and development, in Ohio and Illinois the larger cities have greater independence, whilst in Georgia and Nebraska the cities are closely controlled by the State (Elazar 1972, 147).

Sharkansky (1970; see Fig. 2.1) analyzed differences in State politics and policies, tested for consistency within contiguous regions, and sought to evaluate the relative significance of resources and political variables in explaining political cultures. Three major realms were identified in political terms: the Southeast, with centralized State government, preoccupation with local bills, in receipt of major Federal aid, yet with low scores on voter turnout, party competition, or equitable legislative apportionment (p. 60); the North, with greater prominence of local government, lower State expenditures, little use of sales tax, lower levels of Federal aid, but high scoring on equitable legislative apportionment. The third region, west of the Mississippi, was very diversified but generally showed higher levels of government spending and taxation, high levels of Federal aid and, in the Mountain States, small

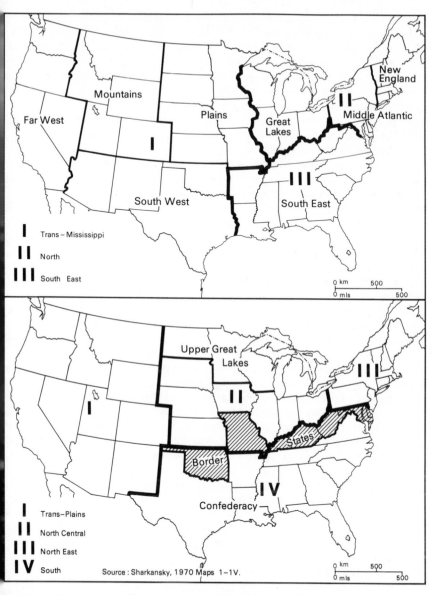

Regional demarcations (Sharkansky 1970, © Bobbs-Merrill)

and less active legislatures. Below the macrolevel Sharkansky tested 17 contiguous regional groupings on 61 measures of politics and policy (p. 17). Three regions, the Upper Midwest, the Great Lakes, and the Mountain States, stood out as having the most uniform political traits. The Upper Midwest (Michigan, Wisconsin, Minnesota, and North Dakota; p. 136), was originally settled from New England and has a tradition of 'progressivism' in politics, with strong political links between farmers and urban labor. Voter turnout is high, party competition is strong, State and local tax spending is high and local government is a clear beneficiary. The Great Lakes States (Ohio, Indiana, Michigan, Illinois, and Wisconsin) partly overlap the previous region. Party competition in this former Republican area has increased; income tax and government debt levels are lower; the cities have fair representation in State legislatures; and levels of Federal aid are relatively low (p. 68). The Mountain States (Montana, Wyoming, Colorado, Idaho, and Utah) were the last major settlement area, peopled by contrasting migrant strains from North and South. More than 30 per cent of land in each State is in the public domain and there is a heavy dependence on Federal aid. Voter turnout is the highest nationally, somewhat surprising in view of the less than average level of economic development (p. 138). In spite of a conservative political tradition, levels of public spending are high.

Other political regions showed greater internal diversities. Often thought to be a coherent political entity, New England was clearly divided between a relatively rural, Protestant, Yankee, Republican north, and a predominantly urban Catholic, multi-immigrant industrial Democratic south. In the Mid-Atlantic States (New York, New Jersey, Pennsylvania, Delaware, and Maryland) the New York–Washington megalopolis was to be differentiated, in its cosmopolitan population, urban-industrial congestion, and immense problems of public funding, from the States south of the Mason–Dixon line with traces of their antebellum heritage (p. 69). The nuances and complexities of regionally differentiated political life could be pursued much further. Suffice it to say that the composition and complexion of State and local governments, and of the Congressional representatives from those areas, condition their political reactions within the Federal system and their attitudes to regional and area policies which originate therein. Such reactions are more than simply a reflection of the spatial taxonomy of problem regions, and the complicated nature of regional political culture must also be taken into account.

There would seem to be strong forces working towards a more homogeneous national political culture: networking on television, nationwide newspaper chains, multinational or increasingly large-scale business corporations, equalizing patterns of consumer demand under universal advertising, nationwide labor markets, and the deeper and wider intrusion of Federal funds (Sharkansky 1970, 78). To these Brunn (1974, 267) adds 'national legislation gains in civil rights, housing, education, consumer protection and environmental quality as further ingredients of a national political culture'. Yet in the face of political realities qualifications must be made at every turn. The speed, if not the distance, of moves towards greater uniformity are countered by regional historical experience (Sharkansky 1970, 78) and by the mounting evidence of special regional problems and issues. As in the general trend towards convergence in regional economic and social conditions, so likewise in regional political cultures there are checks and balances along the route. In political cultures these are less easily defined or assessed but nonetheless potent on that account.

In a sense the voting patterns of the American electorate reflect both the continuity elements of regional or local political culture and, at the same time, specific reactions to changing events and circumstances. Realignments between the two political parties from one election to the next may be nationwide, or there may be, and often are distinct regional differences within the overall national pattern. This distinction has already been convincingly demonstrated for Presidential elections (Archer and Taylor 1981; Archer 1982). In both studies a tripartite subdivision of the US was used, derived from an S-mode factor analysis of the long-term (1872–1980) trends of Democratic voting proportions by State. The three regions were: the North-east, the South, and the West, broadly corresponding to Sharkansky's sub-division (1970; see Fig. 2.1). Brunn (1974) reviewed the entire US electoral process, from precinct to national scale, to detect variations in voting patterns which 'can be analyzed in conjunction with particular social, economic or political cultural characteristics' (p. 271).

2.5 REGIONAL AND AREA POLICIES

We do not believe a meaningful plan can be created without dealing with the important geographical dimension for public investment, or without dealing with matters of
urbanization and the creation of at least a small number of critical masses in human
settlement. (Federal Advisory Commn. on Regional Development 1977)

To European eyes, accustomed to more deliberate intervention by the State in the space-economy, with both negative and positive intentions, it may seem that the US has no regional or coherent area-based sets of policies (Romus 1974, 2). As recently as 1979 the abortive Public Works and Economic Development Act made no mention of regions. Nor was the term much used in the White House Conference on Balanced National Growth and Economic Development (1978). Certainly, too, the sums directly devoted to regional or area development have been very limited. For example, the amount spent by the Economic Development Administration (EDA) and the Appalachian Regional Commission (ARC) over 10 years equalled the cost of but one metro subway in Washington DC, whilst the sum expended on unemployment insurance benefit in 1975 alone was four times the total Federal aid to depressed areas for a decade (Levitan and Zickler 1976, 45). Yet though Federal policies rarely designate regions or areas as such there is a great spectrum of area-specific programs (Cameron 1970; Levitan 1964). Alonso (1975, 776) writes of a 'geographic fallacy' by which the name of a particular territory may be used as a surrogate for its population. Yet any unplanned solution for territorial problems will be at the expense of people rather than place. Somewhere between cloudy rhetoric and intermittent, uncertain prac-tice there exist regional and area-based policy intentions. Regional refers to the first-stage subdivision of the nation, area-based to more local units. There is some consensus that national and both regional and area-based policies need to be harmonized for the good of all, but an equal recognition that such a reconciliation will take a long time (OECD 1980, 41) and is never likely to enjoy more than a low national priority. Indeed, there has been movement away from regional or area-based planning towards concentration on human resource problems, including particularly that of the inner city, but in structural rather than in spatial terms.

There has never been an overarching national economic development policy, nor are regional considerations taken systematically into account (OECD 1980, 32). Policy has responded pragmatically to regional problems as they occur, defining distressed conditions under which areas may qualify (low income, high unemployment, persistent outmigration). Qualified areas are then entitled under their *own initiative* to participate in a variety of Federal programs (Alonso 1975, 774). In order to muster the necessary coalitions in Congress spatial policies have had to be very loosely defined, flexible, and with an even-handed approach which has often ended up favoring virtually *all* areas. Emphasis has been laid on self-help, though local efforts could hardly bring about large results in such a complex system. The local economic base was to be strengthened with a preoccupation on infrastructure improvement. Yet, unlike many European spatial policies, there has been a prohibition on direct grants to industry or, for that matter, any policy of negative restraints, to avoid aid which could distort competition or influence the working of market forces (OECD 1980, 48).

Prime political responsibility for implementing regional or area-based policies has lain with the city, the county, or the State, in applying 'medication for a localized disease' (Alonso 1975, 775). Since politics often constrained policy to 'an attempt to reproduce an industrial revolution in every county' (Zysman 1980, 123), a hopelessly impracticable task, there was little the social scientist could contribute to such spatial-policy thinking. An interim verdict must be that spatial policies in the US have had but a limited, marginal effect. The type of problem dealt with has not been significantly diminished by regional policy (OECD 1980, 44) and 'even with substantial modification, greater priority and more funding, the capacity of federal (spatial) programs to alter, and particularly to reverse geographical patterns of development is extremely limited' (Hansen 1974, 299). Indirect Federal policies, as on highways, major public works, construction, investment in defense, aerospace, or other R and D programs have been cumulatively more significant. Not least because spatial policies have often been uncertain in their aims, particularly on efficiency–equity trade-offs, confused with the War on Poverty, wavering as between 'worst-first' and 'best-first' priorities. Moreover, the failure of similar schemes elsewhere has been ignored (Hansen 1974, 296), and yet there have been worthwhile achievements in spatial policies.

2.6 FEDERAL SPATIAL POLICIES

2.6.1 *Range and impact*

Table 2.3 shows the composition of Federal development assistance (US Dept. Commerce 1977, IV–9), to which must be added the contributions from State governments. Federal grants-in-aid to State and local governments in the late 1970s had indeed risen to 18 per cent of all Federal outlays, compared with less than 10 per cent during the 1950s and 1960s. It is of course true that rather more than one-third of all Federal aid had been derived from State and local revenue received by the Federal government. The Federal agencies, other than EDA, directly concerned with regional development include: HUD, Federal housing assistance, community block grants, and urban action development grants; USDA, loans, or grants systems; EPA, particularly for public water supply and sewerage; DOL (Labor), for employment and training programs; DOT (FHA, UMTA); and HEW, for vocational and technical training. Interagency cooperation, or the lack of it, is an endemic problem in all US spatial policy-making.

Table 2.3 highlights the low levels of direct regional and area-based aid (EDA, ARC, Title V Regional Commissions, TVA). Not surprisingly, the fate of regions or localities is more substantially affected by Federal expenditures which are only indirectly spatial in character (Estall 1977, 361). There is indeed a long history of Federal involvement in the space-economy, through regulation of natural-resource pricing, transportation rates, and specific investment projects. During the past few decades the creation of the interstate highway system (from 1956) and programs for water-resource development have had major repercussions. On one view, the 67,200 km. interstate highway network facilitated metropolitan decentralization, opened up non-metro America, and aided the regional dispersal of population and economic activity (OECD 1980, 26). Yet, on another judgment (Briggs and Rees 1982), the same network was said 'not to have been a determining factor in non-metro growth since 1950'. Water-resource programs have been prime catalysts in the regional development of the arid West and Southwest. The Federal control of rail charges has been instrumental in the rundown of the rail system, though the regulation of airline rates has sustained marginal and unprofitable routes. The maintenance of low gasoline rates, until recently,

TABLE 2.3   *Federal development assistance (FY 1978)*

Dept./Agency	General Development Amount ($M)	Percentage	Economic Development Amount ($M)	Percentage
Commerce (EDA)			400	9.0
ARC			300	6.7
Title V Reg. Commns.			64	2.2
TVA	45	0.2		
HUD	3,600	12.0	550	12.3
USDA	5,780	19.4	927	20.8
EPA	4,500	15.1		
DOL			1,880	42.2
HEW	650	2.2		
DOT	10,500	35.2		
SBA	3,100	10.4	100	2.2
Other	1,647	5.5	203	4.6
	29,822	100.0	4,424	100.0

Source: US Dept. Commerce (1977).

has led to the profligate use of fuel and stimulated dispersal of both people and workplaces.

The differential regional distribution of Federal payrolls and the impact of procurement policies is supplemented by the uneven pattern of Research and Development (R&D) spending (Fig. 6.4). Since World War II Federal sponsored R&D has concentrated upon the aerospace, missile, electronics, and nuclear energy industries, with a budget of 17 billion dollars already in 1970. Even in 1963 expenditure in only half the States accounted for 96.8 per cent of the total and this polarization has continued (Murphy 1971, 8). Manufacturing receives about three-quarters of all Federal R&D investment. Part goes into the major SMSAs in the Northeast and Midwest, and to Pacific coast cities. Defense spending and, in particular, aerospace R&D is concentrated on the Pacific Coast and in the Southwest (Malecki 1981, 79). It must, however, be taken into account that States receiving prime contracts are not necessarily the locations where all the work is performed; about 50 per cent of a defense prime contract is subcontracted, in many cases out of State (ch. 6, p. 236; Figs. 6.4a/b). Though this pattern of Federal R&D spending is said to be inequitable the ramifications are extremely widespread, through linkage and multiplier effects (Malecki 1981, 72), and the regional imbalance is likely to be much less than it at first appears. Moreover, the concentration of such expenditures renders the favored regions and localities very vulnerable to the shifts of government policy (see ch. 6).

The regional patterning of Federal revenues and expenditures (Brunn and Hoffman 1969; Browning 1973) has altered significantly over the past 25 years, with an annual level in 1974–6 about four times that of 1952 (Labovitz 1978, 16). By 1974–6, despite the Vietnam war, national defense spending had fallen from 59 to 26 per cent of total Federal budget outlays. Transfer payments, especially social security benefits, and aids to State and local governments, had become major categories of expenditure. On the revenue side, payroll taxes and other social insurance contributions had become a major source, increasing from 7 per cent in 1952 to 30 per cent of total revenues in 1974–6. The ratio of Federal expenditures to revenues by State has changed significantly (Fig. 2.2), in the general direction of convergence and the reduction of differentials. Greater similarity of ratios is due to the progressive equalization of revenues rather than of expenditures, which remained almost as differentiated in the late 1970s as they had been three decades earlier. The tendency for revenue contributions by States to come closer probably relates to the narrowing of geographical disparities in levels of personal income and the more uniform, graduated Federal income-tax system (Labovitz 1978, 22).

Johnston (1978, 1980) has tested for political variables in the differential Federal expenditure by States and regions, exploring, in particular, the hypothesis that there may be a geography of the 'pork-barrel'. He found no conclusive evidence that 'inter-State variations in government spending reflect the political variables of electoral geography'. Congressmen do seek membership on the committees most relevant to the needs of their constituents and decisions *are* taken for electoral reasons, but in the *overall* pattern this seemed to be unimportant. Unless the 'pork-barrel' has 'over many years

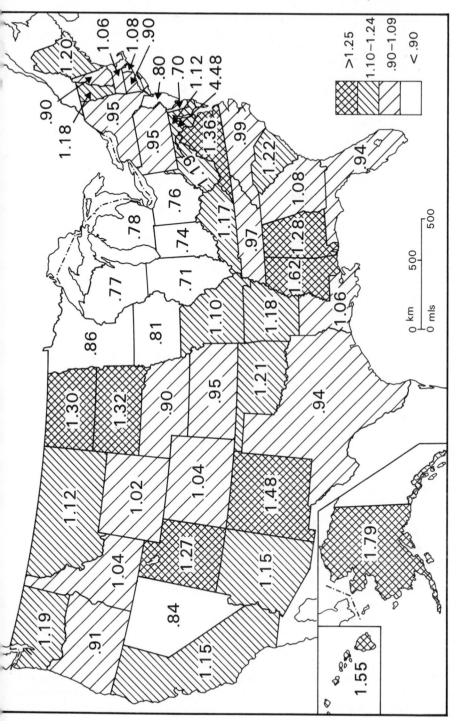

2.2   Federal expenditure/revenue ratios, by State, 1974–6

determined the pattern of spending' (1980, 162) and thus become the con-vention for decision-taking, most self-seeking action by Congressmen is 'often to protect an existing pattern of allocation rather than introduce new "pork-barrel" activity'. At the State level he found that 'spending very much depends on the volume of resources available and political influence largely evaporates' (1980, 163). It has to be said that these conclusions are in opposition to those of political scientists, such as Sharkansky (1970), who underline the importance of political culture in policy decisions.

2.6.2 *Prototypes*

As in Europe, regional planning in the US enjoyed a 'brief Indian summer' in the 1930s (Levin 1969, 5), the product of utopian thinking and the rigorous practice needed to combat mounting economic depression. The Regional Planning Association of America (RPAA) was opposed to metropolitaniza-tion, rural decay, urbanward migration, and social polarization, seeking 'an ecological and social balance' (Friedmann and Weaver 1979, 40). The New Deal legislation under President Roosevelt broke away from city and land-use planning, establishing regional and nationwide programs for public works and the management of natural resources by comprehensive river-basin development. The National Planning Board (1933) became the National Resources Committee two years later, whilst in 1937 the concept was launched that State plans could be federally funded. Of the then 48 States, 47 had created Planning Boards, 1,000 city planning organizations had come into being, and 400 for individual counties. Fears of 'New Deal sovietism' soon surfaced (Levin 1969, 6) and the comprehensive planning dream faded as quickly as it had been born. Even the renowned Tennessee Valley Author-ity (TVA) was not immune. Created in 1933 'to advance the economic and social well-being of the people living in the river basin' (Levin 1969, 5) the Authority was a far cry from the limited munitions factories from World War I, with their associated electric power needs. General plans for the entire river basin were to be promulgated, covering 'flood control, navigation, electric power, the proper use of marginal land, reforestation and the promotion of general well-being' (Friedmann and Weaver 1979, 73). For political survival in the 1930s and 1940s, however, the TVA 'narrowed its concerns to electric power' (Levin 1969, 5) and in time became largely a development corpora-tion 'to encourage urban/industrial expansion' (Friedmann and Weaver 1979, 79). It nevertheless remains a vast enterprise, supplying electric power to 6 million people, managing a 650-mile water network and 28 barrages, for navigation, power generation, flood control, and recreation (Co. State Planning Agencies 1977, 8). Yet it remains a unique institution and after 45 years it has not been imitated.

After World War II the major US national problem was stimulation of aggregate demand, by the promotion of maximum employment. With a healthy national economy, the interim difficulties of lagging or distressed regions would dissolve with time. Through the 1950s the regional policy debate was conducted in terms of 'the costs of the weak to the strong' (Zysman 1980, 133), with a focus on lifting the scattered local pockets of poverty or stranded areas towards some national standard, so that industrial or social capital should not lie unused. The price of inefficiency and the external costs of uneven development were the important questions, not the matter of regional equity. Similarly, the individual States competed with each other to attract industry in an era of 'smokestack planning' (Levin 1969, 9).

2.6.3 *The Economic Development Administration (EDA)*

In 1980 the EDA regional strategy for the investment of resources was defined as 'the promotion of long-term recovery and growth in rural and urban areas with a lagging economy' (US Dept. Commerce 1980, 2). The reduction of unemployment and underemployment, an increase in the income of residents and the fostering of local capital were to be the means. This represents some shift from the initial 1965 policy (Martin and Leone 1977) concerned with pockets of the lagging nonmetro hinterland, with its resource-based problems, towards greater recognition of the difficulties of the older inner cities (OECD 1980, 19). Indeed, in the abortive House Bill 1979 (US Congress, House 1979) more than 90 per cent of the national population would have been eligible for EDA assistance, though President Carter and the Senate (US Congress, Senate 1979) had favored an extension to only 67 per cent (*Congressional Quarterly Almanac* 1979, 310). The emerging crisis of the American cities in the 1970s 'put depressed regions off the back burner' (Zysman 1980, 149), whilst the Revenue Sharing Programs of the Nixon Administration transferred responsibility to the States for some of the policies EDA had operated. The Reagan administration is accelerating this process under a New Federalism, intended to strengthen the decision powers of the States, though with a somewhat diminished financial provision. Regional EDA policy thus held center stage only briefly, because it was founded on a very fragile political alliance. Only a policy which could simultaneously have dealt with declining industrial areas and backward rural regions would have been politically acceptable in the longer term (Zysman 1980, 156), and no such utopian policy has yet emerged from among even the most concerned of social scientists.

The Area Redevelopment Administration (1961) was the precursor of EDA (1965). The political bargaining to create the ARA diffused the original purpose of the 1955 Douglas Bill, which had been intended to combat urban unemployment in the North (Zysman 1980, 143). Low-income and underemployed rural areas in the South also became eligible. Under the 1961 Act delivery of Federal aid was at the county level. Each county had to prepare an Overall Economic Development Program (OEDP), to be approved also by the State, before very limited Federal investment funds became available. Funds could not be used for the relocation or expansion of firms in new areas, and outmigration might not be encouraged. Such a piecemeal, undiscriminating approach 'simply opened the "pork-barrel"' (Zysman 1980, 143) and did not achieve the intended objectives. Yet the ARA nevertheless provided a useful test platform for local economic development policy (Romus 1974, 45).

In the heyday of President Johnson's Great Society program the Public Works and Economic Development Act (PWEDA) of 1965 created the Economic Development Administration (EDA) and, in the same year, from a different Congressional political base, the Appalachian Regional Development Act created the Appalachian Regional Commission. Regional and area-based programs thereafter developed not so much in tandem as in a measure of agency opposition. ERA and ARC failed to agree on priority districts for development or on the designation of growth centers. In such a political melee social science theory was reduced to being 'an occasional weapon of rhetoric in bureaucratic infighting' (Zysman 1980, 140). Under the 1965 Act counties became eligible for public works grants (Title I of EDA), the lion's share of development funding, on the basis of 6 per cent or greater unemployment. The single county basis of designation under ARA was abandoned in favor of creating Economic Development Districts (EDD), Title IV, defined by high unemployment, population loss, low median income, a sudden rise in unemployment, or economic distress in an Indian reservation (ACIR 1978B, 23). Since 1965 there have been shifts in the general thrust and purpose of EDA policy, the criteria for EDDs have become broader, and the political support has waxed and waned, mostly in a negative direction.

A major conflict of purpose has been between a 'worst-first' and a 'best-first' or Big Bang policy. The early 'worst-first' priority, severely criticized by social scientists, targetted aid to areas with the least potential for growth, a policy dropped in 1968 in favor of a more creative growth-center approach. A growth-center strategy postulates benefits for a hinterland from such polarized growth, in 'spread' effects but also in commuting or migration to the core. A growth center should have 'sufficient population, resources, public facilities, industry and commercial services to ensure that its development can become relatively self-sustaining'. At first a notional population of 250,000 was envisaged, progressively reduced in the face of political pressures of self-interest in widespread designation and the scarcity of both funds and expertise to implement the policy. Growth potential could not be unambiguously defined and many centers with clear potential were, for that very reason, excluded from development aid. The EDA-designated centers were generally much smaller than the 50,000 population that Berry had found to be the minimum for a positive hinterland influence. The average population was only 38,192, the median only 24,145 (Hansen 1970, 152–3). EDA simply did not have the funds to create the many external economies needed to induce or reinforce economic growth. Most growth centers did not stimulate the hinterland, absorbed all the investment with little spread effect, drew workers in from outside the EDD, and did not solve local unemployment (Estall 1977, 347). The prime beneficiaries were the residents of the growth center and less than 10 per cent of jobs created went to workers in the hinterland (Levitan and Zickler 1976, 142). The growth-center concept was formally abandoned by EDA though it has lingered on in the rhetoric of the ARC. It may well have been a technically correct policy but it lacked the necessary backing in the political marketplace.

EDDs (Fig 2.3) have been described as 'an experiment on the frontiers of creative federalism' (Levine 1969, 169), development bodies composed of local government, private sector, and minority representatives. Each district contains one or more 'redevelopment areas' and must include one or two

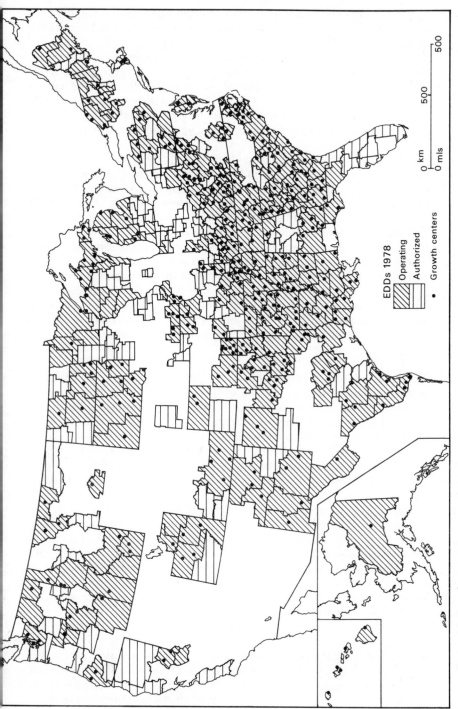

2.3   Economic Development Districts (EDDs), 1978

growth centers within 20 to 30 miles commuting range. An OEDP has to be prepared before designation and approved by both State and Federal governments. Though the EDD has weak powers and the policy has been cynically described as providing 'resident strong backs and migrant strong minds for the nation' (Levin 1969, 217) it has on balance succeeded, and certainly spread. By 1977, 214 EDDs covered 70 per cent of the counties within the continental US and 62 per cent of all EDA-designated areas. On the other hand, the EDA financial commitment in the areas had fallen from 70 per cent in the 1960s to only about 7 per cent by 1977 (US Dept. Commerce 1977B, v–7).

During the 1970s EDA was weakened through the transfer of powers to the States under Revenue Sharing and by the loss of authority for rural development to the Department of Agriculture (Rural Development Act 1972). On the other hand, though economic development planning faded to a set of immediate public investment projects and countercyclical programs, EDA assumed new responsibilities: for non-District Rural counties; large distressed inner-city areas and neighborhoods; and in promoting planning, and redevelopment strategies for metropolitan areas. This has meant considerable diffusion of EDA efforts and finances, with 2,281 areas in receipt of aid in 1978 (OECD 1980, 26), a fatal weakness of making virtually universal what had been intended as a geographically discriminant policy. Yet this alone would not justify the even lower priority for economic development assistance, intended under the New Federalism of the 1980s.

2.6.4 *Multistate regional organizations*

The Appalachian Regional Commission (ARC), created in 1965, has in many respects been a prototype for the 11 Title V Regional Commissions (1965 onwards) which have today become virtually 'wall-to-wall' throughout the USA (Fig 2.4). Additionally, at the regional level, there are five Title II River Basin Commissions (Water Resources Planning Acts, 1962, 1965); the Delaware (1961) and Susquehanna (1970) Basin Federal-inter-State Compact Commissions; some 150 generally single-purpose regional interstate compacts; and 10 Federal Regional Councils, established by Presidential Order (1972).

The range, proliferation, and diversity of such Federal–multistate bodies responds to two needs. The first concerns redistribution of political authority, which neither the traditional compact between States nor the Federal–single State relationship adequately satisfied (ACIR 1972, 169). The State pattern was seen as too artificial, with too many dissimilar units to 'encompass the necessary externalities' (Derthick 1974, 5) in a modern economic system. Secondly, major national economic and social problems, such as drought, flood control, energy shortages, urban disintegration, or rural poverty, far transcended the scale of States. To tackle such problems effectively larger programming authorities were required, though Derthick (1974, 8) argued that regional organizations could not be justified solely as responses to the scale level of issues. Though technically justifiable, the Federal–multistate bodies were regarded by some (Derthick 1974, 4, 182) as 'excrescences on the constitutional system' or 'deviant new growth in a governmental landscape', lacking in an electorate and barely visible to the public. On the other hand, such bodies might counterbalance the burgeoning power of specialized Federal agencies, even though it was feared they risked becoming no more than additional 'Federal instrumentalities' (Derthick 1974, 194).

Multistate regional organizations have certain similarities: representation by Federal and State, but not local, governments; planning or priority setting functions; dependent partly on annual Congressional funding; with a co-ordination role, and their own technical staff. All have had difficulties in performance, none has posed a threat to sponsoring levels of government, and their agency status has never risked establishing a fourth tier of government (Walker 1972). Yet there are both subtle and fundamental differences: in the prime source of initiatives for their creation; the nature of the constituent areas; the legal or statutory character; functions and powers; levels of funding; the basis and balance of political representation; and in the range of planning or programming undertaken. Among the most important differences is that between the bodies concerned with economic development and those with water-resource planning functions. Mandates differ widely and so does the extent of independent operational control in decision-taking.

Given these differences, no neat classification of organizations is possible. Strong forms include the ARC and the two Federal–interState River Basin Compacts, all with vigorous political backing from within the areas concerned. The Title V Regional Commissions and the Title II River Basin Commissions lacked grass-roots regional support and represented the weak organizational and financial outcome of political bargaining at the national level. The ARC and the Title V Commissions had a wide remit for stimulating activities and allocating resources in a controversial field of planning and programming. The Title II Commissions and the River Basin Compacts had a clearer focus, on multipurpose basinwide water resource development and management. The ARC and the Title V Commissions had to rely more heavily on the Congressional purse and both were weak in the face of intransigence by their constituent States. Whereas the ARC had specific program funding for nine headings and a good range of planning instruments, the Title V Commissions had only limited powers for planning or demonstration projects and supplementary grants. Ironically, it was the Title V Commissions which were responsible for drafting comprehensive regional plans and action programs, whilst the ARC covered only the guidelines for the annual review of State plans. Yet the Title V Commissions lacked any statutory connection with the multicounty economic development districts within their regions. Similarly, the Title II Commissions faced problems like those of the River Basin Compacts, but they had only concurrent jurisdiction with State and Federal governments and not the clearly defined responsibilities and authority over Federal agencies enjoyed under the Compacts.

Many Federal–multistate organizations are thus not quite what they at first seem and, moreover, they have waxed and waned with the changing political climate. Most have been weakened or remained weak, 'institutional frailties as intermediaries among traditional government entities' (Co. State Planning Agencies 1977, 2). State governors and officials have been ambivalent, but generally in opposition, seeing the added Federal financial or technical contributions outweighed by frustrations and burdens. On the positive side, the organizations are often seen as mechanisms for diffusing Federal power and assisting States in intergovernmental program management. Some States wish to replace the Federal–multistate organizations by Governors' coalitions, adding aggregate State powers to bodies such as the Southern Growth Policies Board (1972); the Coalition of Northeastern Governors (CONEG 1976); and the Western Governors' Policy Office (WESTPO 1977).

The Appalachian Regional Commission (ARC) has been a proving ground for regional policy and for intergovernmental cooperation (Rothblatt 1971; Newman 1972; Estall 1982). Low incomes, high unemployment, the lack of urbanization, deficiencies in public services, low living standards, and persistent outmigration of the young and able identified Appalachia as a victim of technological change (ACIR 1972, 18). The Commission thus grew from the identified needs of the region, highlighted by the findings of the President's Appalachian Regional Commission (PARC 1963) and born under the 1965 PWEDA legislation (Appalachian Regional Development Act 1965), which had also created the EDA. The Federal–multistate character was reflected in the membership of 13 State governors and a Federal co-chairman. The remit and how it might be conducted was very much less clear. The region was loosely termed Appalachia, but there was general internal geographic, social, and economic diversity. Three or four major subdivisions identified different problem mixes, from the rugged mountain tracts to the hill country, the Piedmont, and the lowlands. Northern Appalachia is the more urbanized and developed, with inbuilt coalfield and marginal farming problems; the center has the lowest incomes, the least urbanization, the poorest public services and housing stock; the south has a developing economy, with metro and urban counties rising towards the national average. Individual States had the responsibility for drawing the ARC boundary within their territory.

The problems differed spatially, but other issues too were potentially divisive. The ARC has been described as 'the triumph of geography over logic' (Zysman 1980, 144) for the State governors wanted an institutional framework for attacking the common problems of a single region, yet in practice the problems tackled were almost exclusively those of local areas. Furthermore, there was a lack of clear policy perspectives. Both backward rural and declining mining or industrial areas were included and the dilemma on priorities reflected that of the EDA at the same time. The regional problem involved the lack of skills and capacity to adapt, but also deficiency of demand in the economy. Any attempt to alleviate these shortcomings required different policies, but both were tackled without sensible discrimination, and with scarce financial means. Then there were physical resource and human resource problems and the priority to people or to place controversy. Responsibility for many social programs remained with other Federal agencies and the ARC progressively became more concerned with public works and area development. In economic development there were major achievements, since the ARC was the only Federal-multistate organization with sufficient investment powers to alter the character of a region (Co. State Planning Agencies 1977, 8).

The 1965 Act authorized special Federal financial aid to build and operate public facilities considered basic for economic expansion, such as roads and health services, and to restore environmental resources (timber, water, strip-mined land) ravaged by neglect and misuse. No program could be undertaken in a State without its consent and no funds could be used for relocation of firms or facilities. One-half ARC expenditure has been on highways, one-quarter on health facilities and 'topping up' the Federal share (not more than 80 per cent) of matching grants (Zysman 1980, 148). The logic of concentrating on highways was twofold: to break down the sense and the reality of isolation, to permit greater commuting and the influx of new industry; but also because highways have always been politically popular weapons (ACIR 1978B, 27).

The development strategy has been to improve the environment for entrepreneurial growth through an improved urban/industrial pattern. Spatially, this has meant two contrasting policies, for growth centers ('with significant potential for future growth' and a good return on the investment dollar), and Local Development Districts (LDDs). Funds were lacking for an effective growth-center policy, but political will by the States was even more so. Though Federal consultants prescribed growth centers, the States wanted dispersal of investment, and on balance they won the day (Zysman 1980, 147). Each State chose its own growth centers and there was great diversity in the 13 methods employed. Surprisingly, almost half the approved projects were in fact concentrated in the growth centers, though there was virtually no interstate cooperation. LDDs too were chosen by the States, 69 covering the 397 counties. Each LDD prepares an area-wide action program (AAP) but has only an advisory role and little political voice. Relations between LDDs and the State legislature varied, usually more effective in housing, education, and social services than on issues of economic development (ACIR 1972, 51). There is no clear coordination between the LDDs and the Economic Development Districts of the EDA.

Overall verdicts on the ARC are inclined to pessimism. Attempts to coordinate areawide planning are said to have been abandoned, in favor of planning by States and communities (Zysman 1980, 147). Only in highway development and interstate transfers of Federal funding has there been positive regional cooperation (Appalachian Conf. 1978, 22). Yet there have been major achievements. The development strategy has influenced programming decisions of Federal agencies, especially in vocational education and health services, whilst the highway program has been an outstanding development. Figures too speak for themselves. Between 1965 and 1977 Appalachia gained 1.5 million jobs and per capita income increased from 78 to 85 per cent of the national average. People in poverty fell from 31 to 14 per cent and out-migration had been stopped and locally set into reverse. How much these achievements may be directly ascribed to the ARC and how much to the working out of market forces continues to be the focus of partisan political debate.

Title V Regional Development Commissions   The Title V Commissions were created under the 1965 PWEDA legislation, as Federal–multistate organizations to promote regional development by 'reducing or removing

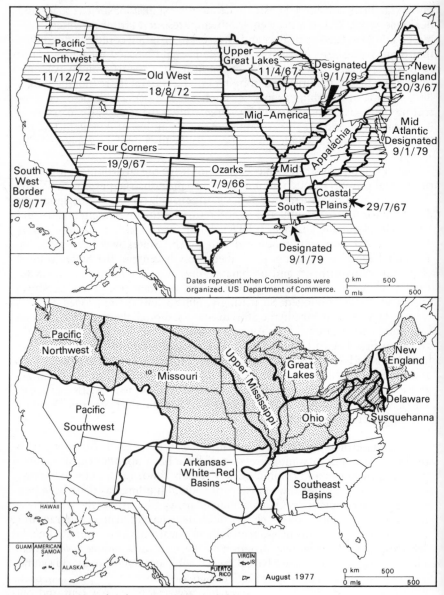

2.4   Economic development regions, 1982

2.5   Title II River Basin Commissions: Inter-state Compact Commissions;
and Interagency Committees

obstacles to growth through planning, research, technical assistance and
supplemental funding of Federal grant-in-aid programs'. Section 501 of the
1965 Act laid down the criteria for designation, mainly indicators of lagging

development, stagnation, or decline. The initiative for proposing a Commission came from the Governors of States in the intended region and the Secretary of Commerce decided the issue. At the outset, misunderstandings crept in. Some Governors saw the Title V Commissions as 'Little Appalachias' whilst the Bureau of the Budget likened them to the investigative Presidential Commission (PARC) which preceded the Appalachian Commission proper (Derthick 1974, 112). Such differences involved contrasting political authority. In reality a new degree of intergovernmental partnership was envisaged, a catalyst for comprehensive regional development planning and action programming. They were not to be 'regional artifacts of Federal policy (Derthick 1974, 129), but rather a Federal–multistate forum 'for accommodating the diversities of the nation whilst ensuring the national interest being met' (US Congress, Senate 1979, 676). The role of 'catalyst, convenor, coordinator and consensus-builder' sounded impressive (US Congress, Senate 1977, 128), but unlike the ARC, the Title V Commissions failed to attract funding.

Originally in 1966 five Title V Commissions were designated: for New England, the Coastal Plains, Four Corners, and Ozarks, and the Upper Great Lakes. The Old West and the Pacific Northwest were added in 1972, and the Southwest Border in 1976. The Coastal Plains, Four Corners, Ozarks, and the Southwest Border have subsequently had boundary changes, usually for expansion. In 1979 three new economic development regions were designated, but Commissions have not been appointed: Mid-America, Mid-Atlantic, and Mid-South (Fig 2.4). Though each designation is of contiguous areas and corresponds to either a distinctive set of problems or a corporate identity based on 'geography, culture, history, or economic relationships' (ACIR 1972, 62), there are very great differences between the regions (Table 2.4). Apart from area, size of population, or mean per capita income, there are fundamental contrasts in the problem mix and in regional political cultures. New England is distinctive, in focus on urban/industrial decline, accessibility, unemployment, and marginal farming. The Coastal Plains, on the other hand, are internally very differentiated, adjusting to sharp urban and industrial growth after 1945 in the south and a more agricultural, rural structure in the north. In the Four Corners region the social, economic, and environmental challenges to dispersed populations in the fragile lands of the arid West are a more severe version of the natural and economic hazards of rural and small-town tracts of the Old West. In the Pacific Northwest, too, the Federal government administers 50 per cent of the land. Agriculture and the aerospace industries are matters of structural concern and the problems of isolated communities or environmental conservation are not far behind. Since 1979 the Ozarks region reaches well down into Texas, with major energy-, water-, and land-use preoccupations. The Upper Great Lakes have high unemployment, poor energy resources, suffer from inaccessibility, and face severe problems of adjustment to twentieth-century decline in timber and iron or copper resources. The Southwest Border has all the frontier problems of the interface with the developing world in Mexico (House 1982B).

From an initial concern with pockets of economic distress the Commis-

TABLE 2.4   *Title V Commissions: area, population, and per capita incomes (1977)*

	Date of designation	Area (1,000 sq. miles)	Percentage of US	Population (1,000s)	Percentage of US	Per capita income ($)	Percentage of US
Coastal Plains	1966	129	3.6	12,669	5.8	5,938	84
Four Corners	1966	535	14.8	7,214	3.3	7,014	100
New England	1966	66	1.8	12,242	5.6	7,183	102
Ozarks	1966	323	8.9	16,003	7.4	6,338	90
Upper Gt. Lakes	1966	116	3.2	3,175	1.5	5,710 (est.)	81
Pacific NW	1972	248	6.9	6,891	3.2	7,156	102
Old West	1972	469	13.0	4,070	1.9	6,480	92
SW Border	1977	116	3.2	4,254	2.0	6,045 (est.)	86
		2,006	55.4	66,518	30.7	6,535	93
US		3,615	100.0	216,320	100.0	7,019	100.0

Source: US Dept. Commerce, Office of Regional Economic Development (1980).

sions have widened their remit to developing and counseling on growth management. Long-range economic development plans are prepared, advice given on EDDs, private investment stimulated, comment made on proposed legislation affecting the region, plans for the component States developed in common, and the maximum use made of Inter-state Compacts (ACIR 1972, 62). The development plan is a research-based inventory, formulating a strategy and action program and emphasizing goals for closing the income or employment gaps (Derthick 1974, 118). Though basically a 'top–down' process, with no citizen participation, the plans have increasingly become a compendium of State plans with minimal interrelationship. Each plan is reviewed by the Federal Advisory Council (FACRED) and passed to the President for approval. It should then become a set of guidelines for regional program and project funding. In practice, plans have either proved to be unsatisfactory, have been swallowed in the Federal structure with little response, or have been approved but remained dormant without application.

The weaknesses of the Title V Commissions are directly political in origin. There is no articulated national policy for the regions to give context to the plans; and since virtually all the national space is now covered by Commissions, their distinctive voices are correspondingly muted (US Congress, Senate 1977, 10–12). Furthermore, the formative years for regional policy were under two hostile administrations, which were said to have 'provided just enough funds to ensure failure' (Appalachian Conf. 1978, 23). Though the legislative branches of government were territorially based, Federal agencies preferred structural frameworks, cutting across jurisdictional boundaries (US Congress, Senate 1979, 673). As the Federal interest in the Commissions subsided the commitment of Commission officials to regionalism usually waned no less speedily (US Congress, Senate 1977, 77). States increasingly tended to view the Commissions as but another Federal grant-in-aid program or a means of leverage against the Federal government.

With severely limited funding (only $63 million in 1977) and lacking a firm political constituency, the Commissions could at best have limited success. The allocation of resources to create jobs or to deal with unemployment was minimal, and often in competition with those of Federal agencies. Congressmen preferred the direct political feedback from having initiated public works projects rather than the concealed benefits and loss of spending control in block grants to the Commissions. Nevertheless, the Regional Commission concept had merits and achievements. Apart from the data banks, research reports, and recommendations, the Commissions acted as a valuable discussion forum, contributing also to a sense of regional identity with which to face the major economic and social problems transcending State boundaries. Such a need remains and is likely to grow under the energy and environmental crises. For its fulfillment it awaits the necessary political goodwill, founded upon enhanced self-interest and to mutual advantage. Government actions in the early 1980s seen destined to ensure that such hopes will be indefinitely deferred.

The *Title II River Basin Commissions* (Fig. 2.5) have also, in a sense, flattered to deceive. Unlike the TVA, they lack operational powers or funding for development. Given the limited legislative mandate under the Federal

Water Resources Planning Act (1965) and the wide remit for multilevel, basinwide water resource planning (ACIR 1972, 96) it is not surprising that planning and priority setting has had to be conducted by cooperation and consensus. The Title II Commissions have concurrent, not overriding, jurisdiction with State and Federal agencies. Presented with difficult issues of soil and water conservation, irrigation, water supply, or flood control, and limited funding, the Commissions have pragmatically focussed on immediate problem areas. There have been major achievements in identifying, researching, documenting, and monitoring water resources, but 'comprehensive, coordinated joint planning' (CCJP) has faded in the face of independently exercised Federal and State powers, resisting modification of their own plans and projects (Co. State Planning Agencies 1977, 2); of $32 million spent in the Missouri basin in 1977 only $2 million passed through the Commission.

Thirty-three States belong to one or more of the River Basin Commissions, for the Great Lakes, Ohio, Upper Mississippi, Missouri, New England, and the Pacific Northwest. Other States have rejected this Federal–multistate concept, preferring to deal direct with Federal water agencies or to treat with the Congressional Committees on which water-scarce States in the South and West have traditionally been well represented and powerful.

The Delaware and Susquehanna basins are administered under Federal extensions of an Interstate Compact (1961, 1970). The remit is 'to plan, construct and operate water resources projects and facilities and to develop plans for water use, control, conservation and management' (Co. State Planning Agencies 1977, 11). The Federal Agencies here are legally bound to accept the Compact decisions, promoting a more orderly and rational development of the river systems than Title II Commissions could hope for.

Interstate Compacts (Barton 1965) are legal and statutory instruments for administering common policies transcending the boundaries of a single State. The device has been in use in America for more than 150 years, initially for the delimitation of administrative boundaries. All Compacts are in a sense regional, but at many scale-levels from local to nationwide. The topics covered are equally varied, from Great Lakes basin management to forest fire protection, water resource sharing, metropolitan transit, nuclear energy, or higher education. Many are between only two States, others more extensive. All are legally binding instruments. Some have the Federal government as signatory, others require Congressional sanction, whilst yet others have no need of Federal approval. In a complex economy and society the Compact is a flexible means of cooperative endeavor for mutual benefit, without infringement of the sovereignty of either State or Federal governments.

Federal Regional Councils are a limited expression of Federal decentralization, mainly as 'listening posts' and for consultative purposes. Four were created experimentally in 1968, enlarged to eight a year later and ten today, covering the entire nation. The aim was for better coordination of Federal agencies and programs, to rationalize delivery of funding and decentralize decision-taking. The regional boundaries were to be common for the principal agencies (DOL, HEW, HUD, OEO, and SBA; later EDA and Law Enforcement Assistance Administration), but this has been only partially realized. There was a mismatch with Title V Commission boundaries: for example, the Four Corners Commission fell into three Federal regions! The States have generally been unresponsive to the FRCs and the Title V Commissions have preferred to liaise directly with Washington.

In a more rational and coherent space-economy there should no doubt be uniform subnational units with common boundaries for all development and planning purposes. In a federal society, with coordinate divisions of political powers, this is likely to remain chimeral, even more so than in the admittedly unsatisfactory state of affairs in western unitary States such as Britain or France (House 1978, 1982A).

2.7 SUBSTATE REGIONALISM

The rapidity of population growth and technological change impacted severely upon a jurisdictional maze of local government, in which the 'preservation of mild chaos is an important goal of the American Federal system' (Grodzins 1960, 78). Local government units and functions were designed for the simpler needs of a smaller population, a system now outmoded in organization and excessively fragmented, with a proliferation of special-purpose districts (ACIR 1978C, 7). In both metro and nonmetro areas the polycentric political system has been fractionalized by a host of single- or multipurpose areawide bodies, growing intermittently and incrementally, often without context or relationship to others. Most States have been 'silent partners in local regionalism' (ACIR 1973, 16), with functions irregularly and excessively diffused to units responsive to Federal rather than to State policies.

There are some 78,000 jurisdictions in the American political landscape: 3,044 counties; 18,517 municipalities; 17,000 townships; 15,780 independent school districts; 23,885 special districts; 530 substate districts; and 281 metro areas (ACIR 1978C, 4), containing 16,802 general purpose local governments, or over one-fourth of the total. Among these the most politically feasible are usually the least effective, and vice versa. Many special districts are Federal agency fiefdoms, regional counties lack powers to achieve their purposes, whilst there are also many obsolete, non-viable general purpose local government units. Indeed, it is precisely the weakness of local government that has led to the creation of substitute special-purpose districts by State and Federal governments. Though the situation is chaotic there is no consensus for reform, and the mosaic is different in almost every State. At least five schools of thought are in the field (ACIR 1977, 31–2): the public choice or pluralistic free-market paradigm; for consolidation, by full-scale local-regional mergers; for a two- or three-tier (city/county + Council of Government) system; for voluntary, piecemeal change; or, pragmatically, for any option, including the status quo.

Federal policy towards local jurisdictions had been rather narrowly function-orientated, focussed on delivery of a multitude of Federal programs. Some pass through local governments, but most are delivered through regional counties (COG, RPC), areawide planning agencies, or A-95 clearing houses, for intergovernmental cooperation. Though there is Federal support for local government improvement, the flexible system of special districts is a bureaucratic preference (ACIR 1978D, 3). Local government is entirely a creature of individual States, created by elected representatives or determined by the State Constitution. Only the State can establish general-purpose local governments and there has been great reluctance, on the part of both politicians and the public, to accept any thoroughgoing local reorganization (ACIR 1977, 1).

Planning and development programs have been a stimulus to local reform. Comprehensive growth plans or land-use regulations have been adopted by 44 States, but only since 1960, following upon HUD (1954) guidelines, under the HHFA 701 program. This was concerned with land-use, transportation, or natural-resource management in the longer-term. In metro areas the organizational problem for planning remains acute, the more so in that State boundaries along riverlines often carve up the major cities. At least four tiers of jurisdiction are common: interstate areawide, single-state subarea, single county, and municipality, to which must be added countless special districts (ACIR 1973, 8). On average there are 90 local governments per SMSA, made up of 2 or more counties, 13 townships, 21 municipalities, 18 school districts, and 30 to 35 special districts, a triumph for democratic representation, a nightmare for coordination or programming. In nonmetro areas are located 70 per cent of the municipalities, 85 per cent of counties, 80 per cent of townships, and 67 per cent of special districts. The economic and social problems there may be less pressing, but the apathy of local government toward reform is even more deeply entrenched.

Because of the inertia of local government, special districts and Councils of Government are likely to spread further and accumulate more functions. The special district authority is usually self-sufficient fiscally, technically specialized, efficient, and geographically flexible, able to span local or State jurisdictional boundaries. Councils of Government (COG), or Regional Planning Commissions (RPC) in metro-areas are multifunctional, voluntary regional associations composed of local elected officials or representatives. Common problems can be discussed, information exchanged and consensus attempted, but action thereafter must originate in State or local governments.

Regional and area development policies at Federal, multistate, State, or local levels reflect the geographical diversity, the contrasting heritage, and the differentiated political culture of the US. To Europeans the spectrum of such policies may seem fragmentary, inadequate, partial, lacking in direction, strength, or power, with correspondingly limited achievements arising from too scarce funding, and the lack of political goodwill. To social scientists the tardy and piecemeal nature of incremental policies, or the lack of coherence within and between them, represents a perennial frustration, even more so when theory or prescription may advocate a clear direction and set of concepts or principles for creating or managing change. If this is to be regarded as unsatisfactory and to be improved, then there must be a closer dialogue among social scientists, politicians, and policy-makers, a dialogue which all must positively seek and from which all must surely stand to gain.

References

ADVISORY COMMN. INTERGOVTAL. RELNS. (1967) *State–local taxation and industrial location* (Washington, DC).
—— (1972) *Multistate regionalism*, A-39 (Washington, DC).
—— (1973) *Regional decision-taking: New strategies for sub-state districts: Sub-state regionalism and the federal system*, Vol. I (Washington, DC).
—— (1977) *Regionalism revisited: recent areawide and local responses* (Washington, DC).
—— (1978A) *The role of metropolitan organizations in national growth and development* (White House Conf.: Washington, DC).
—— (1978B) *Non-metropolitan growth and development* (White House Conf.: Washington, DC).
—— (1978C) *Assessing the inadequacies of government structure and processes: The state–local perspective* (Washington, DC).
—— (1978D) *Federal and State roles in building the capacity of subordinate units* (Washington, DC).
—— (1980) *Regional growth: history perspectives*, A 74 (Washington, DC).
—— (1981) *Regional growth: Inter-State tax competition*, A 76, (Washington, DC).
ALONSO, W. (1975) 'Aspects of regional planning and theory in the US', ch. 36 in FRIEDMANN and ALONSO, 773–87.
Appalachian Conference on Balanced Growth and Regional Development (1978) *Issues Papers* (Charleston, W. Virginia).
ARCHER, J. C. (1982) 'Some geographical aspects of the American presidential election of 1980, *Pol. Geogr. Q.* 1 2, 123–6.
—— and TAYLOR, P. J. (1981) *Section and Party: a political geography of American Presidential elections from Andrew Jackson to Ronald Reagan* (Chichester: Wiley).
BARTON, W. V. (1965) *InterState Compacts in the political process* (Chapel Hill: Univ. N. Carolina Press).
BERRY, B. J. L. and DAHMANN, D. C. (1977) *Population redistribution in the US in the 1970s* (Washington, DC: Nat. Acad. Sci.).
BEYERS, W. B. (1979) 'Contemporary trends in the regional economic development of the United States', *Prof. Geogr.* 31 1, 34–44.
BORTS, G. H. and STEIN, J. (1964) *Economic growth in a free market* (New York: Columbia Univ. Press).
BRIGGS, R. and REES, J. (1982) 'Control factors in the economic development of non-metropolitan America', *Environ. and Planning*, A (forthcoming).
BROWN, A. J. (1972) *The framework of regional economics in the UK* (Cambridge: CUP).
—— and BURROWS, E. M. (1977) *Regional economic problems* (London: Allen & Unwin).
BROWNING, C. E. (1973) 'The geography of federal outlays', *Univ. N. Carolina at Chapel Hill, Stud. in Geogr.* 4.
—— and GESSLER, W. (1979) 'The Sunbelt–Snowbelt: a case of sloppy regionalizing', *Prof. Geogr.* 31 1, 66–74.
BRUNN, S. D. (1974) 'Political cultures', ch. 9 in *Geography and Politics in America* (New York: Harper & Row), 237–70.
—— and HOFFMAN, W. L. (1969) 'The geography of Federal grants-in-aid to States', *Econ. Geogr.* 45 236–9.
BURNS, L. S. and VAN NESS, K. (1981) 'The decline of the metropolitan economy', *Urb. Stud.* 18 2, 169–80.
CAMERON, G. C. (1970) *Regional economic development: the Federal role* (Baltimore, Md.: John Hopkins Univ. Press).

CASETTI, E. (1981) 'A catastrophe model of regional dynamics', *Ann. Ass. Am. Geogr.* **71** 4, 572–9.

CLARK, T. A. (1980) Regional and structural shifts in the American economy since 1960', ch. 8 in BRUNN, S. D. and WHEELER, J. O. (eds.) *The American metropolitan system* (London: Arnold), 111–25.

CLAVEL, P., FORESTER, J., and GOLDSMITH, W. W. (1980) *Urban and regional planning in an age of austerity* (New York: Pergamon).

Congressional Quarterly Almanac (1979) (Washington, DC).

COUNCIL OF STATE PLANNING AGENCIES (1977) 'State Strategies for Multistate organizations', *State Planning Ser.* 8 (Washington, DC).

CRUICKSHANK, A. B. (1980) 'Development of the Deep South: a reappraisal', *Scott. Geogrl. Mag.* **96** 2, 91–104.

—— (1981) 'USA Census '80: a Note', *Scott. Geogrl. Mag.* **97** 3, 175–82.

CUMBERLAND, J. H. (1971) *Regional development: experiences and prospects in the USA* (The Hague: Mouton).

DERTHICK, M. (1974) *Between State and Nation: regional organizations of the USA* (Washington, DC: Brookings Instn.).

ELAZAR, D. J. (1972) *American federalism: a view from the States* (New York: Crowell).

ESTALL, R. (1977) 'Regional planning in the United States: an evaluation of experience under the 1965 Economic Development Act', *Tn. Plann. Rev*, **48** 4, 341–64.

—— (1980) 'The changing balance of the Northern and Southern regions of the US', *J. Am. Stud.* **14** 3, 365–86.

—— (1982) 'Planning in Appalachia: an examination of the Appalachian regional development programme and its implications for the future of the American Regional Planning Commissions', *Trans. Inst. Br. Geogr.* NS 7 1, 35–58.

FLORESTANO, P. S. and MARANDO, V. L. (1981) *The States and the metropolis* (New York: Dekker).

FRIEDMANN, J. (1966) *Regional development policy: a case study of Venezuela* (Cambridge, Mass.: MIT Press).

—— and ALONSO, W. (1975) *Regional policy: Readings in theory and applications* (Cambridge, Mass.: MIT Press).

—— and WEAVER, C. (1979) *Territory and function: The evolution of regional planning* (London: Arnold).

GOTTMANN, J. G. (ed.) (1980) *Core and periphery* (Beverly Hills, Cal.: Sage).

GRODZINS, M. (1960) 'The Federal system' in *Goals for Americans* (Englewood Cliffs, NJ: Prentice-Hall).

HALLETT, G. (1973) 'The political economy of regional policy', ch. 1 in HALLETT, G. RANDALL, P. and WEST, E. G. (eds.) *Regional policy for ever?*, IEA Readings 11 (London: Inst. Econ. Aff.), 1–16.

HANSEN, N. M. (1970) *Rural poverty and the urban crisis* (Bloomington, Ind.: Indiana Univ. Press).

—— (1974) 'Regional policy in the US', ch. 9 in HANSEN, N. M. (ed.) *Public policy and regional development* (Cambridge, Mass.: Ballinger).

HERMANSEN, T. (1971) 'Spatial organization and economic development', *Devel. Stud.* 1 (Univ. Mysore, India).

HOLLAND, S. (1976) *The regional problem* (London: Macmillan).

HOUSE, J. W. (1978) *France: an applied geography* (London: Methuen).

—— (ed.) (1982A) *The UK Space: resources, environment and the future* (London: Weidenfeld & Nicolson) 3rd edn.

—— (1982B) *Frontier on the Rio Grande: A political geography of development and social deprivation* (Oxford: Clarendon Press).

JOHNSTON, R. J. (1978) 'Political spending in the US: analyses of political influences on the allocation of federal money to local environments', *Environ. and Plann.* A, X, 691–704.

—— (1980) 'The geography of federal spending in the United States of America', *Geogr. Res. Stud. Ser. 2* (Chichester: Wiley).

JUSENIUS, C. L. and LEDEBUR, L. C. (1976) 'A myth in the making: the southern economic challenge and northern economic decline', EDA, *Econ. Devel. Res. Rept.* (Washington, DC: US Dept. Commerce).

KASARDA, J. D. (1980) 'The implications of contemporary redistribution trends for national urban policy', *Soc. Sci. Qa.* 61 373–400.

KLAUSEN, T. A. (1973) 'Regional comparative advantage in the US', *J. Reg. Sci.* 13 1, 97–105.

LABOVITZ, I. M. (1978) 'Federal expenditures and revenues in States', *Intergovernmental Perspective*, 44, 16–23.

LEVIN, M. R. (1969) *Community and regional planning* (New York: Praeger).

LEVITAN, S. (1964) *Federal aid to depressed areas* (Baltimore, Md.: Johns Hopkins Univ. Press).

—— and ZICKLER, J. (1976) *Too little but not too late: Federal aid to lagging areas* (Lexington, Mass.: D. C. Heath).

MALECKI, E. J. (1981) 'Government funded R & D: some regional economic implications', *Prof. Geogr.* 33 1, 72–82.

MARTIN, C. H. and LEONE, R. A. (1977) *Local economic development: the federal connection* (Lexington, Mass.: D. C. Heath).

MILNE, W. J., GLICKMAN, N. J., and ADAMS, F. G. (1980) 'A framework for analyzing regional growth and decline: a multiregion econometric model of the US', *J. Reg. Sci.* 20 2, 173–89.

MORRILL, R. L. (1979) 'Stages in patterns of population concentration and dispersion', *Prof. Geogr.* 31 1, 55–65.

—— and WOHLENBERG, E. H. (1971) *The geography of poverty* (New York: McGraw Hill).

MURPHY, T. P. (1971) *Science, geopolitics and federal spending* (Lexington, Mass.: D. C. Heath).

MURRAY, A. (1981) 'Redistricting still plagued by confusion', *Nat. J.* 39 2, 69–73.

MYRDAL, G. (1957) *Economic theory and underdeveloped regions* (London: Methuen).

NEWMAN, M. (1972) *The political economy of Appalachia* (Lexington, Mass.: D. C. Heath).

NORTH, D. C. (1975) 'Location theory and regional economic growth', ch. 13 in FRIEDMANN and ALONSO, 332–47.

ODUM, H. W. and MOORE, H. E. (1938) *American regionalism* (New York: Henry Holt).

OECD (1980) *Regional policies in the United States* (Paris: OECD).

O'ROURKE, T. G. (1981) 'The Frostbelt–Sunbelt controversy', *Newsletter, Univ. Virginia,* 57 8.

PACK, J. R. (1978) 'Frostbelt and Sunbelt: Convergence over time', *Intergovernmental Perspective,* 4 4, 8–15.

PATTERSON, S. C. (1966) *The political culture of the American States* (Iowa City: Univ. Iowa Press).

PERLOFF, H. S. and DODDS, V. W. (1963) 'How a region grows: Area Development in the US economy', *Comm. for Econ. Devel. Supp. Pap.* 17 (New York: CED).

PETERSEN, J. E. (1977) *Frostbelt vs Sunbelt, Pt. I: key trends of the Seventies,* Pt. II *Changing Federal policies* (Boston, Mass.: First Boston Bank Corp.).

PHILLIPS P. D. and BRUNN, S. D. (1980) 'New dynamics of growth in the American metropolitan system', ch. 1 in BRUNN, S. D. and WHEELER, J. O, (eds.) *The American Metropolitan System* (London: Arnold), 1–20.

RIFKIN, J. and BARBER, R. (1978) *The North will rise again: pensions, politics and power in the 1980s* (Boston: Beacon Press).

ROMANS, J. T. (1965) 'Capital exports and growth among US regions', *New England Res. Ser.* 1 (Middletown, Conn.).

ROMUS, P. (1974) *La Politique régionale des États Unis d'Amérique* (Bruxelles: Univ. de Bruxelles).

RONDINELLI, D. A. (1975) *Urban and regional development planning: policy and administration* (Ithaca, New York: Cornell Univ. Press).

ROSTOW, W. W. (1977) 'Regional change in the Fifth Kondratieff upswing', ch. 3 in PERRY, D. C. and WATKINS, A. J. (eds.) *The rise of the Sunbelt cities* (Beverly Hills, Cal.: Sage), 83–104.

ROTHBLATT, D. N. (1971) *Regional Planning: The Appalachian experience* (Lexington, Mass.: D. C. Heath).

—— (ed.) (1974) *National policy for urban and regional development* (Lexington, Mass.: D. C. Heath).

SALE, K. (1972) *Power shift: the rise of the Southern rim and its challenge to the Eastern establishment* (New York: Random House).

SHARKANSKY, I. (1970) *Regionalism in American politics* (Indianapolis, Ind.: Bobbs-Merrill).

SMITH, D. M. (1973) *The geography of social well-being in the US* (New York: McGraw Hill).

STERNLIEB, G. and HUGHES, J. W. (1977) 'New Metropolitan and regional realities', *J. Am. Inst. Plann.* 43 227–41.

STILWELL, F. J. B. (1972) *Regional economic policy* (London: Macmillan).

TIEBOUT, C. M. (1975) 'Exports and regional economic growth', ch. 14 in FRIEDMANN and ALONSO, 348–57.

ULLMANN, E. L. (1958) 'Regional development and the geography of concentration', *Pap. and Proc. Reg. Sci. Assoc.* 4 179–98.

US CONGRESS HOUSE (1979) *To amend the PW & EDA Act of 1965, to extend authorizations for three more years*, HR 2063 (Washington, DC.: USGPO).

—— SENATE (1977) Committee on Environment and Public Works, *Review of Title V Commission Plans*, 95–9, S322–10 (Washington, DC: USGPO).

—— SENATE (1979) *An Act to extend the Appalachian Regional Development Act and Title V of the PW & ED Act of 1965, and to provide for multistate regional development Commissions to promote balanced development in the regions of the Nation*, S.914 (Washington, DC: USGPO).

—— SENATE (1979) Committee on Environment and Public Works, Sub-Committee on Regional and Commercial Development, *Extension of the Appalachian Regional Commission and the Title V Regional Commissions*, 96-H. 14 (Washington, DC: USGPO).

US DEPT. COMMERCE, EDA (1977) *The development of a Subnational Economic Development Policy* (Washington, DC: USGPO).

—— (1980) *Annual Report 1979* (Washington, DC).

VANHOVE, N. and KLAASSEN, L. H. (1980) *Regional Policy: A European Approach* (Farnborough: Saxon House).

VAN WEESEP, J. (1980) 'The change to regional fortunes in the USA: a review', *Tijd. Econ. Soc. Geogr.* 71 3, 187–9.

VILE, M. J. C. (1970) *Politics in the USA* (London: Hutchinson).

WALKER, D. B. (1972) 'Interstate regional instrumentalities: a new piece in an old puzzle', *J. Am. Inst. Plann.* 38 359–68.

WEINSTEIN, B. L. and FIRESTINE, R. E. (1978) *Regional growth and decline in the United States: the rise of the Sunbelt and the decline of the Northeast* (New York: Praeger).
WEST, E. G. (1973) '"Pure" versus "operational" economics in regional policy', ch. 5 in HALLETT, G., RANDALL, P., and WEST, E. G. (eds.) *Regional policy for ever?* IEA Readings 11 (London: Inst. Econ. Aff.), 103–40.
WHEATON, W. C. (ed.) (1979) *Interregional movements and economic growth* (Washington, DC: The Urban Inst.).
WHITE HOUSE CONFERENCE (1978) *Balanced national growth and economic development* (Washington, DC).
WILLIAMSON, J. G. (1965) 'Regional inequality and the process of national development', *Econ. Devel. and Cult. Change*, 13 4, 3–84.
WINNICK, L. (1966) 'Place prosperity versus people prosperity: welfare consideration in the geographic redistribution of economic activity' (L. Ang. Cal.: Univ. Calif., Real Estate Res. Progr.).
ZYSMAN, J. (1980) 'Research, politics and policy: regional planning in America', ch. 4 in OECD *The utilization of the social sciences in policy-making in the USA* (Paris: OECD), 121–58.

3. Social Problems and Policies

JUDITH W. MEYER*

(*University of Connecticut at Storrs*)

3.1 INTRODUCTION

The tradition of government involvement in social issues is a long one, beginning with the earliest public schools, courts of law, and poor houses. However, most of this long tradition was on a local scale, with towns or townships shouldering local social responsibilities. During the Depression of the 1930s the Federal government became significantly involved in social welfare, developing employment programs, social insurance, and early forms of housing subsidy. After World War II, health care deficiencies drew national attention, and Federal funds were made available, often with required matching funds from the State governments, to build hospitals and train doctors.

In the 1960s Federal social commitment increased further with civil rights legislation and the War on Poverty. Federal involvement in racial desegregation issues began, nutrition programs were developed, special education projects were funded, and national health insurance programs were created for the poor and elderly. Federal funds have also been allocated to various crime prevention efforts, to making legal services available to the poor, and to providing a plethora of services for the elderly.

The general aim of government has been to ameliorate the social problems of individual citizens or groups of citizens, and provide a minimum standard of living for all residents under their jurisdiction; Federal involvement implies a national standard, unvarying from place to place within the nation. In addition, the theme of equality of opportunity for each American resonates through US history and provides legitimization for much social legislation (Lewis 1978, 3–5). Ideally, if governmental programs are successful, social problems of poverty, poor health, inadequate education, institutional and personal racism should be minimized. Given the substantial involvement of the Federal government in social policy, an important question is not only the extent to which social problems are being ameliorated, but the extent to which the regional differences in social problems are being reduced.

The United States as a nation has espoused both social and geographical mobility. Some geographical mobility has been in the pursuit of social mobility; witness the migration of many households to the American frontier, of Mormons from Midwestern areas of discrimination to a western area they dominated, of countless individuals from rural to urban areas, of southern rural blacks to northern cities, and of Puerto Ricans and other Latins to the farms and cities. The primary motive for migration has always been econo-

*Dr Meyer wishes to acknowledge financial support from the University of Connecticut Research Foundation, and the cartographic services of Randy Sands and the University of Connecticut Cartographic Laboratory.

mic. Geographical mobility continues in the US, but with some intriguing differences. At least some of the current migration patterns may be the result of government social policies. Whether migration in the 1980s will contribute to further reduction in social differences among individuals and among places remains an open question; in fact, some processes appear to exacerbate certain social problems. Because US mobility is not legally restricted by political boundaries, the effectiveness of local governments' efforts to deal with social ills may be confounded. Thus the role of population distribution in social problems and policies is a further theme.

A third theme grows out of the dual issues of regional as well as personal equalization of social needs and population redistribution. What level of government—local, State, or Federal—should be the principal arbiter and funder of social policy? As chief source of funds the Federal government has been able to serve as primary policy-maker. Considerable controversy exists in the early 1980s, however, concerning the appropriateness of this role.

3.2 SOCIO-CULTURAL PROBLEMS

The United States is a large, socially heterogenous nation. Considering the general affluence of its population in comparison with most of the world's population, its social problems are more modest and yet more appalling both to Americans and to foreign observers.

3.2.1. Poverty

The most central US social problem is the percentage of its citizens who live in poverty, basically a product of the market economy. Sufficient funds enable a household to eliminate most other potential problems, such as poor housing, health care, education, or even poor economic opportunity. Poverty is spatially omnipresent, and its causes (or at least its suggested causes) are numerous. However, concentrations of poor Americans exist at both the local and national scale, justifying a discussion of the geography of poverty. In addition, many of the solutions to poverty involve either direct spatial policies (see ch. 2) or policies applied differentially according to concentrations of impoverished people. Some of the spatial dimensions of the poverty problem must be considered, and some specific correlates of poverty concentrations must be identified, particularly racial and ethnic concentrations, variation in the age structure of populations, and variation in employment opportunities.

The extent of the poverty problem can be measured by the number of households whose incomes do not attain a particular standard set by the Federal government. Another mechanism for determining the extent to which income resources may be inadequate to live an average life is median per capita income or median family income in an area. Although per capita income and incidence of poverty have a high inverse correlation (Morrill and Wohlenberg 1971, 20; Smith 1972, 38), they are not equivalent measures. One further qualification must be noted before the geographical distribution of poverty is explored, namely the difference between the absolute number of people or households in poverty and the proportion of the total population that is in poverty. Both are useful measures, but they may tell rather different stories. California, for example, has a relatively low proportion of its households in poverty, but the absolute number of poor households in California is greater than in any other State (US Bureau of the Census 1980, 467).

a. *Geographical patterns.* Relatively small-scale analysis of the poverty issue and a summary of State-level variations are both relevant. First, a State-level approach offers a general perspective on the location of poverty. Secondly, and more importantly, much of the policy concerning poverty takes State characteristics into account. A State's involvement in welfare is obviously based in part on its citizens' ability to support such efforts. In addition, much of the allocation of Federal funding for welfare needs has been based on State-level statistics.

Remarkable consistency is apparent at the State level for the last two decades in terms of per capita income and proportion of all households in poverty (Table 3.1). Only nine States changed rank by 10 or more between 1960 and 1979 on per capita income; three New England States and two Mountain States declined dramatically; Virginia and three Western Plains States substantially increased their rank. Southern States retained their position at the bottom of the State rankings, joined in 1979 by two Mountain States and two northern New England States (Fig. 3.1). The ten States with the highest per capita incomes are more scattered, with three small States on the East Coast, Illinois in the Midwest, Wyoming and Nevada in the West, and all the Pacific States except Oregon.

An intercensal sample survey of income and education, conducted in 1976 to estimate the number of poor children in each State, provides recent information by State on economic characteristics (US Bureau of the Census 1979). Although the South continued to lag behind the remainder of the nation, the median family income in the region was the only one to register a significant increase in real terms during the 1970s; the other three regions all registered modest decreases. When the analysis of poverty change is restricted to children, 11 of the 17 Southern States showed substantial declines in proportions of children in poverty. Compared to the rest of the nation, that performance is promising, because only 8 of 34 non-Southern States showed a significant decrease in the poverty rate of children. The more general decline in poverty rates throughout the US appears closely linked to the substantial decline in poverty among the elderly during the 1970s.

An important distinction must be made between metropolitan and non-metropolitan poverty areas. Of the approximately 25 million people below the poverty level, almost 10 million lived in nonmetropolitan areas, compared to slightly more than 9 million in central cities and 6 million in suburban areas. Central cities have the highest rate of poverty (15.4 per cent), followed closely by nonmetropolitan areas (13.9 per cent); suburban areas, as expected, have comparatively low rates (6.8 per cent) (Seninger and Smeeding 1981, 383). However, adjusting income for a variety of deductions and the cash value of in-kind food and medical care transfers, Seninger and Smeeding (1981, 383–9) found that nonmetropolitan poverty was more serious than central-city poverty: on 1974 data, 5.2 million city residents were in poverty (8.5 per cent of all city residents) and 7 million non-

TABLE 3.1   *Families in poverty and per capita income rank, 1960–1979*

Region and State	Families below poverty level		Per capita personal income rank	
	1969 (%)	1975 (%)	1960	1979
South	16.2	12.1		
Delaware	8.2	6.6	4	8
Maryland	7.7	6.2	13	12
Virginia	12.3	8.3	33	22
W. Virginia	18.0	11.5	43	36
N. Carolina	16.3	12.1	44	39
S. Carolina	19.0	12.9	48	47
Georgia	16.7	14.6	42	34
Florida	12.7	11.0	29	25
Kentucky	19.2	14.9	46	40
Tennessee	18.2	12.6	44	42
Alabama	20.7	12.9	47	48
Mississippi	28.9	20.4	50	50
Arkansas	22.8	14.1	49	49
Louisiana	21.5	15.0	41	35
Oklahoma	15.0	11.1	35	31
Texas	14.6	11.7	32	21
West	8.9	8.2		
Montana	10.4	8.9	28	38
Idaho	10.9	8.2	38	37
Wyoming	9.3	7.0	17	7
Colorado	9.1	6.3	15	15
New Mexico	18.5	15.5	37	43
Arizona	11.5	10.8	27	28
Utah	9.1	7.0	31	45
Nevada	7.0	7.0	2	2
Washington	7.6	6.6	10	9
Oregon	8.6	6.7	18	17
California	8.4	8.5	5	4
Alaska	9.3	5.2	3	1
Hawaii	7.6	6.4	14	10

Source: US *Bureau of the Census* 1980, 447, 467.
(For North East and North Central see p. 124.)

metropolitan residents were impoverished (10.5 per cent). Central-city residents benefit considerably more than rural people from transfer benefits and various in-kind services. This difference is aggravated by the fact that many of the nonmetropolitan impoverished are black in the South. Blacks in the nonmetropolitan South experienced the least reduction in poverty when in-kind transfers were considered.

Combining regional and metro/nonmetro perspectives reveals that extensive poverty concentrations are found in the central cities of the North and the Pacific Coast, and in the nonmetropolitan areas of the South and West. The State-level statistics showing the South as the major poverty region are amplified with statistics showing central-city and nonmetropolitan poverty rates above the national rate throughout the South. Only the Middle Atlantic

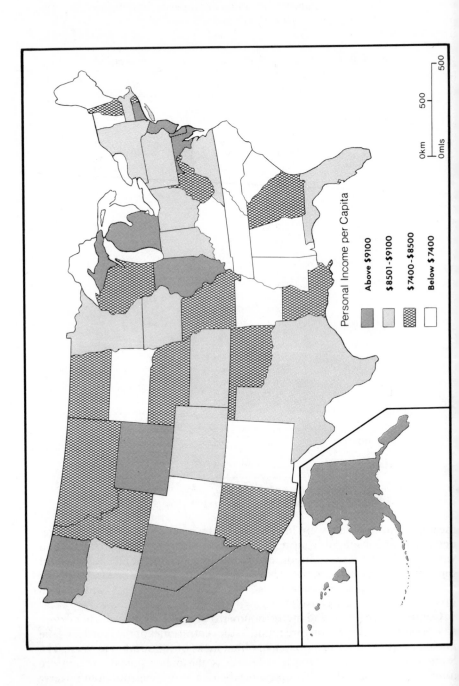

Personal Income per Capita

Above $9100

$8501–$9100

$7400–$8500

Below $7400

central cities and the nonmetropolitan areas of the mountain States also have poverty rates above the national norm. Between 1968 and 1974 poverty rates increased in northern and Pacific central cities but declined in those regions' nonmetropolitan areas. The nonmetropolitan areas of the South and Mountain States uniformly experienced declining poverty rates from 1968 to 1974, but central cities in the South Central region experienced slight increases in their poverty rates, perhaps the result of rural to urban migrations of poor households. On the other hand, taking in-kind transfers into account, poverty rates did decline in both central cities and nonmetropolitan areas throughout the US (Seninger and Smeeding 1981, 391–3).

Morrill and Wohlenberg (1971, 49–88) suggested that explanations for poverty fell into three major categories: geographic, economic, and social. The geographic factors include resource availability and population-resource ratios as well as accessibility to opportunity. The economic factors are based on our competitive economic system, and result in an imbalance in the supply and demand for labor, changing demands for labor with different occupational skills, and concentrations of low-wage industries in areas of excess labor supply. The social characteristics of people may be the most overt reasons for poverty or success: sex, race or ethnic characteristics, and age are differentially related to economic opportunity despite the American myth that anyone can become rich and successful. Education and family structure, also closely linked to poverty, are social characteristics that are somewhat amenable to change based on individual effort; the poverty household whose strong family ties and desire for education see them through hard times to ultimate success is the model cited by the conservative American. The social policies of the late 1960s and 1970s, to the extent that they were successful in reducing poverty, focussed primarily on alleviating problems caused by social characteristics.

b. *Economic factors.* The most intractable poverty areas in the 1980s are concentrated in the nonmetropolitan South and Southwest and in the central cities of the North. The poverty concentrations in central cities are the result of available housing and the impact of public policy, certainly not because they are well placed for those seeking employment (see ch. 7.3.5). A large proportion of the manufacturing and sales jobs are now in the suburban areas, and most of the central-city poor are not qualified for the increasingly white-collar jobs of the city, but must be satisfied with the service jobs generated by that white-collar employment. Unemployment rates are high in many central cities, but curiously they are relatively low in many of the rural poverty areas. A study of four very poor nonmetropolitan counties in the South revealed the explanation for this anomaly: substantial levels of under-employment (Briggs 1981, 375). Many workers were involuntarily employed part-time or were self-employed in marginal business endeavors. The labor force participation rate was very low because so many potential workers were discouraged. Only about one-third of the poverty households in those counties had a head of household who was working full time.

The major explanation offered for these economic problems is the inadequate level of human capital investment in these poverty areas: the central-city and nonmetropolitan populations are relatively unskilled and uneducated and cannot hope to participate effectively in a postindustrial economy. However, other economic explanations also merit mention, given the depth and longlasting nature of the poverty. In a capitalistic, complex society noncapitalistic production systems are increasingly eliminated; labor performed by the household for itself or for the surrounding community—child care, construction, food preparation—becomes commercialized (Howes and Markusen 1981, 446–51). Some political economists argue that unemployment and poverty provide a reserve army of labor to maintain profitability and flexibility for capitalistic production. The movement of blacks to the North and of the Spanish-speaking population to the Southwest and East Coast cities provides some support for this argument. Finally, the working poor of the nonmetropolitan South provide evidence that the structure and dynamics of American industry also maintain poverty areas. Industrial development in poverty areas—central-city slums or rural areas—invariably is low-wage, slow-growth industry which must take advantage of surplus labor to be profitable. Monopoly of a local labor market, cyclical production patterns, and high commuting costs are reasons that full-time workers remain impoverished. Local investment in improving human capital (e.g. education) may not be encouraged, or, at best, equips the young adults for migration to areas of opportunity.

Population redistribution processes of the 1970s and 1980s, both the back-to-the-city and out-to-the-country movements, are likely to have only modest effect on these poverty areas. Metropolitan areas, especially the smaller ones, continue to be the destination for most migrants.

c. *Social factors.* In the 1970s and 1980s age structure and racial characteristics appear to have had strikingly different relationships with poverty, even though both age and race have been important criteria for social policies during the last two decades. Elderly population concentrations are no longer synonymous with poverty. Where concentrations of children are coterminous with poverty, the racial or ethnic minority characteristics of those children suggest that family size may be less important than ethnicity in explaining poverty.

The proportion of the American population that is elderly has been increasing at a steady rate for several decades. This increased proportion results from the high birthrates and immigration rates in the early 1900s and current low birthrates. Because of poor health, loss of regular income from employment, and widowhood, large proportions of the elderly have been poor. However, income levels of the elderly have been increasing steadily, even when inflation is taken into account. The ratio of elderly income to income of similar but nonelderly households has also increased in the last decade (Pampel 1981, 22). The principal propellant toward higher incomes has been improved retirement benefits, both public and private. Women recently becoming elderly entered the labor force earlier than their predecessors, and thus improved their retirement benefits; their incomes also raised now-elderly couples' preretirement income levels. Finally, newer cohorts of elderly obtained higher levels of education and occupational status than cohorts of the elderly who were born before World War I, and therefore they receive higher retirement incomes. These households are also likely to have accumulated nonincome assets—substantial savings and a fully furnished home, for example (Pampel 1981, 29–36).

Social security benefits were the largest source of growth in personal income in the 1970s in many nonmetropolitan areas with high concentrations of elderly (Seninger and Smeeding 1981, 414–15). Many of the nonmetropolitan aged received relatively lower benefits than metropolitan elderly, either because they were farmers or self-employed and thus gained coverage only recently or because they may have had intermittent work histories and/or low wages and thus earned only low benefits. In addition, in the poorest rural States of the South and Southwest, no State funds were used to supplement the minimum Federal welfare payment (Supplemental Security Income) received by the poorest elderly (Seninger and Smeeding 1981, 416). Nevertheless, according to national averages, income inequality among the elderly has been declining steadily (Pampel 1981, 90–101), and only minimal spatial correlation exists between nonmetropolitan counties with high percentages of older Americans and nonmetropolitan low-income counties (Brown and Beale 1981, 42).

A more obvious correlation is apparent between poverty concentrations and concentrations of racial or ethnic minorities in the US (Brown and Beale 1981). Three groups deserve special attention, although they vary considerably in size and characteristics: (a) the smallest group is the Indian population, to whom the nation has a long-standing obligation; (b) the largest group is the black population, which, despite decades of effort, remains substantially poorer than the majority white population; and (c) the most rapidly growing group is the Spanish-speaking population from Puerto Rico, Mexico, and other parts of Latin America (Fig. 3.2). A brief examination of the patterns of concentration, the factors contributing to those patterns, and the problems of these minority clusters helps to explain why so many are still in poverty.

The American Indian population is the most highly concentrated group, primarily as a result of Federal policy. Since colonial times, the national government has been involved in resettlement efforts; throughout the nineteenth century this effort was primarily motivated by the desire to clear the land for white settlement (Niels 1971, 4). Much of this resettlement was accomplished on a tribal basis. Of the approximately 1½ million Indians in 1980 one-half lived in rural areas. Federal policy has vacillated between treating Indian tribes as traditional cultural groups (and so facilitating tribal development) and emphasizing assimilation of individual Indians to the white majority culture, thus facilitating individual development, including migration.

Rural concentrations of Indians on and near reservations have been maintained by a variety of government policies as well as Indian preferences. The Bureau of Indian Affairs provides a variety of services on the reservations, including health care, subsidized housing, education, and employment, particularly in service occupations. Leaving the reservation may therefore involve forfeiting substantial in-kind benefits. In addition, many Indians prefer reservation life, because of tribal loyalties and a value system that is not very compatible with white middle-class values (Sorkin 1978, 129–31).

Urban concentrations of Indians are in two types of cities: urban areas near

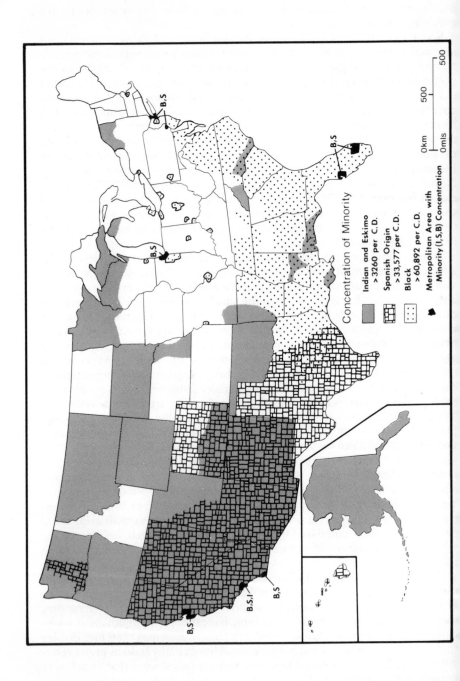

Concentration of Minority

Indian and Eskimo
>3260 per C.D.

Spanish Origin
>33,577 per C.D.

Black
>60,892 per C.D.

Metropolitan Area with
Minority (I,S,B) Concentration

0km   500

0mls   500

large rural Indian populations and large cities some distance from rural Indian populations. Indian populations in cities such as Minneapolis, Seattle, Albuquerque, and Tulsa are predominantly from local tribes and many have moved to these cities in a typical rural-to-urban migration process. Large cities such as Chicago, Los Angeles, and San Francisco–Oakland have attracted Indians from across the nation because of their economic opportunities, and, in the case of the California cities, also because of the climate (Niels 1971, 14–45). Since the mid-1950s the Bureau of Indian Affairs has operated a program of directed migration from reservations to selected urban centers. This program included job training and employment assistance, subsidy for moving and initial maintenance costs, and various counseling services (Niels 1971, 46–67). The importance of this project compared to independently developed channelized migration processes is difficult to determine, but even with this program of assistance a substantial number of Indians have returned to their reservations rather than becoming permanent urban residents. Like other minority groups, Indians tend to be spatially concentrated within urban regions in areas that reflect their economic capabilities.

Despite government assistance, rural Indians remain economically worse off than other minority groups (Durant and Knowlton 1978, 159–67). Reservation Indians have low per capita incomes, high infant mortality rates, low levels of education, and low levels of labor force participation. The low levels of labor force participation are a function of limited education and may be related to isolation from employment opportunities. Until recently, the education provided for Indian children by the BIA was not valued highly. This perception is not surprising, given the educational effort spent at imparting Anglo-culture, even to the extent of emphasizing boarding schools. As Indian schools have increased emphasis on traditional culture, as well as skills for survival in the Anglo world, the dismal educational characteristics of the Indian population may improve, and with it their labor force participation (Murray and Tweeten 1981, 14; Durant and Knowlton 1978, 162, 163; Vinje 1977, 40). The isolated location of many rural Indian concentrations may also be a significant factor in labor force participation. In Wisconsin participation rates were significantly greater on those reservations whose communities contained more manufacturing plants and in which there was a relatively high percentage of young adults; a notable proportion of Indians living off the reservation also was positively related to labor force participation rates (Snipp 1980, 43, 44). However, findings from a study of the 24 largest reservations are less encouraging: labor force participation rates were not related to the proportion of the labor force employed in manufacturing and government jobs (Vinje 1977, 39).

Urban Indians are less likely than rural Indians to be unemployed, with little education and low incomes, although a direct income comparison is unrealistic because of the benefits of housing and health care available on the reservations. This is partly the result of standard migration behavior: the young, healthy, educated individuals leave, but the BIA's relocation and occupational training programs have amplified the differences (Sorkin 1978, 9–20). Education remains a problem for the urban Indian population as well as the rural nonreservation Indians, for several reasons. Except on the reservations and in the BIA boarding schools, Indians are a small minority and thus their culture and traditions, quite different from the white majority's, receive little attention in the curriculum. Although urban Indian families are more likely to value education than their counterparts on the reservations, family pressure to complete school is not as great as most majority children receive. Indian lifestyles, including time-consuming obligations to kin and tribe, also interfere with standard education practices (Sorkin 1978, 87–91), and may enhance the likelihood of lower incomes for current and future Indian households.

Spanish-speaking or Spanish-heritage residents in the US comprise a rapidly growing minority population with a very mixed composition. In the 1980 census, for example, the category 'Spanish origin', numbering more than 15 million, could include the Hispanos of New Mexico (who have resided in that area since the seventeenth century); Mexican Americans, both legal immigrants and their descendants as well as aliens; Cuban Americans, and recent Cuban emigrees; Puerto Ricans resident in the States; and immigrant and alien Latin Americans. This minority, like the Indians, is a young population, with 44 per cent of Spanish-heritage residents under 18. High birthrates plus the greater propensity of young adults to migrate explain this youthful population, but the youthfulness contributes to economic hardship (US Bureau of the Census 1979, 3).

The great majority (more than 80 per cent) of Spanish-heritage residents live in metropolitan areas, clustering near urban economic opportunities. Puerto Ricans are found as a substantial minority in the East Coast cities of Pennsylvania, New Jersey, New York, and Connecticut, and in the Chicago area. Some of these urban residents are, or were, farm workers in the intensive agricultural areas of Megalopolis but they tend to reside in the central cities. Latin American emigrants are even more concentrated on the East Coast, primarily in New York City. Transportation connections to the Island and to Latin America contribute to this spatial distribution, but channels for Puerto Rican migration were often established by labor contractors for agricultural and manufacturing concerns. The other major urban areas for Latin American settlement are in Florida, particularly Miami. Florida is also the major area of concentrated Cuban settlement, with Little Havana in Miami serving as the cultural and economic center of this most successful of the Spanish-heritage minorities. The Spanish population of Florida tends to be older than the Spanish-minority population as a whole, and it has fewer households below the poverty level than the other Eastern States (US Bureau of the Census, 1979, 3).

With approximately two-thirds of the Spanish-heritage residents, the Southwest has the most spatially extensive concentration of the minority. These States are the locus of most of the rural Spanish-speaking population, comprised of Chicanos, recent migrants from Mexico, and Hispanos. Southwestern cities also have substantial Spanish minority populations; some urban Chicanos on the West Coast are farmworkers in the surrounding agricultural areas, although many are service or factory workers.

Even within the individual ethnic groups of this minority population considerable diversity exists. Because if its size, the Mexican-American population has received the greatest attention, but its diversity undoubtedly is typical of other subgroups. In an areal typology created using 1970 socioeconomic data, Boswell and Jones (1980, 88–98) identified several types of Mexican-American concentrations. The largest group, comprising more than 50 per cent of all Mexican-Americans, were a disadvantaged minority within a wider society of Arizona and California and in scattered Midwestern metropolitan areas, but compared to the migrant workers of California, Florida, and the Northwest, and to the large, very poor rural population of Texas, Colorado, and New Mexico, they are 'average'. Outside the Southwest, notably near Minneapolis–St. Paul, Chicago, the industrial cities of Michigan, and in the New York area, as well as near Seattle, Salt Lake City, Denver, and San Francisco, there are relatively better educated, more affluent, and more mobile Chicanos; however, even these groups were below the median standards of the white population. Many of the Chicanos outside the Southwest are related to families who 'settled out' of the migratory farm labor stream, were strike-breakers, or reserve workers during labor shortages (Tienda 1981, 512–15).

The Southwest is the area of most concentrated poverty for the Spanish-heritage population. In the mid-1970s, 23 per cent of the Mexican-origin families were below poverty, with even higher proportions of rural families in poverty. Only modest improvement occurred during the 1970s and in general the Chicano population's economic standing did not improve in comparison with that of the total American population. Low levels of formal education and vocational training, language problems, and the continued concentration of workers in low-paid blue-collar employment, coupled with discriminatory practices and continued legal and illegal migration, do not suggest simple solutions (Tienda 1981, 529–34). The proportion of Chicanos who were farm laborers declined dramatically during the 1970s, but unemployment increased for both men and women, despite high labor force participation rates and expanded employment in clerical, service, and operative jobs (Tienda 1981, 522–9).

A complicating factor in the Spanish-heritage population's relation to the majority society is the continual flow of legal and illegal migrants. While the abilities of these migrants are not unlike those of others at the point of origin and of their peers in the US, they enter the US with minimal formal employment skills. Nevertheless, the economic disparity between the place of origin and the destination is sufficient to justify migration, even for the illegal Mexican agricultural laborer headed for the migrant labor camp (McPheters and Schlagenhauf 1981, 2–8). It is primarily increases in real American, rather than declines in Mexican, agricultural income that lead to increased illegal migration, and increased Border Patrol activity would have little effect on reducing that flow (House 1982). A further unresolved issue is the importance of culture conflict versus discrimination in the economic advancement of the Spanish-speaking population. Their substantial concentrations in the Southwest, in some of the central cities of the Northeast, and in Florida facilitates maintenance of the Spanish language and other cultural traits. Continued early marriage and large families among subsequent generations are further evidence of the retention of Hispanic culture. However, the problems of limited education, in part the result of the system itself, and limited opportunities for obtaining good jobs, may result in realistically lower aspirations (Tienda 1981, 510).

The largest of the minority groups in the US, the black population, is also characterized by spatial concentrations of two types. Approximately one-half of blacks live in the South, where they comprise close to 20 per cent of the total southern population; approximately one-third of southern blacks (about 4 million) lived in nonmetropolitan areas, predominantly as nonfarm residents. The other half of the black population is distributed among the major metropolitan areas of the Northeast and North Central States and a few western cities; most of these nonsouthern blacks live in racially segregated areas of the central cities and inner suburbs.

Like the southwestern concentrations of the Spanish-heritage minority, the southern concentration of blacks is directly linked to the early migration of blacks to America as slaves to work in the agricultural economy of the South. Until 1920 almost 90 per cent of the black population had lived in the South, but then migration streams began to redistribute the population, pulled by northern opportunities and pushed by social discrimination and deteriorating agricultural opportunities. From the Atlantic Southern States blacks headed towards Atlantic Coast cities, particularly during the war years when demand for labor was high; the midwestern industrial cities drew blacks from the South Central area and the western cities attracted blacks from the West South Central states. Most of these migrants have settled in the central cities, and in several northern cities blacks now have a majority or at least a substantial plurality.

The history of racism and discrimination against blacks in American society is well documented. Despite migration to the North or to the metropolitan South; despite the successful sports and entertainment figures; despite the increased awareness and legislation, the black population continues to lag behind the white majority on social indicators. The median family income of blacks remains about 60 per cent of the median white family income, and nonmetropolitan black families had a median income less than 60 per cent of nonmetropolitan white families' income. More than one-third of the nonmetropolitan black families were below the poverty threshold, with even higher proportions in Louisiana and Mississippi (Moland 1981, 485). Given that 40 per cent of black families in several northern areas (Maryland, Washington DC, Ohio, and Michigan) have incomes above the median income for the US, it is not surprising that young adults are encouraged by parents and peers to leave the rural South for economic opportunity, further weakening rural southern communities.

Several factors are consistently associated with low economic status for black households. Like the other minority groups, blacks have a larger proportion of their population under 18 (40 per cent) than the white majority population. More than one-third of black households, both North and South, are headed by women, and the majority of these households are impoverished (Watson 1979, 71–3). Educational levels are lower than the white majority's, blacks are concentrated in the lower occupational levels, and unemployment or underemployment is a serious problem in the nonmetropolitan South as well as in the central cities (Moland 1981, 483). Because of limited employment opportunities and continued discrimination, young blacks have left the South's Black Belt, making it one of the few nonmetropolitan areas that did not experience a population turnaround in the 1970s. Unfortunately, given the characteristics of the remaining population, predominantly youths and unskilled middle-aged or elderly, opportunities are unlikely to improve except in government service activities.

The correlation between minority status and increased likelihood of poverty is primarily a social problem. However, the spatial concentration of large numbers of blacks, Indians, or Spanish-heritage residents in different areas results in problems at a regional scale. Solutions to the poverty of these groups is not likely to come through normal processes of regional development, given the physical and social isolation of their rural concentrations. Ironically, their urban concentrations are frequently in the locations formerly deemed most accessible, the central cities, but are now just as physically and socially isolated. Alleviating the symptoms of this poverty has been the focus of much social policy for almost two decades, but the correlation persists, and the regional patterns of poverty also persist.

3.2.2. Other societal inequalities

Several other social problems have received substantial policy attention over the last decade or two, in efforts to alleviate inequalities in society that prevent Americans from functioning effectively. Health and education have received the most attention, naturally, and improvements in both health and educational status can be noted for the whole population and for particular groups and areas. Housing has also been a concern, particularly in metropolitan areas (see ch. 7.3), but subsidized housing, especially for the elderly, has been constructed in nonmetropolitan areas as well. Inadequate housing remains closely related to household income. Crime is a social problem with an idiosyncratic spatial pattern: obvious correlation with poverty and opportunity can be observed, but other factors are also at play that are less easy to delineate (see ch. 7.5).

a. *Health.* To understand the health problems of the American population requires an analysis of the interaction between population characteristics and the characteristics of the health-care system. Lower income, minority racial or ethnic status, and increased age are all related to more serious health problems, including hunger. However, considerable evidence exists for a geographical factor as well, determined by population density and proximity to sources of health-care services.

Health problems can be measured by the presence of various types of disease, by symptoms, such as infant mortality, that provide an indication of the health of young women and infants as well as the adequacy of health care, or by causative factors such as inadequate diets. The spatial variation at the regional scale of death rates due to various diseases is intriguing more for the questions that can be raised than for any policy usefulness (Table 3.2). Medical geographers and epidemiologists do study spatial patterns of disease, usually for counties or even smaller units, for potential causative

TABLE 3.2   *Regional distribution of death rates for various diseases, 1978*

Rates per 100,000 residents

Region	Diseases of heart	Cancers	Cerebrovascular diseases
US	334.3	181.9	80.5
New England	347.7	203.3	76.0
Middle Atlantic	398.4	208.9	74.1
East North Central	351.2	179.9	79.8
West North Central	351.7	184.3	93.9
South Atlantic	338.2	186.5	85.5
East South Central	332.0	175.2	100.1
West South Central	298.6	163.3	85.4
Mountain	232.6	135.9	57.6
Pacific	274.5	168.7	72.9

Source: US Bureau of the Census (1980), Table 117.

relationships, and for service delivery decisions (Pyle 1979, 59–79). The three major causes of death among adults, heart disease, cancer, and stroke, have rather different spatial patterns. The highest death rates for heart disease and cancer are in the industrialized Northeast and Midwest, a spatial pattern that has been relatively stable since the mid-1960s despite advances in medical care. The Southern States and States of the Great Plains have above-average rates of death from stroke, while the States around the Great Lakes have dropped to below average since the mid-1960s. Among explanations for these patterns are environmental factors such as pollution and urban stress, dietary variations, race (particularly for the southern concentration of stroke victims), and concentrations of aged populations. More than 70 per cent of all deaths from heart disease and stroke occur among the elderly; half of all cancer fatalities are elderly (Pyle 1971, 41–61). Rural and small-town populations appear to be somewhat less healthy than urban populations, particularly among the elderly (Rosenblatt 1981, 616–19).

Infant mortality is a standard measure of the health of a population and highly correlated with poverty and minority racial or ethnic status (Fig. 3.3; Smith 1972, 38, 39). The States with higher than average rates of infant mortality for whites and minorities include the Appalachian States of Tennessee, West Virginia and the Carolinas, Arkansas, Texas, and three Western States. Almost all States with a minority population of 10 per cent or more have above-average rates of mortality for nonwhite infants, simply because the nonwhite rate is so much higher than that for white infants. Only Oklahoma, New Mexico, and Alaska, with Indian minorities who receive government health care, were near the national norm for minority infant mortality. Infant mortality rates in the US have improved fairly steadily over time, but the gap between the white and black population remains considerable, as does the gap between metropolitan and nonmetropolitan populations (Table 3.3).

Hunger, caused by insufficient or inadequate diets, is a health problem that

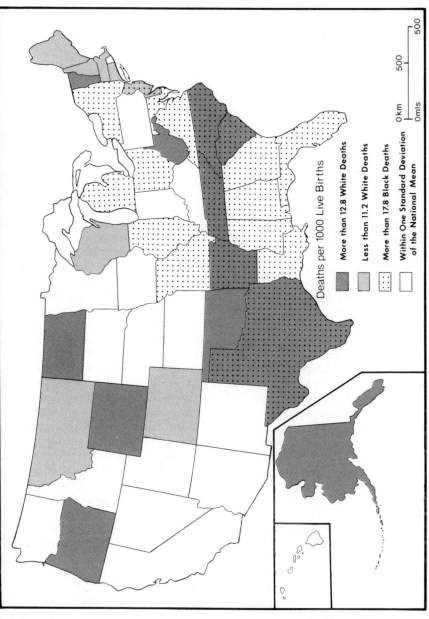

Deaths per 1000 Live Births

More than 12.8 White Deaths

Less than 11.2 White Deaths

More than 17.8 Black Deaths

Within One Standard Deviation
of the National Mean

3.3   Infant mortality, 1978

TABLE 3.3   *Infant mortality, 1968–1978*

| | Deaths per 1,000 live births | | |
	Total	White	Nonwhite
1968			
Metropolitan	21.1	18.6	32.5
Nonmetropolitan	23.0	20.2	39.3
1973			
Metropolitan	18.8		
Nonmetropolitan	20.7		
1978			
Total	13.8	12.0	21.1

Sources: US Bureau of the Census (1980), 77; Rosenblatt 1981, 617.

received considerable attention in the 1960s, when the US realized that it too had hungry people. During that decade the correlation between the proportion of households with inadequate diet and the general social well-being of the population was very high (Smith 1972, 38, 39). More recent statistics on hunger are elusive, although the population participating in various nutrition programs—food stamps, school lunches, meals for the elderly, to name a few—continues to increase. Most of these programs are run with the assumption that poverty and hunger remain highly correlated.

Availability of health care is also a factor in the healthiness of the population, both for emergency care and preventive care. Shannon and Dever (1974, 97–102) cite several studies that show substantial declines in physical consultation and hospital utilization with distance from the provider in urban and rural areas. The lower health ratings of rural elderly populations and the continuing gap in infant mortality rates between metropolitan and nonmetropolitan areas also reflect the importance of accessibility to care. Medical personnel are not distributed equitably throughout the US. The greatest disparity lies between metropolitan and nonmetropolitan areas (Table 3.4) although variation among the regions also occurs. Despite government attention to the shortage of doctors and an overall increase in their numbers, the maldistribution has become steadily worse. Most doctors, particularly the increasing proportion who are specialists, prefer to practise in large metropolitan areas. Not only are there fewer and less affluent people in nonmetropolitan areas, but those who do live there are less likely to have adequate health insurance. These economic factors are coupled with the importance to professionals of consultation, good facilities, and so forth. Ironically, hospital beds are much more evenly distributed, in large part because of the funding provided by the Hill Burton Act (1946) (Rosenblatt 1981, 620–24).

Availability of care is a particular problem for the elderly, even though Medicare and Medicaid have alleviated the major problem of economic access to health care. Compared to the entire population, higher proportions of the elderly live in rural and small town areas where medical care is less available. The older elderly (over 75 years of age) are also less likely to be

TABLE 3.4   *Health care service availability, 1972–1976*

	Within SMSA	Outside SMSA	Overall
Active non-Federal physicians, 1976			
(per 100,000)			
US	19.3	8.0	16.2
Northeast	22.3	10.9	20.6
North Central	17.3	7.5	14.2
South	17.6	7.2	13.8
West	20.2	9.5	17.9
Registered nurses employed in nursing, 1972			
(per 100,000)			
US	38.0	27.0	38.2
Northeast	46.7	47.7	51.4
North Central	36.7	29.6	38.4
South	32.2	18.7	28.8
West	35.3	28.8	36.5
Beds per 1,000 resident population, 1976			
US	4.6	4.3	4.5
Northeast	4.5	4.3	4.5
North Central	5.1	4.9	5.0
South	4.8	4.2	4.6
West	3.8	3.7	3.8

Source: Adapted from Rosenblatt (1981), 622, 624.

mobile, whether by auto in the nonmetropolitan areas or by public transit. However, providing the range of health services needed by the elderly to live independently—medical care, nutrition services, homemaker help—is more difficult in sparsely populated areas.

b. *Education.* Like health, direct measures of education need are not readily available, by school district, county, or State. As more States institute mandatory proficiency testing, some measure of variation in need among the State's districts will become available, but such measures are unlikely to be comparable among States because different testing instruments are employed. In addition, these tests measure needs of the existing school-age population, not the educational deficiencies of the entire population. Yet it is the educational deficiencies of the working-age population that hampers participation in an increasingly white-collar labor force.

Traditionally, two measures of educational attainment have been used as indicators of educational status: the median school year completed for all adults, and the percentage of high school graduates. As long as there was significant variation from place to place or group to group, these measures were satisfactory despite the potential lack of comparability among school systems. However, at the State level at least, these measures are converging. In 1976 the median school years completed for the population 18 years and older was 12.5; the lowest States were in the South, with 12.1 to 12.6 State medians; the highest were in the West, with medians of 12.6 to 12.8. Such figures do not suggest substantial regional educational deficits, particularly compared to the range of 8.7 to 12.2 observed in 1960 (US Bureau of the

Census 1980). The greater variation among States in the percentage of high-school graduates among adults over 25 compared to the variation among young adults suggests that young Americans of the 1970s and 1980s are more likely to finish high school than their parents were (Table 3.5). The lowest region (East South Central) had 15.7 per cent fewer high-school graduates among young adults than the highest region (West North Central), but it was 22.7 per cent below the Pacific States when only the older adults were considered.

Educational expenditures per student are one indicator of the quality of education available, although these figures are affected by salary levels for teachers which may be related to unionization and cost of living rather than to quality of teaching. Expenditures varied from $1,120 to $2,759 per pupil, a range which cannot be attributed solely to wage levels (US Bureau of the Census 1980, 162). Those States with low expenditures per pupil—most Southern States—also had lower educational attainment records. However, some Southern States with relatively less-educated older populations (West Virginia, North Carolina, Alabama, Louisiana, and possibly Georgia) are currently spending more for education than other States whose populations are more educated.

Both educational expenditures and educational attainment are positively correlated with income of the population. Although educational attainment is a causative factor in income variation, educational expenditures depend on community resources to a great extent. Much of the cost of the first 12 years of schooling is borne by local communities, financed by property taxes. Poor communities and poor States are therefore limited in their ability to spend for educational purposes.

c. *Crime.* Both health and educational status are strongly correlated with general social well-being, but crime and other measures of social disorganiza-

TABLE 3.5   *Regional distribution of high school graduates, 1976*

	Percentage of male high school graduates[a]	
	18–24 years	25 years and over
US	78.2	64.1
New England	81.3	68.1
Middle Atlantic	81.4	63.1
East North Central	79.7	64.3
West North Central	82.9	65.7
South Atlantic	72.4	59.6
East South Central	67.2	50.6
West South Central	74.7	61.1
Mountain	81.2	72.9
Pacific	81.4	73.3

[a] In only two regions did male and female percentages differ by more than 2 per cent. Older females were more highly educated in the Pacific region and older males were in the West South Central Region.
Source: Adapted from US Bureau of the Census (1980), Table 242.

tion are not as clearly related to economic resources. Using data from the 1960s, Smith (1973) found that at metropolitan, county, and State scales of analysis, spatial patterns of crime, venereal disease, and drug addiction were different from patterns of other measures of well-being, but did correlate with patterns of rapid population change and high concentrations of urban population. For 1980 the same relationship would hold: the States with very large urban regions (e.g. Illinois, Michigan, New York, California) and States with predominantly metropolitan populations and high rates of growth had the highest rates of crime (Fig. 3.4).

Metropolitan crime rates for each State, for both violent and property crime, ranged from 4,050 to 9,660 incidents per 100,000 inhabitants in 1980, compared to rural crime rates, which ranged from 1,050 to 4,825 per 100,000 inhabitants. In most States the rural rate was less than 40 per cent of the metropolitan rate. However, in States with very urbanized rural settlement, like Florida, Nevada, Connecticut, and Delaware, the rural crime rate approached one-half or more of the metropolitan rate (FBI 1980). Opportunity, as measured by size of population, wealth, and business activity, is obviously an important factor in variation in general crime patterns (Harries 1974, 49, 50).

Patterns of violent crime differ somewhat, with high concentrations in areas with substantial urban-minority populations and lower income levels (Harries 1974, 50–2). In 1980, as in previous decades, the Southern States have the highest homicide rates. This pattern of homicides, primarily associated with personal arguments, has been attributed to a variety of factors, but particularly to the large, impoverished black population and to a more generalized 'cultural' difference between the South and the rest of the US (Harries 1974, 30–6). The association of high crime rates with rapid population increase, explained in part by the opportunity factor, may also be related to social disorganization at both the personal and the community level.

Others (Gibbs 1968) argue that criminal homicide rates correlate inversely with the certainty and severity of punishment. Certainty of punishment (those subsequently imprisoned divided by the number of homicides) varied from a low of 21 per cent in South Carolina to 87 per cent in Utah. Severity of imprisonment (median months served) ranged from 24 in Nevada to 132 months in North Dakota.

d. *A mobile population.* Identifying mobility of the population as a social problem may seem inappropriate for a society that highly values both physical and social mobility. However, mobility can be a problem in a society where the private sector is responsible for most adjustments to economic and social change (Berry and Silverman 1980, 6, 7). Public problems can be identified in two categories: insufficient mobility of population and capital to realize differential market opportunities; and endangered public welfare caused by change, because market prices do not reflect full social costs or benefits, because certain groups would not receive what have become identified as basic rights, or because of short-term or periodic hardships. Unlike the previously discussed social problems, problems caused by mobility are no longer characterized by long-term stability in spatial patterns or causes.

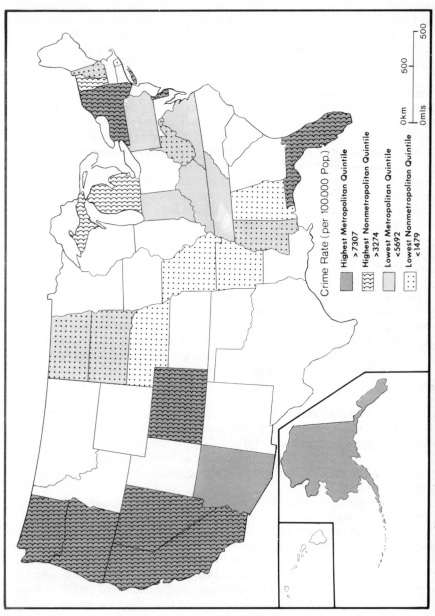

Metropolitan and nonmetropolitan crime rates, 1970

From the Great Depression until the early 1970s mobility was actually lower in the US than it had been during the nineteenth and early twentieth centuries, at least when measured by persistence rates, i.e. percentage of population living in same area at beginning and end of a time period (Allen 1977, 580–2). Migrants in the nineteenth century were more likely to be unskilled and poor, compared to late twentieth-century migrants who are better educated and more affluent than the nonmigrants. Some of the variation in mobility over time may reflect variations in the age structure of the population because young adults are more prone to mobility than any other age group. The US population was more youthful in the nineteenth century, and it is currently experiencing a 'bulge' of young adults who were born in the post-World War II baby boom.

Current mobility is composed of several flows. The highest proportion of mobile Americans is continuing to move within or between metropolitan areas. Within metropolitan areas, the general pattern of residential mobility continues to be from the central city and inner suburbs to new suburban areas (see ch. 7.2.2). Among metropolitan areas, the flow of migrants is increasingly away from the old, large industrial cities of the Midwest and Northeast to the smaller, more recently built-up metropolitan areas of the South and West. By the late 1970s, blacks had joined this flow or were remaining in the South; net interregional migration of blacks was significantly different from zero (US Bureau of the Census 1981a, 1). Rural to urban migration continues, but at a lower rate, because not only are many rural areas relatively depopulated, but the young people who remain are now slightly more likely to stay and take advantage of newly emerging economic opportunities. The significant migration trend since the mid-1970s is the increased number of migrants moving from metropolitan areas to nonmetropolitan regions, either near existing metropolitan complexes or to more remote locations.

In the early 1970s the mobility problem was still identified as rapid urban growth, uneven expansion of urban development, and decline in rural areas; the solutions included policies favoring alternative locations for growth and reversal of migration and physical growth trends (Berry and Silverman 1980, 4–6). By 1978 Carter's Urban Policy Group was listing mobility problems as migration from northern regions to the South and West, slower growth of metropolitan areas, and movement from central cities to suburbs; solutions favored included compact development and revitalization rather than new development. Two of the major issues identified with current mobility trends are the differential rates of participation in mobility and the expense and/or waste involved in creating new public infrastructures and reduced use of existing systems, including schools, housing, streets, and other public services.

The continued exodus of middle-class households from central-city and even inner suburban areas, and the minimum number of such households selecting inner-urban residences has steadily increased the proportion of central-city populations that are poor and of minority status (see ch. 7.2.3). Unfortunately, by living elsewhere in the metropolitan regions, these middle-class households also deprive the central cities of their tax resources, leaving cities with a greater 'problem' population and fewer resources to manage the problem. Poor and minority households are less able to make the same mobility decisions. Problems and the perception of social problems become greater in the central cities, further reducing their attractiveness to households which can afford to live elsewhere. The increased mobility to non-metropolitan areas appears to be fueled by similar perceptions as well as by the long-standing attraction of rural and small town environments for the American population (Meyer 1981, 64–80). Participants in the metropolitan–nonmetropolitan flows are also most likely to be middle-class, educated households, predominantly white. Even the migrating elderly households tend to fit this model.

The differential participation in mobility also contributes to variation in employment and economic-growth opportunities from one part of the country to another. Already during the period 1965 to 1970 the South Atlantic, Mountain, and Pacific States were experiencing substantially higher net migration of college graduates, particularly young college graduates, and the Northeast and Midwest (except New England) were losing proportionately more (Greenwood 1980, 144–6). The possibilities for entrepreneurial activity and increased demand for private goods in areas receiving such an influx of educated migrants are considerable, and this influx has undoubtedly helped to equalize opportunities from region to region in the US. The same areas have received disproportionate shares of the small flow of elderly migrants who likewise benefit the receiving areas, because of their demand for goods and services without concomitant demand for employment opportunities (Greenwood 1980, 126–9, 140–3; Longino and Biggar 1981, 283–90). Coupled with industrial changes due to the growth of markets, the lack of unionization, lower wages, and advantageous climate (see ch. 6.2.2), migration behavior in the 1960s and 1970s has thus made a substantial impact on the perceived problem of inequality of regional development.

The problems for areas losing population are readily apparent. A less competent population remains behind, heavily dependent on public services. The cost of providing public services does not decline directly with decreasing population although revenues do. In fact revenue decline is magnified because, as population declines, property values, on which much local revenue is based, decline from lack of demand for the property. For areas gaining population the problems are somewhat more diverse. In metropolitan areas, expansion of the service infrastructure may lag behind population growth, causing pressure on schools, utilities, and other services. As long as the inmigrant population is reasonably affluent, these problems tend to be only short-term. In nonmetropolitan areas, infrastructure problems loom large, but land-use control also becomes an issue as pressure for development threatens desirable physical environments. For some areas growing primarily because of retirement migration and the concomitant growth of supporting services, immediate pressure on the public infrastructure is less because the elderly do not need schools or elaborate park and recreation programs and often desire low-tax, low-service environments. However, a younger population is attracted to the larger market potential both for public and private sector services, and infrastructure costs and taxes rise. In addition, as they age, the elderly tend to need more services so the long-term welfare impact of elderly migration may be substantial.

In general, mobility within the US appears to be contributing to greater homogenization at the State or regional scale, although at the local scale very distinctive voluntarily segregated groups may emerge. The movement of more educated, middle-class residents from North to South and from metropolitan to nonmetropolitan areas is already reducing the per capita income gaps among these regions (see ch. 2.1.2). The movement of younger households into some of the more remote rural areas—upper New England, the Ozarks–Ouachita Uplands, the Upper Great Lakes—reduces the concentration of elderly and impoverished and improves the quality of life. Even the migration of the elderly to selected Sunbelt locations is unlikely to result in large-scale concentrations, because the economic possibilities generated by this large market attracts young migrants as well.

However, mobility from central city to suburb and from metropolitan to nonmetropolitan areas increases racial and class segregation within metropolitan areas. In addition, those nonmetropolitan areas with substantial minority populations—the southern coastal plain and Mississippi Delta and the Rio Grande Valley (House 1982)—are not attracting industry or migrants at the same rate as other nonmetropolitan areas (Brown and Beale 1981, 54–71).

3.3 GOVERNMENTAL POLICIES

In the US a complex system of local, State, and Federal governments is responsible for most efforts to alleviate social problems. The Federal role has increased over time, both in terms of establishing programs of assistance to meet general or specific needs and in terms of financial efforts. Although individuals in need were the designated beneficiaries of most of this Federal assistance, much of the funding and even program guidelines were funnelled through State and local government agencies; final fiscal results often reflect variation in community characteristics more than directly measured need.

Federal grants to State and local governments for social problems have a long history, beginning with grants for education through the land grant colleges. During the 1930s Depression, employment was provided, welfare grants were increased, and a national insurance and pension program established for dependent children, the old, blind, and disabled. In the 1950s and 1960s, housing, medical, educational, and economic development grants were provided. Since the mid-1960s, more general-use grants have been provided, for community development, employment, transportation, and crime control. From a modest 1 per cent of State and local revenues, Federal assistance has risen to 16 per cent during the twentieth century (Bennett 1980, 380–2).

Not all government efforts have involved fiscal assistance for social problems. Another major concern has been social inequities due particularly to minority status, and more recently to gender. Federal passage, and more importantly, enforcement of voting rights legislation and civil rights legislation have had a slow, but inexorable, impact on black life, particularly in the South. As more blacks have been able to vote, they have gained control of political power in areas where they are the majority. If nothing else, this control has enabled blacks to have some responsibility for dispensing Federal assistance, and through their legislators, to push for relevant programs at the State and Federal levels. The South's net inmigration of blacks, a result of lower outmigration and higher inmigration, suggests that black perceptions of life in the South have changed (US Bureau of the Census 1981A, 1). Black leaders are quick to point out that despite affirmative action regulations, minority households remain disadvantaged, particularly in the private sector; the discussion about poverty and race earlier in this chapter confirms these perceptions. Social legislation affecting women's rights, with its potential impact on the entire American population, is less likely to have spatial implications than legislation dealing with minorities with substantial spatial concentrations. Lee and Schultz (1982, 32–41) found that regional variations in the economic status of women reflected the general pattern of economic well-being. However, when women's economic status was compared to men's within a region, the more affluent regions (Middle West and Northeast) showed greater disparity between the sexes than anywhere except Mormon country.

3.3.1 Economic well-being

The general goals of most social policy have been the elimination of gross inequalities of opportunity and the maintenance of a minimum standard of living for all Americans. Policies that affect economic well-being, measured in terms of adequate household income, employability, and job opportunities, have focussed directly on the problems or have provided indirect economic benefits as an attractive extra to the stated goals of the program. The outcomes of these programs have not always matched their stated intentions, however, and the interaction of public policy and private decision-making is not always beneficial.

a. *Direct assistance programs.* The best-known programs dealing with economic well-being are the welfare programs devised and coordinated through several tiers of government and the employment training programs and unemployment insurance programs. Much of agricultural policy also had as one direct goal the well-being of the family farm household. One of the most successful programs in terms of improving economic well-being, the social security system of elderly pensions, is not generally perceived as a welfare program.

Public assistance programs that provide funds to impoverished households and individuals are a conglomeration of Federal, State, and local programs and funds, including aid to families with dependent children (AFDC), old age assistance, aid to the blind, permanently and totally disabled, and general assistance. Wohlenberg (1976, 440–50) raised several questions about the varying effectiveness of public assistance programs from State to State. In the early 1970s States in the Northeast (from Minnesota, Iowa, and Missouri east to the Atlantic), on the West Coast, and Colorado and Oklahoma were considerably more successful than the southern and most western and Plains States in bringing families out of poverty with public assistance. In attempting to explain this variable pattern, Wohlenberg found that several public attitude variables that identified intensity of conservative perspectives were negatively related to effectiveness. However, the program characteristics developed by public officials were much better predictors of variation in effectiveness. The fiscal effort of a State (what proportion of total local and State expenditures went to public assistance) and the proportion of all public assistance funds provided from the State and localities were positively related to effectiveness of the program. The Federal share of public assistance declines as a State's per capita income rises, but among States and localities fiscal effort is not related to fiscal ability. Wealthy states like Connecticut, Maryland, and New Jersey devoted less than 1.5 per cent of their total expenditures to public assistance, while Oklahoma, then a relatively poor State in terms of per capita personal income, spent more than 2.5 per cent for public assistance. Wohlenberg also found no association between fiscal effort of States and localities and the proportion of public assistance for which they were responsible. States that expended low effort for public assistance ranged from those that paid less than 35 per cent of their welfare bill to those that paid 60 per cent.

Current welfare programs do not benefit nonmetropolitan poor as much as poor residing in metropolitan areas. Although 40 per cent of the poor lived in nonmetropolitan areas in the late 1970s, they received less than 20 per cent of the Federal AFDC money and a third of the Supplemental Security Income (SSI) funds (Seninger and Smeeding 1981, 415–20). The poor in nonmetropolitan areas are served particularly badly by the major cash welfare program AFDC. More than 70 per cent of the nonmetropolitan poor reside in States which are below the median in AFDC benefits. These States also have low nonmetropolitan participation rates because of limited information availability, lack of outreach, and inaccessibility to welfare offices. Ironically, fewer poor children are eligible for the basic AFDC program in nonmetropolitan areas because only 36 per cent of them live in female-headed families compared to 61 per cent of metropolitan poor children. Most of the nonmetropolitan poor live in States that do not extend welfare benefits to unemployed fathers in two-parent families, even though 26 Northern and Western States do offer such benefits. The elderly nonmetropolitan poor, however, have benefitted substantially from the Federal takeover of aid to the indigent elderly and disabled. The minimum payment under the SSI program is pegged at 80 per cent of the poverty line and enables most elderly to move out of poverty.

Of the 13 States that ranked highest on number or percentage of nonmetropolitan poor (all except New Mexico were southern), 8 were providing at least intermediate levels of fiscal effort for public assistance in the early 1970s; 3 of the 'wealthier' States—Florida, Texas, North Carolina—were expending only modest efforts (Table 3.6; Seninger and Smeeding 1981, 416; Wohlenberg 1976, 449). The proportion of total personal income coming from public assistance in several of these States—West Virginia, Georgia, Alabama, Mississippi, Arkansas, and Louisiana—has declined, moving closer to national norms over the past 15 years. Most of these States experienced economic growth during that period and therefore rising personal income, while at the same time they continued to devote below-average proportions of their State budgets to welfare.

In general, public welfare expenditures are lower per capita in small

TABLE 3.6   *Welfare programs in States with rural poor (1970s)*

	Number and percentages of rural persons who were poor in 1975		AFDC recipients as percentage of State poor (%)	Welfare percentage of State budget	Rating of fiscal effort[a] 1970	Change in ratio of income maintenance to total personal income US ratio = 100[b] 1965–78
	(1,000s)	(%)				
Texas	658	20.3	34.4	15.5	Low	101–55
Georgia	560	23.2	56.7	16.8	Interm.	128–96
N. Carolina	528	15.8	43.4	10.5	Low	101–93
Mississippi	513	27.6	50.5	12.4	Interm.	190–165
Kentucky	426	22.2	47.5	17.2	Interm.	143–121
Florida	414	16.7	33.1	9.7	Low	85–74
Louisiana	394	25.0	53.0	13.1	Interm.	280–119
Tennessee	355	17.0	52.2	15.0	Low	97–103
S. Carolina	330	21.2	46.2	9.9	Low	66–99
Alabama	329	21.3	53.3	13.3	Interm.	186–115
Arkansas	279	19.8	49.7	16.2	Interm.	180–116
W. Virginia	218	17.5	43.0	11.8	Interm.	157–119
New Mexico	186	24.4	39.0	9.5	Interm.	139–124
US totals/averages	9480	14.3	59.2	19.3		100–100

Sources: Seninger and Smeeding (1981), 416, 417; [a]Wohlenberg (1976), 449; [b]US Bureau of the Census (1980), 448.

communities and grow with increased population size (Rainey and Rainey 1978, 128–39). Part of this variation is the result of biases in Federal funding, but rural and small-town governments are frequently unenthusiastic about administering such programs, both for ideological reasons and because of the expense involved in setting up and administering small programs to serve a widely scattered population. In addition, potential recipients may be embarrassed to request assistance, a less serious problem in large urban areas where anonymity is more feasible.

Employment is obviously an important key to resolving poverty problems, and governmental efforts have been expended to provide job and skills training, help match the unemployed with job opportunities, and offer unemployment insurance. Spatial variation in the availability and effectiveness of these programs is not optimally matched with need.

Employment and training funds have been made available by the Federal government under several programs, but ironically the unemployed poor of the richer States (based on per capita income) received more Federal benefits than the unemployed poor in poorer States like the South (Schroeder *et al.* 1980, 395–407). This pattern was particularly apparent with skill training programs, despite the great need and lack of infrastructure for such training in poorer States. Under the Manpower Development and Training Act (1962) skill-training funds were allocated on the basis of grantsmanship, high levels of coverage for unemployment insurance, high unemployment compensation, and vocational programs. States with high rural underemployment, low-wage unskilled industries, and minimal vocational training did not receive as much. As the most important legislation in President Johnson's War on Poverty, the Equal Opportunity Act (1964) was designed to create greater equity in job programs by encouraging participation of the poor and using family income criteria. However, using population size as further criteria for funding meant that the poor in more populous (and usually richer) States received more funds.

CETA, the Comprehensive Employment and Training Act (1973), an outgrowth of both programs, allocates funds according to several criteria: (a) 40 per cent according to previous allocations, (b) 30 per cent according to the percentage of total US unemployment found in each State, and (c) 10 per cent according to the percentage of all poor who live in each State. This program is strongly biased toward metropolitan areas, with 88 per cent of the outlays in 1975 in metropolitan counties, which had 72 per cent of the American population (Seninger and Smeeding 1981, 411–13). Only the special Federal response and the Job Corps even approached 20 per cent outlay in nonmetropolitan counties. Part of the special response was a program focussed on migrant and seasonal farm workers, and more of the Job Corps programs were physically located in rural areas, although their clientele included metropolitan and nonmetropolitan individuals who were hard to employ.

Unemployment insurance also is paid out disproportionately in metropolitan areas, particularly in the Northeast and the West (Seninger and Smeeding 1981, 413–15). Many nonmetropolitan jobs are not covered, or benefits are very low, both in terms of weekly income and number of weeks of payment;

southern nonmetropolitan areas have lagged far behind other areas of the US in this respect. In addition, unemployment in certain traditional industries located in the American Manufacturing Belt—steel and automobiles, for example—has led to special compensation programs which differentially benefit unemployed workers in those industrial States.

Finally, unemployment and job service programs, like many social service programs, are more available in metropolitan areas than in nonmetropolitan locations where the population is smaller and the jobs are fewer. This disparity is unfortunate because information about job opportunities is also scarce in such areas. To illustrate the positive potential of information, a massive flow of poor black migrants to the Chicago area was instigated by the *Chicago Defender* in the first half of the twentieth century when it circulated information in the deep South about economic opportunity (Davis and Donaldson 1975, 88–9).

Federal farm policies have historically been directed primarily toward benefitting the rural farmer, although over time the emphasis has changed toward greater concern for food production (Schaller 1978, 200). Initial assistance for farmers provided them with resources—land, credit, water, transportation—and encouraged skill development, in conservation programs, land-grant colleges, and experimental stations, and in extension education. In the twentieth century, policies emerged that directly affected the incomes received by farmers: price supports and production controls, enhanced demand through school-lunch programs and foreign aid, and support for marketing cooperatives (Schaller 1978, 200–1).

Unfortunately, considerable evidence exists that these programs have benefitted primarily the largest, most commercial farmers (Schaller 1978, 202). Higher land values, created by higher support prices, have put small farmers and potential farmers at a disadvantage. In the South, agricultural policy benefitted the white landowners; black tenant farmers lost their right to farm when white owners took that land out of production and pocketed the fees (Davis and Donaldson 1975, 55–60). Many of the agricultural skill development programs were not as readily available to black farmers either, putting them at a significant economic disadvantage. More recently, complaints have surfaced in California about the bias of research and extension efforts in that State toward large-scale and mechanized agricultural activities, thereby reducing the potential value of farmworkers' labor.

The largest economic transfer program in the US, dating from the Social Security Act (1935), is the social security (OASDI) program of old age, survivors, and disability insurance. Because beneficiaries have contributed to this program during their working years, it is not a welfare program, but in an inflationary period the benefits received are greater than actually earned. The major impact of this program, coupled with the supplementary security income program, is the substantial decline of poverty among the nation's elderly population by providing a pension base that is inflation-proof.

The number of beneficiaries in the OASDI program has increased steadily over the last decade, particularly for the old age and disability programs; from 17 million to 21.6 million retired workers between 1970 and 1977 and from 2.7 million to 4.9 million disabled workers. The dollars involved in this program have increased at a greater rate because of inflation; in 1970, $31.9 billion was spent for OASDI benefits and during 1977 $84.6 billion was allocated. Individual monthly retirement benefits increased from $118 to $243 during that same time span (US Bureau of the Census 1980, 341). As noted earlier, these income transfers can have a substantial impact on local economic conditions in areas with concentrations of the elderly.

If social security payments are combined with other government funded pensions and Medicare (because it is financed through OASDI and benefits only the elderly) for each State, these transfer payments averaged 11 per cent of total personal income in 1978, up from 6.4 per cent in 1965. Some States are substantially above that average, particularly those that have received elderly inmigration, have large residual elderly populations or large military bases that would attract military retirees (Fig. 3.5). States with low percentages of total personal income derived from this type of transfer payment include small wealthy Atlantic Coast States, heavily unionized Midwestern States (whose labor forces are well paid and have substantial pension programs), and growing Western States.

b. *Indirect assistance.* A variety of government programs have an impact on the economic well-being of the population without providing funds directly to the impoverished. All these programs tend to be spatially biassed towards areas which have economic problems. The variety of development programs funded with Federal money, the plethora of social service programs funded by all levels of government, and the revenue-sharing funds dispensed by the Federal government all provide economic benefits in areas of need. Government expenditures for general operation and especially defense activities also affect local economic well-being, but need is rarely a consideration in these decisions.

Efforts to deal with development problems at the regional scale have focussed on public works and resource development to induce economic growth. These regional development policies (see ch. 2.6.1) attempted to deal comprehensively with problems of unemployment and low per capita income (Hansen 1980, 10) offering more than the palliative provided by the various direct assistance programs. By improving transportation, providing facilities for industrial development, and investing in health, education, and vocational training, these programs were designed to attract business to areas with a surplus labor force. The most recent source of this type of effort is the Economic Development Administration (see ch. 2.6.3), whose funds, despite leveraging efforts, are probably too widely scattered to have any significant impact (Hansen 1980, 11). The Rural Development Act (1972), created to pull together under the auspices of the Department of Agriculture many efforts at improving the quality of rural life, also focussed on places rather than people; the results primarily emphasized planning and policy development (Schaller 1978, 207–9).

Several dilemmas arise with the development approach to economic welfare (Briggs and Rungeling 1980, 34). The crucial questions of whether all places can or should be 'developed', and of the impact of new development on existing 'developed areas', are usually left unanswered because of their highly political nature. Most areas in need of development do not have a qualified

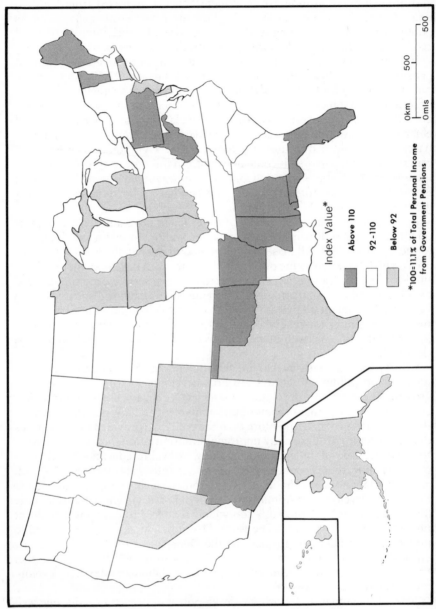

3.5 Government pension index, 1979

labor force; bringing in skilled-labor activities therefore requires importing the necessary labor or engaging in extensive training programs. Training programs prior to the arrival of employment may simply encourage out-migration of the most effective members of the labor force. Those activities attracted to low-skilled, high-unemployment areas pay such low wages that their impact on development may be negligible as well as unstable. Finally, particularly in the rural South, local leaders responsible for development decisions may be opposed to any activities that might affect the existing wage structure. Thus industries employing minority females are welcome, but high-wage industries are not encouraged in agricultural or mining communities.

Programs focussed on smaller-scale development efforts, particularly the community-development block-grant programs (see ch. 7.3.4) for large and small urban areas, are also designed to improve indirectly the economic welfare of a population by encouraging new or expanded business efforts and improving the housing stock. As in the case of regional development programs, political issues have diluted the impact of these programs on economic well-being by dispersing the funds to a full range of communities for a wide variety of purposes (Bennett 1980, 382–4).

One of the indirect economic benefits of all of these development efforts has been the creation of a wide variety of white-collar jobs in planning and administration. This not inconsiderable benefit for a population with a 'bulge' of young educated adults is increased by the array of professional and paraprofessional jobs made available by the vast expansion of government-funded social services in the last decade or so. Concentrations of the elderly, for example, require an array of planning, administrative, and service employees to provide the public services funded by various legislation. Similarly, improvements in education, health care, job training, and counseling programs in poverty areas have meant job opportunities for local educated people or migrants from outside the area. Many of the newly middle-class minority households are the beneficiaries of these social service jobs in central cities and rural poverty areas. These economic benefits, not for poverty households, but for households that might otherwise have had only moderate income levels, are spatially concentrated in areas of need or in administrative centers such as State capitols and Washington, DC. Affirmative action guidelines for minority hiring, a standard accompaniment to funds from the Federal government, and the political power of minorities in areas of concentration, have assured educated minority citizens a share of these and other public-sector jobs.

In addition to the direct assistance grants from the Federal government and the indirect benefits flowing from a variety of government programs, the Federal government has been allocating slightly less than 10 per cent of its total grants to local populations for general and countercyclical revenue sharing. These funds, allocated with a complex formula which considers population, fiscal effort, and per capita income, can be used by State and local governments for any purpose. As Bennett (1980, 379) summarizes, the program has been reasonably satisfactory:

... fiscal disparities have been reduced, fiscal pressures have been relieved, local service expenditures have been increased or stabilized, some measure of greater progression has been introduced in to the U.S. system of taxation . . . some particularly needy areas of poverty in both rural and urban areas have been aided, especially in black-dominated jurisdictions.

A further source of indirect economic benefits in certain areas comes from expenditures of government funds for projects. At the State level, development of educational or correctional institutions or parks provides jobs in certain areas. On a much larger economic scale, Federal expenditures for office activities and, more importantly, defense needs can inject substantial sums into the local economy (see ch. 6.3.3). Location of military bases can have a substantial impact on the local retail economy, creating many low-skilled service positions. Firms that receive defense contracts are very unevenly distributed in the US (see Fig. 6.4). In the early 1970s the 12 States with the biggest military contractors received 8 times as many dollars per capita as the 12 States with minimal military contracts, a substantial infusion of funds (Cox 1979, 218–19). Political manipulations are a strong factor in these allocations. US Senate and House committees tend to be controlled by legislators from those States that will be affected by the committees' deliberations; Connecticut, for example, always has a legislator on the Armed Services Committee because of its substantial defense-related industries (Cox 1979, 227–9). Most government expenditures of this operational character are not directed to areas of economic need, but they are widely distributed throughout the US.

3.3.2 Social services

In addition to various direct and indirect approaches to improving economic well-being, governmental agencies have developed service programs targeted to particular social needs. Although some services are provided directly by government agencies, many of the programs either supplement household income for private consumption of certain goods, for example food stamps and Section 8 housing assistance, or pay for services obtained in the market-place, such as health care. These programs are based on assumptions about the basic welfare needs of the American population and are targeted to meet those needs rather than simply providing additional income. Many of these services are not easily accounted for when determining economic well-being. The difference between the impact of in-kind benefits in metropolitan and nonmetropolitan areas has already been mentioned. The general assumption for most of these programs has been that low-income households need social services, but measuring the impact of these services on physical or social well-being is difficult.

Although government agencies have become involved in an amazing variety of social services, each of them of crucial importance to both recipients and dispensers of the service, the spatial implications of many of these policies are limited, even though regional planning organizations were frequently created as part of the service delivery process. Services to the elderly, for example, are coordinated by Area Agencies on Aging which receive funding from the

Federal and State levels to contract for, and oversee, various nutrition, health, homecare, and social services. These regional agencies, for aging and other services, were set up to provide opportunities for local input and feedback in the programs. Of course, to survive and flourish, these agencies must emphasize the local need for their services, and they are frequently the major source of data on the social needs of their constituency. The other spatial issue of importance for many social services is delimitation of areas of need. Even the wealthiest States have local communities that would qualify for certain targeted social services if small spatial units were considered. A typical example of this problem, reported in local newspapers, is the recent controversy between health planners in Hartford, Connecticut, and the Federal Department of Health Services. Certain types of financial assistance were no longer to be available for running clinics in the slums, because the county as a whole did not meet the criteria of high levels of health-care needs. The planners argued that census tracts, not counties, were the appropriate unit of analysis within densely built-up urban areas because the poor could not get to facilities outside their neighborhoods.

Three of the most basic social services, housing, education, and health and nutrition, are worthy of further consideration because of additional locational issues that have emerged in policy formation and results. Housing policies have facilitated population redistribution, and will be discussed later (see also ch. 7.3.5).

a. *Education.* Two major education policy issues have received attention from the courts and law-making bodies of the States and the Federal government. Both focus on the importance of equality of opportunity for education, regardless of race or ethnicity and of location of residence.

Cox (1979, 186) describes education policy as a classic example of the 'dependence of public provision on tax base geography'. The differences from State to State in expenditures per student have already been mentioned, but equal variability exists within each State. In Connecticut, for example, school expenditures vary from $1337 to $3793 per pupil, depending on whether the town is an affluent suburban community or rural, relatively isolated, and impoverished (Connecticut Department of Education 1980). One solution, tried in the 1970s in Ohio, is to encourage consolidation of school districts to reduce tax-base discrepancies (Cox 1979, 189). Alternatively, State and Federal governments have become involved in funding programs to help break the vicious cycle of poor education: poor jobs, low incomes and cheap housing, low taxes, and so poor education. Towns in Connecticut with low expenditures per pupil receive noticeably higher percentages of their budgets from Federal and State grants than towns with high expenditures; the average expenditure for the five 'lowest' towns was $1410 in 1977–8, with 6 per cent coming from Federal grants and 33 per cent from the State, compared to an average expenditure of $3254 for the five 'highest' towns, with 1.3 per cent from the Federal level and 13 per cent from the State (Connecticut Dept. Education 1980). Connecticut now contributes to local education costs with an equalization formula pegged to a standard above the median expenditure for the State's towns.

Unfortunately it is not entirely clear how effective various grant programs have been in equalizing quality, or even expenditures, for education. Nord and Ledford (1979, 16–19) found that grants to local school systems in North Carolina in the early 1970s did not reduce the gap in spending between rich and poor schools. In fact, equalization grants tended to reduce local funding in poorer districts, freeing funds for competing public services. Richer communities, on the other hand, responded to grants by increasing local funding.

Alternative approaches for equalization of educational opportunity are emerging, particularly for rural school systems (Rainey and Rainey 1978, 138, 143–4). With technological advances in telecommunications, certain types of educational opportunities may be made available through television and telephone linkages, both for students and staff. Small school districts are increasingly combining some of their efforts by forming special-service districts. State or Federal grants are sought to help fund these districts which may provide special education services or programs for gifted children in a number of schools.

The other major area in which the Federal and State governments have become involved in education has been the issue of equal educational opportunities for minorities. After a series of Supreme Court decisions, and the Civil Rights Act (1964), rapid change occurred in the South's systems of segregated schools (Lord 1977, 6–8). From a position of having the most segregated systems of schools in the US, the southern school systems in large and small cities as well as in rural areas desegregated dramatically. By 1978, only Texas, Louisiana, and Alabama had more than one-third of their minority students enrolled in schools that were predominantly (90 per cent or more) minority. On the other hand, black students in Midwestern and East Coast States with large black populations in their cities were very likely to be attending schools with predominantly black enrollment. Desegregation of large city school systems has proven most troublesome in both the North and the South (Lord 1977, 8), despite Federal and State court orders and threatened withholding of funds. In large part this problem results from continuing patterns of residential change in cities that are bounded by more affluent, predominantly white suburbs (see ch. 7.2.3).

Although the problem of racially segregated education continues, an additional problem of the 1970s and 1980s has been education for nonEnglish-speaking youngsters. If a modest concentration of such children exists in a community, they must receive special services according to Federal law; Federal funding has been available, through categorical grants, to set up such programs. The Spanish-speaking population is clearly most concerned about this issue, and States and cities with large Spanish minorities must expend additional funds, but certain areas of the West and scattered communities throughout the northern part of the US have also received substantial numbers of Southeast Asian migrants. An additional concern in Texas and California has been the legal rights of illegal aliens to educational services; a combination of national policy and proximity create tremendous potential costs for communities in these areas.

b. *Health and nutrition.* Policies relating to health and nutrition have been promulgated primarily from the national level, although State governments have been involved both in service decision-making and funding. Health-care programs are by far the most expensive of the in-kind services provided, in part because of the escalation of costs of medical care. While some of the policies have improved disparities in health-care availability, others have aggravated problems in areas with minimal facilities. The impact of nutrition programs is difficult to measure, but the delivery of these national programs shows considerable spatial variation.

Probably the most important health policies of the last decades have been the Medicare and Medicaid programs for payment of health-care costs; these two programs provide a national insurance program for the elderly and for low-income residents. The Medicare program is wholly financed through the social security system, but funding for Medicaid is shared by the States and the Federal government. States with higher per capita incomes pay a larger share of Medicaid costs, similar to the AFDC funding process. In effect, these programs offer additional Federal subsidies in poor States and provide effective demand for health services in areas formerly too poor to support a health care infrastructure adequately.

Medicare and Medicaid, along with private health insurance programs, account for most of the health-care payments in the US. These third-party payments are biassed towards certain types of services, particularly specialty medicine and hospital care (Rosenblatt 1981, 626–34). As was noted above, medical specialists tend to agglomerate in metropolitan areas, so third-party payments are also disproportionately concentrated; nonmetropolitan general practitioners receive lower fees. In addition, new types of medical personnel, particularly various types of health practitioners such as midwives and nurse practitioners, whose services are well-suited to areas with limited health care, are often not covered by third-party reimbursement systems. This lack of coverage has discouraged such personnel from establishing practices in rural and inner-city areas. Ironically, another innovation in health-care delivery, the Health Maintenance Organization, is also most successful in metropolitan areas where the density of potential consumers and of participating medical personnel is highest.

Because it has not been easy for certain areas to attract competent medical personnel, even with additional funding, the National Health Service Corps was created to provide direct placement of health-care providers. These providers, mostly physicians, are obligated to serve in areas of need in return for the financial support they received during medical school (Rosenblatt 1981, 631–2). The most successful programs for providing service in medically underserved areas, such as the WAMI program of the Pacific Northwest and the Rural Services program in North Carolina, coordinate educational resources with the delivery system by combining medical education, dispersed residency training, and subsidies for establishing practices. These programs have placed special emphasis on family medicine as a specialty (Rosenblatt 1981, 637).

Such comprehensive programs require explicit linkages among various levels of a health-care delivery system, one of the goals of the Health Systems Agencies mandated by Federal legislation in 1974 (Pyle 1979, 215). These agencies, responsible for health planning and coordination, for annual implementation plans, and for review of applications for Federal health funds, now cover the entire US. Agencies are nested within States, and each normally includes a metropolitan area (Pyle 1979, 215–17). Although necessary coordination and consumer input have resulted from these agencies' efforts, some negative results have also developed. Differences in the availability of health care between metropolitan and nonmetropolitan areas have been aggravated, because efficient planning suggests closure of small, inefficient units and reliance on larger, more sophisticated ones. A case in point is the proposed closing of small, personalized obstetrics units in community hospitals in order to concentrate funding and demand in larger, more technologically sophisticated units (Rosenblatt 1981, 626–37).

The various nutrition programs are predominantly targeted toward people in need: poor people, poor young mothers and infants, poor school children, and the elderly. Although most nutrition programs are funded nationally, they are administered locally, resulting in differential delivery. For example, the participation rate of eligible households in the food-stamp program varies considerably by State. States in the Great Plains and Mountain areas average only one in three eligible households participating compared to New England, where 70 per cent of eligible households participated (Kodras 1981). Unlike some of the other measures of well-being, food-stamp distribution in the South is only slightly under the national average. Access to nutrition programs for the elderly, particularly the congregate meals program, is also strongly affected by local government decisions such as selection of meal sites, the targeting of efforts towards poor and isolated elderly, and the effectiveness of the administrative agencies. In West Virginia, elderly some distance from the larger urban areas were not able to participate in the State's meal program; in contrast, through targeting efforts and agency outreach, higher proportions of rural elderly in Connecticut participated in the program than did city or suburban elderly (Meyer 1981B, 311–23).

3.3.3 Population mobility and services

Although few explicit government policies exist concerning population mobility, and cause and effect relationships cannot be clearly identified between policy and population change, the obvious potential for indirect relationships requires attention. A variety of government policies have facilitated mobility from central city to suburb and from metropolitan to nonmetropolitan areas, just as earlier governmental action encouraged concentration in cities. In addition, population change undoubtedly requires policy responses in both growing and declining areas.

Direct policies concerning mobility have focussed on people in need— Indians, unemployed workers, and metropolitan blacks—and have been limited in time and financial support. The efforts of the Bureau of Indian Affairs to assist migration of Indians from reservations to urban areas were described earlier as achieving only modest results. During the late 1960s a series of Labor Mobility Demonstration Projects were undertaken by the US Employment Service and 18 State agencies to assist those workers for whom no local employment alternatives were feasible (Hansen 1971, 271–84). The results of these projects indicated the wide range of supportive services necessary, the economic and political conflicts of interest in supply-and-demand areas, and the relatively high cost. Supporters nevertheless argued that benefits would outweigh costs, but no national policy was ever developed. The final policy effort that was designed to affect mobility was the State and Federal 'fair housing' legislation passed in the 1960s. This legislation was specifically enacted to enhance the mobility alternatives of American minority households and by the early 1970s more than 80 per cent of the American housing stock was legally available to households of any race. However, legal inhibitions have been only one factor in the racial residential change patterns in American urban regions (see ch. 7.3.3).

Other government policies have had an indirect impact on American mobility patterns. Construction of the Interstate highway system, for example, affected the spatial pattern of accessibility within metropolitan regions as well as, by general consensus, substantially enhancing the accessibility of nonmetropolitan areas; for a contrary view see ch. 5, p. 225. The pattern of residential settlement on the periphery of the urban region was not dependent on that highway system, but some system of flexible transportation would otherwise have been demanded. Given the pervasive atttachment of Americans to privacy, individualism, and mobility, the result would probably have been similar (Zelinsky 1973, 39–58).

Various kinds of housing policy have also facilitated residential mobility and the emergence of large suburban residential areas. The variety of Federal mortgage insurance programs have enabled moderate and middle-income households to acquire single-family dwellings, and the tax benefits of home-ownership have provided additional incentives for residential mobility (see ch. 7.3.1). The Farmers Home Administration (FmHA) housing assistance programs provide loan assistance for single-family home purchases and construction of multifamily housing in rural areas, thereby encouraging existing residents to remain and others to move to rural areas. Again, the subsidies have made feasible the ambitions of American households, although they can hardly be considered the cause of those goals. According to Coelen and Fox (1981, 604–5), the evidence is clear that water and sewer developments are catalysts for development. Both the FmHA and the Environmental Protection Agency programs for developing these facilities in nonmetropolitan areas have benefitted developers and contributed to residential sprawl rather than fostering concentrated development.

Finally, the increased availability of various government and private transfer payments relieves a larger proportion of the American population from daily journeys to work. Between 1950 and 1975 the percentage of personal income derived from dividends, interest, transfer payments, pensions, and rental income increased from 18 to 29 per cent (Beyers 1979, 35). People receiving this type of income, particularly the elderly, are able to move to amenity areas rather than being tied to existing employment areas.

Although policy responses are necessary in growing areas, evidence is gradually emerging that suggests that many of the problems have been overrated (Baldassare 1981). Particularly in nonmetropolitan areas, growth is often associated with affluence, which allows for investment in the service institutions of the area. In fact, as population increases, the per capita cost of many services declines (Coelen and Fox 1981, 603–5). Short-term problems may emerge, but can be resolved because funds are generally available from local sources. For example, some northern and western migrants may be dissatisfied with conservative educational practices in southern public schools. Because the large physical size of school districts in the South prevents the creation of suburban enclaves in which the newcomers could exercise control, these migrants may find themselves supporting private schools, but they will be able to afford them (Katzman 1980, 265).

Policy problems in areas of declining population, as mentioned earlier, are not as easy to resolve, nor are the implications of these problems limited to the impacted localities. For example, significant outmigration of young adults can provide substantial discouragement for high investment in education in an area (Cox 1979, 245). In fact such localities may feel entitled to national subsidies because they are educating other areas' labor forces. For the largest areas, declining population size can actually reduce costs of service provision by eliminating diseconomies of scale; however, such reduction demands difficult short-term adjustments in the service bureaucracy (Coelen and Fox 1981, 603–5). Such adjustments are particularly necessary since, in many cases, per capita costs of services such as police, fire, and housing services are much higher in large, declining cities than they are in large growing cities (Bennett 1980, 75).

3.4 QUESTIONS FOR THE FUTURE

Several questions were raised in the introduction to this chapter concerning the amelioration of social problems, the significance of population redistribution, and the appropriate level for policy response. Over the last several decades, Federal involvement in social issues has clearly increased. Although problems of poverty, unemployment and underemployment, poor health, poor education, and unsatisfactory housing persist, most evidence suggests that measurable improvement has been made. Disparities between minority groups and the majority population and among regions of the nation have not been eliminated, however. Bennett (1980, 63–5) suggests that this results from the increased concern of jurisdictions with 'fiscal prudence' rather than willingness to be 'Samaritans'. Fiscal prudence requires that affluent geographical regions maintain local autonomy and remain free of commitments that would help to raise the social welfare of less affluent regions. This behavior is most apparent within metropolitan regions, but amenity areas throughout the US are increasingly exercising such prudence. Legislators are also quick to ask what the fiscal impacts of legislation will be on their constituents before committing themselves on an issue. Such behavior is in contrast to the several decades of fiscal support offered to the developing but problem-ridden Southern and Western States by the more affluent residents of the Northeast through Federal programs—the Samaritan effect.

The patterns of population redistribution observed in the last decade— increased net flows of population to the South and West, higher rates of growth for smaller metropolitan areas, and net migration gains in nonmetropolitan areas near metropolitan regions and in remote amenity areas—are undoubtedly the result of interacting forces (see also chs. 2, pp. 48–9; 6, pp. 224–6; and 7, pp. 266–70). The migration flows may indicate that Americans have recognized the reduction in social problems and reduced regional disparities, and are responding by remaining in certain areas or considering them as viable alternative destinations. The redistribution pattern may, on the other hand, be the result of the search for better amenities, made possible by the greater affluence of most Americans. Amenities have also become more significant in locational decision-making by business corporations. A third alternative, perhaps interacting with the first two, is suggested by what Bennett (1980, 62) calls 'local service clubs'. Interpreting several models of fiscal migration, he argues that individuals may be migrating to communities that offer a bundle of goods—amenities, jobs, public-service levels—that accord with their preferences. If such an interpretation is valid, further attempts to create homogeneity, once basic social needs are met, would be counterproductive for freedom of choice.

An important question being debated in the 1980s is the extent to which the Federal role in providing solutions to social problems should now be diminished, with States and local communities assuming more of the responsibility for social welfare. Federal responsibility has evolved occasionally because of widespread evidence of need, but more frequently has been the result of interest groups bypassing less-sympathetic local governments and stating their needs directly to decision-makers at the Federal level. The response has been a plethora of categorical grants, designed to meet specific social needs, and administered by Federal, State, and local agencies. Federal funding has been perceived as appropriate because the 'progressive' nature of the Federal income-tax system compared to more regressive State and local tax systems facilitated a modest redistribution of wealth. Continued Federal involvement, and perhaps complete assumption of the costs of a basic welfare policy, strongly advocated by many interest groups, would primarily benefit those cities, counties, and States that have minimum resources to provide social services (Perlman 1980, 248–9). Current migration patterns would continue, and potentially involve less affluent citizens who could risk migration for better opportunities because of the guarantee that basic needs would be met. Regional disparities in the social well-being of society would be further diminished, but the potential cost in dollars as well as dependence on the government cannot be estimated.

Those who support a devolution of responsibility for social services from Federal to State and local levels argue that Federal programs are not as responsive to local situations, involve high proportions of red tape, and are not an appropriate Federal activity. Alexander (1981, 35–41) provides an example of the potential problem with Federal responsibility in his analysis of the Federal role in assisting communities in distress. Such communities have social, economic, and fiscal needs that must be met with both short-term consumption policies such as welfare and unemployment insurance and long-range investments in community development and education. Federal policies, including revenue sharing, public works employment, most CETA programs, and housing and community development, primarily provide investment in short-term consumption and affect fiscal needs of the community, that is the fiscal imbalance between public-resource needs and the community's fiscal capacity.

Since 1980 significant changes have been made and proposed which would slow, and finally reduce, Federal involvement in social problems. Many of the Federal categorical grant programs have been combined into block-grant programs of assistance, giving State and local authorities more discretion on how to allocate funds for health programs, education programs, and the like. Continuing with that philosophy, President Reagan, in his 1982 State of the Union message, suggested that States assume responsibility for housing, transportation, education, welfare, and food stamps while the Federal government would completely finance the Medicaid and Medicare programs. Of course, both the block-grant programs, which had fewer dollars than their predecessor categorical grants, and the eventual State responsibility for many social needs are designed to reduce the proportion of the Federal budget allocated to social needs.

Given the almost 50-year pattern of ever-increasing Federal involvement in social welfare, these proposals have generated substantial opposition. The special interest groups have expressed serious concerns about impacts on their constituents, and questions have been raised about the ability and willingness of the poorest States and localities to meet national minimal standards for health care, nutrition, and welfare (Heller 1982, 30). This latter concern would be particularly worrisome if the distribution formulas for general revenue sharing were not designed, as they have been in the past, to redistribute at least some of the funds from richer to poorer areas. Geographers have raised an additional concern, identified by Bennett (1980, 64–5) as the State's dilemma, a modification of the classic game-theory concept of the 'prisoner's dilemma'. The problem for social welfare is that without collusion or cooperation between jurisdictions, investment by individual States or localities is more costly and provides potential indirect benefits to neighboring units; for example, a high-quality educational system produces competent adults who may move to nearby localities or States and contribute to their economies. The result is a tendency to underinvest, to keep taxes low so that indirect benefits flow into the locality rather than out of it. Only coordination among units, currently guaranteed in many cases by Federal funding and legislation, can avert potential long-term crises.

If Federal involvement in social welfare services is diminished, the impacts on the American population are unclear. The philosophy underlying such diminished involvement assumes that the private economy would improve, providing more jobs and thus reducing both high unemployment and the sense of economic hopelessness among the poor. Because some of the traditionally poorer areas of the nation have been experiencing substantial economic development, the need for social welfare in those areas should decline. For example, some nonmetropolitan poor families have been able to climb out of poverty by means of multiple earners and multiple jobs, even when the jobs are low-paying (Till 1981, 222–3). These areas might be able to offset the reduction in social subsidies they currently receive and maintain a comprehensive program (Perlman 1980, 249). However, according to analysis of mid-1970s AFDC programs, a sample of metropolitan areas in Sunbelt States have not passed on to welfare recipients any significant proportion of increased local revenue (Thrall 1982, 264). Thus the poorest residents, unable to participate in the economic development process because of limited skills, health problems, or discrimination, would potentially be in worse straits. Declining economies in Northeastern metropolitan areas, coupled with reductions in Federal assistance, would probably require reductions in the relatively generous benefits in those areas, creating hardship for their dependent populations, especially for minorities.

Whether Americans would 'vote with their feet' if variation in social welfare increased dramatically from place to place is unclear. Affluent households would clearly be free to pick the locality that offered their chosen bundle of services and amenities, and invest their surplus funds as they desired, rather than have them taxed away. Moderate-income households would be motivated to search for economic opportunity, perhaps trading off costly service benefits for a secure job and self-help activities. Impoverished households currently dependent on society have been relatively less mobile than other groups in the last several decades, although historically poor Americans moved as freely as affluent citizens in search of opportunity (Allen 1977, 587). Such households, faced with serious deprivation because of minimal social welfare caused either by the impoverished character of their environment or the refusal of their locality to fund social services, might migrate to areas of economic opportunities (as blacks did in the early twentieth century and Spanish-heritage migrants do today). Alternatively, these households might be incapable of such behavior for economic, social, or psychological reasons and will suffer silently or violently in the midst of more general affluence.

Although the United States Constitution does not guarantee the social well-being of its inhabitants, a minimal standard of living has increasingly been assumed to be the right of each of its citizens. The 1980s appears to be a decade during which the mechanisms for guaranteeing such a minimum standard will be debated more seriously. Each new social welfare program of the past has been scrutinized before adoption, but under a prevailing philosophy that Federal responsibility for social welfare was the best solution to the problem. This philosophy is now under question, not only by the Reagan administration, but by many American citizens who are concerned about the distortions in their society introduced by ever-higher levels of Federal involvement in social-welfare programs. Changes in the current approach to social problems, either by further increasing Federal responsibility or by substantially reducing Federal involvement and relying on more local units of government, will have substantial spatial implications for the geography of social well-being.

References

ALLEN, J. P. (1977) 'Changes in the American propensity to migrate', *Ann. Ass. Am. Geogr.* **67** 4, 577–87.

122   *United States Public Policy*

ALEXANDER, J. R. (1981) 'Policy design and the impact of Federal aid to declining communities', *Growth and Change*, 12 1, 35–41.
BALDASSARE, M. (1981) 'Local perspectives on community growth', ch. 3 in HAWLEY and MAZIE, 116–43.
BENNETT, R. J. (1980) *The geography of public finance: welfare under fiscal federalism and local government finance* (London: Methuen).
BERRY, B. J. L. and SILVERMAN, L. P. (eds.) (1980) *Population redistribution and public policy* (Washington, DC: Nat. Acad. Sci.), 'Introduction', 1–7.
BEYERS, W. B. (1979) 'Contemporary trends in the regional economic development of the United States', *Prof. Geogr.* 31 1, 34–44.
BOSWELL, T. D. and JONES, T. C. (1980) 'A regionalization of Mexican Americans in the United States', *Geogrl. Rev.* 70 88–98.
BOURNE, L. S. (1981) *The geography of housing* (New York: V. H. Winston).
BRIGGS, V. M. JR. (1981) 'Unemployment and underemployment', ch. 9 in HAWLEY and MAZIE, 359–81.
—— and RUNGELING, B. (1980) 'A poverty solution for the rural South?', *Growth and Change*, 11 4, 31–5.
BROWN, D. L. and BEALE, C. L. (1981) 'Diversity in post-1970 population trends', ch. 1 in HAWLEY and MAZIE, 27–71.
COELEN, S. P. and FOX, W. F. (1981) 'The provision of community services', ch. 15 in HAWLEY and MAZIE, 589–613.
CONNECTICUT DEPT. EDUCATION (1980) *The condition of public, elementary and secondary education in Connecticut*, vol. 2, *Town and school district profiles* (Hartford, Conn.).
COX, K. R. (1979) *Location and public problems* (Chicago: Marroufa Press).
DAVIS, G. A. and DONALDSON, O. F. (1975) *Blacks in the United States: a geographic perspective* (Boston: Houghton Mifflin).
DURANT, T. J. JR. and KNOWLTON, C. S. (1978) 'Rural ethnic minorities: adaptive response to inequality' ch. 9 in FORD (ed.) *Rural USA*, 145–67.
FEDERAL BUREAU OF INVESTIGATION (1980) *Uniform crime reports* (Washington, DC: US Dept. Justice).
FORD, T. R. (ed.) (1978) *Rural USA: persistence and change* (Ames, Iowa: Iowa St. Univ. Press).
GIBBS, J. P. (1968) 'Crime, punishment and deterrence', *Soc. Sci. Q.* 48, 515–30.
GREENWOOD, M. J. (1980) 'Population redistribution and employment policy' in BERRY and SILVERMAN, 114–68.
HANSEN, N. M. (1971) *Rural poverty and the urban poor* (Bloomington, Ind.: Indiana Univ. Press).
—— (1980) 'Policies for nonmetropolitan areas', *Growth and Change*, 11 2, 7–13.
HARRIES, K. D. (1974) *The geography of crime and justice* (New York: McGraw Hill).
HAWLEY, A. H. and MAZIE, S. M. (eds.) (1981) *Nonmetropolitan America in transition* (Chapel Hill, NC: Univ. N. Carolina Press).
HELLER, W. W. (1982) 'Federalism and the State–local fiscal crisis', *Wall Street J.* Friday, 2 Jan.
HOUSE, J. W. (1982) *Frontier on the Rio Grande: A political geography of development and social deprivation* (Oxford: Clarendon Press).
HOWES, C. and MARKUSEN, A. R. (1981) Poverty: a regional political economy perspective', ch. 11 in HAWLEY and MAZIE, 437–63.
KATZMAN, M. T. (1980) 'Implications of population redistribution for education', in BERRY and SILVERMAN, 253–86.
KODRAS, J. E. (1981) 'The geographic perspective in policy evaluation: a spatial and temporal evaluation of the US food stamp program', Paper presented at annual meeting of AAG, Los Angeles, April.

LEE, D. and SCHULTZ, R. (1982) 'Regional patterns of female status in the United States', *Prof. Geogr.* 34 1, 32–41.

LEWIS, M. (1978) *The culture of inequality* (Amherst, Mass.: Univ. Mass. Press).

LONGINO, C. F. JR. and BIGGAR, J. C. (1981) 'The impact of retirement migration on the South', *Gerontologist*, 21 3, 283–90.

LORD, J. D. (1977) *Spatial perspectives on school desegregation and busing*, Resource Pap. for College Geogr. 77–3 (Washington, DC: Ass. Am. Geogr).

MCPHETERS, L. R. and SCHLAGENHAUF, D. E. (1981) 'Macroeconomic determinants of the flow of undocumented aliens in N. America', *Growth and Change*, 12 1, 2–8.

MEYER, J. W. (1981A) 'Migration to near-metropolitan areas: characteristics and motives', *Urb. Geogr.* 2 1, 64–80.

—— (1981B) 'Equitable nutrition services for the elderly in Connecticut', *Geogrl. Rev.* 71 3, 311–23.

MOLAND, J. JR. (1981) 'The black population', ch. 12 in HAWLEY and MAZIE, 464–501. .

MORRILL, R. L. and WOHLENBERG, E. H. (1971) *The geography of poverty in the United States* (New York: McGraw Hill).

MURRAY, S. and TWEETEN, L. (1981) 'Culture, education and economic progress on Federal Indian reservations', *Growth and Change*, 12 2, 10–16.

NIELS, E. M. (1971) 'Reservation to city', *Univ. of Chicago Dept. Geogr. Res. Pap.* 131.

NORD S. and LEDFORD, M. H. (1979) 'Overlooked causes and implications of school finance disparities', *Growth and Change*, 10 4, 16–19.

PAMPEL, F. C. (1981) *Social change and the aged* (Lexington, Mass.: D. C. Heath).

PERLMAN, R. (1980) 'Social services and population redistribution', in BERRY and SILVERMAN, 228–52.

PYLE, G. F. (1971) 'Heart disease, cancer and stroke in Chicago', *Univ. of Chicago Dept. Geogr. Res. Pap.* 134.

—— (1979) *Applied medical geography* (Washington, DC: V. H. Winston).

RAINEY, K. D. and RAINEY K. G. (1978) '*Rural government and local public services*', ch. 8 in FORD (ed.) *Rural USA*, 126–44.

ROSENBLATT, R. A. (1981) 'Health and health services', ch. 16 in HAWLEY and MAZIE, 614–42.

SALTZMAN, A. and NEWLIN, L. W. (1981) 'The availability of passenger transportation', ch. 7 in HAWLEY and MAZIE, 255–84.

SCHALLER, W. N. (1978) 'Public policy and rural social change', ch. 12 in FORD (ed.) *Rural USA*, 199–210.

SCHROEDER, L. D., SJOQUIST, D. L., and STEPHAN, P. E. (1980) 'The allocation of employment and training funds across States', *Pol. Analysis*, 6 4, 395–407.

SENINGER, S. F. and SMEEDING, T. M. (1981) 'Poverty: a human resource–income maintenance perspective', ch. 10 in HAWLEY and MAZIE, 382–436.

SHANNON, G. W. and DEVER, G. E. A. (1974) *Health care delivery: spatial perspectives* (New York: McGraw Hill).

SMITH, D. M. (1972) 'Towards a geogrpahy of social well-being: interstate variations in the United States', in PEET, R. (ed.) *Geographical perspectives on American poverty*, Antipode Monographs in Social Geography (Worcester, Mass.: Antipode), 17–46.

—— (1973) *The geography of social well-being in the United States* (New York: McGraw Hill).

SNIPP, C. M. (1980) 'Determinants of employment in Wisconsin native American communities', *Growth and Change*, 11 2, 39–47.

SORKIN, A. L. (1978) *The urban American Indian* (Lexington, Mass.: D. C. Heath).

THRALL, G. I. (1981) 'Regional dynamics of local government welfare expenditures',

Urb. Geogr. 2 3, 255–68.
TIENDA, M. (1981) 'The Mexican-American population', ch. 13 in HAWLEY and MAZIE, 502–48.
TILL, T. E. (1981) 'Manufacturing industry: trends and impacts', ch. 5 in HAWLEY and MAZIE, 194–230.
US BUREAU OF THE CENSUS (1979) *Current population reports*, Series P-20, **334** 'Demographic, social and economic profile of States: Spring 1976 (Washington, DC: USGPO).
—— (1980) *Statistical abstract of the United States: 1980* (101st edn.) (Washington, DC: USGPO).
—— (1981A) *Current population reports*, Series P-20, **368** 'Geographical mobility: March 1975 to March 1980' (Washington, DC: USGPO).
—— (1981B) *United States summary, final population and housing unit counts*, 1980 Census of population and housing: Advance Rep.
VINJE, D. L. (1977) 'Income and labor participation on Indian reservations', *Growth and Change*, 8 3, 38–41.
WATSON, J. W. (1979) *Social geography of the United States* (London: Longman).
WOHLENBERG, E. H. (1976) 'Public assistance effectiveness by States', *Ann. Ass. Am. Geogr.* **66** 3, 440–50.
ZELINSKY, W. (1973) *The cultural geography of the United States* (Englewood Cliffs, NJ: Prentice-Hall).

TABLE 3.1   *Families in poverty and per capita income rank, 1960–1979* (continued from p. 83)

Region and State	Families below poverty level		Per capita personal income rank	
	1969 (%)	1975 (%)	1960	1979
North East	7.6	7.2		
Maine	10.3	9.3	36	46
New Hampshire	6.7	5.9	21	30
Vermont	9.1	10.8	34	44
Massachusetts	6.2	6.1	9	16
Rhode Island	8.5	6.9	19	29
Connecticut	5.3	5.6	1	3
New York	8.5	7.6	6	13
New Jersey	6.1	6.9	7	6
Pennsylvania	7.9	7.4	16	24
North Central	8.3	7.4		
Ohio	7.6	7.3	12	18
Indiana	7.4	6.0	22	20
Illinois	7.7	8.3	8	5
Michigan	7.3	7.6	11	11
Wisconsin	7.4	5.8	20	26
Minnesota	8.2	6.4	25	19
Iowa	8.9	5.8	30	23
Missouri	11.5	9.5	23	32
North Dakota	12.4	8.0	40	33
South Dakota	14.8	10.6	39	41
Nebraska	10.1	7.1	26	27
Kansas	9.7	6.1	24	14

Source: US *Bureau of the Census* 1980, 447, 467.

4. Federal Environmental Management: Some Land-use Legacies of the 1970s

4.1, 4.2, 4.3 RUTHERFORD H. PLATT (University of Massachusetts);
4.4 GEORGE MACINKO and 4.5, 4.6 KENNETH HAMMOND (Central Washington University)

4.1 INTRODUCTION

It could be argued that the golden age of environmentalism in the US lasted from 1 Jan. 1970 when President Nixon signed the National Environmental Policy Act (NEPA) until 20 Jan. 1981 when President Reagan took the oath of office. NEPA declared 'a national policy which will encourage productive and enjoyable harmony between man and his environment; to promote efforts which will prevent or eliminate damage to the environment . . .' The Act required each Federal agency to prepare an Environmental Impact Statement on proposed 'major actions significantly affecting the quality of the human environment' and established the Council on Environmental Quality (CEQ) to monitor the preparation and circulation of such statements. One of the first acts of the Reagan administration was to discharge all staff members of CEQ, thus signalling the downgrading, if not the demise, of NEPA and its national policy.

The achievements of the past decade are not so easily dismantled. NEPA was perhaps the visible tip of the iceberg of programs, policies, and perceptions which characterized the 'environmental movement'. To be sure, NEPA was not merely symbolic: during the 1970s it generated over 11,000 environmental impact statements and was the basis for several hundred lawsuits, 114 in 1978 alone (US Co. on Environmental Quality, 1979, 589). Many Federal project regulations and expenditures have been altered or canceled as a result of NEPA scrutiny (Anderson and Daniels 1973). Yet criticism has been expressed that NEPA had become a paper mill and a paper tiger, no longer relevant to the day-to-day process of environmental management (Fairfax 1978). In a hopeful sense, this may mean that environmentalism matured during the 1970s from a 'brushfire' posture, based on challenges to decisions made by the 'establishment', to being a part of the establishment itself. When law students headed for corporate practice began routinely to take courses in environmental law, the movement had come of age.

Let us therefore look beyond NEPA to the rest of the iceberg. The machinery of environmental management in the US is complex, specialized, and, like any other governmental activity, bureaucratic and cumbersome. For every public interest lawyer filing a NEPA lawsuit, there are thousands of civil servants processing permits, organizing training sessions, conducting research, gathering field samples, and so forth. Many of the programs now in place were established during the heady 1970s. In the words of CEQ:

In 1970, Congress began to enact a body of legislation which by the end of the decade would have a major impact on people's lives and the nation's way of doing business, possibly comparable with such earlier political changes as the New Deal in the 1930s or the civil rights reforms of the 1950s and 1960s. In 1970 alone, Congress passed amendments to the Clean Air Act, requiring establishment of national ambient air quality standards; the Occupational Safety and Health Act, mandating Federal air pollutant and physical hazard standards for workplaces; and the Resources Recovery Act, calling for demonstration programs in waste recycling and better hazardous waste management. In that same year the President, by Executive Order, reactivated a long dormant portion of the 1899 Rivers and Harbors Act and established the nation's first Federal permit system for control of water pollution. The President created the Environmental Protection Agency (EPA) out of several existing Federal offices to oversee and manage pollution control programs. (CEQ 1979, 1)

These measures were soon followed by the Coastal Zone Management Act (1972), the Federal Water Pollution Control Act Amendments (1972), the Noise Control Act (1972), the Endangered Species Act (1973), the Safe Drinking Water Act (1974), the Resource Conservation and Recovery Act (1976), the Surface Mining Control and Reclamation Act (1977). Just to list the leading Federal enactments suggests the breadth of the legislative attack on environmental degradation, but to pass a law is scarcely to solve the problem. Some of these statutes have been responsible for the spending of billions of dollars, as in the case of the 1972 Water Pollution Amendments. Others like the Resource Conservation and Recovery Act, have barely become operative. While the nation's waterways are generally improving in quality as a result of the huge investment in sewage treatment plants, many water supplies remain polluted and certain types of harmful substances, such as viruses, escape conventional treatment processes. There is also the question as to whether the benefits of a particular approach justify the costs involved.

In essence, the quest for environmental improvement cannot rest with adoption of a law or the funding of a program. Past experience must be evaluated and new approaches formulated. In the words of Gilbert F. White (1969), in place of single solutions to individual problems, we must pursue multiple goals with multiple means. Other industrial societies have mastered this concept better than the US. In Tokyo, for instance, a new regional sewage-treatment plant has a landscaped park and playground on its roof. In West Germany the world's largest open-pit lignite mine is providing topsoil and overburden to restore earlier mined areas to agricultural productivity. There are American examples as well, such as the facility at Muskegan, Michigan, where sewage waste-water is trickled onto marginal farmland, allowing it to produce bumper crops while yielding groundwater purified by filtration through the soil mantle. However, such experiments are exceptional in the US; we need greater flexibility in our response to environmental degradation (Davis 1968).

The decade of the 1970s was therefore a period of intense and prominent environmental activity, but was neither the beginning nor the end of the environmentalism of this country. The roots of these efforts lay not just in NEPA but in the creation of the national forests in 1891, the founding of the National Park Service in 1916, the national planning programs of the New

Deal, the outdoor recreation and open space movement of the early 1960s, and so on. Many of these phases seemed to run their course and expire, but their fruits lived on. The National Resources Planning Board, for instance, was terminated by Congress in 1943 (Clawson 1981) but its concept of basinwide water-resource planning inspired the establishment of river basin commissions (Fig. 2.5) under the Federal Water Resources Planning Act (1965); these are to be eliminated under the Reagan administration.

Handwringing is nothing new in the environmental literature. A collection of environmental papers by geographers (Cooley and Wandesforde-Smith 1970), prepared on the very eve of NEPA and the 'environmental decade' opened with the same lament heard frequently in 1981:

And what about the future? There is some indication that the close of the 90th Congress late in 1968 may mark the end of this remarkable period in the history of conservation politics in the United States. Some members of Congress, as well as of the new Republican administration, have suggested that we are reaching the end of a long wave of significant and highly visible progress, and that the widely hailed 'environmental crisis' has, in a certain sense, passed the peak of critical national interest and public concern. (p. xvi)

Short of economic or political cataclysm, it can fairly be predicted that the legacy of past environmental reforms will substantially survive the fluctuations of the present time. To be sure, there will be casualties and the CEQ is a major one, but environmental improvement is now embedded in the American legal and economic system. To rout it out would be equivalent to repealing the reforms in social services, consumer protection, financial disclosure, civil rights, and other progressive elements of American society developed since 1933.

Much attention in the environmental literature has been devoted to air or water pollution, solid waste disposal, and environmental litigation (Davies and Davies 1975; Jones 1979). Federal legislation in the 1950s established enforcement action against residuals dischargers, if specific interstate damage could be proved, whilst modest Federal subsidies for waste-water treatment and water quality planning were also introduced at an early stage (Kneese 1980, 263). By the Water Quality Act (1965) Congress required States to set standards for interstate and boundary waters whilst in the Air Quality Act (1967) State standards for ambient air quality were set and a State implementation plan was required.

In the Clean Air Amendments (1970) the Federal role in setting and enforcing standards was greatly expanded and stringent new emission standards for automobile emissions were promulgated. Two years later the Water Quality Amendments (1972) introduced a system of permits for point-source waste discharges and increased subsidies for municipal waste-water treatment plants (Kneese 1980, 265). National goals for the elimination of discharge of all pollutants into rivers were set for 1985, with best available technology to be utilized by industries and municipalities by 1983. EPA was authorized to initiate legal action against polluters (Dye 1981, 203). The setting of such high standards was unrealistic to some, but by the 1980s significant improvements to clean air and clean waters had been made. The impact of government environmental protection policy upon industrial location and regional development is discussed in chapter 6 (section 3.3d). Figures 6.6a and b show the varied spatial impacts of manufacturers' capital expenditure on air- and water-pollution controls in 1977. The implications of environmental policies for the cities are treated in chapter 7 (section 4.3).

Solid waste disposal in affluent mass-consumption society is a major problem. Present per capita waste disposal of 6 to 8 lb. per day is expected to double in the next 20 years, with huge quantities of cans, bottles, jars, automobiles, and paper on municipal dumps (Dye 1981, 204). This is a spatial problem concentrated around the great cities and leads to an increasingly costly operation of seeking out landfills and transporting an ever larger mass of discarded materials. Federal legislation was consolidated in the Solid Waste Disposal Act (1965), amended by the Resource Recovery Act (1970) and the Resource Conservation and Recovery Act (1976).

This chapter concentrates on other Federal programs, more specifically relating to the management of land resources.

4.2 THE NATIONAL FLOOD INSURANCE PROGRAM

4.2.1 Geographic origins

Floods have long been a cause of great financial and personal distress in the US, and an object of considerable attention by geographers. Possibly the nation's greatest flood occurred in the Lower Mississippi Valley in April 1927. Levees were breached in some 200 locations and 18 million acres of bottomland in 6 States were inundated. At least 313 lives were lost and property damage was estimated to amount to $284 million in 1927 dollars. This led to the Lower Mississippi Flood Control Act (1928) which established a dominant Federal role in the reconstruction of the devastated valley (Hoyt and Langbein 1955, 261). Subsequently, President Roosevelt in 1933 established the Mississippi Valley Committee and charged it with reviewing the broad problem of flooding throughout the Mississippi drainage basin, encompassing 40 per cent of the US land area. This committee was soon converted into the Water Planning Committee—one of a series of national planning units culminating with the National Resources Planning Board. A key member of the Water Committee from 1933 on was Harlan H. Barrows, of the University of Chicago Department of Geography.

Barrows early brought one of his graduate students, Gilbert F. White, to Washington to serve on the Committee's staff. Thus began a long association between professional geographers and the problem of floods.

On the basis of work with the Water Committee between 1933 and 1940, White (1945) challenged the conventional wisdom regarding public response to floods. This wisdom, fostered by the Corps of Engineers and the 'Rivers and Harbors' lobby in Congress, advocated strictly an engineering approach to the problem of floods. This approach was solidly endorsed by Congress in the Flood Control Act (1936) and its successors which authorized a multibillion dollar program of dams, reservoirs, levees, diversion channels, and coastal protection works. White demurred that unless such structural measures were accompanied by land-use controls to restrain unwise flood-plain development, the greater losses would ensue in the event of floods exceeding the design limits of the flood-control projects. More broadly, White advocated the use of 'multiple adjustments' including: land elevation above expected flood levels; upstream reduction of surface runoff through forestry, soil conservation and other measures; structural flood control projects; emergency measures to remove people and property in the path of a flood; floodproofing to strengthen buildings and utilities against flood damage; floodplain zoning and other land-use restrictions; public disaster relief; and National Flood Insurance.

After 23 years and much further articulation of these concepts by White's students and others (e.g. Murphy 1958; Sheaffer 1960; Kates 1965), Congress adopted the National Flood Insurance Act (1968). Like the 1927 Lower Mississippi Flood Control Act, this marked another turning-point in national flood policy.

4.2.2 The intent of the framers

The objectives and theory of the National Flood Insurance Program (NFIP) may best be understood by reference back to the statements of those most closely concerned with its establishment. In the absence of private insurance coverage against flood losses, public deliberation on the possible need for a national flood insurance program arose in the early 1950s. In 1956 Congress adopted a Federal Flood Insurance Act which, however, was subsequently abandoned. Efforts to revive the concept in the early 1960s culminated in a directive in the Southeastern Hurricane Disaster Relief Act (1965) that the Department of Housing and Urban Development prepare a feasibility study on flood insurance. At about the same time, the Bureau of the Budget commissioned a special task force to review all aspects of national flood policy. These two reports, prepared under the direction of Marion Clawson and Gilbert F. White respectively, were prepared in parallel and submitted to Congress in late 1966. Both reports recommended establishment of a national flood insurance program with important qualifications.

The Clawson report (US Congress, House 1966A) recommended establishment of a national flood insurance program to serve two purposes: to spread the costs of financial assistance to flood victims among all occupants of flood hazard areas, and to help prevent unwise use of land where flood damages would increase in the future. The report stressed the importance of two safeguards to limit future growth in floodplains. First, the use of *actuarial rates* to charge floodplain occupants a premium consistent with the risk inherent in their location. However, the report admitted that rates might have to be subsidized by the Federal government for existing buildings in order to attract widespread participation. Secondly, 'there should be incentives for State and local governments to practice *wise management of flood-prone areas*, by means of such devices as effective channel encroachment laws, good land use zoning, and others'.

Both these approaches, actuarial rates and floodplain management, required detailed and accurate studies of hydrologic risk within each flood hazard area. The report discussed at some length the relationship between the statistical probability of flooding at a particular site and the dollar cost of average annual flood damage. A determination of this relationship was considered crucial both to the setting of actuarial rates and the adoption of floodplain management measures. The Clawson report thus envisioned detailed flood-risk mapping of all areas where flood insurance would be offered. In subsequent practice, however, flood insurance has been offered in advance to many communities, with detailed mapping following at a later date.

The White report (US Congress, House 1966B) considered the feasibility of flood insurance as one of many possible public adjustments to floods. This report was even more cautious than the Clawson report regarding the danger of unwarranted floodplain encroachment:

A flood insurance program is a tool that should be used expertly or not at all. Incorrectly applied, it could exacerbate the whole problem of flood losses . . . It would not be improper to subsidize flood loss insurance for existing property. That might be done, provided owners of submarginal development were precluded from rebuilding destroyed or obsolete structures on the floodplain. However, to the extent that insurance were used to subsidize new capital investment, it would aggravate flood damages and constitute gross public irresponsibility.

The White report went on to identify floodplain management as critical to a national flood insurance program:

Planning and coordinating the development of the floodplain is required as part of any significant effort to break the pattern being fostered by present federal policies concerning flood damage prevention, namely the continuing sequence of losses, protection, and more losses. This requires leadership of the federal government in a fashion that will gain effective participation by the state and local governments. Although the federal agencies can exercise direct control over federal installations in the floodplain, the far greater number of decisions affecting new development are made by private individuals and corporations within the limits set by state and local plans and regulations. (p. 25)

The theme that flood insurance must be contingent upon floodplain management was restated by Robert C. Wood, Undersecretary of Housing and Urban Development, at committee hearings on the proposed program in 1967 (US Congress, House 1967A):

It would not be logical as a matter of public policy to permit insurance to be made available in localities which did not, on their own initiative, or on the initiative of state or local authorities, take whatever steps would be appropriate to assure that their citizens would not unknowingly acquire and develop property where it is subject to known flood hazards.

4.2.3 Floodplain mapping

The National Flood Insurance Act (1968) was faithful to the intent of the framers in requiring floodplain management and actuarial rates for new construction as conditions for participating in the program. In reality, both these requirements were contingent upon the availability of detailed and reasonably accurate floodplain maps and associated flood data for each stream and coastline in the US. Without such maps and data floodplain management could not proceed because there was an inadequate basis for land-use regulations or land acquisition. And without flood data actuarial rates could not be determined since the flood risk pertaining to specific sites was unknown.

In the absence of floodplain maps and studies for most of the country, Section 1360 of the 1968 Act required the Federal Insurance Administration to: 'identify and publish information with respect to all flood-prone areas, including coastal areas located in the United States, which have special flood hazards, within five years following . . . this Act, and to establish a flood-risk zone in all such areas . . . within fifteen years following such date.'

This provision generated a two-stage program of floodplain mapping and analysis, one of the most ambitious mapping programs in US history. The first stage involved the preparation of Flood Hazard Boundary Maps for approximately 20,000 communities with flood problems. These maps were prepared very quickly, based on available information and were not particularly scientific. They did, however, serve the twofold purpose of informing communities that they in fact had floodprone areas and identified property which should be covered by flood insurance.

The second stage of mapping consisted of detailed 'flood insurance studies', indicating differential areas of flood risk for the calculation of actuarial premium rates and the boundaries of the 'floodway': that part of the 100-year floodplain subject to stringent controls against encroachment. This second stage was slow to get started. By the end of 1975, seven years into the program, detailed studies had been initiated for 1,156 communities, but only 550 had been completed. By the end of 1980 about 10,000 studies had been initiated of which 5,800 were completed. This delay in the completion of maps and studies thus deferred the application of both floodplain management and actuarial rates for many years in most communities. But insurance coverage under the program has nevertheless grown in leaps and bounds during the 1970s, by virtue of two important changes to the original Flood Insurance Act.

4.2.4 Mid-course corrections

To return to the development of the program—the first year of NFIP was not encouraging. Only 4 communities entered the program and 20 policies were sold. Two obstacles were identified which hindered implementation of the program. First, many communities did not have detailed flood insurance studies or floodplain maps available upon which to base regulations. Secondly, many communities were unwilling to adopt floodplain zoning voluntarily due to concern about limiting investment and hindering growth of their local tax base. These two obstacles were addressed in subsequent legislation in 1969 and 1973 (Platt 1976).

The emergency phase   Congress amended the National Flood Insurance Act in 1969 to waive the requirement for application of actuarial rates on a provisional basis: '. . . for the purpose of providing flood insurance coverage at the earliest possible time, the Secretary . . . shall provide insurance coverage without regard to any estimated risk premium rates which would otherwise be determined under Section 1307.'

The authority established the 'emergency phase' of NFIP under which communities might enter the program on a provisional basis and property owners therein might purchase limited flood-insurance coverage. Communities were exempt from the full application of floodplain management criteria, pending completion of their flood-insurance studies and rate maps. Instead, a community need only acknowledge that it had a flood problem and agree to enforce minimal flood-mitigation policies. Similarly, actuarial rates were not applicable even for new construction since they cannot be determined in the absence of a flood-insurance rate map. Limited levels of coverage were provided for any structure, at flat rates subsidized by the Federal government.

The Flood Disaster Protection Act (1973)   Two major floods of 1972, Hurricane Agnes in the mid-Atlantic States and a flash flood at Rapid City, South Dakota, brought to Congressional attention that flood insurance was still not widely in effect. This led to enactment of the Flood Disaster Protection Act (1973) which placed NFIP on a new footing. It required flood insurance to be obtained by any property owner in an identified flood-hazard area as a condition to receiving any 'Federal or federally-related' financial assistance for purchase or development of such property. This effectively foreclosed the marketability or improvement of floodprone property in communities which were not participating in NFIP or where a property owner failed to purchase insurance in participating communities. The 1973 Act also denied disaster assistance from any Federal agency in communities not participating in NFIP.

This Act elicited a tremendous increase in NFIP activity (Table 4.1). The number of participating communities increased from 2,000 in 1973 to about 17,000 in 1980, of which about 11,000 were in the 'emergency phase'. Policies in effect have grown from about 300,000 to over 2 million while total coverage has grown from $4.6 billion to $100 billion (December 1980).

The Flood Disaster Protection Act (1973) thus greatly expanded the insurance activity of the program. Most of this coverage, however, has been issued at subsidized rates under the 'emergency phase'. As of 23 April 1980, out of approximately 1.8 million policies, only 50,500 were based on actuarial rates. This reflects the slow pace of completion of flood-insurance studies upon which such rates can be based.

Reclassification and technical asistance   A third mid-course correction in the NFIP in 1980 was a redirection of the program to reduce the number of communities scheduled for detailed studies and to concentrate attention upon the needs of the most floodprone communities: 'The reclassification of a large number of communities in the NFIP's current inventory and the refocus of [FIA's] mapping and flood insurance study efforts on seriously flood-prone communities will permit a refocussing and concentration of [FIA's] efforts on floodplain management technical assistance to communities' (Jimenez 1979). Under this policy, States were asked to identify communities having minimal

TABLE 4.1   National Flood Insurance Program, 1971–1980

Fiscal Year	Premiums ($1,000)	Loss Payments ($1,000)	Participating Communities	Policies in Effect	Coverage ($ billion)
1971	$ 6,341	$ 251	158	75,864	$ 1.1
1972	7,003	2,500	637	95,123	1.5
1973	15,315	15,007	2,271	272,448	4.6
1974	25,777	36,638	4,090	385,478	8.4
1975	40,950	26,235	9,625	539,888	13.7
1976	57,524	81,359	14,502	793,779	22.7
1977	83,783	59,190	15,585	1.1 million	33.6
1978[a]	40,235	50,887	16,000+	1.2 million	37.1
Calendar Year					
1978	99,456	135,568	16,000+	1.3 million	NA
1979	117,069	482,375	16,448[b]	1.6 million	60
1980	NA	NA	16,957[c]	2 million+	95

[a] 1 July–31 Dec. 1977.
[b] As of 11 July 1979. This figure included 3,381 communities in the Regular Program and 13,107 in the Emergency Program.
[c] As of 15 Nov. 1980, including 5,571 Regular and 11,386 Emergency.
NA = Not Available.
Source: Federal Emergency Management Agency data.

flood hazard or development in floodplains for reclassification. Flood insurance would be made available thenceforth in such communities at regular program levels of coverage but at a subsidized rate. Reclassification of emergency program communities was abandoned in 1981 upon criticism that it would 'dilute' the regular program.

4.2.5 Current status and issues

The current status of the National Flood Insurance Program may be summarized before we turn to some unresolved issues. Statistically the program is very substantial. Some 17,000 US communities are participating in NFIP, with 10,250 in the 'regular' program with floodplain regulations in force, and the rest in the 'emergency phase'. This means that most communities with any kind of flood problem have at least acknowledged the existence of such problems by entering NFIP. Most of the nation's larger and more seriously floodprone communities are, or soon will be, enrolled in the regular program. With 2 million policies in effect and $100 billion in total coverage of buildings and contents, the program now represents a major component of public response to flood disasters. By early 1981, 198,000 claims had been filed on flood-insurance policies; total payments to victims was nearly $1 billion.

There is evidence the NFIP is achieving progress in the management of floodprone communities (Table 4.2). It appears that many localities have voluntarily exceeded the minimum standards for floodplain management established by FIA.

Another encouraging finding is that NFIP participation is not limited to larger metropolitan places. Table 4.3 indicates that a surprising 49 per cent of regular program communities (including counties) are located outside

TABLE 4.2   Floodplain management measures used by NFIP communities, 1981

	Regular Phase (N = 798)	Emergency Phase (N = 405)
	(%)	(%)
Minimum elevation	84	63
Zoning	77	71
Subdivision regulations	76	75
Floodproofing requirements	68	40
Floodway regulations	60	35
Sedimentation and erosion controls	31	24

Source: Burby and French 1981.

SMSAs, essentially rural communities and isolated cities of fewer than 50,000 inhabitants. For many of these outlying areas, compliance with the minimum floodplain-management standards of NFIP is their first modest effort towards land-use planning and control, albeit not always a popular step in terms of local sentiment.

We may now consider a few critical issues that confront the National Flood Insurance Program in the 1980s.

Fiscal solvency   Like the US Social Security Program, NFIP is faced with a grave disparity between revenue and payments. To date the vast preponderance of policies have been written at subsidized flat rates (25 cents per $1,000 of coverage for residential structures). Such rates of course do not reflect the actual risk of loss at particular locations or elevations. Payments on claims have far exceeded premium revenue, in 1979 alone by $482 million to $117 million (Table 4.1), and this does not include the operating costs of the program itself. To date, the US Treasury has paid over $1 billion into NFIP to defray its deficits on inadequate premium revenue and administrative costs. This approximates to the total of payments made on flood-insurance claims so far. Thus premium revenue is about covering the operating costs of the program with all payments to victims coming from the Federal treasury.

TABLE 4.3   Nonmetropolitan activity of the National Flood Insurance Program (8 April 1981)

	SMSA[a]	Non-SMSA	Percentage of non-SMSA
Regular program	3,139	3,055	49
Emergency program	2,598	8,236	76
Number of policies	1.4 million	603,000	30
Amount of coverage	$73 billion	$22 billion	23
Number of claims	145,110	53,024	27
Amount of claims	$781 million	$197 million	20

[a] Standard Metropolitan Statistical Areas.
Source: Federal Emergency Management Agency data.

NFIP is therefore really no better than conventional disaster assistance. The program has not yet begun to shift the costs of floods from taxpayers to floodplain occupants.

An important question is what happens when a community moves into the regular phase and actuarial rates begin to replace subsidized rates. In theory this would bring premium revenue more closely into line with claim payments. In practice there is little experience to draw upon. In the first place, actuarial rates apply only to 'new' structures started after the date the community is converted to the regular program, and to higher levels of coverage on 'existing' structures. With a building recession in progress, relatively little new construction has occurred in or out of flood hazard areas since 1978 when communities began to convert to regular phase status in large numbers. As noted above, only 50,500 policies were written at actuarial rates as of April 1980.

Coastal issues   In many respects coastal hazard management is the 'Achilles heel' of the National Flood Insurance Program. Although its adoption was originally triggered by a series of coastal disasters in the 1950s and 1960s , NFIP has been notably deficient in coastal areas. A disproportionate amount of flood-insurance coverage is found in hazardous coastal settings, especially on barrier islands along the South Atlantic and Gulf shorelines (Fig. 4.1). According to FIA, 38 per cent (670,500) of all policies in effect in the US are found in four highly floodprone coastal metropolitan areas: Miami/Fort Lauderdale; Tampa/Fort Myers; New Orleans and Houston/Galveston. Each of these areas has been narrowly missed by recent hurricanes; a square hit will mean billions of dollars in claims. Each has experienced rapid development in hazardous areas over the past decade. Indeed, it has been argued that coastal development has occurred *because of*, rather than *in spite of*, the NFIP (Miller 1975; US Congress 1981).

Management of coastal flood hazards is complicated by related physical phenomena such as shore erosion, subsidence, landslides, earthquakes, tsunamis, and seiches. Shorelines which are susceptible to any of these hazards can expect aggravated flooding as a result. Yet NFIP is limited in its ability to develop comprehensive hazard maps or management regulations which treat the coastal setting realistically. In other words, flooding is viewed abstractly rather than in the context of natural conditions which give rise to it or worsen its impact. Coastal erosion, for instance, has had very little attention in the delineation of coastal high-hazard areas, even though certain areas are experiencing landward movement of the shoreline by several meters per year.

Post-disaster recovery   Public disaster assistance, including flood insurance, is frequently used to rebuild structures *in situ* and thereby set the stage for the next flood disaster. The immediate aftermath of a flood is theoretically an ideal time to mitigate future losses through such measures as relocation of floodplain inhabitants, removal or flood-proofing of structures, land acquisition for parks and open space. In actual practice the sentiment of private and public interests alike is to return to normal as quickly as possible by restoring the status quo.

NATIONAL FLOOD INSURANCE PROGRAM

NUMBER OF POLICIES PER STATE AS OF APRIL 1981

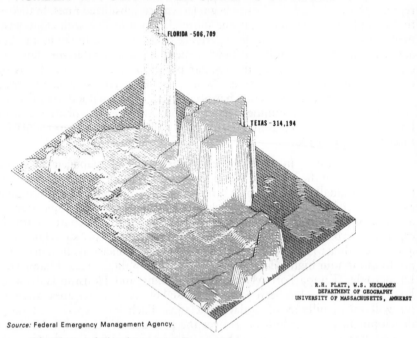

FLORIDA -506,709

TEXAS -314,194

R.H. PLATT, W.S. NECHAMEN
DEPARTMENT OF GEOGRAPHY
UNIVERSITY OF MASSACHUSETTS, AMHERST

Source: Federal Emergency Management Agency.

4.1   The National Flood Insurance Program

During and after the heavy flood losses of 1979, the Carter administration began to explore a new approach to post-disaster recovery; one that would emphasize the identification and realization of opportunities for mitigation of future losses. A study conducted for the US Water Resources Council (Platt 1979) documented experience in Rapid City, South Dakota, and elsewhere in replanning flood-ravaged communities. The small rural village of Soldiers Grove, Wisconsin, for instance, with considerable Federal and State assistance has undertaken to move its central business district out of the floodplain of the Kickapoo River to an upland site, where innovative design of new commercial buildings also permits application of alternative energy sources (National Science Foundation 1980).

In July 1980 the Office of Management and Budget directed Federal agencies involved in post-flood recovery to collaborate in seeking ways to reduce future flood losses. Under an Interagency agreement, signed in December 1980, 10 Federal agencies agreed to cooperate in performing post-flood assessments of mitigation opportunities under the leadership of the Federal Emergency Management Agency which now administers the NFIP. This places NFIP at the center of the recovery process with influence not only over its own activities but all other Federal efforts as well.

Thus an exciting opportunity is at hand for continuation of the long tradition of geographic contribution to the management of flood losses. Post-flood assessment of mitigation options is inherently a geographical exercise involving the assembly and analysis of a wide variety of data: physical, economic, demographic, structural, ecological, and so forth. This is to be no leisurely field exercise, however. In order to make the results available to agencies before they have committed their recovery funds, the survey and report must be completed within 15 days after the disaster declaration.

4.2.6 Conclusion

The National Flood Insurance Program (NFIP) is a study in contradictions. Originally sponsored as a housing and insurance measure, it has achieved prominence (and notoriety) as an incentive to the adoption of land-use restrictions against development in floodprone areas. Inspired by a series of coastal hurricanes during the 1950s and early 1960s, it has had least success in stemming development of coastal hazard areas, but has been more effective along inland streams. It is administered by a very small staff (by Federal standards) of about 400 persons, yet it is one of the largest domestic programs in terms of contingent liability: over $100 billion of flood-insurance coverage is currently in effect. It was intended to save Federal expenditures on disaster relief by transfer of the costs of assistance to occupants of hazard areas through the medium of insurance premiums. So far it has experienced costs well in excess of premium revenue, with the deficit supplied by a Federal subsidy of over $1 billion. It is castigated by many environmentalists for allegedly permitting, and even subsidizing, new development in coastal areas, especially on fragile barrier islands. Yet it has introduced many thousands of communities to the notion of floodplain management, including many rural areas which have had no prior experience of land-use planning.

In short, the National Flood Insurance Program is highly complex and widely misunderstood, both as to its goals and as to its operation. Its very complexity reflects the nature of the problem which it addresses; flood losses are not susceptible to convenient remedies. The ultimate issue then is whether the complexity of NFIP serves or defeats its objectives to reduce future flood losses and Federal costs.

4.3 COASTAL ZONE MANAGEMENT

Coastal zone management has been a major instrument in the nation's efforts to upgrade its environment and rationalize the use of its natural resources during the 1970s. Public efforts to manage coastal areas have emerged in two forms. Beginning in 1970, a number of States, notably California, Washington, and Rhode Island, passed new legislation establishing strong coastal management programs within their own jurisdictions. These were important examples of an expanding role of State governments, in certain cases at least, in exercising greater control over land planning and management within their borders (Bosselman and Callies 1971; Healy and Rosenburg 1979).

The other expression of public policy in coastal areas was the Federal Coastal Zone Management Act (1972). This Act was adopted at the height of efforts in Congress to pass a National Land Use Policy Act (US Congress, Senate 1973). The controversy that prevented adoption of a truly nationwide Act apparently could not withstand the charm of the seacoast. The Coastal Zone Management Act passed the Senate by a vote of 68–0, and the House of Representatives by 376–6.

Although they both relate to the management of coastal areas, the Coastal Zone Management Program (CZMP) differs from the National Flood Insurance Program (NFIP) in nearly every respect (Platt 1978). While NFIP was conceived as a housing and insurance measure of little interest to the general public at the time of its adoption, CZMP epitomized the environmental mood of the times and was widely acclaimed.

In place of the NFIP 'carrot and stick' approach, CZMP offers a 'lollipop' of Federal grants with conditions attached. NFIP directs its efforts to local communities while CZMP largely deals with State governemnts. NFIP focusses upon flood hazards while CZMP addresses a broad range of coastal planning issues, e.g. mining, fisheries, natural area preservation, recreation and beach access, economic development, navigation facilities, offshore oil development (Conservation Foundation 1977; Ditton *et al.* 1978).

4.3.1 The nature of the CZM Act

The original CZM Act followed closely the principles of the defeated national land-use Bills: declaration of a national policy favoring better management of (coastal) land and water resources; creation of a process to facilitate Federal–State collaboration in planning these resources; authorization of funds for Federal grants to assist States in developing and administering their own management programs. Its benefits are limited to coastal States and territories, 35 in number, which border the oceans or the Great Lakes. Geographically the program addresses the 'coastal zone', defined to extend seaward to the limit of each State's jurisdiction (normally 3 miles) and landward to a boundary determined by each State to encompass all land 'strongly influenced by' coastal waters. Federally owned lands are excluded.

The CZM Act enumerates areas of national concern but does not overtly mandate Federal policies. According to the Senate Committee Report: 'There is no attempt to diminish State authority through Federal preemption. The intent of this legislation is to enhance State authority by encouraging and assisting the States to assume planning and regulatory power over their coastal zones' (US Congress, Senate 1972). The program is thus more concerned with process than with substantive results. This again differs strongly from the National Flood Insurance Program wherein authority to establish national floodplain management standards is delegated by Congress to the Federal Emergency Management Agency.

Several kinds of planning grant to coastal States are authorized by the CZM Act (as amended). Originally the Act provided grants for the purposes of formulating a coastal plan (Section 305) and administering the plan (Sec. 306) after approval by the Federal Office of Coastal Zone Management (OCZM). Additional grants are available regarding urban waterfront revitalization and beach access (Sec. 306A), coastal energy impacts (Sec. 308), interstate planning (Sec. 309), and estuarine sanctuaries (Sec. 315).

All 35 eligible States and territories have collectively received a total of $64.5 million under Section 305 and that phase is now completed. As of January 1981, 26 States and territories had received approval of their coastal plans and were eligible for plan implementation grants under Section 306. By early 1980, $34 million had already been allotted for this purpose. Federal grants cover 80 per cent of program costs; the balance must be provided by each State. Approved programs cover 75 per cent of the nation's shorelines, including the Great Lakes, and encompass most of the nation's coastal population. In the words of CZM Administrator Robert Knecht (OCZM 1979, 1): 'With the approval of these programs, the job of coastal management begins in earnest, as States, localities, and Federal agencies put into effect newly developed and organised coastal management practices.'

4.3.2 The content of CZM plans

While OCZM does not dictate the substance of State coastal plans, it does expect certain planning tasks to be performed and specified issues to be addressed. The first order of business for State coastal planners has been to delimit the inland boundary of their coastal zones. This has been accomplished in most cases through a process of detailed planning studies, public hearings, and State legislative or executive action (Robbins and Hershman 1974; OCZM 1975). States have differed greatly in their approach to this task. Some States, such as California, sought a very wide coastal zone so as to extend the influence of CZM planning as broadly as possible. Others, like Texas, sought a very limited coastal zone so as to qualify for Federal grants while causing minimum interference with private property owners. This task was completed in most States by the mid-1970s.

A second task has been to identify 'permissible land and water uses' within the coastal zone or subareas thereof. This implies some form of 'State zoning' of coastal areas, a notion stoutly opposed by local governments in most areas of the US. States thus have walked a tightrope between adopting significant restrictions upon the use of coastal land as demanded by OCZM while minimizing disturbance to the prerogatives of local governments and private owners. The Act limits State discretion in two ways: reasons must be given for prohibiting any particular use, and facilities of 'regional benefit' may not be excluded from the coastal zone.

A third task is to identify and designate 'areas of particular planning concern' within each State. These include coastal sites of special significance for many reasons, including natural qualities, geology, history, cultural resources, and so forth. These areas essentially comprise mini-planning areas within the coastal zone wherein the State may establish special regulations and policies. Naturally the interpretation of this task varies greatly from one State to another, but it may prove to be the cutting edge of the CZM process where diligently applied.

A fourth element of a coastal plan is the development of a State capacity to influence land-use decisions within their coastal zones, forcing States to preempt a certain degree of land-use control authority from local governments. It may be achieved in various ways: e.g. State adoption of criteria for local implementation; direct State land-use regulation; or State review of local actions for consistency with the State CZM plan. In its 'Five Year Report' (1979) OCZM cites widespread adoption of new State legislation despite local opposition in some cases. Among the 35 eligible States and territories: 22 have enacted some form of coastal management legislation; 31 have new wetlands statutes; 20 have measures to protect unique or endangered flora and fauna; 26 are dealing with the need to protect their beaches and primary dunes; 16 have measures regulating offshore sand and gravel mining and/or oil and gas extraction.

As previously noted, the adoption of a law is not equivalent to the solving of a problem. The content and administration of these laws would need to be examined closely to determine what effect, if any, they are exerting upon the management of coastal zones. Like the local floodplain management measures adopted under the National Flood Insurance Program, they are at least a step in the right direction.

4.3.3 Additional coastal issues

As CZMP gathered momentum, certain additional planning issues gained prominence. Amendments in 1976 added several new elements to the program with special grant funds provided in some cases. Most important among these was the 'coastal energy impact program' (Sec. 308). In recognition of the existing and pending development of offshore energy resources, this section authorized grants for planning studies and projects relating to 'economic, social, or environmental' impacts upon the coastal zone of 'new or expanded energy facilities'. These include port expansion, terminal facilities for liquefied natural gas (LNG) and coal, as well as petroleum refineries, and staging facilities for offshore drilling operation. The potential magnitude of energy-related activites upon coastal areas (see ch. 5.6.1 and 3) is already visible along the Louisiana and Texas Gulf coasts where isolated fishing villages have been transformed into supply ports for hundreds of offshore rigs. The advent of drilling at several locations off the New England and Mid-Atlantic coast foretells major adjustments for port communities and the coastal environment in those regions. Thus Massachusetts, Rhode Island, New York, New Jersey, and Maryland have received significant CZM planning assistance under Section 308.

Another issue addressed in amendments to the CZM Act is beach access. Initial planning studies in many States documented a prevalent lack of public access to shorelines. Although coastal waters are subject to public control up to the mean high-water mark in most States, it is frequently impossible for the public to reach the water's edge because of private property lining the shorefront. Furthermore, many States have only a small proportion of shoreline in public ownership, Federal, State, or local. In Massachusetts, for instance, only about 10 per cent of the State's shoreline is in public ownership, mostly the Cape Cod National Seashore; otherwise, private holdings impede public access to coastal waters. CZM, through its beach-access program, has facilitated the planning, and in some cases the acquisition, of easements, rights of way, parking areas, boat ramps, and other means for promoting access to the shoreline. The Land and Water Conservation Fund has been an important source of Federal matching funds to States and local governments for coastal recreation facilities (see p. 154).

An important 'process' issue in the administration of CZMP has been 'Federal consistency'. Section 307 requires that once a State plan is approved: 'Any Federal agency which shall undertake any development project in the coastal zone . . . shall insure that the project is, to the maximum extent practicable, consistent with approved State management programs.' This provision has triggered controversy and litigation with respect to Federal leasing of offshore oil and gas rights in coastal waters covered by approved State plans. In *American Petroleum Institute* v. *Knecht*, the US Court of Appeals (9th Circuit) upheld OCZM approval of California's plan despite fears by the oil industry that this would limit future Federal lease sales. This same decision and the lower court decision from which it arises (456 Fed. Supp. *889* 1978) provide a comprehensive review of the legal aspects of CZMP. The Reagan administration has announced its intention to proceed with lease sales (see ch. 5, pp. 184, 192–3) as well as to eliminate CZMP Federal funds; the future role of CZMP in the oil-lease process is therefore unclear.

4.3.4 Conclusion

Management of the nation's coasts under both Federal and State laws has barely begun. Approved CZM plans cover 75 per cent of the nation's shorelines, but most of these have been in effect only since 1978 or 1979. Experience is therefore extremely limited in the application of CZM policies to specific developmental and resource management efforts. Continued Federal funding is deemed crucial to the survival of State CZM programs. In a poll of 25 States with approved CZM programs in March 1981 only 5 indicated that they would be able to continue their programs without Federal assistance, at much reduced levels (Coastal Society 1981). Of course, such polls of program officials may be self-serving. The real question is whether coastal zone management can continue without a CZM program, through the normal process of government.

The problems certainly do not ebb with the tide of Federal funds. The Coastal Society (1981, 11) lists the following among critical problems of coastal zone management awaiting further public response:

From 1975 to 1977, more than 23,000 spills occurred in coastal waters releasing over 38 million gallons of oil.

Over 40 per cent of the nation's coastal wetlands have been damaged or destroyed; over 75 per cent of those remaining have experienced some degree of degradation through dredging, filling, or pollution.

Less than 5 per cent of the nation's shoreline is in public ownership.

Nearly two dozen American ports have announced plans for new coal export facilities (see ch. 5.6.3).

Many other ports are rendered obsolete by the container revolution and face decline and disuse.

Perhaps the most perplexing issue which also haunts the National Flood Insurance Program is what to do about the surge of population and investment in coastal hazard areas, especially along the South Atlantic and Gulf coasts. Congress has recently enacted legislation prohibiting flood insurance and other Federal benefits for new development on undisturbed barrier islands. This should help to curb further expansion of hazard-prone development and provide indirect protection to barrier islands remaining in their natural state. It is too late, however, to deter settlement of the coastal zone which has already taken place. It is estimated that 6 million people from Maine to Texas live within reach of a '100-year' storm surge (Am. Met. Soc. 1976). Most structures are not strengthened or elevated, and most of this population has little personal experience of hurricanes (White and Haas 1975).

The seminal issues of offshore leasing, natural hazards, recreation, and protection of natural areas, will continue to confront governmental bodies whether or not there is a Federal or State coastal zone management program. Basically CZMP has helped to elucidate the issues and promote scientific analysis of alternative lines of action. Like the National Environmental Policy Act, the CZM Act has not guaranteed that harm will not come to the coastal environment. Rather it has sought to ensure that key decisions are made with knowledge of potential consequences and with opportunity for broad public involvement. It is to be hoped that these two principles will survive as tenets for coastal decision-making, regardless of the future of the CZM Program itself.

4.4 THE SURFACE MINING CONTROL AND RECLAMATION ACT (1977)

The effects of surface mining on the environment first emerged as a prominent public issue in the early 1970s. According to Rosenbaum (1978, 54): 'No technique of fossil-fuel recovery inflicts a more violent, pervasive, or devastating impact upon the land than surface mining for coal.' Traditional indifference toward the environmental impact of surface mining was to change as, in a climate of heightened public awareness, coal reemerged dramatically as a strategic national energy resource.

4.4.1 New emphasis on coal and surface mining

The oil embargo of 1973, together with the natural gas shortage early in 1977, focussed attention on coal (see ch. 5.6.3) which represented over 90 per cent of US domestic hydrocarbon reserves (McDaniel 1978, 290). Declining domestic reserves of oil and gas and increasing uncertainty regarding Middle East petroleum supplies point to a dramatic increase in coal production by the end of the century (Table 4.4). Further, the switch from underground to surface mining as the dominant method of coal production promised greatly to increase environmental impacts associated with coal production. This switch gained momentum in the 1950s when coal had to compete with very cheap imported oil and with natural gas regulated federally at very low rates. If environmental costs were ignored, surface mining was more efficient than underground mining and required far less capitalization to start up new operations. Vietor (1980, 228) put it thus:

TABLE 4.4   *US coal[a] production by method of mining 1947–1979 and projected*

Million tonnes	Total	Surface	Underground	Percentage Surface	Underground
1947	631	140	491	22	78
1950	516	123	393	24	76
1955	465	121	344	26	74
1960	416	131	285	31	69
1965	512	179	333	35	65
1970	603	264	339	44	56
1975	648	355	293	55	45
1979	776	469	301	60	40
1985	1,034[b]				
1990	1,257[b]				

[a]Bituminous and lignite.
[b]DOE mid-level projection assumes medium economic growth and medium availability of energy with constant oil prices.

Source: President's Commn. on Coal (1980) *Coal Data Book*, Washington USGPO.

Before 1941, strip mining coal was a marginal sort of business endeavour, suited only to isolated pockets of very shallow coal seams. But during the 1950s manufacturers were able to produce ever-larger and more energy-intensive strip-mining equipment that made stripping profitable at greater depths and thus over a far wider area.

Surface mining accounted for 23 per cent of total production in the US in 1953, but 60 per cent by 1979, rising to a probable 75 per cent by 1985. In 1977 surface mining of coal was disrupting about 4,000 acres of land each week (US Congress, House 1977, 73). Rising coal production, both *in toto* and from surface mines, heightened public awareness of the environmental and social costs of surface mining. In the absence of effective State policies this set the stage for Federal regulation.

4.4.2 *Surface mining and the environment*

Reflecting the perspective of Appalachia, Wooley (1979, 628) reminds us that the problems addressed in the SMCRA

did not originate with the first irate citizen or meddling environmentalist. They also did not begin with the passage of environmentally oriented laws and regulations, or with the first visits by government inspectors. Rather, these problems arose from the basic fact that the interaction of strip mining and Appalachian hydrology naturally tends to produce the terrible morass of landslides, impassable haulroads, topsoil loss, aggravated flooding . . . stream pollution and other conditions which . . . inflame the local populace.

Harvey (1978, 1148) adds loss of fish and wildlife resources and a decline in natural beauty to the social environmental costs of surface coal mining. Rodgers and Schaecter (1979, 258) refer to the Congressional notation in the SMCRA that strip mining can destroy or diminish 'the utility of land for commercial, industrial, residential, agricultural, and forestry purposes'. McDaniel (1978, 292–3) adds that increased sedimentation had impaired water supplies, reduced waste-assimilation capacity, and diminished the water-storage capacity of impoundments, and then goes on to outline some of the special problems surface coal mining poses for the subhumid American West, such as the revegetation of mined lands in arid and semi-arid environments and the heavy demands energy development projects place on already limited water supplies (see ch. 5.6.3).

4.4.3 The need for national legislation

Vietor (1980, 229) contends that free enterprise failed to provide the incentive necessary to internalize all the costs of surface mining because voluntarism was 'inconsistent with competition and with management's obligations to maximize profit'.

The Chairman of the Committee on Interior and Insular Affairs of the US House of Representatives and sponsor of the SMCRA, said (Udall 1979, 553) that throughout the Committee's hearings a recurring problem of competitive disadvantage was perceived to stem from variable State regulatory patterns. As a consequence, Title I of the Act recognizes that: 'Surface mining and reclamation are essential in order to insure that competition in interstate commerce among sellers of coal produced in different States will not be used to undermine the ability of the several States to improve and maintain adequate standards on coal mining operations within their borders.'

McDaniel (1978, 297) seconds the notion that effective State programs depend on State officials knowing that essentially similar standards are being rigorously enforced in neighboring States. Similarly, operators mining in States requiring high levels of reclamation, who must add such reclamation costs to the price of their coal, should not have to fear being undercut by operators in States requiring little or no reclamation of mined lands.

Other reasons for national standards include the fact that pollution, such as acid mine drainage, does not respect State boundaries. Further, the large-scale mining of western lands involved complex mixtures of Federal and non-Federal lands which could be handled best by relatively uniform rules. For these and similar reasons, Udall and his committee saw surface coal mining as a national environmental problem needing a national solution. More telling than the competitive disadvantage factor was the generally poor record of the States as regulators of mining activities. Vietor (1980, 192) interprets this record in terms of inadequate technical and material resources available at State level. Many States simply were not equipped to evaluate or refute the contentions of industry.

Pennsylvania, one of the leaders in State regulation of surface mining, is cited by Vietor as an example of the relationship between the mining industry and State regulatory Agency that he labels 'clientelism'. Following an initial period in which policies established in 1961 and 1963 prescribed rigid enforcement goals, the zeal of the Pennsylvania Bureau of Surface Mine Reclamation weakened and 'the bureau began dealing with, rather than dictating to, the strip-mining industry' (Vietor 1980, 82). By 1969 there had been a sharp decrease in the number of both bond forfeitures and formal hearings as the environmental regulatory process had degenerated into a bargaining process geared more to achieving satisfactory day-to-day working arrangements than to achieving any systematically determined environmental results.

McDaniel (1978, 295) agrees that the State response to problems of surface mining has been less than adequate. Though he acknowledges that most State surface mining laws between 1970 and 1975 were superior to earlier laws, he finds them 'seriously deficient with respect to administration, mine inspection, and enforcement'. State mine-inspection programs, necessary to assure compliance with reclamation laws and subsequent enforcement efforts, were judged largely ineffective by McDaniel for 'where the coal industry dominates the economy of a State as a major source of jobs and taxes, political influence, subtle or otherwise, may be used to moderate enforcement laws'. But he judges the failure to require performance bonds adequate to allow reclamation upon forfeiture by the operator as the most serious deficiency in most State surface mining regulations (op. cit. 296). Bonds were sometimes set so low that operators were encouraged to forfeit the bond in lieu of adequate reclamation. Furthermore, given such low bond amounts, States were unable to reclaim the land with forfeited monies.

4.4.4 SMCRA in brief

Congressman Udall has characterized the deliberations attending the Surface Mining Control and Reclamation Act (1977) as follows:

It took six years of tenacity and bitter debate to pass Public Law 95–87. The history of the Act would serve as a textbook for any national legislator desiring to thwart the clear will of the majority of the Congress. . . . a legislative endeavor involving 183 days of hearings and legislative consideration, eighteen days of House action, three House–Senate Conferences and Reports, two Presidential vetoes, approximately fifty-two recorded votes in the House and Senate, and the machinations (and statesmen-like conduct) of three Presidents is an activity ripe for scholarly analysis, let alone the stuff for a pretty good novel. (Udall 1979, 554)

The result of the collective labor alluded to by Udall was an 88-page Act establishing a national program for regulating all surface mining as well as the surface effects of underground mining. The Act created a new agency, the Office of Surface Mining Reclamation and Enforcement (OSM), within the Department of the Interior, to administer an ambitious program that attempted to 'strike a balance between protection of the environment and agricultural productivity and the Nation's needs for coal as an essential source of energy' (Sec. 1202F).

The SMCRA is a compromise whose essential requirements fall within three categories: pre-planning, mining practices, and post-mining reclamation (McDaniel 1978, 299). The first requires that permit applications be accompanied by a reclamation plan that specifies the method of reclamation, provides a timetable for its execution, and gives evidence of research into pre-mined land use, hydrologic conditions, and the character of both coal and overburden. The second mandates mining practices that minimize damage to the environment or to public health and safety. Included here are restrictions on the placement of overburden, blasting regulations, and pollution control requirements. Finally, requirements are set for the restoration of land to its pre-mined condition. Backfilling requirements, revegetation, and water quality and quantity considerations figure prominently here.

The SMCRA (Sec. 1201) was intended:
(a) to establish a nationwide program to protect society and the environment from the adverse effects of surface coal mining operations;
(b) to assure that rights of surface landowners are fully protected from such operations;
(c) to assure that surface mining operations are not conducted where reclamation is not feasible;
(d) to assure that adequate procedures are undertaken to reclaim surface areas as contemporaneously as possible with the surface coal mining operations;
(e) to strike a balance between protection of the environment and agricultural productivity and the nation's need for coal as an essential source of energy;
(f) to assist the States in developing and implementing a program to achieve the purposes of the Act;
(g) to promote the reclamation of mined areas left without adequate reclamation prior to the enactment of the Act;
(h) to assure that appropriate procedures are provided for public participation in programs established under the Act;
(i) to establish effective and reasonable regulation of surface mining operations for other minerals;
(j) to encourage the full utilization of coal resources through the development and application of underground extraction technologies;
(k) to stimulate research investigations, experiments, and demonstrations, in the exploration, extraction, processing, development, and production of minerals and the training of mineral engineers and scientists.

Harvey (1978, 1160–1) judges Section 515 which sets performance standards regulating surface mining and Section 516 which establishes standards governing the surface impacts of underground mining to be the substantive heart of the Act. These provisions are aimed at restoring the land to a condition capable of supporting the uses it could support before mining took place.

4.4.5 Commentary

The performance standards set forth in the SMCRA were to be implemented in two stages. First an interim transitional program lasting nearly three years in which the Federal government was to have primary responsibility, and secondly a permanent regulatory program in which State governments were to exercise considerable autonomy. From the time the interim regulations were issued in draft form (Sept. 1978), they were assailed by the mining industry as too costly and too strict. Environmental groups took a more favorable view.

The industry view (Gage 1979) maintains that OSM failed to appreciate the cost to industry of the regulations or to recognize the benefits of a more flexible program than that promulgated by OSM. Industry contends that OSM paid insufficient attention to the coalmine operators' costs of compliance with the regulations, and, consequently, to the operators' ability to produce coal at a reasonable cost. Finally, it argues that the regulations unduly restrict the operator because they often set forth rigid design criteria and invariable standards. The economic arguments used by Gage echo those previously used by the Ford Administration to justify its veto of strip mine legislation proposed in 1975. The Congressional study (US Congress, House 1975, 161) that examined the justification for veto found the arguments to be generally unfounded and highly questionable.

A satisfactory balance between protection of the environment and agricultural productivity and the nation's need for coal as an essential source of energy could be achieved, according to industry, only if OSM's regulations were more reasonable, more flexible, and based on a better understanding of what was physically, technologically, and economically possible. In particular, inflexibility in regulations were said to hurt small operators, disrupt energy supplies, and increase costs to the consumer. Further, it was claimed that OSM's inflexible regulatory approach would stifle technological advances by effectively 'freezing' the 'state of the art' in surface mining, and land-reclamation technology (Gage 1979, 604).

The environmentalist view (Wooley 1979, 641, 667–9) disagrees with the above and argues that variances permit all the flexibility needed; and that the regulations are more than reasonable given the poor performance of State regulatory activity, the coal industry's history of environmental abuse, and its hostile attitude toward the merits of environmental protection.

Wadsworth (1980) examines the regulatory controversies surrounding the SMCRA and distinguishes between 'hardship' issues caused by OSM's delay in promulgating permanent regulations, and 'specificity' issues concerning the degree of regulatory specificity allowed under the Act. The regulations which run to nearly 150 pages and include more than 400 pages of explanatory comment have generally stood up well in court. OSM has argued that a high degree of specificity is in accord with the Congressional intent of preventing unfair competition among coal producers that might result from widely differing State procedures. Further, OSM argued that detailed regulations were needed because the Act was worded too broadly to be self-implementing. Terms such as 'environmentally sound reclamation efforts' and 'reasonably stable water levels' used throughout the Act, required further clarification. More generally, because numerous provisions of the Act require definition and clarification, the courts will be required effectively to redraft the regulations via a series of decisions (Wadsworth 1980, 769).

The most recent of these decisions saw the Supreme Court reverse lower-court decisions in Virginia and Indiana that had challenged the constitutionality of provisions requiring mine operators to restore mined land to approximately original contours and permitting the designation of areas as unsuitable for surface coal mining. Justice Marshall said the regulations are 'reasonably related to the goals Congress sought to accomplish. The Act's restrictions on the practices of mine operators all serve to control the environmental and other adverse effects of surface coal mining' (*Herald Republic* 1981). As of late 1981, the Reagan administration appeared to be reducing the Federal role in the enforcement of the Act (Smith 1981, 762).

In the absence of Federal oversight, many States gave evidence that they have neither the technical competence nor the financial resources, and often not even the will, to regulate the surface mining industry. As but one example, Wooley (1979, 655–6) observes that 'until the Federal dollars began to flow in late 1978, the West Virginia Reclamation Division had no geologist, hydrologist, or soil scientist working directly and constantly to review permit applications. Yet West Virginia is one of the premier coal mining states.'

One then comes down to the question of balance between coal production and environmental protection. Crucial here is the starting point from which perspective is to be determined. If one starts with legislation (US Congress, House 1971), that would have completely banned surface mining, the 1977 SMCRA looks moderate. If, on the other hand, one takes the coal operators' view of the halcyon days when public regulation was nonexistent, then SMCRA is an unwelcome intrusion into the business of private enterprise, but those days presumably are gone for good. The concept of public stripmine regulation, Federal and State, appears sufficiently established to withstand the vicissitudes of individual administrations.

4.4.6 *Conclusion*

Passage of the Surface Mining Control and Reclamation Act (1977) ended a long and bitter effort to regulate the surface mining of coal. In SMCRA Congress has created a regulatory structure with more promise than past State efforts, although one that still needs revision to incorporate more effectively regional and local differences in slope, soils, climate, and vegetation. Performance standards, rather than design criteria, should be emphasized in the revision, to allow for innovation and flexibility in reclamation practice. Whether the Act can accomplish its dual objectives of allowing for an expansion of coal production, while at the same time minimizing the environmental damages attendant upon surface mining of coal, will depend on effective implementation and enforcement of a sensibly and sensitively revised Act. Implementation has been very difficult in the face of industry challenges. The coal industry has successfully fought previous legislation considerably more lenient than that enacted in SMCRA.

There is some concern that a national regulatory program administered by the States within a framework of Federal standards may be 'susceptible to many administrative ills that have reduced most State mine regulation programs to a charade' (Rosenbaum 1978, 7). In fact, some see a paradox in a program that has recognized the near failure of States to regulate, and yet gives regulatory powers to them (Rochow 1979, 559). In particular, a two-tier regulatory structure in which Federal agencies supervise State agencies, which, in turn, implement strip-mine controls may simply compound enforcement problems.

An offsetting factor may be the gradual emergence of what Rosenbaum (1978, 152) calls the 'quality of life public'. This essentially middle-class, well-educated, white, politically active group shares a broad concern for promoting cultural, environmental, and aesthetic values in the political process. Though perhaps numbering no more than 25 per cent of the American populace, it has become an increasingly influential force committed to balancing traditional preoccupations with economic growth by moral, ethical, and aesthetic values. The saga of strip mining may provide a test of its mettle for one of the Reagan administration's earliest reversals of environmental policy seems to be occurring in the regulation of strip mining. Secretary of the Interior, James Watt, is said to be 'recasting virtually every rule written' in the four years since Congress passed the Surface Mining Control and Reclamation Act' (Smith 1981, 759). If Watt is successful in his attempt to remove specific criteria for reclamation and to reduce Federal involvement, the program may be left with lofty goals, but negligible enforcement.

In short, in the SMCRA one finds a flawed piece of much-needed legislation, with laudable goals embodied in an immensely complicated and discretionary set of administrative rules. That it needs streamlining is beyond question; that it can survive the direct onslaught now directed at it is doubtful. Meanwhile the social and environmental effects of a rapid rise in the surface mining of coal cannot be wished away.

4.5 HERITAGE CONSERVATION

Environmental conservation or preservation as used herein includes both the natural world and the built environment. Though the Federal government missed many opportunities to preserve natural areas, the built environment has fared worse, for it was long ignored (Hosmer 1965, 1981). Few of the early European settlers had respect for the thousands of years of history of the native Indian, and transient frontier settlement made it difficult to differentiate from the welter of current events those of lasting significance. There were significant exceptions where the Federal government held the title to national shrines and monuments, but even the acquisition of the Robert E. Lee property, now the location of Arlington National Cemetery, was more an act of post-Civil War vengeance than of appreciation of historic value.

Johnson (1976, 372) suggests the recent rapid public acceptance of historic preservation is in part due to the fact that 'preservation issues have tended to be more simple and the goals more tangible. And because preservation efforts have been largely non-threatening to most members of society, they have frequently offered avenues for opponents on other issues to work together.' This is in contrast, for example, to the complex and less-defined controversies over energy and pollution control.

While admitting the difficulty of finally defining 'quality of life' Biddle (1980, 195) notes five goals that historic preservation seeks to promote:

Through finding new and productive uses for sound old structures, preservationists keep familiar landmarks in our environment, thereby making it easier for us to tolerate other stresses and changes that we cannot control. Preservation rehabilitates and maintains buildings of human scale that, in ensemble, provide visually pleasant and hospitable streetscapes. Both adaptive use and rehabilitation are helping to revive the cities, bled for thirty years by the suburbs and their malls. Through their demonstrable commitment to conservation, preservationists apply a counterforce to America's throwaway culture, and demonstrate their belief that intangibles must be considered when applying the 'highest and best use' criterion in judging value. Finally, preservationists encourage a renaissance of the tradition of the craftsman who signed his work and stood behind it.

4.5.1 Early legislation

Before the Antiquities Act (1906) the limited Federal role in historic preservation required that Congress be persuaded to act on each site. Historic site designations by Congress were rare, though Gettysburg National Cemetery was created in 1872 and in the same year Yellowstone was set aside. Congress also protected other natural wonders that later became National Parks. The Sequoia and General Grant areas in California and Mt. Rainier in Washington are prominent examples. The first historic national monument was El Morro in New Mexico, created by executive order in 1907. Numerous sites have since been designated. Authority to designate landmarks was extended to the executive branch by the Antiquities Act. The President could then establish national monuments to protect 'historic landmarks, historic and prehistoric structures and other objects of historic or scientific interest' provided that they were in Federal ownership and of national significance. Destruction at the hands of Federal agencies was not addressed in the Act.

A modest declaration of a national policy came with the passage of the Historic Sites Act (1935): 'it is declared that it is a national policy to preserve for public use historic sites, buildings, and objects of national significance for the inspiration and benefit of the people of the United States'. The Act required federal agencies to consider historic preservation in their plans and programs. It authorized the Secretary of the Interior to initiate what became the National Survey of Historic Sites and Buildings. The survey highlighted the richness of the heritage of the American people and provided a marker against which its loss could be measured. Private owners of property listed on the survey could have their structures and/or land designated as a National Historic Landmark. This voluntary commitment by the owner could be rescinded without penalty. The designation would be removed if the historic value was destroyed.

In 1949 Congress chartered the National Trust for Historic Preservation, a nonprofit corporation funded in part by membership dues. Its main purpose is to facilitate public participation in the preservation of sites, buildings, and objects of national significance or interest as well as to accept and administer donated properties and funds. In 1970 the National Trust had 23,670 members; by 1980 membership exceeded 160,000, a sign of the popularity of historic preservation during the 1970s. Even with private efforts, the National Trust could not cope with the destruction of the 1950s and early 1960s, much of it caused by Federal programs and policies.

4.5.2 Economic issues

In the absence of direction to the contrary, transportation officials seek routes for new facilities where initial dollar costs are minimized. By contrast, little weight is given to cultural and ecological losses, long-range values, or losses from the disruption of social ties or sense of community. Parks, open space, marshland, and older or rundown buildings all attract the eye of the engineer. Congress provided some protection from the highway bulldozer when the Department of Transportation Act (1966) included as an article of national policy that 'special effort' should be made to preserve parks and historic sites. This applied to sites either on the National Register of Historic Places or with historic significance as determined by appropriate officials at the State and local level. It did not become impossible to destroy such sites for highway purposes, but it did make it unlawful and probably much more expensive to do so routinely (Gray 1971).

The Urban Mass Transportation Assistance Act (1970) contains similar restrictive language. The Airport and Airways Development Act (1970) contained more general, but adequate, language concerning the protection and enhancement of environmental quality.

Rapid escalation of developmental land values easily overcame any reluctance on the part of private developers to destroy the American heritage in the name of profit and progress. Indeed, haste to develop before any historic values could be identified was not unknown. The Housing and Urban Development Agency operated under the Housing Act (1949) to carry out urban-renewal projects (see ch. 7.3.3). Ancient buildings of historic value are often commingled with other old buildings. All of them may be run down, be part of a slum, and thus constitute a prime area for renewal. The Act required indiscriminate razing of the area, so historic structures were destroyed and communities disemboweled to provide space for new businesses or housing.

Congress was well aware that urban renewal frequently caused the loss of historic buildings and the Housing and Urban Development Act (1965) permitted relocation of historic buildings where a public or nonprofit organization would renovate and maintain the structure for historic purposes. It authorized HUD to provide financial assistance for local surveys of historic structures and sites, to recognize historic and archaeological preservation within the definition of urban renewal, and to include that purpose within the open space and urban beautification programs. These HUD programs, however, were terminated by the Nixon Administration in 1974 in favor of Community Development Block Grants.

4.5.3 The broader view

In 1966 a study by a special committee of the US Conference of Mayors (Hyman *et al.* 1966) recommended broader Congressional action on historic preservation. Congress responded with the National Historic Preservation Act (1966), which extended protection to cultural items of national significance and to property with historical, architectural, archaeological, or cultural significance to a community or State.

In its statement of purposes, the Act recognized our obligations to future generations to preserve legacies of the past. It noted inadequacies of prior Federal efforts, both in comparison with private efforts and in the face of accelerated destruction. In general, Congress declared: that the spirit and direction of the Nation are founded upon and reflected in its historic past; and that the historical and cultural foundations of the Nation should be preserved as a living part of our community life and development in order to give a sense of orientation to the American people. The role of history and culture as a stabilizing and spiritual force was a new perception and it was somewhat radical to suggest that preservation should be a living part of the community rather than consisting solely of shrines or museums. Moreover, the Act included 'districts' and 'sites' as worthy of preservation. Thus areas with no outstanding specimen of architecture and without association with a particular individual or event could still qualify if in fact they represented an example of culture or 'roots' worthy of perpetuation. Nor was ancientness now a requisite for preservation. Association with important events, representative examples of a rapidly vanishing present, and commercial opportunities to recycle old, abandoned but substantial buildings were all now adequate reasons for preservation. Recently construction and energy costs (Advis. Co. Hist. Preservn. 1979) have increased imaginative reuse of older structures where embodied energy and location are advantages. Moreover, the rising numbers of singles, childless couples and of small families, as well as the costs and hassle of commuting, reduce the lure of the suburbs. Living in a renovated mill, barn, or warehouse in a historic district is now fashionable and, except where public subsidies are provided, largely restricted to people of some means. Improvement of the tax base, employment opportunities, and general revitalization of the community in consequence of preservation and restoration are not overlooked by public decision-makers. Building reuse is directly responsive to the 'living part of our community life' policy enunciated by Congress. The Public Buildings Cooperative Use Act (1976) directs the General Services Administration to give preference to historic buildings for Federal office space.

The National Register of Historic Places has 20,000 or so entries and some 1,500 are historic districts only locally significant individually but nationally significant in the aggregate. The Act required an expansion of the National Register and provided assistance to States for their own surveys and plans for preservation, acquisition, and development of historic properties. Matching grants were provided both to States and to the National Trust for Historic Preservation for actual preservation projects that might include appropriate 'protection, rehabilitation, restoration, and reconstruction' of eligible property.

Section 201 created the Advisory Council on Historic Preservation, with rather sweeping duties to advise, recommend, and inform the President, Congress, and State and local governments on needs, studies, and guidelines to achieve preservation purposes. It must submit an annual report and may recommend needed legislation. Section 106 requires that Federal entities allow the Advisory Council to comment on any undertaking 'prior to the issuance of any license' when anything listed on the National Register may be affected. The responsibilities of Federal agencies were to include review for property that might merit inclusion on the National Register. The Advisory Council recommends that each State adopt programs similar to those of the Federal government, appoint a State Historic Preservation Officer, and adopt legislation to enable local governments to carry on historic preservation.

4.5.4 Tax incentives

Before the Tax Reform Act (1976) (Koch 1977; Oldham 1980; Powers 1980), historic properties were frequently a liability. When zoning prevented destruction and rebuilding the owner suffered an income loss and was denied the tax advantages of new construction. It is rare that a private owner of commercial property will place patriotism, civic responsibility, aesthetics, and a sense of history above profit. In those rare instances where the owner was motivated to expend funds for restoration, the prompt reward was a property-tax increase.

The 1976 Act denies accelerated depreciation for a new building erected on the site of historic structures, and disallows any deduction for the expenses of clearing a historic structure from the site. This denial applies individually to buildings on the National Register and, in the absence of permission from the Secretary of the Interior, to all buildings in a Registered Historic District. Owners who expend substantial sums on rehabilitation can use the accelerated depreciation advantage of new construction. If an owner chooses to make a charitable donation of a long-term interest in the property a tax deduction can be taken. The Revenue Act (1978) allows a 10 per cent investment tax credit for rehabilitation of buildings 20 years or older. The generosity of such a tax shelter for the wealthy investors has not been lost either on the wealthy or on critics of such Federal largesse (Nesson 1978). Money succeeds where directives and duty fail.

The 1966 Act provides financial incentive for States to take a greater role in preservation. Matching grants are available for both acquisition and development. Many have adopted their own preservation laws, their own tax-incentive programs, created their own register of historic sites, and provided incentives for local preservation efforts. The local efforts are crucial, for in virtually all States it is the local government that has power over land-use, zoning, and building standards.

4.5.5 The Penn Central decision

A crucial test of local power to control the fate of historic sites came with the Grand Central Terminal case in New York (Costonis 1977; Brooks 1979), which reached the Supreme Court of the US. The rights accruing to an owner of the property, however powerful in America, are never absolute. Taxation is the most common sovereign demand on private property and has been used to discourage and to encourage specific uses. Eminent domain and zoning have evolved as the most-used vehicles of public control or taking of private property. The Grand Central Terminal case in New York City has added yet another tool.

That the world-renowned Beaux Arts style terminal was worth preserving was never seriously in doubt. The question was whether the owner, Penn Central, should be allowed to destroy its character by significantly extending its height. This was allowed on adjacent properties and a 59-storey office building would return several millions of dollars per year in rental fees. If this development was to be disallowed the question was how to do so with some fairness.

Neither the total loss of the value of development rights that would have fallen on Penn Central under a sustained zoning decree nor the crushing financial burden on the already strapped treasury of New York City required by eminent domain was adopted. Instead Penn Central was allowed to transfer to adjacent properties they owned or market to other owners in the area the development rights which they had, but could not exercise, on the site of the Grand Central Terminal. Such Transferable Development Rights (TDR) are valuable and, to ensure a market, the city agreed to relax restrictions on building size for the nearby properties. The case tended to remove any doubt about the validity of landmark designation of even very valuable properties and ought to reduce the number of claims of 'taking' when property is so designated. As Dennis (1980, 343) comments, '. . . future cases are likely to concentrate on reasonable return questions and the adequacy of the procedures used by the local preservation commissions rather than on the decisions they reach.'

No discussion of the legal protection for historic or cultural areas and objects would be complete without mention of the National Environmental Policy Act (1969). Though it does not specifically provide protection from demolition or serious alteration, it does state that all major Federal actions that significantly affect the 'quality of the human environment' require an 'environmental impact statement'. The Federal agency must make a conscious decision to destroy. If specific procedures to identify the values are not followed, interested citizens have legal grounds to prevent or to delay the action significantly, and may provide alternatives.

Both individual buildings and entire districts have been preserved and recycled under the widespread application of the recent laws. Some of the results have become a source of regional and even national pride—for example, the Vieux Carré Historic District in New Orleans, Pioneer Square in Seattle, Ghirardelli Square in San Francisco, and Quincy Market in Boston. They nicely complement the earlier preservation of national shrines and monuments such as Mount Vernon, Monticello, Independence Hall, and Williamsburg.

4.6   RECREATION

4.6.1   *The Land and Water Conservation Fund Act (1964)*

The Land and Water Conservation Fund Act (LWCF) or 'LAWCON' has been a mainstay of public efforts, Federal, State, and local, to acquire space and develop public recreation. The achievements of the fund have exceeded and outlasted several other Congressional initiatives of that era, e.g. the Federal Water Projects Recreation Act (1974), the HUD Urban Open Space program, and the Greenspan program.

The Bureau of Outdoor Recreation and the Fund itself were in part inspired by the influential report of the Outdoor Recreation Resources Review Commission (ORRRC) published in 1962. In fact, the Commission did not originate or advocate the idea of a dedicated recreation fund in the form the LWCF eventually assumed. That idea came from the so-called Committee of

Fifteen organized by the National Park Service to counter the formation and activities of the ORRRC. It included five members each from the National Park Service, the American Institute of Park Executives, and the National Conference on State Parks. The Committee represented an unsuccessful last-ditch effort by the Park Service to retain its limited existing authority for nationwide recreation planning. Taken together, the history and results of the ORRRC and the Land and Water Conservation Fund comprise an important success story in American resource conservation.

4.6.2 *The Outdoor Recreation Resources Review Commission*

In 1958 Congress established the Outdoor Recreation Resources Review Commission (ORRRC) to assess both demand and opportunities for outdoor recreation. Its many reports and recommendations led directly to the establishment of the Bureau of Outdoor Recreation (BOR) in 1962 and the LWCF in 1964.

At the time ORRRC was established recreation was generally associated with the wide open spaces of western and rural America; the use of outdoor recreation facilities greatly exceeded their carrying capacity; and responsibility for recreation planning and provision was divided among many agencies at each level of government. ORRRC was intended to be bipartisan and nonpolitical, and recreation opportunity was coming to be viewed as the right of all citizens. The ORRRC was created as a compromise because there were 'so many agencies involved in these various recreational fields that no single agency could handle it without being under suspicion of grinding its own axe' (Engle 1958, 11369).

Active support for creation of ORRRC came largely from the traditional conservationists and preservationists. Support also came from most States and some Federal agencies. Nottably absent or opposed were urban-oriented organizations, including the National Council of Mayors, the National Association of Manufacturers, urban planners, the US Chamber of Commerce, or any group concerned with the underprivileged, the handi-capped, or racial minorities. This lack of urban support is reflected in the Bill as finally passed. The Commission was to be concerned with *outdoor* recreation in a nonurban sense. '"Outdoor recreation resources" shall not mean or include recreation facilities, programs, and opportunities usually associated with urban development such as playgrounds, stadia, golf courses, city parks, and zoos.' Recreational activity was seen by Congress as an important need of the mind and body, an activity often missing in the urban setting. The Commission's summary quoted philosophers of ruralism, including Jefferson who 'saw the land as the country's ballast against the rootlessness of city living', and Thoreau, who asked 'in words that still compel': 'Why should we not . . . have our national preserves . . . for inspiration and our own true recreation? Or shall we, like villains, grub them all up, poaching on our own national domains?' (ORRRC 1962, 13).

On balance, the Commission emphasized urban needs and called for recreation opportunity in and near urban areas. Its chairman, Laurance Rockefeller (1965, 13), summed it up later:

When we were first setting up the Commission there was still a very general feeling that outdoor recreation meant the wide open spaces; that there wasn't much that could be done about the cities except to provide its people more recreation areas somewhere else.

But all of us were getting an education. When we submitted our final report three years later, the gist of our recommendations was that we were really concerned with a better environment where most people live—in our urban areas.

Both Congress and the Commission avoided the prospect that a growing population and finite resources might require a reduction of individual demand. It can be reasonably argued that to raise the issue of limits at that time would not have been productive. They turned instead to multiple use, better planning, and program coordination to utilize space, shoreline, or water more effectively.

In spite of the emphasis on urban areas, the Commission did not see a need for the Federal government directly to acquire recreation land within urban centers. Rather the appropriate Federal role was deemed to be: first, continuing Federal acquisition of large areas of national significance, and secondly, encouraging State and local government acquisition efforts through a Federal matching grant program. In 1962 the President asked Congress to establish a 'Land Conservation Fund', limited to Federal acquisition of recreation lands. Grants to States, proposed in another Bill, could only be used for outdoor recreation planning. Urban recreation needs were not discussed and the Bills did not pass. In 1963 a proposal was made to establish a 'Land and Water Conservation Fund' so as to assist States with their recreation planning. From a modest beginning the Fund became the nation's primary source of funding for planning, acquisition, and development of park and recreational programs.

The purposes of the fund were rather sweeping:

To assist in preserving, developing, and assuring accessibility to all citizens of the United States of America of present and future generations and visitors who are lawfully present within the boundaries of the United States of America such quality and quantity of outdoor recreation resources as may be available and are necessary and desirable for individual active participation in such recreation and to strengthen the health and vitality of the citizens of the United States.

In spite of what would appear to be an ongoing need, a termination date of 1989 was nonetheless built into the fund legislation.

Funding was initially from sales of surplus Federal real estate, a diversion of Federal motorboat fuel taxes from the highway trust fund and from admission and user fees at certain Federal recreation areas. The total income soon proved inadequate, user fees being especially disappointing. It was administrative policy to provide 60 per cent of LWCF appropriations to the States on a matching basis and 40 per cent to Federal agencies. With one exception the Federal share of the fund was restricted to acquisition. Funds could be used to reimburse the Treasury for enhanced fish and wildlife values at Federal water-development projects. The emphasis was on expanding recreational opportunities in National Parks, National Forests, and Federal

Wildlife Refuges. All purchases had to be authorized by Congress and restrictions were placed on National Forest purchases, so that no more than 500 acres could be purchased outside any one forest and no more than 15 per cent of all acreage added to the forests could be west of the 100th meridian.

Initial grants to States were for planning. A State Comprehensive Outdoor Recreation Plan (SCORP) was required as the basis for approval of requests for State acquisition and development projects. In theory, the individual SCORPs would be coordinated with a national recreation plan. The formula for allocation of funds to States required that two-fifths be apportioned equally and three-fifths on the basis of need, but did not allow any one State to receive more than 7 per cent of the total allocated. This effectively favored the less-populated States over the more populous ones, an initial bias which has shifted with time and changing events.

4.6.3 The urban thrust

The initial size of the fund—about $100 million—could not make a dent in the urban needs, but could preserve some natural areas from immediate destruction. By 1968 riots had swept urban areas across the nation. Most concerned members of Congress still thought of recreation in traditional terms, but some began to comment on urban needs and even talked of forcing States to use more of their share in urban areas as they proceeded to double the level of the fund using receipts from Outer Continental Shelf Mineral Leasing.

In 1970 LWCF authorization was increased to $300 million for each year through FY 1989, the last year of the fund. The record shows a decided shift toward favoring urban areas. The need for States to emphasize an urban thrust was officially noted as was the importance of acquiring and developing facilities within and near urban areas. It was also acknowledged that the Federal share of the LWCF was necessarily involved in urban recreation.

The HUD open-space program was eliminated as a categorical grant program in 1974 and became a part of the new block-grant scheme. This automatically meant that in the poorest cities many other needs would have priority and little money would be allocated to open space. Congress later increased the LWCF authorization to $600 million in 1978, $750 million in 1979, and $900 million in FY 1980 through 1989. In 1977 Congress advanced the date for $900 million by two years, to cope with the backlog of authorized but unacquired lands for the National Park system and the National Recreation Areas. Congress further favored urban areas by changing the apportionment formula to shift funds to more populous states and directed the Secretary of Interior to submit to Congress 'a comprehensive review and report on the needs, problems, and opportunities associated with urban recreation in highly populated regions'. Actual appropriations, of course, frequently did not match authorizations. In addition, the inability of States to match or to obligate their mandated share plus frequent executive impoundments of appropriated funds meant that actual outlays often did not approach authorizations (Table 4.5).

The study submitted in 1978 (US Dept. Interior) cited not only the numbers of people living in urban areas and the role of recreation as a 'key component

TABLE 4.5   *Land and Water Conservation Fund: appropriations and expenditures, 1965–1982*

Fiscal Year	Amounts available for appropriation[a] ($1,000s)	Appropriation ($1,000s)	Actual Outlays ($1,000s)
1965	28,398	16,000	1,254
1970	288,500	145,537	112,489
1975	562,221	307,492	283,617
1980	1,015,354	508,794	595,242
1982 (estimate)	1,927,567	520,365	556,000

[a] Cannot be summed as portions represent balances carried forward.

Source: *Budget of the US Government*, Appendix, Washington, DC: USGPO.

of physical and mental health' but also the vastly altered energy picture which had created new demands for recreation opportunities close to home. The study documented needs, cited problems associated with lack of coherent urban policy, and sought to improve the supply of recreation facilities in urban areas. Congress responded with the Urban Parks and Recreation Recovery Act (1978) for rehabilitation of existing indoor and outdoor recreation sites and associated historic or otherwise significant structures. The program had barely begun in 1981 before being threatened by the Reagan administration.

The 1978 Act was a belated attempt to rectify problems created by Congress. First, Congress authorized numerous new National Recreation Areas, National Seashores, and National Parks without providing adequate funds for their purchase. Further, delay in acquisition drove the prices to unimagined levels. Attempts were made to allow greater flexibility in apportionment discretion by the executive, but the States held fast to their 60 per cent share in exchange for support of the program.

4.6.4 *Development* versus *acquisition*

President Kennedy's letter to Congress proposing recreation legislation (1963) mentions 'planning and acquisition and development', emphasizing the urgent need for acquisition. Any physical changes or improvements to the area required would be considered development. As adopted, the LWCF Act limited development expenses to 10 per cent of total grants to States in each of the first 10 years. This limitation was intended to encourage early acquisition of open space so as to avoid both quality degradation and price escalation. Opponents of limits on development contended that enough land was already available and development of facilities would reduce the public resistance to user fees. Some States had little desire for an acquisition program and desired instead to shift current development, operation, and maintenance expenses to the LWCF grants. Further, it can fairly be said that recreation facilities attractive to tourists were often preferred to open-space acquisition, in order to derive local economic benefits. Even Secretary of the Interior Udall (US Congress, House 1963A, 58) placed the limitation in an unfavorable light: 'The 10 percent limitation on development may mean that about $375

million of estimated State needs for development would not be accommodated within the first 10 years.' It is clear that the 10 per cent limitation on
development was an offspring of the Bureau of the Budget. It found little
favor with other executive agencies, Congress, or the States. The hearings
record suggests that a development funding maximum between 25 and 50 per
cent would have been acceptable to the States, but to attempt to restrict them
individually or collectively to a miserly 10 per cent meant that all opportunity
for any limitation on their use of the LWCF development was lost.

Several times it was pointed out that the States had to present a plan
acceptable to the Secretary of the Interior. It was contended that this safeguard would prevent irresponsible State use of funds. The critical role to be
played by the State plan was now obvious, but without legal limitation it
seems naive to expect that most States would faithfully adhere to the guidelines advanced:

In most States emphasis during the first few years of the program will be on planning
projects. As comprehensive planning is completed, land acquisition projects will take
first place in importance.

. . . it is unlikely that any very substantial part of the moneys made available to the
States under the bill will be devoted to development projects . . .'. (US Congress, House
1963B, 1, 10).

The Federal share of the fund was essentially restricted to acquisition.
Some opponents of Federal purchases have a philosophic aversion to any
extension of public ownership; others feel that Federal holdings hamper their
economic development; and some, most notably the timber industry, see
Federal holdings as a threat to their business operation. Those who wish to
strengthen the role of the State see additional Federal acquisition as a threat.
There was also a conviction that the real need was for development. In the
early years Congress aggressively favored State acquisition and the Appropriations Committees expressed their dissatisfaction with the emphasis on
development on several occasions. This is highlighted by two quotations:
First, 'In the opinion of the Committee, a proper ratio between development
and acquisition for the States would be about one-third for development and
two-thirds for acquisition' (US Congress, House 1967B, 5). Secondly, 'The
committee urges a limit on development costs at about 35 per cent of the total
annual appropriations allocated to the States' (US Congress, Senate 1968, 9).
The States favored development and the Bureau of Outdoor Recreation
(BOR) wanted to get funds committed, but under pressure from Congress
BOR Director Crafts apologetically wrote: '. . . it is necesssary for me to take
steps to seek to carry out those directives; therefore I believe we must work
toward that goal of at least a 50–50 ratio of acquisition to development
expenditures' (US Bur. Outdoor Recreation 1967). Another step toward
development was taken when the 1976 amendments allowed up to 10 per
cent of the allocation to any State be used for 'sheltered' facilities for swim-
ming pools and skating rinks. Even when restricted to States with 'severity of
climate'—high winds, extreme cold, or heavy snow—the door was opened

another crack. Though not true of every State, in the aggregate, both in numbers of projects and amount of money expended by States, development exceeded acquisition.

4.6.5 *Planning*

A major purpose of the Land and Water Conservation Fund was to promote comprehensive, coordinated Federal, State, and regional resources planning. A share of the LWCF was immediately available for State planning, but eligibility of States and territories for the much larger acquisition and development matching funds was contingent upon the approval by the Secretary of the Interior of a State Recreation Plan. A quality State recreation plan was absolutely crucial to set the pattern for a long-range coordinated recreation effort. It was to be a part of a comprehensive plan and was to evaluate demand and supply, set priorities, and be creative. Approval of the State Plan by the Secretary would constitute certification at the Federal level. A major criterion for BOR approval of individual projects subsequently submitted by the States was whether the project was in accord with the State plan.

The requirement for an approved State recreation plan created some resentment, but nearly all States wished to qualify for the Federal funds and they therefore carried out at least some minimum amount of required planning. Many States had limited experience in recreation planning and to obtain sufficient and talented planning staff at any price was not easy. When every State was simultaneously vying for recreation planners it was not possible. To produce a sound, creative, coordinated plan is time-consuming; vested interests resisted coordination, while to delay any longer than was absolutely necessary to qualify for Federal funds was politically inexpedient. By mid-1968, with States actually expending funds in accordance with their plans, a survey of State Liaison Officers indicated that nearly one-third rated their existing State plan as inadequate or useless.

If State planning had been the sole consideration, BOR might have disapproved inadequate plans, but BOR wished Congress to establish the precedent that all the fund income would be appropriated annually. The formula for division of the appropriations to States provided some money for every State. Thus to obligate all the money, approved plans were needed from all of them. Consequently, officials of the BOR were, if anything, more anxious than the States for all the plans to be submitted and approved at an early date. The plans ranged from sophisticated policy plans downward to a shopping list of pet projects which had long been gathering dust on the shelves of State land-management agencies. The solution of the dilemma was a fairly liberal set of BOR guidelines for plan development and a scheme of provisional approval, which enforced revisions and updating of plans.

If the State planning efforts were not exactly sterling, the early Federal planning effort was solid lead. A comprehensive plan was required and, though delayed, was to be released in 1969. The plan did not suit the new Nixon administration and a new one was prepared and released in late 1973. It was a thin document on slick paper, full of photographs, generally descriptive, and devoid of substantive policy or program guidelines (US Bur. Outdoor Recreation 1973). Senator Henry Jackson obtained a copy of the far more meaty original plan and had it published, including some scathing comments on the Nixon administration's attitude toward recreation programs.

A third national plan produced during the Carter administration was heavy on data with volumes of background studies to support recommendations and programs (Heritage . . . Service 1979). It included a new policy, funds for historic preservation, and an expanded LWCF. The newly articulated and funded urban thrust provided a solid base from which to move into the decade of the 1980s. With the election of President Reagan, however, recreation and historic preservation were among the first programs scheduled for cuts or elimination. Some of the functions of HCRS vanished in 1981 and others were shifted to the National Park Service. Though launched under the banner of fiscal restraint, the attacks on these programs demonstrated a lack of intellectual appreciation of the value of the past as a stabilizing social force or for the long-run health of ecological systems. Twenty years' intensive effort on behalf of the future was in jeopardy.

4.7 CONCLUSION

The Federal role in environmental management began to take shape in the years 1957–69, and came of age during the following decade. In almost all respects the first Federal steps were halting and incremental. There was a reticence to intervene in traditional State functions, unless there was a clear interstate issue at stake. Federal budgets were limited for environmental matters and on all questions affecting air or water pollution there was usually a powerful and effective industrial lobby (ACIR 1981, 54). The environmental decade of the 1970s was powered by a widespread commitment to the belief that a clean environment was a democratic birthright and, moreover, technology could as readily create it as continue in its course of pollution.

Environmental legislation was prompted by public demand, as focussed by the mass media and private environmental and conservation organizations. Traditional lobbying in Congress, States, and communities was reinforced by lawsuits to compel industry or public agencies to conform with environmental legislation. Such legislation proliferated, in all environmental fields, with standards beyond the capacity for Federal enforcement. Furthermore, a counteraction set in. Public concern waned, though environmentalists continued to be active. States or local governments complained that Federal actions were contradicting or impeding their resource-management policies. Conflicts arose, as between air-quality standards and urban economic revitalization, or maximum coal extraction in the West and maintenance of environmental standards. The onset of recession promoted the resurgence of economic over social priorities. The decision of Congress to exempt the Trans-Alaskan pipeline environmental impact studies from review by the Courts and the 1977 Water Pollution Control Act Amendments were signs of the times (ACIR 1981, 55). Under the Reagan administration policies to correct an unstable economy and to exploit energy resources are in conflict with policies favoring environmental protection.

The stage is thus set for a quick return to an earlier incrementalism in policy. To some, the outcome of group struggle over the environment has been to produce 'a virtual stalemate over policy direction and a paralysis of government action' (Dye 1981, 208). Yet the cumulative experience will not have been lost and, it is hoped, will resurface once growth momentum resumes and environmental concerns take their rightful place in the quest for 'quality of life'.

Public Acts

Airport and Airways Development (1970) PL 91-258
Antiquities (1906) PL 59-209
Clean Air Amendments (1970) PL 91-604
Department of Transportation (1966) PL 89-670
Endangered Species (1973) PL 93-205
Federal Coastal Zone Management (1972) PL 92-583
Federal Flood Insurance (1956) PL 84-1016
Federal Water Pollution Control Amendments (1972) PL 92-500
Federal Water Projects Recreation (1974) PL 93-251
Federal Water Resources Planning (1965) PL 89-80
Flood Control (1936) PL 74-738
Flood Disaster Protection (1973) PL 93-234
Historic Sites (1936) PL 74-292
Housing (1949) PL 81-171
Housing and Urban Development (1968) PL 89-117
Land and Water Conservation Fund (1964) PL 88-578
Land and Water Conservation Fund Amendments (1976) PL 94-422
Mississippi River Flood Control (1928) PL 70-391
National Environmental Policy (1970) PL 91-190
National Flood Insurance (1968) PL 90-448
National Historic Preservation (1966) PL 89-665
National Trust Charter (1949) PL 81-408
Noise Control (1972) PL 92-574
Occupational Health and Safety (1970) PL 91-596
Outdoor Recreation Resources Review Commission (1958) PL 85-470
Outer Continental Shelf Mineral Leasing (1968) PL 90-401
Public Buildings Cooperative Use (1976) PL 94-541
Refuse Act (1899) PL 55-425
Resource Conservation and Recovery (1976) PL 94-580
Resources Recovery (1970) PL 91-512
Revenue (1978) PL 95-600
Safe Drinking Water (1974) PL 93-523
Solid Waste Disposal (1965) PL 89-272
Southeast Hurricane Disaster Relief (1965) PL 89-339
Surface Mining Control and Reclamation (1977) PL 95-87
Tax Reform (1976) PL 94-455
Urban Mass Transportation Assistance (1970) PL 91-453
Urban Park and Recreation Recovery (1978) PL 95-625

References

ADVIS. COMMN. INTERGOVTAL. RELNS. (1981) *The Federal role in the Federal system: The dynamics of growth* (Washington, DC), A-83.

ADVIS. CO. HISTORIC PRESERVATION (1979) *Assessing the energy conservation benefits of historic preservation: Methods and examples* (Washington, DC).

AMERICAN METEOROLOGICAL SOCIETY (1976) 'The hurricane problem', *Bull. Am. med. Soc.* **57** 8, 996–7.

ANDERSON, F. R. and DANIELS, R. H. (1973) *NEPA in the courts: A legal analysis of the National Environmental Policy Act* (Baltimore, Md.: Johns Hopkins Univ. Press).

BIDDLE, J. (1980) 'A tribute to Robert Stipe', *N. Carol. Cent. Law J.* **11** 2, 195–203.

BOSSELMAN, F. P. and CALLIES, D. R. (1971) *The quiet revolution in land use control* (Washington, DC: USGPO).

BROOKS, R. A. (1979) 'Historic properties gain greater protection under new interpretation of the National Historic Preservation Act: WATCH v. Harris', *Conn. Law Rev.* **12** 1, 156–73.

BURBY, R. J. and FRENCH, S. P. (1981) 'Coping with floods: the land use management paradox', *J. Am. Plann. Ass.* **47** 3, 289–300.

CLAWSON, M. (1981) *New Deal planning: The National Resources Planning Board* (Baltimore, Md.: Johns Hopkins Univ. Press).

COASTAL SOCIETY (1981) 'Coastal zone management under the Reagan budget', *Bull. Coastal Soc.* **5** 1, 3.

CONSERVATION FOUNDATION (1977) 'The coasts are awash with disputes', *Conserv. Fdn. Newsl.* March.

COOLEY, R. A. and WANDESFORDE-SMITH, G. (1970) *Congress and the environment* (Seattle, Wash.: Univ. Washington Press).

COSTONIS, J. J. (1977) 'The disparity issue: a context for the Grand Central Terminal decision', *Harv. Law Rev.* **91** 2, 402–26.

DAVIES, J. C. and DAVIES, B. S. (1975) *The politics of pollution* (Indianapolis, Ind.: Bobbs-Merrill).

DAVIS, R. K. (1968) *The range of choice in water management* (Baltimore, Md.: Johns Hopkins Univ. Press).

DENNIS, S. N. (1980) 'An annotated list of major Historic Preservation Court decisions', *N. Carol. Cent. Law J.* **11** 2, 341–61.

DITTON, R. B., SEYMOUR, J. L., and SWANSON, G. C. (1977) *Coastal resources management* (Lexington, Mass.: D. C. Heath).

DYE, T. R. (1981) *Understanding public policy* (Englewood Cliffs, NJ: Prentice-Hall).

ENGLE, Rep. (1958) *US Congressional Record*, 85th Congr., 2nd Sess. CIV 9, 11351–99.

FAIRFAX, S. K. (1978) 'A disaster in the environmental movement', *Science*, **199** 4330, 743–8.

GAGE, R. J. (1979) 'The failure of the Interim Regulatory Program under the Surface Mining Control and Reclamation Act of 1977: the need for flexible controls', *W. Virginia Law Rev.* **81** 4, 595–625.

GRAY, O. S. (1971) 'The response of Federal legislation to historic preservation', *Law and Contempt. Probl.* **36** 314–26.

HARVEY, D. M. (1978) 'Paradise regained? Surface Mining Control and Reclamation Act of 1977', *Houston Law Rev.* **15** 5, 1147–74.

HEALY, R. G. and ROSENBURG, J. S. (1979) *Land use and the States* (2nd edn.) (Baltimore, Md.: Johns Hopkins Univ. Press)

HERITAGE CONSERVATION AND RECREATION SERVICE (1979) *The Third Nationwide Outdoor Recreation Plan: The assessment* (Washington, DC: USGPO).

HOSMER, C. B. (1965) *Presence of the past: A history of the preservation movement in the US before Williamsburg* (Washington, DC: Preservation Press).
—— (1981) *Preservation comes of age: From Williamsburg to the National Trust, 1926–49*, 2 vols. (Charlottesville, Va.: Univ. Press Virginia).

HOYT, W. G. and LANGEBEIN, W. B. (1955) *Floods* (Princeton: Princeton Univ. Press).

HYMAN, S. *et al.* (1966) *With heritage so rich* (New York: Random House).

JIMENEZ, G. M. (1979) 'A redirection of the National Flood Insurance Program' (Washington: Federal Insurance Administration) mimeo.

JOHNSON, H. D. (1976) 'The role of public attitude and involvement in the preservation movement', *Conn. Law Rev.* 8 2, 371–81.

JONES, C. O. (1976) *Clean air* (Pittsburgh, Penn.: Univ. Pittsburgh Press).

KATES, R. W. (1965) 'Industrial flood losses: damage estimation in the Lehigh Valley', *Univ. Chicago, Dept. Geogr. Res. Pap.* 98.

KNEESE, A. V. (1980) 'Environmental Policy', ch. X in DUIGNAN, P., RABUSHKA, A., and CAMPBELL, W. G. (eds.) *The United States in the 1980s* (London: Croom Helm), 253–83.

KOCH, L. A. (1977) 'State and Federal tax incentives for Historic Preservation', *Univ. Cincinn. Law Rev.* 46 3, 833–45.

McDANIEL, J. A. (1978) 'The Surface Mining Control and Reclamation Act of 1977: an analysis', *Harv. Environ. Law Rev.* 2.

MILLER, H. C. (1975) 'Coastal flood plain management and the National Flood Insurance Program: A case study of three Rhode Island communities', *Environ. Comment*, November issue.

MURPHY, F. C. (1958) 'Regulating flood plain development', *Univ. Chicago, Dept. Geogr. Res. Pap.* 56.

NATIONAL SCIENCE FOUNDATION (1980) *A report on flood hazard mitigation* (Washington, DC: NSF).

NESSON, R. L. (1978) 'Treasure houses: taking shelter in old buildings', *Harpers*, 257 1543, 16–20.

OFFICE OF COASTAL ZONE MANAGEMENT (1975) *Boundaries of the coastal zone* (Washington, DC: OCZM).
—— (1979) *The first five years of coastal zone management: an initial assessment* (Washington, DC: OCZM).

OLDHAM, S. G. (1980) 'Federal tax provisions and the Federal framework for Historic Preservation', *Urb. Lawyer*, 12 1, 66–73.

OUTDOOR RECREATION RESOURCES REV. COMMN. (1962) *Outdoor Recreation for America*, Rept. to President and to Congress. (Washington, DC: USGPO).

PLATT, R. H. (1976) 'The National Flood Insurance Program: some midstream perspectives', *J Amer. Inst. Planners*, 42 3, 303–13.
—— (1978) 'Coastal hazards and national policy: A jury-rig approach', *J. Amer. Inst. Planners*, 44 2, 170–80.
—— (1979) *Options to improve Federal nonstructural response to floods* (Washington, DC: US Water Res. Co.), NTIS PB 80–160146.

POWERS, L. A. (1980) 'Tax incentives for Historic Preservation', *Urb. Lawyer*, 12 1, 103–33.

ROBBINS, J. M. and HERSHMAN, M. J. (1974) 'Boundaries of the coastal zone: a survey of State laws', *Coastal Zone Mgt. J.* 1 305–31.

ROCHOW, K. W. J. (1979) 'The far side of paradox: State regulation of the environmental effects of coal mining', *W. Virginia Law Rev.* 81 4, 559–93.

ROCKEFELLER, L. S. (1965) *A new sense of urgency. The General Electric forum for nat. security and free world progress*, VIII 4, 5–6.

RODGERS, D. R. and SCHAECHTER, N. J. (1979) 'Environmental law: Federal regulation of strip-mining', *Ann. Survey Amer. Law*, 2 227–83.

ROSENBAUM, W. A. (1978) *Coal and crisis: The political dilemma of energy management* (New York: Praeger).
SHEAFFER, J. R. (1960) 'Flood proofing: an element in a flood damage reduction program', *Univ. Chicago, Dept. Geogr. Res. Pap.* 65.
SMITH, R. J. (1981) 'Watt carves up strip-mining policy', *Science, 212*, 4496.
UDALL, M. K. (1979) 'The enactment of the Surface Mining Control and Reclamation Act of 1977 in retrospect', *W. Virginia Law Rev.* 81, 4, 553–7.
US BUREAU OUTDOOR RECREATION (1967) Letter to Clinton W. Burdick from Edward C. Crafts.
—— (1973) *Outdoor recreation: A legacy for America* (Washington, DC: USGPO).
US CONGRESS, HOUSE (1963A) Comm. on Interior and Insular Affairs, *Hearings on S.859: Land and Water Conservation Fund*, 88th Congr., 1st Sess. (Washington, DC: USGPO).
—— (1963B) Comm. on Interior and Insular Affairs, *The Land and Water Conservation Fund Act of 1963: Outline for major provisions*, HR 3846, Comm. Print 14, (Washington, DC: USGPO).
—— (1966A) *Insurance and other programs for financial assistance to flood victims*, Comm. Print 43, 89th Congr., 2nd Sess. (Washington, USGPO).
—— (1966B) *A unified national program for managing flood losses*, House Doc. 4465, 89th Congr., 2nd Sess., (Washington, DC: USGPO).
—— (1967A) *National Flood Insurance Act of 1968*, Hearings before the Sub-committee on Housing of the House Committee on Banking and Currency, 90th Congr., 1st Sess. (Washington, DC: USGPO).
—— (1967B) *Dept. of the Interior and Related Agencies. Appropriations Bill 1968*, 90th Congr., 1st Sess. H. Rept. 206 to accompany HR 9029 (Washington, DC: USGPO).
—— (1971) Sub-Comm. on Mines and Mining of the Comm. on Interior and Insular Affairs, *Hearings on HR 60 and related bills: regulation of strip mining*, 92nd Congr., 1st Sess. (Washington, DC: USGPO).
—— (1975) Comm. on Energy and the Environment and Sub-Comm. on Mines and Mining of the Comm. on Interior and Insular Affairs, *Surface mining veto justification briefing*, 94–23, 94th Congr., 1st Sess. (Washington, DC: USGPO).
—— (1977) Comm. on Interior and Insular Affairs *Surface Mining Control and Reclamation Act of 1977*, House Rept. 218, 95th Congr., 1st Sess. (Washington, DC: USGPO).
US CONGRESS, SENATE (1968) *Interior Dept. and Related Agencies 1968*, 90th Congr., 1st Sess., Sen. Rept. 233 to accompany HR 9029 (Washington, DC: USGPO).
—— (1972) US Code: *Congressional and Administrative News*, 2 4776, Sen. Rept. 92–753 (Washington, DC: USGPO).
—— (1973) *National Land Use Policy legislation 93rd Congr.* Comm. Print for Senate Comm. on Interior and Insular Affairs, 93rd Congr., 1st Sess. (Washington, DC: USGPO).
—— (1977) Comm. on Energy and Natural Resources, *State surface mining laws: a survey. A comparison with the proposed federal legislation, and background information*, Comm. Print 25, 95th Congr., 1st Sess. (Washington, DC: USGPO).
—— (1981) *Federal Flood Insurance Program*, Hearing before a Subcommittee of the Senate Appropriations Committee, 97th Congr., 1st Sess. (Washington, DC: USGPO).
US COUNCIL ON ENVIRONMENTAL QUALITY (1979) *Environmental quality* (Washington, DC: USGPO).
US DEPT. INTERIOR (1978) *National Urban Recreation Study* (Washington, DC: USGPO).
VIETOR, R. H. K. (1980) *Environmental politics and the coal coalition* (College

Station, Texas: Texas A & M Univ. Press).
WADSWORTH, S. (1980) 'Surface Mining Control and Reclamation Act of 1977: Regulatory controversies and constitutional challenges', *Ecology Law Q.* 8 4, 763–5.
WATERS, R. A. (1979) 'A summary of the legislative history of the Surface Mining Control and Reclamation Act of 1977 and the relevant periodical literature', *W. Virginia Law Rev.* 81 4, 775–83.
WHITE, G. F. (1945) 'Human adjustment to floods', *Univ. Chicago, Dept. Geogr. Res. Pap.* **29.**
—— (1969) *Strategies of American water management* (Ann. Arbor, Mich.: Univ. Michigan Press).
—— and HAAS, E. (1975) *Assessment of research on natural hazards* (Cambridge, Mass: MIT Press).
WOOLEY, D. (1979) 'The protection of hydrologic and land preservation values under the Surface Mining Control and Reclamation Act of 1977: a welcome reform', *W. Virginia Law Rev.* 81 4, 627–70.

5. Energy Problems and Policies

JOHN W. HOUSE

(University of Oxford)

The most important, difficult and neglected questions of energy strategy are not mainly technical or economic but rather social and ethical. (AMORY LOVINS, 1977)

The Federal role in national energy production is to bring resources into the energy marketplace while simultaneously protecting the environment. (FEDERAL GOVERNMENT ENERGY PLAN, 1981)

We have a national energy policy and it's basically one of promotion, of pushing the product. (DIRECTOR, FORD FOUNDATION, ENERGY POLICY PROJECT, 1973)

5.1 ENERGY PROBLEMS

5.1.1 The basic natural resource

Though few today might accept President Carter's rhetorical assertion that the energy crisis remains the 'moral equivalent of war', there is no set of problems so complex, so beset by uncertainties and even ignorance, or seen in so many different lights by such a multitude of contending parties and special interests. Politicians, entrepreneurs, consumers, technocrats, environmentalists, and foreign governments are all involved, for 'the structural, systemic and value bases of energy provision are the bases of our society itself' (Burton 1980, 294). In this sense decisions on energy policy are 'a test-bed for conflict over broader social (and political) issues' (Schurr *et al.*, 1979, 543). How far government at any level is responsible for the energy situation or should take powers to effect change, in the public interest, remains a highly contentious issue in the US.

That energy is the basic natural resource and a resource in which the US is incomparably rich is beyond dispute. With only 6 per cent of world population, the US consumes one-third of world energy output, contributing 10 per cent to American GNP (Hammond *et al.* 1973, v). For long used to abundant wealth based upon coal, petroleum, natural gas, hydro power, and, more recently, nuclear potential, US citizens have traditionally had little respect for planning, managing, husbanding, or conserving what are increasingly to be regarded as finite sources and wasting assets. The painful adjustments to a dramatically less favorable world energy scene have been harder to bear in a complex society of continental scale, with a dispersed population and long-distance transportion of people and goods. No less energy-intensive has been the preference for large single-family homes, heated or air-conditioned, with the great majority of citizens mobile in large, powerful cars and used to acting as if energy was to remain for evermore an inexhaustible cheap commodity (Schurr *et al.* 1979, 14).

Though energy costs and availability affect everyone, there persists widespread ignorance or disagreement on the facts, uncertainty about what, if anything, should be done and by whom, with no clear national consensus on goals and how or when they might be reached. Yet energy is a great 'source of social power' (Burton 1980, xxv) leading to concentrations of both wealth and authority in private corporate hands. Particularly for this reason, many in the US see energy problems as basically issues of governance (Goodwin 1981, xvii). To some the powerful oil industry is the bogeyman, confronting 'basic American values, political relations, economic institutions and environmental expectations' (Burton, 1980, xvi). To others the so-called energy crisis 'is a crisis of the political system' (Stobaugh and Yergin 1979, 13), heightened by the traumatic transition from an abundance of energy with concern about falling prices to a condition of increasing uncertainty with sharply rising prices for consumers. In an energy world dominated by the 'geopolitics of oil' (Burton 1980, 34) there can be little doubt that the energy shortage is predominantly a public policy question (Mitchell 1976A, 17). What the role of government should be in combatting energy problems remains a very open issue. While some speak of the need to 'mobilize Federal democracy' (Goodwin 1981, xvi), others (Moore 1980; Dye 1981) emphasize the ineffectiveness and mismanagement resulting from government intervention to date. Given the enormously complex range of energy problems, each with its inbuilt dilemmas and few capable of resolution entirely within national jurisdiction, there must be a place for public policies, even if only in the role of catalyst for change. Energy is inextricably intertwined with major problems of the economy and all must be addressed together (Mitchell 1976A, 48) surely a proper role for government in what has been called 'an energy management morass' (Daneke and Lagassa 1980, 2). Furthermore, 'the energy problem cannot be broken down into individual elements requiring solution; rather it is the whole pattern of the energy system that constitutes the problem' (Anderer *et al.* 1981, 25). Not least there is the interaction of energy policies with problems of the environment, further buttressing the case for intervention in the public interest. To this argument the geographer has a distinctive contribution to make (Wilbanks 1978).

5.1.2   The US energy market

Table 5.1 and Figures 5.1 and 2 show the structure of energy production and consumption in the US. With a consumption of one-third of world energy in 1981, the balance lay between petroleum (43 per cent), of which one-third was imported, natural gas (27 per cent), coal (22 per cent), hydro power (4 per cent), and nuclear power (4 per cent). Coal exports were 10 per cent of production in 1973, rising to 15 per cent in 1981. This structure is the outcome of some two centuries of development resulting from a providential combination of the endowment of energy resources (Cuff and Young 1980), the course of evolution and application of technology, and the timing, direction, and magnitude of colonization. After an economy fueled dominantly by wood until the mid-nineteenth century, coal came to provide 50 per cent of needs by the early 1880s, rising to a peak of more than 75 per cent by 1910. From small beginnings in the latter half of the nineteenth century (5 per cent fuel needs in 1900) petroleum and natural gas became the major energy

	1973	Percentage of total	1981	Percentage of total	1985	Projected[a] Percentage of total	1995	Percentage of total
Production								
Crude oil	19.493	31	18.125	28	17.0[b]	25	19.3	22[b]
Natural gas liquids	2.569	4	2.268	3	2.3	3	1.9	2
Natural gas	22.187	36	20.098	31	18.6[c]	27	18.7	22[c]
Coal	14.366	23	18.700	29	21.9	32	33.7	39
Hydro power	2.861	5	2.734	4	d		d	
Nuclear power	0.910	1	2.897	4	5.4	8	8.6	10
Other	0.046	—	0.127	—	3.3	5	3.6	4
Total	62.433		64.499		68.5		85.8	
Consumption								
Oil	34.840	47	31.998	43	33.9	42	31.8	34
Natural gas	22.512	30	19.927	27	19.4	24	19.4	21
Coal	13.300	18	16.011	22	19.2	24	29.5	32
Hydro power	3.010	4	2.972	4	d		d	
Nuclear power	0.910	1	2.897	4	5.4	7	8.6	9
Other	0.040	—	0.110	—	3.4	4	3.6	4
Total	74.609		73.915		81.3		92.9	
Imports[e]								
Crude oil	6.883		8.864		13.6		9.6	
Oil products	6.097		2.524		1.1		1.0	
Total	12.980		11.388		14.7		10.6	
Percentage of consumption		37		36		43		33
Percentage of energy consumption		17		15		18		11
Natural gas	0.981	4	0.846	4	0.8	4	0.7	4
Coal exports	1.443	10	2.918	15	2.7	16	4.2	
Net *imports*[e]	12.659	17	9.536	10	12.9		7.2	8

* One quad = 172 million barrels crude oil, 969 billion cf gas, or 44.4 million short t. coal.
[a] Estimate from middle world oil price forecasts $33.00/b 1985, $67.00/b 1995.
[b] Includes shale oil production: 0.1 quad 1985, 0.8 quad 1995.
[c] Includes Alaskan and unconventional gas production of 0.7 quad 1985 and 4.3 quad 1995.
[d] Included in 'other' which also covers geothermal and solar.
[e] Imports of electricity and exports of coke not shown.

Source: US Dept. Energy *Monthly Energy Rev.*, March 1982; *Annual Rept. to Congress* (1981).

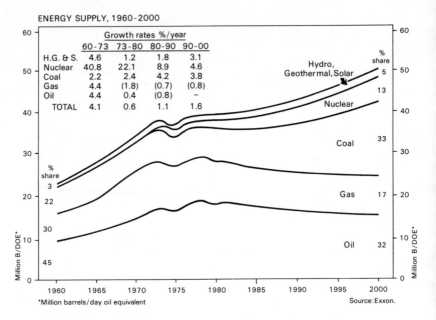

5.1   Energy supply, 1960–2000

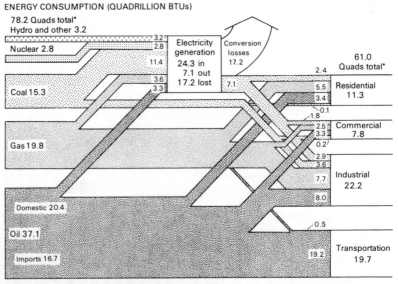

5.2   Energy consumption

source during World War II, peaking at about 75 per cent of needs in the early 1970s. The successive phases of Industrial Revolution were pioneered and implemented in what became the Manufacturing Belt of the Northeast and Midwest. As the frontier of colonization moved west the Appalachian coal-fields, the Interior coalfields, the oil and gas resources of the West and Southwest, and the hydro power of the West were successively exploited, without damage to the market domination of the Manufacturing Belt. The essential regional complementarity in energy resources meant early and growing long-distance transport of supplies, by water, rail, pipeline, or transmission line. Yet the distribution of energy production remains remark-ably uneven. Few States are blessed by an abundance of energy resources. Almost two-thirds of oil and natural gas is produced in only three States: most uranium is taken from two and coal from five. All told, fully 60 per cent of America's energy supplies can be found in just seven States (Mitchell 1976A, 3). The great disparities between energy-rich and energy-poor States add fuel to political controversy and inevitably color attitudes to the so-called 'energy crisis' and its prospective policy solutions. The considerable and long-term interstate movement of energy supplies has inevitably led to a progressive Federal government regulatory role.

Markets too have shifted proportionately during the decades since World War II. Domestic and commercial consumption has risen from 30 (1945) to 37 per cent of the market (1981), industry is down from 44 to 37 per cent, whilst transport has consumed a steady 26 per cent of all energy. The transformation among sources of energy is reflected in the type and pattern of energy consumption by States 1980 (Fig. 5.3). Competition among energy sources, with remarkably regular lead-times for substitution (Anderer *et al.* 1981, 276), changing regional and metropolitan employment structures, the impact of interregional and polarizing migrations of people, and the effect of the cumulative energy problems of the 1970s help to explain both the differentiated pattern and the constraints and potentials for any short-term dramatic improvements in the energy situation. Elements of natural com-parative advantage in fuel balances are clear: petroleum and natural gas in the Southwest and California, coal in Appalachia, the Midwest, and some Mountain States, hydro power in the Pacific Northwest. Imported oil in New England and the New York region highlights fuel deficiency, while many States have sought to diversify the forms of energy used, to minimize cost and maximize efficiency and flexibility in a fast-changing situation. The spatially variable, but as yet minimal, contribution of nuclear power is a further feature of energy consumption.

5.1.3 Critical changes in the 1970s

Though concern about energy supplies was raised much earlier this century, over hydro-power development and conservation (Goodwin 1981, xv), the situation was dramatically transformed in the early 1970s. The rapid multi-plication of oil prices, first in 1973–4 and then in 1978–9, coincided with a peaking of US domestic production and the onset of slowdown in a post-industrial mature economy (Anderer *et al.* 1981, 161). During a period of political instability in the Middle East the US had doubled her oil imports,

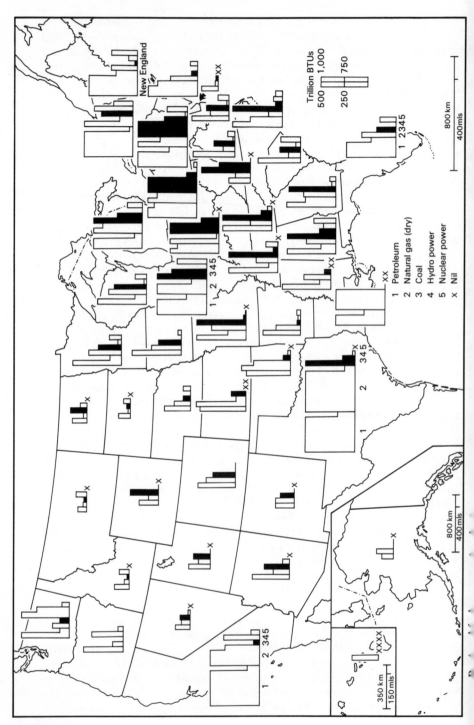

becoming increasingly dependent and vulnerable as a result. Hence talk of 'a threat to the American political system' (Dye 1981, 184; Stobaugh and Yergin 1979, 13) or President Carter's 'moral equivalent of war'. Though US policy-makers have a 'proclivity for *ad hoc* crisis management' (Prast 1981, 8) the difficult energy situation is not a well-defined problem to be solved. It is too extended over time and too nebulous to be identified in crisis terms. To some (Schurr *et al.* 1979, xix) there is a set of interacting problems within one integral energy system, with broad, complex, and multi-facetted issues for which there is 'no easy formulation of general principles to be universally applied' (Burton 1980, 180). To others the issues are seen as the outcome of 'liberal-democratic nongovernance', essentially social and ethical problems rather than problems solely of a market economy. Alternatively, the situation has been 'partly manufactured, partly policy-induced and is partly the result of structural changes in the energy economy' (Burton 1980, 299). As a result, policy for energy will need to be 'more than the juggling of plural interests, more than an academic critique and more than short-term compromise with the powers that be' (Burton 1980, 180).

Energy, economic growth, and urbanization   In a general sense there is a good correlation between consumption of energy, economic growth (GNP), and job provision, though it is far from a simple linear relationship (Allen 1979). From the latter part of the nineteenth century to 1914 energy consumption grew at a faster rate than GNP as the US consolidated its heavy industrial base. Between the world wars the rate of GNP growth exceeded that of energy as less energy-intensive industries and services developed, traditional manufacturers introduced energy economies in processing, and use of the more flexible energy source in electricity became widespread (Schurr *et al.* 1979, 15–16). Since 1945 the GNP—energy—jobs relationship has become more complex. While some see an almost perfect correlation (Burton 1980, 159) others (Schurr *et al.* 1979, 16) emphasize short-term fluctuations, as productivity declined and economic growth became intermittent, and increases in lifestyle meant higher per capita energy consumption in a rising population. The rapid progress of urbanization (1940–70 +80 per cent urban, compared with +47 per cent overall population) meant intensification in the development of industry, use of materials, transport, and energy. This was offset, but only in a limited way, by a general reduction in energy input per unit of output on the part of both producers and consumers (Goodwin 1981, 683). In this process technology was often substituted for labor, trade for self-sufficiency, and oil and gas for coal. Burton (1980, 167) makes an interesting comparison between the urban system and the energy system 'both with a variety of actors and interests; both with significant, even central, collective and aggregate effects which no actor is obliged to take into account'.

A transitional situation   Economic growth is likely to remain uncertain in the 1980s, giving time for an orderly transition from an economy traditionally based upon limited domestic liquid and gaseous fuel reserves, with an increasing vulnerability from once cheaper foreign oil imports, to a more stable base of diversified energy resources (US Dept. Energy 1980A, 1–1).

Transitions have been endemic in the energy industry, but the magnitude and complexity of what will now be required, the external constraints likely to be imposed, and the limited time for achievement of greater balance, diversity, and stability make policy formation and implementation very problematical. Perhaps the scarcest of all factors is time. Though there is regularity within energy substitution and the internal structure of the substitution process is robust, takeover times (from 1 to 50 per cent of market share) are long. Lead times for technological innovation are reduced with difficulty and response times in the energy system are slow and thus a further constraint (Anderer *et al.* 1981, 276). Faced with such constraints either the momentum of economic growth must remain slow in the transitional period, or it must take non-energy-intensive forms. Alternatively, growth must be matched by higher energy prices, whilst conservation practices are maximized and a range of new energy sources is introduced and developed commercially (Burton 1980, 38).

Energy prospects   There is general agreement that the most serious energy problems are those for the short term, to the mid- or late 1980s. Adjustment to potential shortages of domestic oil and gas and the need, for security reasons, to diminish oil imports cannot be achieved by government order; indeed, when the immediate economic recession ends an increase in imports may be required. Increase in coal supplies to substitute for oil will not be a universally acceptable operation, given the environmental implications and the massive capital investments required. Shifts in energy courses for the production of electricity, the 'reference energy system' (Anderer *et al.* 1981, 244) may be more readily accomplished. In the intermediate term (to the end of the century) much will depend on the state of the international oil market. Domestic supplies of oil and gas will continue to be depleted, but new energy sources, such as the conversion of coal to oil, use of oil shale, geothermal or solar energy, and perhaps nuclear breeder reactors may become commercially viable (Hammond *et al.* 1973, 148). In the next century the energy situation should become more manageable, with a range of sources from nuclear to solar making a greater contribution, while the vast coal reserves might be more effectively put to use. That is not to say that the matching of energy resources with rising demand will be easily carried through. Though slower economic growth may reduce the rate of energy consumption and the national population rise more slowly there is still likely to be a sizeable potential energy gap. From a total energy consumption of 73.9 quadrillion (10^{15}) Btus (British thermal units) in 1981 (Table 5.1) an estimated 115 quads will be needed annually by the year 2000, assuming a 1.8 per cent per annum growth in energy and 3.2 per cent expansion in GNP (Schurr *et al.* 1979, 19). A high-growth scenario would require 140 quads per annum; a low-growth projection about 100 quads. To give some order of magnitude, 20 quads represent all the natural gas consumed annually in the US in the mid-1970s, or about 1½ times the then annual coal consumption.

Though the significance of available resources changes with technology and/or demand Table 5.2 shows the general estimate of recoverable reserves of conventional mineral fuels. The conclusion to be drawn is that though there is an abundance of some, there is only an adequacy in others. To realize

TABLE 5.2   *Recoverable reserves of principal mineral fuels*

| Fuel | | Identified[a] | | Undiscovered (hypothetical resources)[b] | TOTAL | Quads (10^{15} Btu equivalent) |
		Reserves[c]	Inferred reserves			
Coal	billion short t.	260	648	895	1,803	37,863
Oil	billion barrels	34	23	82	139	806
Natural gas liquids	billion barrels	6	6	16	28	115
Natural gas	trillion cu. ft.	209	202	484	895	917
Uranium	thousand short t.	890	1,395	1,515	3,800	1,140 LWR 68,400 FBR
Total	Quad (10^{15}) Btu	6,163	14,391	20,287	40,841 LWR	108,101 FBR

[a] Relatively unexplored extensions of known reserves.
[b] Undiscovered materials assumed to exist in known producing regions and under known geological conditions.
[c] As of 1 Jan. 1978, dating back 3–4 years.
Nuclear reactors: LWR, Light Water Reactor; FBR, Fast Breeder Reactor
Source: Adapted from Schurr *et al.* (1980) Table 7-1, p. 226.

these assets a competitive market economy is unlikely to be adequate and thus public policy has a role to fulfill.

5.2 PERSPECTIVES AND ATTITUDES

5.2.1 A spectrum of views

In the conventional view of American society individualism, consumer sovereignty, and the autonomous free-market system rank high in the structure in which 'the interests of particular individuals and groups are maintained in some sort of balance and great decisions facing society are made in cooperative fashion under sets of rules rather than in response to centralized authority' (Goodwin 1981, 684). Given the proliferation and conflicting interests of actors in the energy marketplace, tensions are dominant, reflected in 'bitter struggles in Congress, regulatory agencies, the courts and the press' (Stobaugh and Yergin 1979, 216). Enormous sums of money are involved with widely conflicting perceptions of the national interest, the significance of environmental or other social costs, disagreement over the technical facts on energy, and conflict over basic values. The situation has been described (Daneke and Lagassa 1980, 2) as 'a paradigm case of interest group liberalism' in which competing interest groups of uneven power and fragmented institutions converge to disaggregate and diffuse policy-making, leading to a lack of comprehensive goals and of any coherent energy strategy. Certainly the growth of special interest groups, vocal, strident, and well organized, is a feature of the US energy arena. It is not surprising that producers, who seek to externalize as many costs as possible, consumers, who demand cheap energy, and environmentalists, who wish to protect all environments absolutely, should disagree fundamentally, leading all too often to blockage and stalemate (Burton 1980, 181). Perhaps more unusual is the rapidity with which citizen groups mobilize in defense of local, if sometimes vested, interests. In what many regard as a 'zero-sum' energy game bargaining and trade-offs among interested parties lead to hard-won compromise but inhibit decisive public action on pressing problems.

On many energy issues there is a dualism among the contenders. Expansionists are usually in a clear majority, favoring continuance of economic growth and all necessary energy output to fuel it, believing that science and technological innovation will provide the means. Those committed to limitation stress the reduction of wants, since the impact of growth is outrunning the capacity of earth to sustain it, firmly accepting that in the case of energy more does not necessarily mean a better life (Schurr *et al.* 1979, 401). Though in a minority, the limitationists gained ground in the 1970s, the environmental decade. The American penchant for respecting minority opinion has characteristically permitted obstruction of particular additions to energy supplies, however costly the outcome. Other dichotomies are those between technological optimists and diminishing-return pessimists (Goodwin 1981, 682); between those seeing the need for only tactical energy solutions, by marginal incremental adjustments, and those who insist on major strategic changes, necessitated by basic contradictions in the social and economic system (Burton 1980, 221); and, finally, between those who favor a 'hard' path to energy solutions, through large-scale centralized power and production facilities and those supporting 'soft' path solutions, decentralized and disseminated, with proper respect for people and place.

Public opinion on energy matters is something of an enigma, with views described as being wholly unlike reality (Prast 1981, 90). Widespread ignorance or disagreement on the basic facts about energy is matched by an 'except me' syndrome (Daneke and Lagassa 1980, 265) and an unwillingness to accept personal sacrifices. Disbelief that the real costs of energy have risen colors opinion poll results. In 1977 49 per cent saw no real energy shortage, 59 per cent favored strip mining, and 69 per cent wanted more nuclear power generation (though four years later 58 per cent opposed this): in 1979 85 per cent claimed to be conservationist in outlook and practice. Public mistrust of energy decision-makers has been endemic. Those proposing a quick technological fix are as suspect as those who claim that future economic prosperity can be assured and lifestyles maintained with minimum change (Daneke and Lagassa 1980, 226). Public confidence in the scientific community, too, was shaken after the Three Mile Island nuclear accident. Yet public opinion, however wayward, has on occasion proved to be powerful (Prast 1981, 8), in the *de facto* moratorium on new nuclear reactors after 1979; many court actions; in regional and interstate disputes, and in plebiscites, as on nuclear energy in California and elsewhere. To bridge the gap between the public and the policy-maker a richer dialogue and continuous two-way set of contacts is needed. If a new social consensus on energy is to emerge, there must be an end to 'public relations tactics, biassed agenda setting, and the definition of political problems in economic terms to maintain political peace' (Burton 1980, 191).

Furthermore, energy problems impact unfairly upon silent minorities. Whereas previously underprivileged groups, such as the Indians or the native peoples of Alaska, have occasionally been more favorably treated and indeed have often achieved some control of energy projects on their lands (Burton 1980, 314), the urban poor and those in the ethnic ghettoes have rarely been as fortunate. Low-income groups and ethnic minorities paradoxically prefer 'hard'-path energy solutions, in a situation where the political process has no constituency for overall fairness and benefits categories of people or place without regard for welfare considerations (Schurr *et al.* 1979, 461).

The regional perspective   'Energy policy is now the most divisive regional issue to afflict this country since civil rights' (*Washington Post*, 23 June 1975). Though talk of an 'energy war between the States' is grossly exaggerated there are deep-seated differences among them, a lack of unity on energy which has 'more to do with the ways of nature than of politics' (Mitchell 1976, 3). Energy is potentially short in every region, but the basis of long-standing conflict of interest lies between producer and consumer States, between the northern gas consumers and the southwestern producers, between the western coal States and eastern consumers. These contrasts in energy endowment are reflected, through transfer costs and regulatory practices, in disagreements on energy pricing, tariffs on imported fuels, and the rate of energy growth (Mitchell 1976, 4). Offshore oil and gas exploration and exploitation raises issues of States' rights, natural gas policy heightens regional tensions, while the 'pork-barrel' type of loaded decision on energy plant siting is a further, if local inflammatory issue (Goodwin 1981, 679). Talk of 'national sacrifice areas' (Burton 1980, 156), of unfavorable impacts of boom and bust developments in peripheral locations adds to regional tensions. Yet in a continent-wide integral energy system it might be 'a great mistake if we ever balkanise, if we ever have regional feelings in this country that are so intense that we cannot have a national energy policy' (Secretary of Interior Udall 1976).

5.2.2   Principles for policy

In a complex situation viewed so differently by so many, universal principles or priorities are hard to establish. There is 'a theoretical as well as a real conflict between the marginalist, incremental analysis and implications of micro-economics and the structural relations which are of concern in political economy or sociology' (Burton 1980, 200). The range of parameters is so great, ranging from the pricing of energy resources, the magnitude and type of energy expenditure and issues of 'fairness', to intergovernmental relations, the uncertain effects of proposed policies and market failures, such as social costs unmet or needs ignored (Schurr *et al.* 1979, 435).

Nevertheless, three broad principles are involved: efficiency, equity, and environmental integrity; national security too will figure somewhere. Though not mutually exclusive, trade-offs, leverage, and policy-bargaining have clear limitations. Efficiency relates to a technocratic search for economic optimization, often referring to the laws of thermodynamics seeking to avoid waste of heat energy or to match energy supplies and uses (Burton 1980, 201). Econometric models of considerable complexity, modeling market equilibria, or system dynamics, had an ever-widening impact on Federal policy decision in the late 1970s (Stobaugh and Yergin 1979, 235). Multiregional models have been developed to measure regional economic and demographic effects of particular policy-decisions (Hughes 1979; Holloway 1980). One of the more interesting is the National-Regional Impact Evaluation System (NRIES) used to measure the effects of advanced coal production (Wendling and Ballard 1980, 7). As a medium-run, 5 to 10 years, impact analysis tool, the model comprises 51 State econometric models integrated into a national framework. Within each State model there are 264 equations, of which 68 are behavioral; in addition, the national model has 20 behavioral and 100 total equations, making 3,500 behavioral and 14,000 total equations in all. Multiple case histories and scenarios too have been modeled (Knowles 1980, 325), but many critics have argued that econometric or engineering models have consistently made too optimistic predictions for energy development. 'Insight, not numbers' (Stobaugh and Yergin 1979, 235) is a useful prescription for qualifying the technocratic solutions which may emerge.

The concept of equity or fairness is difficult to define unambiguously and even more problematical to incorporate directly into energy policies. Every policy has an uneven impact, on persons and places, favoring some, disadvantaging others. It is possible to argue that such inequities should be rectified, if at all, through the tax system, income maintenance, or other welfare supports (Schurr *et al.* 1979, 49). In terms of fairness it is easier to raise questions than to find convincing answers. Should energy prices be manipulated to shift income or expenditure among persons or regions? Who is to bear the cost of reductions in environmental quality and who should pay to avoid such? How far should future generations be borne in mind when seeking solutions to contemporary energy problems? (Schurr *et al.* 1979, 460). The urban poor and ethnic ghetto residents have special claims, but these are unlikely to be met through the energy market.

Environmental integrity has a wholesome sound and since the mid-1960s there has been rising concern for environmental conservation (ch. 4). As recently as 1981, however, the Secretary of the Interior (James G. Watt) laid down the dictum that 'environmental sensitivity requires a balance of economic development and environmental preservation'. It is to be hoped that as the economic recession bites ever more deeply in the US, concern for the environment will not 'fall through the cracks'.

National security is a further, more 'shadowy' background principle for energy policy (Deese and Nye 1981), expressing itself through foreign policy-decisions on vulnerable oil imports, creation of strategic stockpiles, priority for military exploitation of nuclear power, or restriction on export of nuclear technology.

Goals for consensus In the community at large there are such varied, at times conflicting, interests that consensus may be hard to find. As Charles Schulz said in testimony before the Senate Budget Committee—'It is literally impossible to define an ideal energy policy . . . [It] is important therefore . . . to seek a set of compromises which minimises the damage to some goals whilst we try to attain others' (Mitchell 1976A, 50). Consensus might begin to be shaped around the need for an adequate and varied supply of energy, available throughout the national space-economy, based as far as possible or profitable upon domestic resources. Conservation, for both the short and the longer term, would have a place and environmental integrity a significant, if uncertain, role to play. Under the pressure of successive oil price escalations during the 1970s and the resultant Federal energy policies, consensus on energy is a little nearer in the 1980s. The multiplicity of supply options appears to offer that flexibility which may ultimately reconcile both expansionists and limitationists within a similar quantum of energy output (Schurr *et al.* 1979, 541). In a limited way the successful National Coal Project (1978) is an indication of how producer, consumer, and regional interests may be reconciled, if not altogether harmonized.

5.3 THE ENERGY ROLE OF GOVERNMENT

5.3.1 *Government or market forces?*

The energy market poses an essentially political problem at all levels. Should government—Federal, State, or local—act as producer, planner, intermediary or catalyst, controller or stimulator of energy resources? The spectrum of views on the government role ranges from none to a central control of some national energy policy, but is strongly weighted in the direction of minimum public intervention. Argument against intervention is on grounds that it is either inappropriate or ineffective, or both, and that free-market forces operating through individual or corporate choice are more efficient and produce more widely satisfying results. As President Reagan put it (July 1981)—'No regulatory practice is to be undertaken . . . unless sufficient information is available to determine that the potential benefit to society . . . outweighs the costs.' It was said that government action had not reduced oil imports, made the US more energy self-sufficient, or led to the development of other ways of using or saving energy at an acceptable price. Federal price regulation of oil and natural gas had encouraged waste and hindered exploration and production. The regulation of electric power by State utility commissions had hampered development and improvement, whilst the costs of Federal environmental protection had been high in relation to benefit (Dye 1981, 186).

Counterargument is both pragmatic and in terms of political principle: 'People have to live through the market solution' (Mitchell 1976A, 71). Furthermore, some organization of the energy market is beneficial in the public interest, without the need to evoke any theory of malicious conspiracy on the part of powerful vested corporate interests (Burton 1980, 303). The US Constitution reduces public power by separation and division and thus there is neither adequate concern nor the means for dealing with private or market power. Given the 'symbiotic relationship between monopolistic industry and a compliant government' (Burton 1980, 301), economic sovereignty cannot now be said to reside in the people and there is unequal access to policy formation and the rewards of policy. To protect the public interest some planning continues to be necessary, but it should be better organized and more discreetly administered. Hitherto in the energy arena planning has resembled 'a series of disjointed reactions to periodic problems rather than the rational formulation of strategy in anticipation of long-term concerns, leading to uncoordinated policies and incremental decision-taking, with too parochial and too short a time-frame' (Prast 1981, 8). Thus policy became defined as what is done. That said, no centrally planned reorganization of the energy marketplace is likely to succeed, for there is a 'political minefield to be crossed by anyone wishing to make major policy reversals in energy legislation'. To be effective, government action must be cautious, supportive, and a catalyst for only those changes in which there is a clear consensus.

5.3.2 Government involvement

Public intervention in the energy market is of long standing, scattered over many individual programs, but it has never been coherent. As far back as 1890 the Sherman Anti-Trust Act broke up the Standard Oil Trust and the oil industry has at intervals since been affected by 'percentage depreciation allowances, tax deduction expenses, intangible drilling cost refunds, foreign tax credits, prorationing, import quotas, price controls, naval reserves, and shipping restrictions' (Burton 1980, 64). The 1920s Texas oil rush led to the regulatory powers of the Texas Railroad Commission and Texan oilmen virtually controlled pricing in the world oil market until World War II. At the height of the New Deal the Federal Power Commission (FPC) was created 'to assure an abundant supply of electricity throughout the U.S.A. with the greatest possible economy and with regard for the proper utilization and conservation of natural resources'. The Natural Gas Act (1938) was to establish 'a just and reasonable price', by regulating the interstate price of gas moving by pipeline, extended later (1954) to a well-head gas price control. In the early 1960s common price ceilings were put on all gas sold within each major field. Critique suggests that prices were not perceptibly lower as a result, that a gas shortage was promoted and that since Federal price control covered only part of the market it led to considerable cost-shifting by electric utility companies. Failure of the FPC was said to lie in the structure of regulation itself (Breyer and Macavoy 1974) leading to 'monopoly without effective control, private enterprise without effective incentive or stimulus, government supervision without the possibility of effective initiative in the public interest' (Kahn 1971, 328). In hydro-power development the one-off experiment of multipurpose river-basin resource management in the TVA was not repeated, though quasi-public and State-supported bodies such as the Bonneville Power Administration have since flourished. Between 1959 and 1973 the Mandatory Oil Import Program preserved US oil prices above world levels but kept energy prices high on the US eastern seaboard.

It may be argued justifiably that US government structure is ill adapted to give coherent leadership on energy issues. By comparison its potential corporate adversaries, in a high-risk, investment-expensive energy business are large in scale, strongly organized with powerful Congressional lobbies and with resources in which there are either spatial monopolies or in which competition can be artifically reduced by agreement among producers. Congress, by comparison, is 'dominated by relatively narrow special interest groups, both regional and industrial, the executive is riven by bureaucratic conflicts, and the Presidency is distracted by larger issues' (Goodwin 1981, 681). In particular, energy issues are addressed by no fewer than 67 Federal agencies and 12 Congressional Committees (Hammond *et al.* 1973, v), a sure prescription for ineffectiveness and frustration.

The Carter years   Successive Presidents and Congresses have formulated fragments of energy policy (Goodwin 1981), among the more ambitious that for Project Independence (1973) under President Nixon, vainly seeking to achieve US energy self-sufficiency by 1980. It is, however, the more comprehensive attempts at nationwide energy planning under President Carter which merit particular consideration, in themselves and for the sharp contrast they offer to the energy policies of his successor, President Reagan.

In the National Energy Plan (1977) the Carter administration sought three objectives: an immediate reduction in 'dark and dangerous dependence on foreign oil'; for the medium term, to keep US oil imports sufficiently low to protect national security and develop capacity use of new higher-priced (backstop) technology, as world production approached capacity limitation; and, thirdly, for the longer term, to develop renewable and inexhaustible energy supplies for sustained healthy economic growth. The instruments were to be: replacement cost pricing, involving controlled removal of regulatory and price ceilings on domestic oil and natural gas (by September 1981); stimulated expansion of coal production; the taking of 'windfall' profits from such deregulation, in part to aid affected low-income Americans; modest nuclear energy expansion; encouragement of dispersed (decentralized) energy technology; new investment in alternative energy technologies including liquefaction and gasification of coal, solar, geothermal, and wind power; changes in electrical pricing, railroad, and trucking regulations; and a strong commitment to energy conservation and the protection and enhancement of environment. A Department of Energy (DOE) was created in 1977, States were to be treated as partners in the energy program, citizens were to participate, and information was to be sought on possible horizontal or vertical divestiture of the powerful oil companies (i.e. their disengagement from takeovers of other energy resources and from raw-material to end-use monopolies).

The Carter Plan was thus a proposal for Government intervention to assist, support, and promote energy development. It faced powerful opposition in Congress, where it was subsequently mutilated, but it was criticized too in academic circles, by neoclassical economists (Mead 1977) and radicals (Cockburn and Ridgeway 1977) alike. Whilst commending replacement cost pricing, reform of utility rates, the expansion of the Strategic Petroleum Reserve (SPR), and decontrol of gasoline prices, Mead questioned tax subsidies to business for solar installations, conservation, or cogeneration equipment, and any mandatory measures on conservation. He saw as counterproductive: the 'myopic' concern with energy conservation, the assumptions on continuing growth in energy demand, and certain proposals on liberalizing intangible oil-drilling tax costs, extending them to geothermal prospecting, and also the amendment of the Outer Continental Shelf Lands Act to give greater Federal control over reserves (Burton 1980, 74–7).

A radical view (Cockburn and Ridgeway 1977) criticized the failure to confront the power of the oil industry, to check the overwhelming automobile culture, the trend to undemocratic changes in which the poor would be the worst affected, and the error in relying upon taxation provisions. The stance on nuclear power was seen as ambiguous, with both costs and safety neglected and the proposals for expansion in coal output insufficiently protective of the environment. The Federal government should be more positive, by itself developing and controlling the use of energy resources on public lands, by fostering mass transit in urban areas, influencing building and car design, and by acting as a model in conservation practices (Burton 1980, 81–6).

Finally passed late in 1978 as the National Energy Act, in much changed form, the Plan would have saved 2.4 to 3.0 million barrels of oil equivalent per day (MBDOE), 1.4 MBDOE natural gas, 1.1 MBDOE by industrial conversion to coal as prime mover and by utility rate regulation, and 0.4 MBDOE by tax breaks for conservation. However, the program was overtaken by political events.

The Reagan administration   An energy-briefing document (Halibouty Rept. 1979), whilst acknowledging the Carter thrust towards reducing dependence on foreign oil, criticized the overall strategy as 'a way to deal with energy by doing away with it . . . tucking it away like a rare bottle of wine.' Curtailing energy consumption had impeded production. The early message from the Reagan administration was 'to break the energy sector loose from government intervention and control, letting the laws of the marketplace determine policy'. Table 5.3 shows the immediate budgetary and funding impact of this transformation of policy.

It is still early to evaluate a policy which has not settled in, but certain implications are clear. They must be interpreted in the knowledge that the economic recession created a world glut of oil, at least for the short term. Economic forces, rather than policy, had caused a reduction of US oil imports by Spring 1981 to no more than their level 10 years earlier. The Federal government is 'to sit back as a neutral referee in the energy marketplace, disengaging from a role as planner or manager of the nation's energy resources' (May 1982). A start is to be made by 'untangling regulations and dismantling procedural blockades', though 'limited government involvement may be warranted to make sure that essential supplies and services continue'. 'The American people themselves will conduct a continuing national plebiscite in the marketplace on what energy they choose to produce, import, consume and save.'

Much has been promised, but in the Fall of 1982 the Department of Energy still existed, though threatened by extinction and dispersal of its functions to the Departments of Commerce, Justice, Interior, or Agriculture. No longer was there an intention to replace oil imports at *any* cost, not seen as an essential criterion for national energy security, nor was indiscriminate subsidy for alternative fuels regarded as an appropriate way forward. In January 1981 all price controls on domestic crude oil and gasoline were abolished, but no acceleration of the rate of natural gas price deregulation programmed by Carter's 1978 Act had been put into effect. Amendment of the Powerplant and Industrial Fuel Use Act (PL95–620) is proposed, to permit power stations to burn natural gas after 1990. The 10-year moratorium on leasing of public land for coal production has been lifted as part of an aggressive program of

TABLE 5.3   *Energy program 1980–1982*

$ Million budgeted	1980 Carter	1982 (proposed) Reagan
Conservation	779	195
Fossil fuels (petroleum, natural gas, coal)	858	441
Solar etc.	751	241
Nuclear fission	350	460
Nuclear fusion	1,198	1,247
Environment	235	231

Source: Financial Times, 28 Apr. 1981.

PROJECTS: *Abandoned*: Magneto-hydrodynamics (MHD); ocean thermal energy conversion (OTEC); solar energy research institute (SERI); conservation in industry.

Reduced: Coal liquefaction; coal gasification; coalmining R & D; heat engines/heat recovery; conservation in transport; conservation in buildings.

Increased: Magnetic fusion systems; commercial nuclear waste; advanced uranium enrichment technology; conventional reactor systems; plutonium/tritium production; naval reactors.

making Federal land available for hydrocarbon exploration and exploitation. Though the 80 million acres of 'wilderness' lands are to be protected until the end of the century, unless there is a national security crisis or a further foreign oil embargo, offshore oil and gas resources of the Outer Continental Shelf (OCS) are to be opened up; even the Arctic National Wildlife Reserve, which has been partly protected under President Carter's legislation. The benign neglect of nuclear power generation was to be reversed, though marketplace cancellations of plants continued and the nuclear industry stagnated under cost and environmental pressures. There were to be fewer export barriers on nuclear technology, help with the disposal of radioactive waste, speedier licensing of new nuclear reactors, and the opening up of nuclear fuel reprocessing to private companies. Public money would be spent on high-risk/high-payoff advanced technological research, but the Synthetic Fuels Corporation would be pared back and loan or cash guarantees would be the limit of Federal involvement in the synthetic fuels industry. As the Chairman of the Synthetic Fuels Corporation put it: 'If the private sector doesn't want it, why should the government want it?', or, to quote Senator James McClure: 'There's a host of technology you could apply to energy, provided you don't have to sell it' (1981).

Late in 1982 there was talk of 'giving the oil companies all the land they can drill on', possibly phasing out the windfall taxes on oil profits, introducing an oil import levy, deregulating tariffs charged by interstate pipelines, relaxing further the Clean Air Act Amendments (1977) and surface mining regulations whilst returning the latter to the States. Yet the energy community continues to contest its separate battles. The free market in energy which 'will allow utilities and everyone else to vote for the energy mix that is most appropriate, economically and regionally' is still very far off. Some politicians continue to show a catholic range of enthusiasms, others to remain wedded to particular, often constituency-based projects. The addicts for benign and renewable energy resources contest the marketplace with the scarcely touched nuclear industry exponents; solar interests are almost in eclipse whilst synthetic fuels will have to progress only to the extent that commercial sponsors will foster. Described by some as 'non-policy' there will still remain the open question on public involvement (Thompson *et al.* 1981). Will the Alaskan natural-gas pipeline be built without some public funding? Will nuclear construction take off again without government finance and what about public safeguards on nuclear operations? Will Federal agencies need to 'hold the ring' between competing interests and regions in conflict over coal development and should that industry be more fully freed from safety and environmental standards? In 'boom or bust' energy developments should government intervene directly in planning or merely fund the social services needed? Will any of the longer-term alternative energies become practicable without continuity, even build-up of public funding? To these and other questions only the future has answers, but some interim assessment is possible.

In any accommodation *intergovernmental relationships* will be important, not least because many of the exciting innovations in energy policy and administration have been at State and local levels (Daneke and Lagassa 1980, 2). Rather than defining and imposing centrally derived policies, a basically noncoercive Federal system will be needed for any solutions. Governments at Federal, State, and local level respond to different political constituencies, with fragmented relations to Federal agencies, jurisdictional jealousies on occasion, or overlapping and wasteful duplication. Harmony may be stimulated by giving subordinate governments a greater stake in the national energy program (Schurr *et al.* 1979, 466–8). However, because of the diversity of their problems regions, States and local governments will wish to determine what that contribution may be, particularly in the siting of new major facilities or the bringing into use of large-scale fuel extraction. Nor is the issue one of simple identifiable impacts of energy policy. Any important energy development will affect macroeconomic variables of income, output, and employment in both energy-producing and nonproducing areas of the country (Wendling and Ballard 1980, 7).

5.4 POLICY FORMULATION

5.4.1 Energy goals and choices

In seeking what energy future people want, what different scenarios are possible, and how many and various paths lead in that direction, the constraints already mentioned both limit the oportunities and set a framework to the vision. There is no ideal energy policy, however administered, no comfortable formulation of universal principles, no easy technological fix, no miracles or short cure, and no solutions to be dictated from Washington. For these reasons and given the nature of American society, policy tends to be 'heavily stacked in favor of the status quo with a strong preference for inaction' (Goodwin 1981, 679). Nor can energy policy be abstracted from other overriding national goals including the fight against inflation, deficit financing, high interest rates, or the promotion of free trade. Likely future world economic conditions will strongly influence the US energy situation and development of a collectively 'shared' worldview will be an important context for energy choices.

Preoccupation with the short, medium, or long term will condition choice among alternative energy options, as will the need to balance efficiency with equity and environmental integrity. In what must be a transitional energy situation orderly transition will be more readily possible if the destination can be unambiguously discerned (Schurr *et al.* 1979, 11) and cost benefit analysis contributes little to identifying an optimum. Time is needed for readjustment to a dramatically changed energy arena, to adjust behavior patterns, the structure of the energy industry, and to lessen the impact unfairly imposed on regions or people. With long technical lead-times for innovation to become commercially useful, the staging of extremely complex technological or investment decisions will be critical. Scientific research needs to focus on diversifying the technological base, highly specialized vulnerable energy systems need to be duplicated, strategic reserves to be built up, and major new facilities carefully sited (Burton 1980, 189). Collective determination among options (Bradshaw 1977, 187) should define an adequacy in energy sources in the short term, while enhancing diversity in the longer term; freedom of action should be promoted, with greater democratic engagement in energy decisions; the transition should be smoothed and potentially disastrous alternatives avoided (some would include the Fast Breeder Reactor), for it is alleged in some quarters (Burton 1980, 320) that nuclear power generation might make only a marginal long-term contribution. Price deregulation will not provide a cornucopia, environmental integrity should be sustained, and conservation, though important, 'may be no more than collateral against which more energy adjustment time is borrowed' (Prast 1981, vii).

Hard and soft paths   A useful dichotomy which polarizes the ways forward is that between so-called hard and soft energy paths (Lovins 1977), whose essential difference 'lies in the technical and socio-political structure of the energy system' (Daneke and Lagassa 1980, 245). The hard path is that almost exclusively followed by US governments since Project Independence (1974). Large-scale, high technology, centralized solutions are favored, such as the massive interconnection of electricity generating systems, nuclear fission and fusion, encouraging fossil fuel production by higher prices and ready leasing of public land, and exploring coal liquefaction or gasification (Cortner 1980, 263). Soft paths (Lovins 1976) focus upon inexhaustible and renewable energy resources, and smaller-scale, decentralized, disseminated units of production; in particular there is a resistance to nuclear technology, and a sensitivity to the views of people.

Critics of hard paths stress the unacceptably high capital costs, environmental, health, and safety risks, and the divorce of control from the sovereignty of the people. The soft-path approach has its critics throughout the energy industry, particularly in electrical utilities, deriding 'utopian visions based on inaccurate facts and overly romantic values' (Daneke and Lagassa 1980, 1). Moreover, the soft path is seen by some as more of an instrument for achieving social change than a carefully considered economic option.

In practice elements of both hard and soft paths will be needed to effect the energy transition and the mix will vary according to the geography, the economy, and the culture of different regions or metropolises of the US.

5.4.2 Key questions

Public policies on pricing and on regulation or taxation are fundamental in the energy arena (Batelle Inst. 1978). It is possible to argue that under the free-market system prices reflect an equilibrium between supply and demand, but the market in energy is, and long has been, one of exceedingly imperfect competition. It is also a market of unparalleled complexity in which external conditions are influential and in which there are many unpaid costs, such as those reflecting insecurity of supplies, particularly from overseas, and the domestic social costs of health, environment, and safety which are rarely, if ever, internalized in energy prices (Schurr *et al.* 1979, 49).

Figure 5.4 shows, first, comparative energy costs in 1982 in terms of the average technical cost of production expressed in dollars per barrel oil equivalent on a thermal basis. Secondly, and germane to the uniting of supplies with market, the comparative energy transportation costs of different media. These 'natural' elements of pricing define the comparative advantage of particular regions and localities in the US, provide a basis from which

HNICAL PRODUCTION COSTS (1982)
nated range in dollars

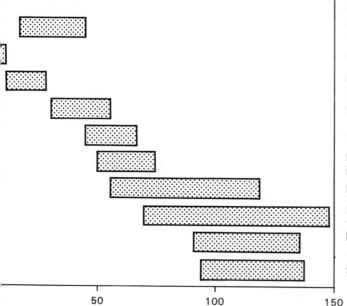

Middle East oil
(existing fields)
Liquids from oil
sands/shale

Coal

Nuclear inputs
(break even value)

LNG imports

SNG from coal

Liquids from
imported coal (Eur.)

Biomass

Electricity (fr. fossil
f./nuclear)

Electricity (fr. solar
/wind

Solar heating

50 100 150

' dollars per barrel oil equivalent on thermal basis

Source:Financial Times, 14/4/82

RGY TRANSPORTATION COSTS (1977)

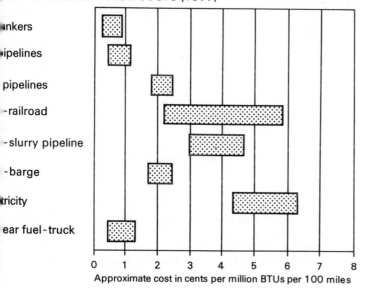

ankers

ipelines

pipelines

-railroad

-slurry pipeline

-barge

tricity

ear fuel-truck

0 1 2 3 4 5 6 7 8

Approximate cost in cents per million BTUs per 100 miles

Source:US Dept. Energy (1979)

5.4   Comparative fuel costs, 1982

to measure price manipulations by public regulatory policies or by artificial distortions, and give a yardstick by which potential substitution of energy sources may begin to be measured. Actual market pricing for categories of energy does not accurately reflect production plus transportation costs, but is the outcome of contention between government regulatory policies and the monopolistic or cartel practice of entrepreneurs. In general, US energy is underpriced and prices do not reflect full marginal costs of energy supply. This was true for oil and gasoline before decontrol in 1981 and will continue to be so for natural gas even after the intended partial deregulation in 1985. Natural gas is presently priced at average costs, but the actual cost of marginal gas may be three times that. The price of electricity is regulated at a fraction of the replacement cost of even conventional power plants and both coal and nuclear power also bear politically controversial external costs (Stobaugh and Yergin 1979, 226). There is widespread agreement, though rarely among consumers, that energy prices should represent the full marginal costs of energy supply. To achieve this in an equitable manner at a time of economic recession and inflation will necessarily require a slow and politically contentious process of adjustment. Producers and importers must receive signals on the true worth of energy to the consumer, consumers signals on what energy is costing society (Schurr *et al.* 1979, 439–49). Hitherto government regulation of price has had an overall effect of inefficient allocation of energy resources, both in form and in location.

The history of government involvement in price regulation, both directly and indirectly, is long-standing, complex, and has had both unintended as well as the intended effects. Prime criteria for evaluating regulations (Thompson *et al.* 1981, 245) at a time of sensitive changes in energy include: do they lead to a reduction in oil imports from insecure sources? Do they contribute additional and diversified domestic energy at reasonable free-market prices? Do they encourage worthwhile conservation? It has been said (Burton 1980, 217) that many past regulations and taxes have led directly to increasing size and company integration within energy industries, and thus to centralization and concentration of economic power. In the future deliberate compensating welfare measures will be justifiable to offset the impact of rising energy prices on low-income households.

Indicative of the variable impacts of regulation the coal severance tax and oil 'windfall' profits tax may be briefly mentioned. Coal severance taxes (Ward 1982) are a tax on extraction (30 per cent in Montana, 10.5 per cent in Wyoming), levied by the State in question to benefit those affected by mining, as well as adding to State revenues. The principal effect of the tax is to shift coal production among the States, benefitting the taxing State and penalizing the consumer in the Middle West and the East. High transport costs on western coal plus some ability to substitute from eastern coal limits the power of Montana and Wyoming to influence the national market, even though the Supreme Court ruled that there is no restriction on the tax which a State may levy. The overall effects on the national coal market, on coal production or on average price have been minor, but the benefits to Montana and Wyoming have been considerable.

The 'windfall' profits tax on the wellhead price of oil was introduced under

President Carter to siphon off the artificially induced gains to the oil companies by the rising price of oil and the rapid escalation in the value of petroleum reserves. President Carter saw the measure as sound in itself, with the revenue so gained to be available for stimulating new technologies, or assisting those unfairly impacted by the oil price rise. Congress wanted the consumer to benefit, while the oil and gas companies wanted return or amelioration of the tax, to stimulate exploration in marginal areas. In the event none of these concerns has been effectively addressed and, on present intentions, by 1986 the windfall tax on newly discovered oil will be halved to 15 per cent.

5.4.3 The supply–demand balance

Transition to a more balanced, secure energy system needs to have regard for some symmetry and stability between supply and demand. Though neither is entirely predictable or programmable, least of all in an inflationary condition of economic depression, energy policies must incorporate basic assumptions on each. Neither supply nor demand will grow exponentially and indeed both may grow slowly, but mismatches between them are still likely, promoting shortages, market distortions and dislocations. The world economic situation is even more difficult to predict far ahead, as recent oil price fluctuations so clearly indicate. The steady decline in world crude oil and product price 1981–2 led to some complacency in the US and a cutback in consideration of alternative and renewable energy resources. Short-term contingency planning not infrequently thus conflicts with long-term options.

On the supply side it is said (Stobaugh and Yergin 1979, 11) that domestic oil, natural gas, coal and nuclear power combined could provide only one-third of the additional energy needs in the US during the 1980s. Unconventional energy resources might do better, but energy planning must focus, in the first place, on the prospects for oil, natural gas, coal, and nuclear power. Oil has traditionally been 'king of the fossil fuels' (Anderer *et al.* 1981, 34) and natural gas the 'ideal fuel resource', but, even with continuing oil imports and natural-gas consumption growing at 2 per cent per annum, conventional oil and gas output will decline seriously by the year 2000 (Schurr *et al.* 1979, 26). For both oil and natural gas the great debate is about price, who determines and who gets the benefit. Coal has the century-long reserves (Table 5.2) and the intended rapid expansion of output may be feasible, but it will not be without difficulties. Reluctance to shift to coal relates to the severe environmentalist (sulphur air pollution, strip-mining reclamation), human (labor relations, health problems), and political constraints on a traditionally backward industry. Nevertheless, coal will have an enhanced role, though perhaps used increasingly in a selective manner, either in traditional industries, such as steel-making, or as major source of secondary fuels (Anderer *et al.* 1981, 28–9). Nuclear power generation and its prospects continue to be a major enigma, stalemated by controversy in the political process, with problems which, though technically severe, are even more intractable socially and politically. Though electricity generated by nuclear power is already lower in cost than generation from coal in some regions (New England, the Coastal West) there remain question-marks against all aspects of the nuclear future.

Influencing the demand side of the energy equation by public policy is as problematical. Given that there is no painless formula for reducing energy consumption and that 37 per cent of all energy is consumed domestically or in commerce, the potentials for influencing demand are there, but it represents a massive unpredictable problem. Taught to regard energy as cheap and abundant, the consumer reacts indignantly to contrary views, with considerable inelasticity in demand in the face of sharply rising energy prices. Self-indulgent and prepared to pay the cost for energy, the consumer is nevertheless aware of the problems of the energy market. With the queues for gasoline and the electricity blackouts, a crisis mood may have fleetingly set in, but a fall in world oil prices soon encouraged complacency and energy consumerism. It may or may not be the case that effective conservation practices could economize up to 40 per cent of present energy use (Stobaugh and Yergin 1979, 12), but a major public relations and education operation will be needed if such a target is even to swim into sight.

5.5   RESTRAINING DEMAND

5.5.1   *Conservation*

Any public conservation policy thus faces difficulties, not least in the political arena, for it is unpopular and has no clear constituency, except perhaps among 'soft' energy path enthusiasts. Perhaps for that very reason claims for what conservation can achieve tend to be very ambitious (CONAES 1979; Hitch 1978; Rawl 1978; Sawhill 1978). Conservation is seen as 'the key energy resource' (Stobaugh and Yergin 1979, 136) and the 'greatest energy opportunity'. At the most favorable, conservation might substitute for 10 to 12 quads (10^{15}) Btu of energy by the year 2000, achieving a 1.1 per cent reduction in energy intensity per annum (Thompson *et al.* 1981, 233). On another estimate (Stobaugh and Yergin 1979, 152) the cumulative fuel saving could amount to 20 billion barrels of oil equivalent, 1975–2000, about double the proven oil reserves of the North Slope of Alaska. It is tempting to think that market forces through the pricing system might largely achieve these objectives. Certainly between 1979 and 1982, with a GNP unchanged in real terms, there was a 20 per cent fall in US petroleum demand, largely induced by price-related conservation and to some extent fuel switching. But the price rises needed to accomplish such large-scale targets would have serious equity effects (Schurr *et al.* 1979, 513) upon the poor, the ethnic minorities, and those living in marginal areas. The fact that such price-induced conservation can have a quick effect makes the social injustice of its potential impact the more unacceptable. The use of a discriminant tax policy to offset such undesirable effects would likely be a nonstarter. As the Chairman of the Texas Railroad Commission put it—'This country did not conserve its way to greatness. It produced itself to greatness.' The general thrust of the Reagan administration is to curtail *public* expenditure on conservation in the public, the industrial-commercial and the private sectors, relying on entrepreneurial and individual initiative to act in the direction of self-interest. Others agree that research and technical needs require public intervention, and indeed also institutional innovation (Burton 1980, 204). If a new conservation ethic is to take root it will need considerable government backing through the education system and the media and also by demonstration of commitment in its own bureaucratic practices.

Conservation may take three forms: first, out-and-out cutback in demand; secondly, and more controversially, shift in the way and where Americans live, including moves against the typical low-density suburban sprawl, which would be seen as a repressive and unacceptable political act, however meritorious in the fuel which may be saved; thirdly, much more specific instances of conservation, such as 'the insulation of houses, more fuel-efficient cars, energy-savings in industrial processing, containing heat presently wasted' (Stobaugh and Yergin 1979, 138). Sixty per cent of conservation savings are said to lie in only four areas (Burton 1980, 204): space conditioning, including heating, insulation, and air conditioning; motorcar fuel consumption; industrial energy cogeneration, the combined production of steam and electricity at industrial sites; and in commercial lighting.

For further consideration the transport, industrial, and domestic energy markets may be isolated. The transport industry consumed 26 per cent of total US energy in 1981, one-half in the form of oil and one-half of that consumed in motorcars. Fuel economies on the railroads were achieved in the conversion from coal-firing to diesel fuel and electrification. Private cars posed a different sort of problem. Distances in general travel and commuting are extensive in a mobile society and in a cheap fuel era cars were traditionally large and covered relatively few miles per gallon. Conservation policy operated on the car manufacturers, stipulating more fuel-efficient models, in addition to the environmental and safety requirements which were pressed at the same time. Pollution emission standards were promulgated and regulation on fuel-efficiency, mandated by Congress, was more readily negotiated in that automobile manufacturing was concentrated in a few large corporations. The prescribing of fuel-efficient cars for government officials was a useful demonstration side effect.

Manufacturing consumed 37 per cent of energy in 1981, spread over a myriad plants and firms in a wide diversity of industries. Some are energy-intensive, such as the steel industry or aluminum production, but a great range of twentieth-century growth industries use less energy per unit of output and can switch more flexibly between energy sources. Generalizations about energy conservation in industry are thus difficult, but decision-takers there are usually well informed, profit-conscious, and respond well to signals in the energy market (Stobaugh and Yergin 1979, 146). High returns are expected on investment and in that sense energy-saving projects, with low returns, may be of secondary importance in many plants and firms. Under the National Energy Act (1978) a 10 per cent tax credit could be claimed on energy investment and, indeed, the greatest short-term progress in conservation could probably be made in the manufacturing sector, in technological innovation, recovery of waste, and better organization of the workplace.

Cogeneration of steam and electricity at industrial sites is regarded as a particularly promising technological innovation, possibly saving up to 20 per cent of existing industrial energy consumption (Stobaugh and Yergin 1979,

160). Though a proven technology and economically viable, particularly if fueled by coal and in medium-sized plants, there are difficult organizational relationships with the electricity industry to be solved. Who is to own and operate the facility, the industrial plant, an electric utility or an independent? What basis should be used for the costing of standby electricity fed from the grid and what terms for any surplus power sent into the grid system? (Schurr et al. 1979, 515). There are, furthermore, certain environmental, safety and health aspects to be taken into account.

Domestic and commercial uses consumed 37 per cent of energy in 1981. Rising personal affluence has been translated directly into higher per capita household energy consumption, whilst the shift of American employment towards the rapidly growing service sector has added its own quantum to greater demand for energy. For both commercial and domestic uses direct heating offers worthwhile energy economies. The design and construction of energy-efficient new building stock has a 10 to 40 year lead time for significant changes to be made. Though a 15 per cent tax credit has been allowable since 1978 for residential conservation investment, there remains widespread ignorance, coupled with a disinclination to bear the often substantial capital costs of installation. Better building design, improved instalation, and adjusting the thermostat offer the most significant prospect for domestic savings.

In short, the energy necessary to produce a given unit of output can be measured by: lowering energy-intensive production; changing the composition of energy consumption; and shifting to a less energy-intensive mix of goods and services (CONAES 1979, 120).

5.6 SUPPLY OPTIONS

5.6.1 Oil

The vast and rapid change in the US oil industry over the past decade makes even the sort-term future hard to predict. The sharp escalation of energy costs, even within two years (1979 37 per cent, 1980 18 per cent, 1981 12 per cent), overlapped with domestic crude oil and gasoline price deregulation, one of the first acts of the Reagan administration (January 1981). Within the years 1979–82, a time of little change in GNP in real terms, the demand for oil in the US fell by 20 per cent, a fall accounted for more by price-induced conservation and fuel switching than by constraints imposed by economic recession. The price of a barrel of oil in the US had risen from $6.74 in 1974, to $31.85 in 1981; oil refineries in 1982 were working at only 64 per cent capacity and there had been 50 refinery closures in 18 months. A world glut of oil in the early 1980s might be only transitory but with unparalleled ferment and political instability in the Middle East the further international oil outlook remains problematical. Table 5.4 shows an official projection of the US oil market to the year 2000.

US domestic oil policy revolves around three basic options (Stobaugh and Yergin 1979, 41): curbing the power of the oil companies, said by some to be excessive; deregulating the price of crude oil and gasoline; and, thirdly, increasing domestic supplies of oil, by developing Alaskan and Outer Con-

TABLE 5.4   *US oil market, 1980–2000*

Million barrels per day (mbd)	Actual	Mid-range projection		
	1980	1985	1990	2000
Domestic production				
Conventional oil: Lower				
48 States	7.1	6.0	5.3	4.2
Alaska	1.5	1.6	1.7	1.8
Enhanced oil (from fields previously worked)	–	0.2	0.6	1.8
Total crude oil	8.6	7.8	7.6	7.8
Natural gas liquids	1.5	1.3	1.1	0.7
Total crude + nat. gas liquids	10.1	9.1	8.7	8.5
Shale and coal liquefaction	–	–	0.4	2.2
TOTAL PRODUCTION	10.1	9.1	9.1	10.7
Refinery gain	0.5	0.5	0.5	0.4
NET IMPORTS	6.3	6.3	4.8	1.2
TOTAL CONSUMPTION	16.9	15.9	14.4	12.3

Source: US Dept. Energy, October 1981, press release.

tinental Shelf (OCS) resources, together with enhanced recovery of residual oil from existing fields. Oil from unconventional means, oil shales, tar sands, or the liquefaction of coal might be longer-term resources of considerable value, but the economics of such operations remain dubious.

The belief that the major oil companies have long been manipulating the US energy market dies hard, but as the chairman of Sun Oil put it (1981)— 'The days when we had two economies, one for the oil industry and one for everybody else, are over.' Many are not so sure (Solberg 1976). Notably consumer interests and divestitures of oil power are the favorite prescriptions: oil companies to pull out of their 'octopus-like' grip on alternative energy production (horizontal divestiture), and also for vertical divestiture to break the chain of control from oil exploration through to marketing. It has been commented that 'though there might be significant psychological and political effects' (Schurr *et al.* 1979, 43), the net economic impact would be slight. Public ownership is a nonstarter.

Oil and gasoline price deregulation (the last 15 per cent in January 1981) replaced no fewer than 17 categories of oil pricing, and completed the decontrol begun under President Carter in 1979. Prices rose, but an 80 per cent 'windfall' profits tax clawed back the greater part of oil company gains. It is still not clear how far those unfairly affected by price rises, the poor, the ethnic communities, and remote, peripheral areas, will be compensated from public funds. Smaller refining companies suffered by the axing of 'entitlement' programs, whereby their purchases of expensive foreign oil were compensated by the refineries processing the then controlled and cheaper domestic product.

Domestic oil output fell from 3.995 in 1973 to 3.772 billion barrels in 1981 and, as Table 5.4 shows, production in the 49 conterminous States will continue to fall according to official estimates. The latest figure for oil reserves (35 billion barrels) is up on the 1978 estimate of 34 billion barrels recoverable, though there is dispute about where the bulk of the yet undiscovered reserves may actually lie. According to oil companies, less than 15 per cent lie onshore, but the US Geological Survey estimates such reserves to be 85 per cent. The drilling boom under way in the early 1980s will clarify the position. Major contributions to future US oil production will come from Alaska and, more speculatively, the Outer Continental Shelf. In both cases, the Federal government has considerable regulatory powers. With one-third of the continental land area and all the Outer Continental Shelf (OCS) in the public domain the Federal government controls access to 85 per cent of oil reserves, 40 per cent of gas and uranium, and 35 per cent of coal reserves. Access to new acreage is indeed rated more important for the oil industry than higher prices (Schurr *et al.* 1979, 43).

Though Point Barrow, Alaska, was designated a Naval Petroleum Reserve as early as 1923 exploration of the North Slope began only in 1958 and substantial drilling in 1963. In the early 1980s proved Alaskan oil reserves were almost 15 billion barrels, with the bulk in the Prudhoe Bay field. 'Every well drilled from Prudhoe Bay to the Arctic Wildlife Refuge has encountered hydrocarbons and would have been commercial if in Texas.' Distance from markets and the problems of transport by land, along the Alaskan pipeline to Valdez on the south coast, or by sea through the ice-bound northern passage have limited and delayed full development (Cicchetti 1972). Offshore drilling costs in the Arctic basin are extremely high with severe environmental difficulties and the need to use ice-resistant drilling cones or to create gravel islands on which to base drilling rigs in the Beaufort Sea. The Federal government has lifted the seasonal restriction on drilling, to permit exploration in 10 rather than 5 months of the year; the earlier limitation was to protect the Bowhead whale migration. The Alaskan government, too, by its initial taxes on both production and retailing of oil, caused restrictions on development. The extended program of Alaskan OCS leasing, from 1982 on, promised to accelerate opening up offshore from both Prudhoe Bay and Kuparuk. Meanwhile the impact of oil development on the Alaskan economy and way of life has been dramatic, for both good and ill (US FEA 1976).

OCS leasing remains a controversial subject, both environmentally and politically (Mitchell 1976B, Mansvelt Beck *et al.* 1977). Apart from Alaska, the Santa Maria basin off California and the Georges Bank off Newfoundland have attracted the greatest interest. Nearly 1 billion acres, the entire OCS of the USA, is to be made available for oil and gas exploration during the 1980s, to be conducted under 'stringent' environmental safeguards' in order to 'enhance the national security, provide jobs and protect the environment while making America less dependent on foreign oil reserves' (James F. Watt, US Sec. Int.). Possibly 35 billion barrels of oil and 115 trillion cu. ft. of natural gas remain to be discovered under the OCS. The opening up of the Arctic Wildlife Refuge (9 million acres) for oil exploration by the mid-1980s is seen by some as a threat to caribou breeding grounds and remains a politically sensitive issue.

TABLE 5.5 *Alaskan oil resources, 1982*

	Discovered	On stream	Thou-barrels per day	Reserves (billion barrels)	Recoverable	Average depth wells (feet)	Oil column (feet)
Prudhoe Bay	1968	1977	1,500	10 (23)[a]	5.5 (9.6)[a]	8,000–9,000	350
Kuparuk	1969	1981	90–250	4.4	1.3	6,3000	50

[a] Different estimates for Prudhoe Bay.

Sources: various, incl. *Financial Times,* 21 July 1982.

Enhanced recovery of oil left in the underground reservoir during earlier extraction may add up to 1 million barrels per day before the end of the century, using the new technology of injecting chemical compounds or heat treatment. Four-fifths of US shale oil reserves occur on the Colorado West Slope, with an estimated 2 trillion barrels of oil of which 600 billion might be recoverable. The Federal government owns 79 per cent of the oil shale basin, operating a restricted leasing program in blocks of 8 square miles at a time. Exxon planned a pilot extraction plant for 47,000 barrels of oil a day for 80 years, but closed the project in 1982, in view of the high construction costs, the likely nonviable price of the oil, and the lack of commitment by the Reagan administration. Oil from coal is discussed under Coal.

The future of oil imports is unpredictable (Bohi and Russell 1978) but the clear intention is to reduce the flow, though not 'at any cost'. A net oil importer ever since 1948 the US government both stimulated overseas development by domestic oil companies and sought to control imports by quota regulations under the Mandatory Oil Import Program, 1959–73. By 1979 foreign oil supplied 55 per cent of US consumption but within two years this had been cut back to 36 per cent; some 32 per cent of imports came from non-OPEC sources in 1981. The Department of Energy forecast of 4.8 million barrels of oil imports daily in 1990 contrasts with the 10 million barrels predicted under the National Energy Plan as recently as 1977. Imports continue for the Strategic Petroleum Reserve (SPR), a projected emergency storage of four months' oil supply, mostly in salt domes in Texas and Louisiana. The Louisiana Offshore Oil Port (LOOP) was completed in 1981 to process 1.4 million barrels per day, pumped 28 miles to storage caves. Talk of a prospective oil import fee of 5 dollars a barrel (1982) might contribute to of stabilization of lower oil imports, but such imports will continue to be required, a constant factor in US foreign policy (Conant 1982).

5.6.2 Natural gas

Natural gas is almost everyone's favorite fuel. 'It burns clean, its extraction and transport offer no environmental difficulties and unlike nuclear power there is no problem of waste disposal' (Stobaugh and Yergin 1979, 56); only 5 per cent of consumption was imported. In 1981 natural gas provided 27 per cent of all US energy consumption and 31 per cent of domestic energy output (Table 5.1). Yet the pricing of natural gas, always complex, has been described as 'one of the great religious wars of American politics' (p. 57), with multiple conflicts of interest on the one hand and the most sophisticated econometric models and computer printouts on the other (US Fed. Trade Commn. 1979). Conflict has raged over the appropriate method of pricing, either by the costs of production or by marketplace value (Gault 1979). Public intervention in gas pricing has had a long history (US Congress, Senate 1972): 1890–1925, local pipelines and distribution companies came under State or local government price regulation as 'natural monopolies'; the Natural Gas Act (1938) created the Federal Power Commission (now the Federal Energy Regulatory Commission) to administer a 'just and reasonable' price to be charged initially by interstate pipeline companies; intrastate companies remained free of wellhead price controls (Stobaugh and Yergin

1979, 61). In 1954 a Supreme Court decision extended the powers of the Natural Gas Act to products as well as pipeline companies. Thus in the interstate market costs of production were a pricing yardstick, but in the intrastate market the value among buyers and sellers was a dominant criterion, with a divergence of prices between the two markets as a result. The Natural Gas Policy Act (1978) was a complicated first step towards partial deregulation of the industry (Stobaugh and Yergin 1979, 76–8). Controls were to be retained in 40 per cent of 'old' gas, but by 1985 there was to be a gradual rise towards parity with oil prices for the 60 per cent of 'new' gas discovered since 1976. The wellhead price of gas consumed intrastate was to be centrally controlled temporarily on the same basis as interstate gas. The complicated outcome was a compromise, benefitting wells producing for interstate markets, interstate pipeline companies, and consumers in nonproducing States. Intrastate consumers and their pipeline or distribution companies stood to lose by the deal, unless they had access to 'old' interstate gas supplies. With a complexity of pricing almost defying economic rationale or the ability to regulate efficiently or equitably it is not surprising that the conflict over natural-gas pricing has continued.

For retaining a measure of control after 1985 it is argued: prices would otherwise 'fly up' by 50 to 100 per cent, adding 2 to 3 per cent to inflation; a 'windfall' profits tax would be needed; a 'gas bubble' of 3 trillion cu. ft. of unsold gas already existed in 1982; and unregulated gas pricing under the 1978 Act already catered for unusually deep, offshore, or 'hard to get' categories. The case for total deregulation was that control stifled development, led to counterproductive underpricing, misallocation of resources, and reduced exploration for new resources. The 23 pricing tiers for gas were seen as distorting market allocations, creating artificial regional advantages (Osleb and Sheskin 1977), and leading to noneconomic distribution.

Though natural gas consumption fell back in the early 1980s, the 1981 reserves of 198 trillion cu. ft. need to be augmented for demand anticipated well before the next century. Prudhoe Bay, Alaska, may be the world's largest gas field with 26 trillion cu. ft. of reserves, yet the proposed Alaskan natural-gas pipeline, without which gas will continue to be pumped back into the oilfield, is almost as controversial as its Siberian counterpart, but for different reasons (US Congress, Jt. Econ. Comm. 1972). The 4,800-mile pipeline across Alaska and Canada will split into two legs, one to California, the other to Illinois. Though full operating capacity might deliver 2 billion cu. ft. of gas daily, the costs of building are so high that the estimated cost of delivered gas (1985–6) would be 9 dollars per 1,000 cu. ft, three times the 1980 weighted domestic price. Anti-Trust waivers have been necessary to enable corporate financing to be assembled and, even so, Federal money will almost certainly be needed. Decontrol of natural gas prices might well render Alaska gas even more uneconomic, since the intention had been to 'roll-in' the higher Alaskan price within the lower regulated price of the national market.

Natural gas imports came mainly from Mexico (300 million cu. ft. per day in 1982) and Canada, but there are political impediments to rapid expansion in both cases. Liquefied natural gas, from North Africa, is unlikely to make much contribution. Gas from coal is considered below.

5.6.3   Coal

Under the National Energy Act (1978) coal was to double in output, to 1.2 billion short tons, within 10 years, playing the role of a 'transitional fuel' towards an energy market dominated in the twenty-first century by nuclear fusion and solar energy. None of this now seems likely, even though, with its century of reserves, coal remains America's most prolific, yet least utilized, fuel reserve (Halibouty Rept. 1979). Table 5.6 shows the essentials of production, consumption, and projected trends.

The coal economy (US Congress, Senate 1978; Zimmerman 1981), however, faces a unique set of difficulties, from its very characteristics (geological and chemical), geographical location involving transport costs, the uncertainty of demand, government regulation, environmental opposition, and the human problems of labor and managerial organization. It is not surprising that from supplying 50 per cent of US energy needs in 1946 the contribution had fallen to 18 per cent in 1973, rising once more to 22 per cent in 1981. From an output of 630 million tons in 1947, production fell to 400 Mt in 1961, rising to 814 Mt in 1981.

Coal is bulky, heavy, dirty, and expensive to mine, transport, store, and use; in burning it creates air pollution, serious if the sulphur content (SO_2) is high. Production had traditionally been concentrated in the Appalachian and, to a lesser extent, the Interior (midcontinent) fields, but marked shifts in the balance and quality of coal are now under way (Deasy and Griess 1967; Clements 1977; Davis 1981). Of US coal reserves, 54 per cent, measured by weight but not in heating value, lie west of the Mississippi. These reserves include three-quarters of all *strippable* (opencast minable) coal, some 70 per cent on Federally owned land, with a further 20 per cent near Federal land. Through land-leasing policy (Kahn and Hand 1976) as well as environmental, health, and safety legislation, the Federal government is in an even more powerful position to influence the coal industry. Fear of the destruction of fragile ecosystems in the West, the possibility of conflicts over scarce water, and the risks of creating 'boom and bust' developments led to a 10-year moratorium on the leasing of Federal lands for coalmining. In 1981 this moratorium was lifted by the Reagan administration, though 'wilderness' areas remained protected.

Markets for coal are still concentrated in the Northeast Manufacturing Belt and other major metropolises, long supplied from the eastern bituminous coal and anthracite fields. Most eastern coal has been deep-mined and mining left an unfortunate legacy of rundown, pollution, and dereliction in many Appalachian settlements (Walls 1976). Eastern coal has a higher sulphur content and is thus unacceptable under the Clean Air Act Amendments (1977), without the installation of expensive scrubbers in the generating plant chimneys. Western coal, by contrast, is almost entirely strip-mined (opencast production) and has a lower sulphur content, an advantage somewhat offset by a lower calorific value and remoteness. Strip-mining produces 60 per cent of all US coal, with a high labor productivity of 27 tons per man per day, compared with 14 tons for deep-mined coal. On the other hand, strip-mining produces serious land reclamation problems (Rowe 1979) and heavy on-costs of restoration under environmental legislation (see ch. 4.4).

TABLE 5.6   *The US coal economy, 1980–1990*

Million short tons[a]	1980	1990
Production		
East	555	827
Percentage	71.5	61.5
West	221	518
Percentage	28.5	38.5
Total	776 (814)	1,345
Domestic consumption		
Power stations	526 (595)	935
Coking plants	77 (60)	74
Industry/Retail	74 (68)	160
Synthetic fuel	–	38
Total	677 (742)	1,207
Exports		
Canada	19	24
Overseas	16	118
Total	65 (110)	142
of which steam coal	14.1	83
Barrel per day oil equivalent	152,512	897,764

1981 figure in brackets.
[a] 1 short ton = 0.9072 metric tonnes = heat equivalent of 3,948 barrels crude oil.

Source: National Coal Association (1981).

Eighty per cent of coal is consumed in electricity generation, where in some regions of the US it competes on equal terms with nuclear power, if the environmental costs of coal are fully weighted. Under the National Energy Act (1978) power station burn for new plant was to be increasingly by coal while natural gas was excluded as a fuel until 1990, though this has been flexibly interpreted in the Southwestern States. A shift in the balance of US coal production westward is apparent from Table 5.6. Program models for the coal industry (Leblanc *et al.* 1979) test the spatial implications of variable levels of total demand, of demand for low-sulphur coal, and transport costs. With fast-rising demand or stricter antipollution (SO_2) regulations there will need to be major expansion of new mines on western Federal lands, focussing on Montana and Wyoming. Serious transport bottlenecks and community problems would arise there, as the traditional westward flow of coal was set into reverse and 'boom and bust' afflicted many remote settlements. Prices of coal would increase more sharply in the East, though local markets for either coal or electricity in the western coal States are likely to remain limited.

Transport problems are central in the coal economy: 65 per cent of coal moves by rail, 11 per cent by water, 12 per cent by truck, 11 per cent is converted to electricity near the mine-mouth, and 1 per cent moves by other means (Stobaugh and Yergin 1979, 87). Eastern railroads are congested, often in deteriorating condition, their networks carrying unprofitable branch lines and hampered in competition with barge or truck lines (Schurr *et al.* 1979, 486). Western railroads face a dilemma. Since capital investment for new lines in a low-traffic region is high, will demand for western coal justify the investment risks in providing additional capacity? If demand for coal increases rapidly, with long lead times in construction of lines how will it be met? Coal-slurry pipelines offer an alternative in some areas, with cost advantage in long-distance, high-capacity movement of water-impregnated coal dust. But there are demerits too: first, a considerable volume of water is required and is not likely to be available in Western States, where water is scarce and States' rights are strong; secondly, the volume of dirty water at the destination represents a considerable pollution disposal problem. Slurry pipelines might contribute to holding down rail freight costs for coal and would cause less disruption than trains to communities along the line. However, opposition to slurry pipelines has been strong. Railroad companies have combined with environmentalists to defeat right-of-way agreements and the use of 'eminent domain' legislation was defeated in the 95th Congress. Larger bulk coal carriers on the Great Lakes (with loads up to 60,000 tons), bigger barge tows on rivers, and the use of unit-trains of 100 wagons, each carrying 100 tons of coal, are already in use to handle the growing volume of coal movement. Conversion of western coal *in situ* to electric power and its transmission over 1,000 miles might be economic, but it would encounter severe difficulties from environmentalists, objecting to the lines of pylons, and also from the ubiquitous scarcity of process water in the West.

The human problems of the coal industry, though long endemic, are less serious than once they were. The difficulty of recruiting and training for dangerous, unhealthy work applied principally to underground mining. The disruptions and strikes plaguing the industry related to the unionized eastern mines, but union membership has declined from 500,000 in 1945 to 160,000 in 1981, most western strip-mines are non-union, and communities no longer have the same attachment to a tightly organized local mining culture. On the management side, one disturbing feature may be the intrusion of petroleum companies into the coal industry, by 1974 forming no less than 17 of the 25 largest companies. Though they are capable of vast capital investments, the fear is that the marketing of coal may be unfairly prejudiced in favor of the primacy of oil.

Table 5.6 shows the projected potential for coal exports. A World Coal Study (WOCOL) in 1980 estimated these to be within the range of 125 to 350 million metric tonnes by the end of the century; the National Coal Association projected 142 Mmt for 1990. Whereas coking coal for the steel industries of Western Europe and Japan had been a traditional US export, it is steam coal that now holds the greatest promise, in spite of competition from Australia, Canada, or South Africa in world markets. Long-term overseas contacts are essential if the major new coal terminals, their feeder lines, and the deepened ship channels are to be created on the US Atlantic and Gulf coasts (Starr 1981). Otherwise the typical congestion with perhaps 100 ships waiting to load off Hampton Roads and Baltimore is likely to become even worse.

5.6.4 Synthetic fuels

For the immediately foreseeable future visions of massive synthetic fuel production have almost completely faded, a sharp turnaround from the heady expectations even as recently as 1980. Gasification or liquefaction of coal to oil were to have led the way, with minor contributions of gasoline from biomass (gasohol). Gasification of coal is to produce a low Btu (British thermal unit) gas from the combination of coal with air and steam, a well-known but uneconomic technology except under economic or political siege conditions. Liquefaction of coal is achieved by the distillation of coal in the absence of air, a process used in wartime Europe and exploited on a larger scale today in South Africa. Both gasification and liquefaction processes require large-scale organization and billion dollar funding; they produce gas ($3.88 to 6.72 per million Btus) or oil ($50 to 75 a barrel) at costs well above natural fuel costs. Thus both seek governmental financial support and are extremely vulnerable to economic recession or falling fuel prices. Environmental problems of air and water pollution are endemic and the impact of plants employing 2,000 workers is often dramatic in small-scale communities. Water supply in the dry West would be an ultimate constraint in any case (Boris and Krutilla 1980).

Federal government involvement has thus been cautious and tentative for the most part. President Ford's Synthetic Fuels Commercialization Program and Nixon's Energy Independence Authority (Inter Agency Task Force 1974) both failed to pass the Congress (Schurr *et al.* 1979, 527). The Energy Security Act (1980) under President Carter was more positive, even extravagantly ambitious: 500,000 barrels of synfuels a day were to be produced by 1987 and 2 million barrels a day by 1992. The Exxon Corporation claims the US could produce up to 15 million barrels a day by the year 2010 but even 8 million barrels a day would require 150 large-scale plants, an unheard of rate of expansion. Several major projects were started; the oil-shale schemes have already been discussed. In Morgantown, West Virginia, a coal liquefaction plant was set up to produce 20,000 b/d oil from 6,000 tonnes of coal. Out west the schemes were more grandiose: in North Dakota a coal gasification plant to produce 12 million cu. ft. gas per day, equal to 20,000 barrels of oil, with a longer-term target of 125 million cu. ft. gas per day; and two major oil-shale-using plants in Colorado (Cathedral Bluffs and the Piceance basin). The Federal Synthetic Fuels Corporation (SFC) was established to oversee public investment and technological progress.

Under President Reagan's National Energy Policy Plan SFC was threatened, the target for synfuels was cut back to 500,000 barrels per day by 1990, and support dollars were limited to loans for only a handful of projects, mainly for coal liquefaction. With the loss of Federal funding and in face of the oil glut the private sector withdrew from most synfuels schemes. Investment which had been given up in other fuel and power resources made continuing synfuel commitment difficult to justify in the marketplace. The fear now is that the necessary infrastructure and rudimentary industrial base will not be created, technological 'know-how' and trained cadres will be dispersed, and the synfuels industry will be restarted with difficulty if and when its time comes in an age of greater energy scarcity.

5.6.5 *The nuclear option*

No energy issues have sparked as much technical controversy or been debated with such violent political emotions as those surrounding nuclear power generation (Addinall and Ellington 1982). For these reasons governmental roles, at Federal, State, and local levels, have been as inevitable as they have been controversial. Public opinion has swung from a majority in support of further nuclear power investment in the 1970s to a majority against further construction in the 1980s. Value judgments on the desirable future for society compete with nakedly political views, whilst entrepreneurs, consumers, and interest groups line up determinedly on both sides of the argument. Nuclear power should be developed slowly, if we are to avoid 'the nuclear garrison state' (Burton 1980, 311). Alternatively, we have reached a 'nuclear stalemate' (Stobaugh and Yergin 1979, 108), on technical, economic, and environmental grounds. Others wish to 'maintain the nuclear enterprise' (Schurr *et al.* 1979, 492), while even more positively (Ahmed 1979, 146) the nuclear option 'preserves the economic integrity of the energy economy for the next thirty years' and 'enables the transition from an oil-dependent nation to inexhaustible energy resources (nuclear fusion and solar energy)'.

Arguments for nuclear power generation are advanced mainly by technocrats and bureaucrats, committed to 'hard' energy paths and 'centralized, high technology and heavy machinery solutions to energy problems' (Burton 1980, 313). Though problems are seen to exist and to be difficult they are regarded as manageable in 'a technology of necessity if not of choice' (Stobaugh and Yergin 1979, 109). To electric utility companies nuclear power is looked on as safe, clean, and, until the recent fallback, the only means to cope with rising demand. Opposition is often total and, even if partial, is conducted with both emotion and reason. Amidst general mistrust of politicians and entrepreneurs in the industry it is felt that 'large numbers [of citizens] are put at risk without their consent' (Schurr *et al.* 1979, 498), that to be acceptably safe needs more resources than can be made available, that the effects of low-level radiation over long periods, the probability and the consequences of accidents are none of them adequately known. Disposal of radioactive waste has not been satisfactorily solved, while thermal pollution, the siting of nuclear plants, and lack of confidence in their construction or performance are other reasons for public disquiet. The early enactment of the Price Anderson Act (1957) 'to satisfy public liability claims' through Federal indemnity, and the reassuring nature of the Rasmussen Report on nuclear accident risks did little to allay such growing public concern (Shrader-Frechette 1980).

In an energy-abundant US economy nuclear power started late, but the technical breakthrough of the light water reactor (LWR), using pressurized steam (PWR) or boiling water (BWR) processes, created a powerful industrial base in the mid-1960s, with four major reactor manufacturers. On the false assumption that private industry would develop from the LWR base (Bupp and Derian 1981), Atomic Energy Commission research was directed to the next technology, the Fast Breeder Reactor family (FBR). Heavy losses were incurred by the LWR reactor manufacturers at the very time, in the early 1970s, that the anti-nuclear movement was gaining powerful momentum.

Project Independence (1974) envisaged nuclear power providing 30 to 40 per cent of US energy by 1989 and even up to 50 per cent by the year 2000, but by 1979 the economics of the nuclear industry were under challenge in its only market, electricity production, and the 'nuclear stalemate' had set in with a vengeance. President Carter's National Energy Act (1978) favored continuance of the LWR strategy, with reluctance, forbade nuclear fuel reprocessing in view of the risks of plutonium proliferation (for weapons), safety issues, and damage to the environment. Though opposed to FBRs, President Carter was forced by Congress to authorize the Clinch River FBR (see below). By early 1978 seven States had enacted legislation against nuclear waste storage and any further nuclear power development until the Federal government had solved the storage problem (Stobaugh and Yergin 1979, 129). President Reagan's nuclear policy (1981) was 'to create a climate which would permit revitalization of civil nuclear power without compromising health or safety'. There were to be fewer barriers to the export of nuclear plants and technology, help was to be given for disposal of the mounting heaps of radioactive waste, speedier government licensing of reactors, and the controversial nuclear fuel reprocessing industry was to be opened up to private enterprise.

In the early 1980s the nuclear industry was in some disarray. In 1981 77 nuclear reactors were operating (58GW, gigawatt = 1 million kilowatt, capacity), 70 of them for commercial purposes. A further 80 (88GW capacity) were under construction and about an additional 70 to 75 were under consideration. Those operating were working at only 65 per cent capacity, compared with 75 per cent in 1978. Nuclear power stations take an average 12 years to complete in the US, in contrast to only 5 years in Japan, though the Nuclear Regulatory Commission (NRC) was seeking (1982) to cut the time in the US to 6 to 7 years. The spatial distribution of the stations (Guinness 1979) relates to the availability of other energy sources, the scale and rate of growth in demand for electricity and the power of antinuclear lobbies. The South Atlantic States lead in absolute terms and in per capita installed nuclear capacity, lacking fossil fuels and with a rising population. New England and the Middle West are prominent too, with one-third of their electricity from nuclear sources. Though California has the need to maximize energy output the antinuclear movement is powerful there, reinforced by the potentially disastrous outcome of the nuclear breakdown in the Three Mile Island plant, at Harrisburg, Pennsylvania (President's Commn. 1979).

Alternative nuclear technologies require brief consideration. Among conventional converter reactors the LWR will continue to hold pride of place for some time in the US, based on a once-through fuel cycle using uranium (UR) 235. On the most optimistic high scenario of the Department of Energy (Schurr *et al.* 1979, 493) LWRs by the year 2000 might have had an energy output equivalent to all 1978 oil imports. This will no longer hold true and, inefficient in the use of uranium, with major radioactive waste disposal problems, the LWR is the 'least socially desirable' nuclear option (Ahmed 1979, 145). More efficient in using uranium, heavy water reactors (HWRs) have no problems with plutonium from waste residues, but are out of favor in the US. The availability of uranium was earlier thought likely to limit the LWR program, but recent discoveries have removed that constraint

(Uranium Inst. 1979). Uranium enrichment, a two-year process from the ore-field to the reactors, remains for the present in Federal hands.

The reprocessing or storage problems of nuclear spent fuel continues to be a major problem. Three reprocessing plants were conceived in the 1960s, but all were closed by the early 1980s without having operated effectively. Opposition to reprocessing during the Carter years, because of the risks of plutonium production for weapons, has been overtaken by the sharp fall in the price of uranium from £40 (1976) to £23 a pound in 1981.

The Fast Breeder reactor (FBR) program obviates the spent fuel problem of the LWRs, but the capital costs are exceedingly high and the technology as yet commercially unproven. Indeed the fall in the rate of electricity demand expansion, coupled with the discovery of large uranium reserves, makes 'FBR development a luxury' (Ahmed 1979, 145). The Clinch River plant, a Liquid Metal Fast Breeder Reactor (LMFBR) project, though a proven technology, is the only potentially commercial venture, with a very checkered political history. Forced upon a reluctant President Carter by Congress, the Clinch River scheme was to provide 4,000 jobs in the Tennessee Valley. After false starts the scheme was finally endorsed (November 1981). Using uranium 50 to 60 times as efficiently as the LWRs, the LMFBR will require 5 to 6 tonnes of plutonium for its full fuel cycle. Britain may help to provide part of this by leasing plutonium from its civil stockpile, to avoid the political risks of processing plutonium from spent LWR fuel generated within the US. Though FBR development is not inevitable, by some flywheel technological momentum, it is certainly not unthinkable (Schurr *et al.* 1979, 506).

5.6.6 Electricity

Electricity has been called 'the reference energy system' (Anderer *et al.* 1981, 244), whose price influences the price of all other energy forms. The energy mix in electricity production varies with the natural resource endowment, the rate and scale of demand, and the costs of alternative source options in the natural energy marketplace. Electricity is a flexible resource, capable of long-distance transmission, economically up to 1,000 miles, by regional or local grid network, but it is not capable of commercial storage. Hourly, daily, seasonal, periodical, and annual demands fluctuate and efficient marketing of electricity depends on meeting base-load requirements and flexibly switching blocks of power through the grid to meet peak demand in different places and at different times. Standby generating capacity is needed and hydro power, when and where available, is particularly suited to meet peak load.

Electric utility pricing is subject to State and local regulation, while the costs of fuel imput are variably affected by Federal, State, or no regulations. Natural gas is, in regulatory principle at least, denied to new power stations until the 1990s, though the cheapest and preferred fuel. The policy trend has been to convert oil-fired stations to coal-burning, though the change has been slow and strongly opposed in Texas and Louisiana. The competition between coal and nuclear power in the electricity industry is difficult to evaluate fairly.

Capital construction costs must be amortized over the 30-year life of nuclear stations or coal-fired power, while technological innovation, fuel costs, Research and Development charges, and inflation accounting all complicate the issue. Among recent comparisons, a Tennessee Valley Authority (TVA) study in 1981, using a 15 per cent interest rate, found electricity generating costs similar for coal and nuclear power for stations starting production in 1995. According to a 1979 comparison (Schurr *et al.* 1979, 286) nuclear power has perhaps a 5 to 15 per cent advantage in New England, which generates one-third of its electricity from nuclear sources, and in western coastal States. Overall in 1979 national average figures for coal and nuclear power costs showed 18.8 mills per kilowatt-hour on a 10 per cent interest rate for coal generation and 16.6 mills for nuclear power; on a 15 per cent interest basis the figures were then respectively 22.8 and 21.4 mills (Schurr *et al.* 1979, 288).

Hydroelectric power supplies only 5 per cent of US energy needs, irregularly distributed according to variable natural endowment of precipitation and storage sites. All major sites have now been utilized, that at Grand Coulee being the largest hydro station in the world (7,460 MW, megawatts, installed capacity, to rise to 10,830 MW). Some think that hydro power has already been overdeveloped, with consequential damage to wildlife and groundwater reserves, and disturbance of silting regimes on rivers. The remaining potential sites, some 2,100 in all, 1,400 of which already have an impounding barrage, are smaller and these would be less efficient, approximately in the ratio of 1 to 3. Once construction costs are amortized electrical output becomes economic at medium-scale sites. Furthermore, when pricing is adjusted to what the market will bear, often in near monopoly conditions, disseminated development of hydro-power production is both economically possible and viable. If all feasible sites were to be developed, about 1 million barrels of oil equivalent per day could be generated, say one-fifth of present oil imports. This is highly improbable within the foreseeable future, but tax credits and indirect aids to small-scale hydro schemes under the Public Utilities Regulation Policy Act (1978) are matched by regulations requiring public utilities to buy electricity from small generating plants at 'least avoidable cost' (often the higher) whilst asking that there should be preferential access to transmission lines for the power thus generated.

One possibility for flexible electrical power which has not been fully exploited is the extension of regional grid transmission networks for switching of blocks of power derived from complementary fuel sources. Presently the reach of both national and local utility policy is territorially restricted by the layout of the grid network and the fragmented nature of utility undertakings. The Pacific Northwest (Daneke and Lagassa 1980, 242) illustrates the possibilities. Earlier, 120 public utility companies concentrated electricity production irregularly at less than State scale. The large hydro stations in the Pacific Northwest were a major force in the regional integration in the electricity industry, with Bonneville Power Administration organizing regional leadership as a marketing agency. Ironically, it took the nuclear age to introduce complications. The Washington Public Power Supply Service (WPPSS) in the late 1960s planned five nuclear power plants, not one of which has been completed 14 years later; two have been scrapped, one mothballed, and the other two are programmed to become operational in 1984 and 1985. Millions of dollars have already been added to electricity costs with no increase in supply. A matching nuclear horror story concerns the Diablo Canyon project in California, a facility of the Pacific Gas and Electricity Company. A site decision was reached in the mid-1960s and indeed was approved by the Sierra Club (environmentalists) in 1967. Construction ran into technical difficulties, enforcing a five-year delay, the anti-nuclear movement mobilized in the 1970s, and further technical problems have prevented any nuclear power being generated commercially (1982). Earthquake precautions had to be increased to cover 7.5 on the Richter Scale, the wrong blueprint was used for earthquake supports, and the pipes were incorrectly installed. Perhaps not surprisingly the PG & E company has decided that all its future power plants will be fueled by coal, while the public is left wondering about the uncertain nuclear future.

5.6.7 Alternative energy sources

As Dr Johnson aptly put it, in a different context, in the case of alternative energy 'All argument is for it, all belief is against it.' Many technological possibilities exist for developing a wide range of alternative energy sources (Modeling Resources Gp. 1978), from solar and biomass, to geothermal, wind energy, and the harnessing of tides. In the early 1980s many of these projects have become even more uneconomic, falling into the 'pricing trap' of lower oil prices; others have always been of dubious economic validity. If alternative sources of energy are to be developed for the longer term, there is a case now for the Federal government to introduce 'balancing distortions' in pricing (Schurr *et al.* 1979, 528), to give such sources 'an equal chance with the *social* costs of imported oil' (Stobaugh and Yergin 1979, 54). With an irregular and widely disseminated alternative resource potential and no clear political constituency for public action, it is not surprising that many programs suffered severe cutbacks in the early 1980s.

Solary energy and biomass (forest, agricultural, and municipal waste) are available in most places. Wind and geothermal energy have a more localized potential, whilst tidal power, for effective harnessing, is even more local. The degree of localized occurrence increases the problem and costs of transmission of energy which for most types is intermittently available, seasonally variable, or in the case of most natural biomass dependent upon a seasonal or depletable resource.

Harnessing solar energy has the greatest potential, but it is difficult to take a balanced view (US ERDA 1977A; US Dept. Energy 1978; Yokell 1980). Enthusiasts, such as the International Sun Day Organization, see as much as 40 per cent of US energy coming from the sun within two decades. More restrained optimists (Stobaugh and Yergin 1979, 183) think 20 to 25 per cent might be possible, but only if given the right economic and political incentives. President Carter was firmly committed to solar energy harnessing, but with the virtual eclipse of Federal funding for solar energy research and the curtailment of tax credits in 1982, further progress is likely to be very slow. Federal research money had favored 'Big Solar' programs (Stobaugh and Yergin 1979, 202), including solar furnaces (power towers) for electric power stations, on the French model with batteries of mirror reflectors. Yet when President Carter said 'Solar energy works. We know it works. The only problem is to cut costs', he was referring rather to the widely disseminated domestic and commercial market, for solar panels and small-scale installations at home, in the office, and in industry. Though sales of solar equipment more than doubled in each year of the early 1980s, underpinned by Federal and State tax credits, there continue to be important economic and institutional barriers (Stobaugh and Yergin 1979, 191–3): the costs of borrowing are high and property taxes stand to be increased for solar installations; skilled labor, for installation and maintenance, is scarce; the legal position on right of access to the direct rays of the sun is uncertain; and electric utility companies continue to be hostile. Nevertheless, progress continues and SOLARCAL, a State solar energy council in California to 'maximize solar energy use in the State in the 1980s' (Burton 1980, 310), shows what public involvement can achieve in pursuit of 'collective energy goals'.

Biomass fuels have a long history in that wood was the dominant source of energy in the US until the mid-nineteenth century. Wood-burning stoves have certainly come back into fashion and in calorific value wood competes well against most western coals (Stobaugh and Yergin 1979, 199). Rather than depleting further the often remote 20 per cent of US forests suitable for commercial fuel, it is wood-waste and the bi-conversion of agricultural manures or municipal rubbish to methane gas that offers the best prospect for development, though usually on a very localized farm or community basis.

Geothermal energy lies either very deep underground or, in remote National Parks, in the forms of geyser pipes or mud-flows (Geothermal Res. Gp. 1979; US Dept. Energy 1980B). Highly localized, it is appropriate that local jurisdictions should have an important say in development, since the environmental, social, and economic impacts are felt at community level. The Geothermal Resource Impact and Planning group of Lake County, California (GRIPS) is an interesting example of such local cooperative endeavor (Daneke and Lagassa 1980, 120). Wind energy has certainly inspired Federal research support and demonstration (US ERDA 1977B). Tax credits are available for wind power installations and 2,200 were registered in 1981 compared with only 1,000 two years earlier. Coast, mountains, and Great Plains sites obviously have the greatest potential but transmission of an irregular, low output resource is neither economic nor practicable. In experimental form US Windpower has a 20-windmill farm at Crotched Mountain, New Hampshire, each windmill capable of generating 30 Kw in 25 mph winds; at Yakima, Washington State, three large Department of Energy wind towers drive turbines, each with 2.5 megawatts generating capacity.

Other alternative energy sources include: tidal power, directly harnessed by flow through turbines; ocean thermal energy conversion (OTEC) designed to suck energy from the sea and requiring gargantuan structures to do so; magneto-hydrodynamics (MHD), to generate electricity without the need for big turbo-generators, by blasting very hot gases between the poles of a magnet; and the use of photo-voltaic cells either for direct heating or electric power generation. These sources are likely to remain items of connoisseur interest to technocrats, at least for the remainder of this century.

5.7   IN CONCLUSION

Energy problems are complex, not well defined, and are very differently regarded by all the diverse actors and interests in the energy marketplace. That energy questions are central to the entire economic growth and urbanization processes is not in dispute. Further than that, decisions on energy policy will inevitably be the catalyst of changes in long-established economic, social, and political structures. For these reasons energy policy has been a highly sensitive political issue. The American political system, with its checks and balances, has traditionally sought to keep some kind of societal equilibrium among the many competing interests of people, jurisdictions, and place. The price of such an attempted accommodation has been the lack of clear, coherent, and effective energy policies and, though perhaps the most cardinal of all domestic policies, energy policy has lagged far behind in the general policy arena.

Granted that no ideal energy policy can be satisfactorily defined, in theory or in practice, all attempts in the direction of optimization have consistently failed. Though efficiency criteria have always ranked high, with market forces seen as the determinant, the constraints of environmental policy also have been influential in many decisions on energy during the 1970s. Unfortunately, priority for efficiency or environmental integrity has often been at the expense of equity or social justice, both for disadvantaged people and places unfairly treated. Widespread and deep-seated tensions characterize actors in the energy game, with a constant search for an elusive consensus on what kind of an energy future people want and are prepared to finance. Furthermore, how are the benefits, the costs and the risks of energy options to be allocated within society, and by whom? The role of governmental intervention, at any level or on almost any issue, remains controversial, though by any reasonable rationale it seems inescapable, if equity is to have a hearing.

The dramatic shifts in the world energy situation during the 1970s were strikingly felt in the US, consumer of one-third of global energy. Ever since, there has been a piecemeal and incremental approach to American energy problems, seeking to adjust to an uncertain, fluctuating situation. Emphasis in policy has been laid upon transition, but transition to what, and when and how? Solar energy and nuclear fusion represent a twenty-first century destination for some, a plurality of diverse energy sources a preferred long-term option for others. Special interest groups, many and politically influential, will press for, or bitterly oppose, particular solutions. Perhaps the most that can be said for energy policy prospects is that there will be governmental action of a deliberately limited kind, on a strict cost-benefit basis (though even this is politically controversial!). States and localities will play a more significant role and Federal funding will be less and more selective. Policy will operate on both the demand and supply sides of the energy equation. Conservation offers perhaps the most dramatic short-term and medium-term prospects, while on the supply side the options are complex and preferred courses of action likely to be matters of considerable dispute. Oil will continue to be imported, though in lesser volume, domestic oil and gas resources will be more intensively prospected and exploited, though the returns may be limited, and coal production will expand, though probably not to the heady annual target of 1.2 billion tons or more. The nuclear option will continue to be controversial, but will be pursued, and the Fast Breeder Reactor technology will continue to be favored officially, though it may flatter technically only to deceive commercially. Minor alternative energy resources will make variable contributions, but only slowly, unless there are further explosions in international oil prices. The consumer will continue to cherish the illusion that he can dominate the energy marketplace. Governments, acting in the public interest, will need to act as arbiter in a policy arena where corporate power has traditionally been strong, competition and fairness notoriously weak, and the public interest all too often a residual loser.

References

ADDINALL, E. and ELLINGTON, H. (1982) *Nuclear power in perspective* (London: Kogan Page).

AHMED, S. B. (1979) *Nuclear fuel and energy policy* (Lexington, Mass.: D. C. Heath).

ALLEN, E. L. (1979) *Energy and economic growth in the United States* (Cambridge, Mass.: MIT Press).

ANDERER, J., McDONALD, A. and NAKICENOVIC, N. (1981) *Energy in a finite world: paths to a sustainable future* (Cambridge, Mass.: Ballinger).

BATELLE MEMORIAL INST. (1978) *An analysis of Federal incentives used to stimulate energy production* (Springfield, Va.: Nat. Tech. Info. Service).

BOHI, D. R. and RUSSELL, M. (1978) *Limiting oil imports: an economic history and analysis* (Baltimore, Md.: Johns Hopkins Univ. Press).

BORIS, C. M. and KRUTILLA, J. V. (1980) *Water rights and energy development in the Northern Great Plains: an integrated analysis* (Baltimore, Md.: Johns Hopkins Univ. Press).

BRADSHAW, T. F. (1977) 'My case of national planning', *Fortune*, 95 Feb.

BREYER, S. G. and MACAVOY, P. W. (1974) *Energy regulation in the Federal Power Commission* (Washington, DC: Brookings Instn.).

BUPP, S. C. and DERIAN, J.-C. (1981) *The failed promise of nuclear power. The story of light water* (New York: Basic Books).

BURTON, D. J. (1980) *The governance of energy: problems, prospects and underlying issues* (New York: Praeger).

CICCHETTI, C. J. (1972) *Alaskan oil: alternative routes and markets* (Baltimore, Md.: Johns Hopkins Univ. Press).

CLEMENTS, D. W. (1977) 'Recent trends in the geography of coal', *Ann. Ass. Am. Geogr.* 67 1, 109–25.

COCKBURN, A. and RIDGEWAY, J. (1977) 'Carter's powerless energy policy', *New York Review of Books*, 24 May 26.

COMM. ON NUCLEAR AND ALTERNATIVE ENERGY SYSTEMS (1979) *Energy in transition 1985–2010* (Washington, DC: Nat. Acad. Sci.).

CONANT, M. A. (1982) *The oil factor in US foreign policy* (Lexington, Mass.: D. C. Heath).

CORTNER, H. J. (1980) 'Developing energy policy with the new sociopolitical realities', ch. 17 in DANEKE and LAGASSA (eds.) *Energy policy and public administration.*

CUFF, D. J. and YOUNG, W. J. (1980) *The United States energy atlas* (New York: Free Press).

DANEKE, G. A. and LAGASSA, G. K. (eds.) (1980) *Energy policy and public administration* (Lexington, Mass.: D. C. Heath).

DAVIS, J. F. (1981) 'Shifts in US coal production: trends and implications' *Geography* 66 304–9.

DEASY, G. F. and GRIESS, P. R. (1967) 'Energy demands, local and regional differences in long-term bituminous coal production prospects in the Eastern United States', *Ann. Ass. Am. Geogr.* 57 519–33.

DEESE, D. A. and NYE, J. S. (1981) *Energy and security* (Cambridge, Mass.: Ballinger).

DYE, T. R. (1981) 'Energy and the environment', ch. 8 in *Understanding public policy* (Englewood Cliffs, NJ: Prentice-Hall), 183–209.

GAULT, J. C. (1979) *Public Utility regulation of an exhaustible resource: the case of natural gas* (New York: Garland).

GEOTHERMAL RESOURCE GROUP (1979) *Geothermal sources and technology in the United States* (Washington, DC: Nat. Res. Co, Nat. Acad. Sci.).

GOODWIN, C. D. (ed.) (1981) *Energy policy in perspective: Today's problems, yesterday's solutions* (Washington, DC: Brookings Instn.).

GUINNESS, P. (1979) 'Nuclear power and the American energy crisis', *Geography* 64 2–16.

HALIBOUTY REPT. (1979). Briefing report to President Reagan by a group of US businessmen and oilmen.

HAMMOND, A. L., METZ, W. D., and MAUGH, T. H. (1973) *Energy and the future* (Washington, DC: Am. Ass. Adv. Sci.).

HUTCH, C. J. (ed.) (1978) 'Energy conservation and economic growth', *Am. Ass. Adv. Sci. Symposium*, 22 (Washington, DC: Am. Ass. Adv. Sci.).

HOLLOWAY, M. L. (1980) *Texas national energy modeling project* (New York: Academic Press).

HUGHES, W. R. (1979) 'National and regional energy models', *Growth and Change*, 10 1, 92–103.

INTER-AGENCY TASK FORCE (1974) *Project Independence, Blueprint*, Final Task Force Rept.

KANH, A. E. (1971) *The economics of regulation* (New York: Wiley).

KANH, M. H. and HAND, R. (1976) *Implications of ownership patterns of Western Coal reserves and their impact on coal development* (McLean, Va.: Mitre Corpn.).

KNOWLES, J. S. (1980) *America's energy famine: its causes and cure* (Norman, Okla.: Oklahoma Univ. Press).

LEBLANC, M. R., KALTER, R. J., and BIOSVERT, R. N. (1979) 'Allocation of US coal production to meet future needs', ch. 25 in ROWE, J. E. (ed.) *Coal surface mining: impacts of reclamation* (Boulder, Col.: Westview Press), 435–61.

LOVINS, A. B. (1976) 'Energy strategy: the path not taken', *For. Aff.* 55 1, 65–96.

—— (1977) *Soft energy paths towards a durable peace* (Harmondsworth, Midd.: Penguin).

MANSVELT BECK, F. W. and WIIG, K. M. (1977) *The economics of offshore oil and gas supplies* (Lexington, Mass.: D. C. Heath).

MEAD, W. J. (1977) 'An economic appraisal of Pres. Carter's Energy Program', unpublished paper.

MITCHELL, E. J. (1976A) *Energy: regional goals and the national interest* (Washington, DC.: Am. Enterprise Inst. for Pub. Pol. Res.).

—— (1976B) *The question of offshore oil* (Washington, DC: Am. Enterprise Inst. for Pub. Pol. Res.).

MODELING RESOURCE GROUP (1978) 'Energy modeling for an uncertain future: study of nuclear and alternative energy systems', *Supporting Pap.* 2 (Washington, DC: Nat. Acad. Sci.).

MOORE, T. G. (1980) 'Energy options', in DUIGNAN, P. and RABUSHKA, A. (eds.) *The United States in the 1980s* (Stanford: Hoover Instn.), 221–53.

OSLEB, J. and SHESKIN, I. M. (1977) 'Natural gas: a geographical perspective', *Geogr.*

Rev. **67** 1, 71–85.

PRAST, W. G. (1981) *Securing US energy supplies: the private sector as an instrument of public policy* (Lexington, Mass.: D. C. Heath).

PRESIDENT'S COMMISSION (1979) *The accident at Three Mile Island, Rept.* (Washington, DC: USGPO).

RAWL, L. G. (1978) 'US energy conservation', ch. 4 in ABRAHAMSON, B. J. (ed.) *Conservation and the changing direction of economic growth* (Boulder, Col.: Westview Press).

ROWE, J. E. (ed.) (1979) *Coal surface mining: impacts of reclamation* (Boulder, Col.: Westview Press).

SAWHILL, J. C. (ed.) (1978) *Energy conservation and public policy* (London: Prentice-Hall).

SCHURR, S. H., DARMSTADTER, J., PERRY, H., RAMSEY, W., and RUSSELL, M. (1979) *Energy in America's future: the choices before us* (Baltimore, Md.: Johns Hopkins Univ. Press).

SHRADER-FRECHETTE, K. S. (1980) *Nuclear power and public policy* (Dordrecht: Reidel).

SOLBERG, C. (1976) *Oil power: the rise and imminent fall of an American Empire* (New York: New Amer. Lib.).

STARR, J. T. (1981) 'American coal exports to Western Europe and Japan', *Geography* **66** 4, 309–11.

STOBAUGH, R. and YERGIN, D. (eds) (1979) *Energy future* (New York: Random House).

THOMPSON, W. F., KARAGANIS, J. J., and WILSON, K. P. (1981) *Choice over chance: economic and energy options for the future* (New York: Praeger).

US CONGRESS, HOUSE (1980) Comm. on Interstate and Foreign Commerce. *The energy factbook*, 96th Congr. 2nd Sess. (Washington, DC: USGPO).

US CONGRESS, JOINT ECONOMIC COMM. (1972) *Natural gas regulation and the Trans-Alaskan pipeline*, Hearings, 92nd Congr. 2nd Sess. (Washington, DC: USGPO).

US CONGRESS, SENATE (1972) Comm. on Interior and Insular Affairs, *Natural gas policy issues*, 92nd Congr, 2nd Sess. Pts I and II (Washington, DC: USGPO).

—— (1978) Comm. on Intergovtal. Affairs. *The coal industry: problems and prospects. A background study*, 95th Congr, 2nd Sess. (Washington, DC: USGPO).

US DEPT. ENERGY (1978) *Solar energy* (Washington, DC: USGPO).

—— (1980A) *Secretary's Annual Rept. to Congress*, DOE/S-0010(80) (Washington, DC: USGPO).

—— (1980B) *Geothermal energy as a source of electricity* (Washington, DC: USGPO).

US ENERGY RES. AND DEVEL. ADMIN. (1977A) *Solar energy in America's future* (Washington, DC: USGPO).

—— (1977B) *Federal wind energy program* (Washington, DC: USGPO).

US FED. ENERGY, ADMIN. (1976) *Economic impact of oil resource development on the Alaskan economy*, RB 251.660 (Washington, DC: USGPO).

US FED. TRADE COMMN. (1979) *The economic structure and behavior in the natural gas production industry*, Staff Rept. Bur. Econ. (Washington, DC: USGPO).

URANIUM INSTITUTE (1979) *The balance of supply and demand, 1978–1990* (London: Uranium Inst.).

WALLS, D. S. (1976) 'Central Appalachia: a peripheral region within an advanced capitalist society', *J. Sociol. and Social Welfare*, **4**.

WARD, M. P. (1982) 'Coal severance taxes. The effect of Western States' tax policy on the US coal market', *Rand Repts.* **2848** (Santa Monica, Cal.: Rand Corpn.).

WENDLING, R. M. and BALLARD, K. P. (1980) 'Projecting the regional impacts of energy development', *Growth and Change*, **11** 4, 7–17.

WILBANKS, T. J. (1978) 'Geographic research and energy policy making', *Geogrl. Survey*, 7 4, 11–18.
YOKELL, M. D. (1980) *Environmental benefits and costs of solar energy* (Lexington, Mass.: D. C. Heath).
ZIMMERMAN, M. B. (1981) *The United States coal industry: the economics of policy choice* (Cambridge, Mass.: MIT Press).

6. Government Policy and Industrial Location

JOHN REES* *(Syracuse University)* and BERNARD L. WEINSTEIN *(Lamar University)*
Lamar University

6.1 INTRODUCTION

During the last 20 years major changes have taken place in the structural and regional fabric of the American economy. These include major challenges to American dominance on the world industrial scene, higher growth rates in the service, compared to manufacturing, sectors, a large amount of population and capital mobility, manifested in the growth of Southern and Western States and in the relative stagnation of the traditional industrial heartland, and unprecedented growth rates in nonmetropolitan areas. More recently (in 1980) these economic changes were accompanied by a major structural change in American politics, which many heralded as the end of the liberalism symbolized by the Great Society programs of the 1960s. This basic change in the character of government policy at the Federal level will also involve, at least for the short term, a deconcentration process, a devolution of power to the State and local levels.

The size and complexity of these fundamental changes in both the political economy and the regional industrial structure of the US, changes that may be paralleled this century only by the impact of the 1930s Great Depression and World War II, make proper evaluation difficult. This is particularly so when one considers their recent vintage. To differentiate cause from effect in these changes and to ascertain the correct role of market forces and government policies as causal mechanisms in a *non ceteris paribus* milieu is the worst dilemma of policy analysis and evaluation. However, this also makes the task more important to undertake.

The impact of government policy on industrial location and regional economic development in different parts of the US has been given much attention by the media in recent years and there is always a tendency for such publicity to capture attention in the political arena. This can result in policy enactment without enough cautionary examination of political expediency or enough time for serious analytical research to explore the full short- and long-term implications of alternative policies. This is particularly so in a dynamic society like the US where the pendulum of change can swing freely from one extreme to another and where the time-honored consensus of 'least government as the best government' can result in reactive, as opposed to anticipatory, solutions to problems. Reactive policy-making can result in a form of disjointed incrementalism wherein policies are arrived at independently and incrementally without careful review of alternative options.

* Dr Rees wishes to acknowledge the partial support of NSF Grant Soc-77-28103 in the writing of this chapter, and the research assistance of Pamela Van Cleve.

Hence, there exists an essential role for geographers as policy analysts and evaluators of the interaction between economic structure, the policy-making process, and the country's regional fabric.

The first part of this chapter (6.2) examines the changes that have taken place in US industrial structure. The second part (6.3) discusses and evaluates the impact of government policies on the industrial geography of the US in recent times; while part three (6.4) discusses some imminent policy changes that may have profound effects on US industrial geography in the future.

6.2 STRUCTURAL AND LOCATIONAL CHANGES

After World War II the US witnessed important changes in its economic structure. The tertiary sectors serving consumers, businesses, and government have been growing at faster rates than the manufacturing sector, at least in employment, if not in productivity terms. Rapid technological changes have also taken place in the service economy as well as in manufacturing. At the same time changes occurred in the location of economic growth and it has been argued (Rees 1979A; Norton and Rees 1979) that these locational changes are linked to structural change.

6.2.1 Structural changes

a. *The relative growth of manufacturing versus services.* The first major change of a structural nature involves the growth of manufacturing activities compared with nonmanufacturing activities. The relatively faster growth of the service economy (banking, insurance, communications) as shown for employment data in Table 6.1 has led some to conclude that we are now living in a post-industrial society where information-intensive and other service activities generate more growth than manufacturing does.

A study by Moriarty (1976) examined whether metropolitan area growth in the US during the period 1959–70 was primarily a function of growth in the manufacturing or the service sector. The study (p. 209) concluded that

both population and total overall employment growth have been more dependent on the growth of the service sector and the growth of the service sector has not been

TABLE 6.1 *Manufacturing as a proportion of total US employment 1947–1977*

Year	Manufacturing employment (millions)	Total nonagricultural employment (millions)	Manufacturing as percentage of total employment
1947	14.294	43.881	32.6
1954	16.099	49.022	32.8
1958	16.025	51.363	31.2
1963	16.958	56.702	29.9
1967	19.323	65.857	29.3
1972	19.029	73.714	25.8
1977	19.590	82.423	23.7

Source: Census of Manufactures; Bureau of Labor Statistics.

totally dependent on the growth of the manufacturing sector alone. . . . The investigation fails to provide sufficient evidence to verify the proposition that the country's metropolitan area growth during the period is primarily a result of the growth in demand for manufactured goods produced in cities.

Similarly Brian Berry (1973) suggested that the rapid growth of the South, Southeast, and West was led by the tertiary and quaternary sectors. In the same vein Miernyk (1976) tested the Clark–Fisher hypothesis which suggests increases in per capita income as a regional economy advances from specialization in the primary or extractive sector through the secondary or manufacturing sector to the tertiary or service sector. For 15 Southern States, between 1940 and 1975, Miernyk found that 'per capita income decreases as dependence on manufacturing increases and per capita income increases as relative dependence on trade and service employment increases.'

To equate the results of such studies with the demise of the manufacturing sector, however, is dangerous, since analyses of employment data alone ignore the impact of technological change, i.e. the substitution of capital for labor and its translation into productivity differentials. Indeed Miernyk (1976, 33) pointed out that 'tertiary activities benefit less from technological change than primary and secondary activities. And it is technological change broadly defined which produces rising real incomes.' The implications of this statement are reminiscent of the early work of the French economist Jean Fourastié, who postulated that a shift in the labor force from the secondary to the tertiary, when it is not the result of technological change, is evidence of economic weakness rather than of strength, or what he called the 'tertiary crisis'.

It may not be mere coincidence therefore that American productivity, which grew fairly rapidly during most of the post-war era, took a puzzling drop in the late 1960s (Denison 1978). In his explanation of why national income per person employed (NIPPE) dropped in the early 1970s, Denison concludes that governmental controls have required 'the diversion of a growing share of the labor and capital employed by business to pollution abatement and to the protection of employee safety and health'. Given the decline of R & D spending as a proportion of GNP in the early 1970s Denison (p. 48) suggested that 'managerial talent ordinarily devoted to developing means of cutting costs may have been absorbed by the need to adapt to a flood of new controls over the conduct of business.' He adds that government regulation could have delayed implementation of decisions that could advance productivity, but does not attribute any of the productivity slump to the relative economic shift to the service sector. This may be due to reasons overlooked in growth studies that merely dwell on employment as the prime variable. One is that growth of service employment may be a direct result of greater productivity in manufacturing which has made available an increased supply of goods at a relatively low price. The other is a factor borrowed from investment theory, the accelerator principle, which emphasizes the importance of an increase in demand for innovation from the service sector (telecommunications, banking, information processing) which in turn results in increased investment and productivity in the manufacturing sector. Despite the relative growth of the service economy in recent times and the relative decline in productivity in the American economy, there is no proof that both processes are causally connected.

b. *Changes within manufacturing industry.* Since 1945 major technological changes have taken place within manufacturing industry, giving rise to a series of growth industries that did not contribute to the economic growth of the US in prior technological epochs. These growth sectors in manufacturing include electronics (SIC 36), computing machinery (SIC 357), chemicals and plastics (SIC 28 and 30), aerospace production (SIC 372), and scientific instruments (SIC 38). The leading growth industry in terms of employment between 1950 and 1970 was electronics, which was also categorized as the leading producer of American innovations in recent years (National Science Board 1977). In many respects electronics has become the leading growth sector of the American economy in the middle part of this century in the same way that the machine tools industry formed the key sector of the industrial boom period at the end of the nineteenth century.

The largest growth sectors in American manufacturing have been both technology-intensive and R & D intensive. Industries with the greatest number of innovations per net sales and higher Research and Development (R & D) expenditures per net sales have strong statistical associations with growth in both added value and employment (Rees 1979A). Though these growth industries in manufacturing have been the most innovative, this does not imply that larger companies within these sectors are more efficient producers of innovations than smaller companies. The National Science Board (1977), Mansfield (1977), and others have shown that large companies are not necessarily the more efficient producers of innovations in proportion to R & D dollars spent.

Any empirical research on the relationship betwen technological innovation, industrial change, and regional economic growth is at best a complex task, which probably explains why spatial differentials in innovation potential and the interregional diffusion of industrial innovation have remained among the *terrae incognitae* of industrial geography for so long (Thomas and LeHeron 1975; Malecki 1979; Rees *et al.* 1981). The definition of technology itself and its natural trajectories can be complex, partly because of the incrementalism implicit in the definition of innovations. One example of this dilemma pertains to the discussion of the changing structure of American industry. Given the previous argument that electronics is the 'industrie motrice' of the American economy in the latter part of this century, one of the major spin-offs of that industry is computer software. The rates of growth in manufacturing versus services in the future may depend on precisely how that industry is defined. Will software be defined as a form of 'high service' within the tertiary sector, or will it (more like the printing industry) be classified as a manufactured product? Such definitional issues may appear mundane; yet their results will have a major bearing on how industrial change manifests itself spatially. Largely because of the complex nature of the American economy in general, discussion of industrial location trends and how these are affected by government policy will be explicitly limited to the manufacturing sector.

6.2.2 Locational changes

The structural changes in the American economy have taken place at a time when major changes also occurred in the location of economic activity. It has been shown that States losing manufacturing jobs over the period 1966–77 also had below-average growth in service employment, while States gaining in manufacturing employment also gained in service employment (Norton and Rees 1979). As suggested by traditional regional development theory, therefore, a State's economic health still depends to a large degree on the competitiveness of the manufacturing sector.

Two interrelated locational changes can be identified in US industrial geography in the last 20 years. One involves the much-publicized Snowbelt–Sunbelt inter-regional shift (see ch. 2.2.1). The other process involves the decentralization of urban America and the revival of non-metropolitan (rural) areas (see chs. 3.2.2a and 7.2.2).

a. *Interregional changes in manufacturing.* The most striking change in the location of US economic activity in recent times has been the growth of States in the South and West and the relative stagnation of States in the northern and eastern parts of the country, the popularized Snowbelt–Sunbelt shift (see ch. 2.2.1). This can be interpreted as the decentralization of economic activity from the core region of the country to the periphery. It can also be viewed as a catching up or regional convergence process on the lines suggested by Jusenius and Ledebur (1976) and the Advisory Commission on Intergovernmental Relations (1978). The traditional manufacturing heartland (defined here as the New England, Mid-Atlantic, and East North Central divisions of the Bureau of Census) has been losing ground to the more peripheral areas of the nation. This resulted initially in the growth of California in the post-war era and more recently in the growth of certain key States of the southeast and southwestern regions.

Table 6.2 shows changes in manufacturing employment by census region for the period 1947–77. The first Economic Census after World War II was taken in 1947 and the most recent in 1977. Over the period 1947–63 the three census regions of the Manufacturing Belt gained over 230,000 manufacturing jobs with the six New England States showing the only absolute decline in employment. During the same time period the other peripheral census regions gained 2.4 million manufacturing jobs with the largest gains occurring in the Pacific region, specifically California. In the period 1963–77 the Manufacturing Belt gained only 1,000 manufacturing jobs while some of the States of the East North Central region made up for the large losses of the Mid-Atlantic States. The peripheral regions continued to show increases in manufacturing employment over this 13-year period, this time of 2.6 million. Thus the period from the mid-1960s to the mid-1970s can be seen as the era when the Manufacturing Belt as a whole just about held its own in absolute employment terms.

The genesis of decline in the Manufacturing belt is seen clearly when manufacturing employment data are disaggregated into production and non-production workers (Table 6.2). It is the people directly involved in production as opposed to administration, wholesaling, and other support activities that form the core of the manufacturing process. Despite the absolute in-

TABLE 6.2 *Changes in manufacturing employment types by region 1947–1977*

REGION	1947–1963			1963–1977		
	Change in total employment	Change in production workers	Change in nonproduction workers	Change in total employment	Change in production workers	Change in nonproduction workers
New England	- 50.2	- 205.7	155.5	- 34.9	- 100.3	65.4
Mid Atlantic	121.3	- 399.1	520.4	- 457.7	- 467.8	10.1
East North Central	160.9	- 333.8	494.7	493.8	242.6	251.2
Manufacturing Belt	232.0	- 938.6	1,170.6	1.2	- 325.5	326.7
West North Central	228.3	78.9	149.4	283.0	176.7	106.3
South Atlantic	600.9	320.3	280.6	697.9	465.7	232.2
East South Central	252.3	153.8	98.5	440.6	322.0	128.6
West South Central	313.8	169.3	144.4	578.1	391.0	187.1
Mountain	143.2	80.6	62.6	177.5	115.9	61.6
Pacific	884.4	444.8	439.6	457.2	314.4	142.8
Periphery	2,422.9	1,247.7	1,175.2	2,634.3	1,785.7	858.6

Source: Census of Manufactures.

crease in manufacturing employment in the Manufacturing Belt between 1947 and 1963 the number of production workers declined by nearly 1 million while the periphery gained 1.2 million. Similarly, the small absolute gain of 1,200 manufacturing jobs in the Manufacturing Belt disguises a large loss of production workers (325,500), while the peripheral region again gained more than 1.7 million such workers.

Two inferences can be made from Table 6.2. One is that the decentralization of key production workers from the Manufacturing Belt to other areas of the US has been going on for at least 30 years: it is *not a new process* of the 1960s and 1970s. Traces of the shift can be traced back to the movement of the textile industry from New England to the ·Carolinas, a shift that has continuously been fueled by the search for cheaper factors of production (Danhof 1964). The reason why the process is of more concern today is not only due to the fact that the Manufacturing Belt witnessed absolute decline in manufacturing employment in the late 1960s and early 1970s. The macroeconomic context of the decline is important. *Since the overall growth rate in the national economic system is lower, the regional allocation within the system becomes even more important.* In a demographic context Alonso (1978, 73) succinctly sums up the process: 'As far back as the beginning of the century the Sunbelt centers such as Phoenix, Houston, San Diego, and Miami were already strong gainers from migration; but as long as natural increase remained high every area was growing and sectionalist jealousies were small.'

A second inference from Table 6.2 is the increasing importance of nonproduction workers within the manufacturing labor force. Production workers accounted for 83 per cent of the manufacturing labor force in 1947, 72 per cent in 1963, and 68 per cent in 1977. The Manufacturing Belt lost nearly 1 million production workers between 1947 and 1963 but gained over 1 million nonproduction workers in manufacturing, roughly the same gain as witnessed in the peripheral region. The Manufacturing Belt still gained in nonproduction workers between 1963 and 1977 but only by 25 per cent of the gain in the periphery. If greater amounts of administrative or nonproduction workers in the region can be equated with a greater degree of control over manufacturing activity, then Table 6.2 shows that the Manufacturing Belt has lost less control over manufacturing than it has lost in actual production. In a study of manufacturing headquarters in the US (Rees 1978A), Census Enterprise Statistics were used to make the argument that in the late 1960s and early 1970s the Manufacturing Belt indeed increased its *de jure* control of manufacturing activity in other parts of the US. This concurs with the study of Dicken (1976) using Federal Trade Commission data on mergers and acquisitions between 1955 and 1968 and is testimony to earlier statements made by Senator Kefauver in 1947. 'The control of American business is steadily being transferred from local communities to a few large cities in which central managers decide the policies and the fate of the far-flung enterprises they control'. Though the trend towards what has become known as 'external control' is not a central issue in this study, it is a process implicit in recent US regional industrial changes.

It has been proposed elsewhere (Rees 1979A, B) that many of the changes inferred from Table 6.2 can be explained by the product cycle model borrowed from international trade theory. The product cycle model has a geographical dimension once it is recognized that the innovation and standardized production stages have different locational requirements. The innovation stage of product development needs a high input of R & D (a high-cost item) and is usually carried out in large urban areas. The standardization phase on the other hand favors low-cost locations (usually peripheral) where labor costs in particular are less. This part of the product cycle explains the early loss of production workers from the Manufacturing Belt in Table 6.2. The essence of this theory of industrial deconcentration is summed up as follows:

The spatial manifestation of the product cycle implies that over time regions can change their roles *from being the recipients of innovations* (via branch plants) *to being the generators of innovation* (via indigenous growth). As the decentralization of production accumulates in the standardization phase of the product cycle, external economies . . . can build up and regional demand can grow to a critical threshold where an industrial seedbed effect can take place. (Rees 1979B, 58–9)

Traditionally, the Manufacturing Belt has served as the seedbed of growth of the American manufacturing system (Perloff and Wingo 1961). Recently, however (Norton and Rees 1979) the diffusion of technology to the more peripheral areas of the US has led to the innovation potential of the Manufacturing Belt being eroded and that of the periphery being enhanced.

So far, trends have been discussed only in macroregional terms in the form of a core–periphery model. It is important to bear in mind, however, when documenting the growth of manufacturing in the 'periphery' in recent times, that this in reality only reflects the growth of a *few key States*, notably Texas, California, North and South Carolina, Tennessee, Florida, Georgia, and Michigan. Figure 6.1a shows the absolute change in manufacturing employment by State between 1963 and 1977. While the core–periphery shift stands out in the form of absolute decline in six States on the *eastern* side of the industrial heartland (most notably New York, Pennsylvania, and Massachusetts), a great deal of interstate variations is revealed. Such variations would suggest that the notion of Snowbelt versus Sunbelt is too simplistic a regionalization procedure, as suggested by Browning and Gessler (1979). Indeed, Figure 6.1a itself hides great variations in industrial structure within each State which makes any regionalization procedure difficult. Six of the eight States recording gains of over 100,000 manufacturing jobs each are located in the southern census region (namely Texas, North Carolina, South Carolina, Tennessee, Florida, and Georgia; the exceptions being California and Michigan). Texas and California experienced the largest absolute gains between 1963 and 1977, with over 300,000 new manufacturing jobs each, while New York was the only State to experience losses over 300,000. During that same period, a number of key industrial States at the western end of the Manufacturing Belt (especially Michigan, Ohio, Indiana, and Minnesota) witnessed healthy increases in manufacturing employment, as did some of the less developed States in the union, namely, Alabama, Arkansas, and Mississippi. Because of the current image of Michigan as an automobile-dominated

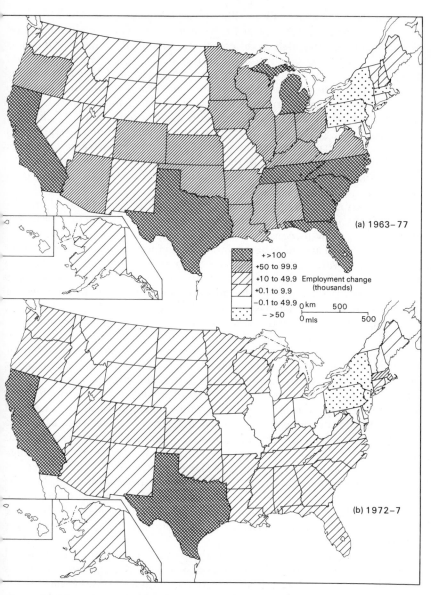

+ >100
+50 to 99.9
+10 to 49.9   Employment change
+0.1 to 9.9   (thousands)
−0.1 to 49.9
 − >50

(a) 1963–77

(b) 1972–7

6.1   Absolute change in manufacturing employment: (a) 1963–77;
       (b) 1972–7

State in permanent recession, one tends to ignore the vast increases in manufacturing employment there during the 1960s and even the early 1970s.

   On examining absolute change in manufacturing employment over a more
recent time period, 1972–7, however (Fig. 6.1b), one finds that absolute
employment decline in manufacturing has spread *westwards* in the Manu-

facturing Belt to include Ohio, Illinois, and Missouri, but not Michigan. Clearly this introduces the notion of changes in employment in different parts of the Manufacturing Belt at different times due to the impact of business cycles. The capital-goods-producing sectors of the Mid-Atlantic States tend to feel the impact of recessions more than other States (ACIR 1978) and this period included the deepest recession since the Great Depression. Patterns in the rest of the country, apart from the revival in Massachusetts and Connecticut, are reminiscent of the changes in Figure 6.1. The dominance of California and Texas as the key growth centers outside the Manufacturing Belt is striking, as is the absolute decline in New York and Pennsylvania. As Figure 6.2a shows, however, all four of these States are still among the seven largest manufacturing States in the country when measured by value added in production.

Clearly any generalizations at the State level hide large potential differences in industrial structure, changes in wage inflation, as well as in the role of key metropolitan growth centers within each State. Without delving into intrastate variations in any more detail, interstate changes in payroll in proportion to changes in value added, show a State-by-State pattern quite repetitive across the country for the period 1963–77 (Fig. 6.2b). The greatest decrease in payroll as a percentage of value added occurred generally in States with a small absolute industrial base in 1963, namely New Mexico, Arkansas, Wyoming, Mississippi, and Louisiana. West Virginia and Delaware are the only two States to show payroll increasing as a percentage of value added. There is a greater State variation in payroll as a proportion of value added for 1977 alone, from a low of 28 per cent in Louisiana to a high of 71 per cent for Delaware. For 45 of the conterminous States, the large increases in wage inflation as well as increases in the number of employees in the growth States are countered by even larger gains in value added, the result of increased capital expenditures in capital-intensive industries in some States as well as increases in productivity measured by value added per employee. Suffice to say that the relationships between changes in industrial structure, wage inflation, and productivity increases have not been given enough serious attention to date, particularly at the metropolitan area level where they can be addressed most appropriately. One can only assume that such endeavors are on the agenda of industrial geographers for the 1980s, particularly as the productivity dilemma of American industry looms large on its agenda for economic recovery.

It is still a moot point, however, whether 1972–7 trends are cyclical instead of structural, since the capital goods sector of the Manufacturing Belt was seriously hit by the Great Recession of 1975, and 'the economies of the Northeast and the Midwest have been robust only when national growth rates have been high' (ACIR 1978, 30). It is quite feasible that the severity of the Great Recession may prove to be the turning-point for the Manufacturing Belt, and a benchmark for continuing slow national growth. As stated in a recent regional growth study by the Advisory Commission of Inter-Governmental Relations (1978, 38) 'continued slow national economic growth could result in the Northeast and Midwest dropping below other regions in relative economic well-being.'

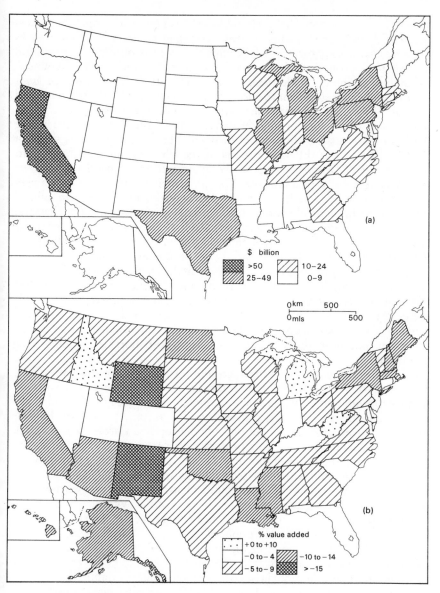

6.2a   Absolute value added by manufacture, 1977
6.2b   Change in payroll as percentage of value added, 1963–77

This product cycle interpretation of regional economic changes under way in the US implies not only that lagging peripheral regions are catching up with the core, but also that regions go through long cycles of growth and decline, with the first regions to decline being those that were first to industrialize.

This notion of a regional life cycle has its antecedents in Schumpeter's process of creative destruction wherein new economic structures in new regions bypass existing structures which become functionally obsolete. The position of any region on this regional S-shaped curve is the result of counterbalancing, seemingly dialectical, forces characterized by the push of *innovation* or new development to ensure future adaptation on the one hand and the pull of *inertia* protecting the status quo on the other. While Norton and Rees (1979) have documented the continued erosion of the Manufacturing Belt's function as a technological seedbed, Malecki's (1979, 32) study of R & D activities in different regions of the US over time concludes that: 'Industrial R & D appears to be evolving away from a dependence on some large city regions, especially New York; it remains at the same time a very markedly large city activity . . . The deconcentration of R & D from some of the major technological regions is difficult to extrapolate into more general trends. Many of the faster-growing areas of R & D activity are located in the Northeast despite signs of economic decline in other regional indicators.' Recently it has become popular once again for economists to think in terms of long cycles: 'It should be of little surprise that the long-term swings in relative economic fortune have been newly rediscovered as the nation's aging industrial regions increasingly appear to be entering the negative phase of such cycles' (Sternlieb and Hughes 1978). The question remaining to be answered is whether the regional economic changes will continue, whether they indeed represent long-term shifts in regional roles or just short-term equilibrating tendencies.

b. *Nonmetropolitan industrial growth.* Another major decentralizing process involving manufacturers in the US concerns the recent growth of nonmetropolitan areas (see also chs. 2, pp. 41–3; 3, pp. 99–103; and 7, pp. 269–70). In many ways this can be regarded as an extension of the suburbanization process into small and nonmetropolitan areas close to large urbanized growth centers. This process began to receive attention in the mid-1970s and to date a number of studies have discussed the process (Beale 1976; McCarthy and Morrison 1978; Briggs and Rees 1982; Lonsdale and Seyler 1979). Perhaps Irving Kristol summed up the process best when he said that we were tending toward 'an urban civilization without cities' where nonmetropolitan areas have the technological capability of being functionally and culturally metropolitan.

Beale, who has made one of the more comprehensive analyses of nonmetropolitan growth since 1970, has shown (1976, 954), however, that 'both adjacent and non-adjacent classes of non-metropolitan counties have had a migration reversal. The force of the reversal has actually been stronger in the more remote non-adjacent class than it has in the adjacent group'.

Beale shows that nonmetropolitan counties with the most rapid growth are retirement counties, though many of these counties have other sources of growth: state colleges, recreation businesses, and manufacturing. He sees the decentralization of manufacturing as one of the major economic thrusts behind nonmetropolitan growth in the 1960s. 'Manufacturing comprised 50 per cent of all growth in non-metropolitan employment in the 1960's. The subsequent slackening of manufacturing and the surge in trade and services in other sectors except government has seen manufacturing jobs amount only to 3 per cent of non-metropolitan job growth from 1970 to 1976' (p. 955). McCarthy and Morrison (1978) generally concur with this. 'Previous growth advantages associated with manufacturing and government related activity appeared to have diminished in the 1970's and retirement and recreation have emerged as important growth-inducing activities in the non-metropolitan sector' (p. 46).

Though the role of manufacturing activity as the economic thrust behind the growth of nonmetropolitan areas may have declined in the early 1970s compared to the 1960s, the period 1970–5 was an unusual one cyclically. Moreover, the factors explaining the decentralization of manufacturing activity at the metropolitan and nonmetropolitan scale are similar to those that explain the decentralization of manufacturing at the interregional scale: the use of underemployed female labor, lower wage rates, better work attitudes, less unionization, availability of cheap land, and improved transportation. Erickson and Leinbach (1978) proposed that the filtering down of industry from metropolitan to nonmetropolitan areas can be explained by the product cycle model, as in the interregional scale interpretation. In testing their filtering-down hypothesis in nonmetropolitan areas of Kentucky, New Mexico, Vermont, and Wisconsin they show that a vast majority of the filtering-down branch plants have corporate headquarters located within the Manufacturing Belt. This may be expected for Kentucky, Vermont, and Wisconsin, given their geographical proximity to the larger cities of the Manufacturing Belt. In New Mexico, as may be expected, companies with headquarters in California and Texas play a greater role in nonmetropolitan industrial development. Yet the Manufacturing Belt still houses the headquarters of 59 per cent of nonmetropolitan plants in New Mexico.

Given that US nonmetropolitan counties have shown a remarkable degree of economic growth and diversity in the 1970s, there remains a need to isolate the realities from the myths of these ongoing processes. Elsewhere, Briggs and Rees (1982) examine three control mechanisms behind these changes and conclude that the interstate highway system was *not* a determining factor in nonmetro growth since 1950. Despite the large growth seen in nonmetropolitan manufacturing, and particularly in wholesaling, in the 1970s, this growth process was not clearly associated with the development of the interstate system, though alternative views are held (see chs. 3, p. 117, and 7, pp. 287–8). A multiple regression analysis showed that the traditional determinants of nonmetropolitan development (economic and social base factors, degrees of urbanization) decreased in importance over time, while the role of government and amenity factors increased in the 1970s, confirming the structural change seen in the economies of rural communities in recent times. In these analyses, however, the presence of open freeways explain a smaller percentage of variation in net migration in nonmetropolitan areas than any other factor considered.

Because branch plants are the dominant type of manufacturing establishment in rural areas, the argument has been made that their nonlocal ownership pattern has led to employment instability in nonmetro areas and a general detrimental impact on local economies. This argument gains little support from detailed empirical work undertaken in Wisconsin and Texas (Briggs and Rees 1982). Indeed, branch plants seemed to contribute to the employment stability of nonmetro areas in the 1970s. Also, the fact that branch plants may be more innovative than anticipated in terms of their production processes implies that they can act as seedbeds for innovation and indigenous growth in rural areas.

Though rates of employment growth were greater than population growth rates in most nonmetro counties and though greater potential for per capita income increases occurred in counties where employment growth exceeded population growth by the largest margins, the relative importance of *unearned income* has increased significantly in nonmetro areas in the 1970s. Nonadjacent nonmetropolitan counties were seen to be more dependent on unearned income than were adjacent counties, and as the size of the largest place in nonmetro counties diminished, the proportion of unearned income increased with a high degree of empirical regularity. While investment income in the form of dividends, interest, and rent accounted for 16 per cent of personal income in nonmetropolitan areas in 1977, transfer payments accounted for 17 per cent of the total and had grown at faster rates since 1969. In only 14 States (three in New England, but most in the Great Plains) did nonmetro counties show larger proportions of investment income compared to transfer payments in 1977. Since annualized growth rates in transfer payments in nonmetropolitan areas exceeded those for unearned income as a whole, which in turn exceeded the growth rates for total personal income in the 1970s, this trend was seen to facilitate the spread of people into the more remote rural areas in the 1970s.

To summarize: two types of industrial decentralization processes have occurred in the US in recent times—an interregional movement that is changing the economic health of the older and newer parts of the country, and a nonmetropolitan movement. Much has been written about these processes of late and it is important to sort out the objective reality from the myths that surround them. Because they are similar processes occurring at different geographical scales, many of the causal mechanisms are common to both, as they are to international decentralization trends. Here it has been shown that market mechanisms working through structural changes brought about by new technology have played significant roles in these industrial decentralization processes. In the same way that market mechanisms can affect these processes, so can different forms of public policy have an impact on the spatial decentralization of industry.

6.3 THE IMPACT OF GOVERNMENT POLICY ON US REGIONAL INDUSTRIAL CHANGE

Major structural changes in American industry since 1960 were earlier seen to be linked to decentralization tendencies at two different geographical scales. Concern for the interregional changes shown first by the media, and then in political circles, stems from the belief that the Federal government has been the major causal element in the process of regional growth and decline. Clearly, when one region gains and another loses, political capital can be made. But much of what has been written may be the result of what some have called 'Newton's Third Law of Journalism', where every overreaction leads to an equal and opposite overreaction (Franko 1978). It is quite easy to be so close to an issue that the proper perspective is lost. This is true not only of the role of government in industrial change, but also of Federal regulation and intervention in general.

Dangers implicit in the debate on the pros and cons of government regulation in the US in the 1970s are well summarized by Okun (1978; see also ch. 1.4.1). In establishing a 'capitalistic democracy' the US has to encounter the uneasy compromises provided by the capitalist ethic with its emphasis on economic efficiency through market mechanisms, on the one hand, and the democratic ideal with its egalitarian aspirations on the other. The search for liberty and equality has resulted in irreconcilable polarities in many societies. Okun sees the blanket indictment of all government regulation and intervention as a polarization that threatens the unique balance of the American system.

Many of the government's functions in promoting and regulating activity in the market place are not controversial; indeed some are conducted so routinely that they tend to be taken for granted . . . The worst enemies of US capitalism are a handful of its ardent proponents, who prescribe fiscal monetary policies that would produce mass unemployment, regulatory policies that would violate the legitimate interests of third parties and reforms of government programs that would provide vivid pictures of economic misery. (Okun 1978, 26.)

This debate on the appropriate role of government regulation is not a new one (see Koch 1974; Bain 1968; Rees 1980). It has a history as long as the American heritage itself, and so there is more reason why perspective can be lent to the issue. Neither is the issue of regional industrial change new to the American arena. Indeed it is the dynamism of the movements from the Old World to the New, the westward expansion, the movement from the South to the North, first of blacks then of whites, that created the American character. Of course, market mechanisms played their role; so did government through, for example, the railroad system in the nineteenth century and the interstate system in the mid-twentieth century. Every government action, every company decision has a regional or geographical impact. Decisions affect people, and people live in a variety of different places. Cameron (1968) interpreted regional development in the US as the clash of two forces: national demand on the one hand and planned adjustments on the other. The crucial issue then becomes how *explicit* or *implicit* government policies are in their regional impact or, indeed, how aware are policy-makers of any direct or indirect regional biases when they design policies. This leads to the importance of 'ex ante' and not 'ex post' policy analysis and this in turn involves problems of classification and measurement made inherently more complex by the perpetual dynamism of regional economies and the existence of *non ceteris paribus* situations (Glickman 1980).

This section initially looks at government intervention in American regional economic development in its historical perspective. Even before the

1970s the battle for Federal funds had surfaced in the US; in many ways the debate is merely new wine in old bottles. A series of policies (mostly at the Federal level) are assessed in the way they potentially have a direct impact on industrial location and regional economic change: taxation policies, economic development assistance, Department of Defense procurement patterns, and policies of the Environmental Protection Agency. The indirect impacts of government policies are also discussed.

6.3.1   The 'conspiracy theory' revisited

In 'Four Decades of Thought on the South's Economic Problem' Danhof (1964) reminded us of the recurring nature of the economic battles between the North and the South, and the recurring concern about the Federal role. In one of various southern strategies to gain further industrialization, the South-eastern Governors' Conference, formed in 1937, formally urged the Federal administration to decentralize the award of defense and war contracts. Though the South has come a long way since June 1938 when Franklin Roosevelt declared the region the nation's 'number one economic problem', the 'conspiracy theory' of North against South raised its head throughout the first part of the twentieth century. 'Sectional conflict, which some held to be inevitable, resulted in a conspiracy, deliberate or fortuitous, on the part of the North, the large national corporations, or some financial groups, with the help of the federal government to thwart the South' (Danhof 1964, 36). Implicit in the economic history of the South, however, has been a recognition that if the Northern States controlled the economic allocation of resources, one way to counter this was through the political process, particularly the seniority system in Congress, the Sam Rayburns and the Lyndon Johnsons, and the political allocation of resources.

By the 1970s the conspiracy theory was being interpreted in reverse, with the North accusing the South of obtaining preferential treatment from the Federal government to fuel its economic growth. (For a general regional interpretation see ch. 2.2.1; for urban implications see ch. 7.2.5.) The 'Second War between the States' of the mid-1970s led to many hurried accusations. *Business Week* (17 May 1976) was the first to report. '*Although detailed data are unavailable*, capital from the Northeast and Mid-West has financed the industrial expansion of the South.' The *National Journal* (26 June 1976) then followed: 'Spending for defense accounts for nearly all the federal spending disparities among the Northeast, Mid-West, South and West. The federal government spent $620 per capita for defense in the West, nearly triple the $210 rate of defense spending in the Mid-West.' This was written without regard for subcontracting data and thus made the erroneous assumption that States in which prime contracts were allocated were also the locations where the products were made and the jobs created. Peterson and Muller (1977) made similar statements, though as a result of more careful study:

Federal spending for purchases of goods and services is more strongly skewed toward the rapidly growing regions of the country than are total federal outlays. On a per capita basis, the Pacific states receive more than twice as much federal revenues as the Great Lakes States and 80 per cent more than the Mid-Atlantic States. *Although a detailed examination of federal spending would be necessary to establish the point conclusively,* data strongly suggest that federal employment, goods and service acquisitions, and direct capital investment have been shaped by the same cost and profitability considerations that have influenced private sector demand for regional output.

Yet without 'a detailed examination of federal spending' the reliability of such claims has to be questioned.

Some consensus now seems to have been reached on these interregional changes and on the Federal role. Jusenius and Ledebur (1976) provide us with a more objective perspective. Among their findings were:

  i. Even if no migration had occurred (between North and South), the population would still have increased more rapidly in the Sunbelt South.
 ii. Even with greater Federal expenditures in the South, per capita incomes in the Sunbelt-South are generally lower than those in the Northern tier.
iii. In contrast to more popular beliefs, the problem of poverty is more pervasive in the South than in the North.
 iv. While the Southern States are among the poorest in the country, they received less than the national average in per capita Federal government expenditures.
  v. The Northern Tier States confront serious economic difficulties, but policy decisions based on the assumption that the experience of 1970–5 represents a new trend may be ill-considered and counterproductive in the long run.
 vi. Debates which focus on the rate of growth of the Sunbelt as a partial explanation of the economic difficulties of the Northern States are detrimental to the goal of achieving national policies that facilitate overall growth among all regions in the US. This conclusion is also shared by Weinstein and Firestine (1978).

In yet another study of regional change in the US (ACIR 1978) similar conclusions, and some additional ones, were reached. The more important findings were:

  i. Over the last 50 years economic activity and population movements have resulted in growing equalization of well-being among eight regions of the country. Indeed it is an expected postulate of neoclassical regional economics that factor mobility will lead to a convergence in regional incomes over time. This convergence in regional welfare has been accompanied by substantial decentralization of economic activity away from the regions of earliest industrialization.
 ii. The regional shifts in economic activity have taken place without substantial disparities in regional unemployment rates. This concurs with another study by Wheaton (1978) which saw very little relationship between growth rates in manufacturing employment in SMSAs and their unemployment rate.
iii. The greatest rates of regional convergence (in per capita incomes) were realized between 1930 and 1950, and since then the rates have slowed. Indeed in the early 1970s variations in regional growth rates have widened and rates of convergence accelerated.

iv. For the last 25 years, the economies of Northeast and Midwest have been strong only when national growth rates have been high. Other regions continue to grow even when national growth rates are slow. This is an important trend to consider if future regional economic change in the US takes place under prolonged periods of slow national growth. Continued slow national growth could result in the Northeast and Midwest dropping below other regions in relative economic wellbeing. It also shows that macroeconomic policy can have a major impact on regional industrial change, a topic we need to know more about.

v. Over the last 25 years the most rapidly growing states of the Southeast and Southwest have received substantially higher Federal payments than their residents have paid to the Federal government in taxes and revenues. The opposite pattern is true of New England, the Mideast, and Great Lakes regions. No causal connections between the growth rates and the expenditure-to-revenue ratios are shown, however, an important qualifier since the data on which the statement is based can still be questioned on the grounds that surpluses in certain regions may actually be spent in deficit regions. The ACIR study also shows that during the last 25 years, disparities in Federal flows of funding between States have been steadily narrowing, a conclusion also reached more recently by the *National Journal* (1981).

Markusen and Fastrup (1978), on the other hand, note that 'alternative accounting of federal government fiscal behavior produces quite different conclusions.' They show that in the case of Federal grants to State and local governments, such payments do not favor the Sunbelt. Yet this is not surprising given the variables influencing the distribution of aid when some States choose not to tax themselves and hence forego Federal Aid. Similarly, it is not surprising that in a program like social security, funds are distributed disproportionately to areas where older people live.

In retrospect, therefore, the repetitive nature of the conspiracy theory between major regions of the US implies that the debate may subside only to become an issue once again, as long as politicians represent people in specific regions and as long as government policies inevitably have a differential regional impact. The regional debate of the late 1970s had at least some consensus: that regional economic disparities within the US are indeed disappearing, and that *the most effective form of regional policy will be maintaining a healthy national growth rate*, a situation that can only seem precarious in the early 1980s. Expert opinion still seems to differ as to what parts of the country benefit most from Federal outlays, and what parts get more than their 'fair share'. In most cases this can be traced back to the weakness of basic data sources and the difficulties of tracing interregional flows of revenues and expenditures in an open economy. One has to sympathize therefore with the pleas for better data sources on Federal outlays, and the need for more comprehensive methodologies to deal with the impact of Federal policies.

6.3.2 Measurement problems

A major problem in assessing the impact of government policy generally is that it is fraught with methodological difficulties. The foremost difficulty is comparing the results of such policy. Another is the problem of measuring the costs and benefits associated with Federal regulation.

Some of the problems associated with cost-benefit and cost-effectiveness analysis have been covered thoroughly by Julius Allen (1978). On the cost data side it is usually difficult to obtain reliable aggregate data. One of the most widely quoted studies was conducted by Murray Weidenbaum: 'The cost imposed on the American economy by federal regulatory activities in 1976 totaled $66.1 billion. This estimate comprises $3.2 billion in administrative costs and $62.9 billion in compliance costs' (Weidenbaum and De Fina 1978). This represents 4 per cent of the GNP, $307 per person living in the US, 18 per cent of the Federal budget. Yet one has to share Allen's skepticism on these and other estimates based on data for different authorities at different times. 'All of these estimates appear to be unavoidably tentative and in no sense completely reliable. Furthermore, they are all estimates of *gross* rather than *net* costs of regulation, in that they do not include estimates of offsetting gains attributable to regulation' (Allen 1978, 20).

Some of the problems involved in measuring the impact of government policy on industrial and regional change (not only in States but also in cities and counties) have also been addressed by Hines and Reid (1977). Since the late 1960s detailed annual reports on Federal spending in small areas have been available in the Federal Outlays series initiated by the Community Services Administration. Earlier editions suffered from serious deficiencies in completeness and accuracy. In 1975 program identification improved by use of the Catalog of Federal Domestic Assistance which in future may help comparisons of Federal outlays over time. However, there is still the problem of assessing whether the county in which a Federal payment was received was the place where that money was spent, and its subsequent multiplier effect. The multiplier effect of Federal outlays will undoubtedly vary from one program to another, while research shows that the tendency of Federal dollars to migrate across regional boundaries may be very high (Bahl and Warford 1971).

There are techniques available for tracing the interregional flow of money, the best-known being the application of input–output analysis. In a multiregional context, input–output analysis itself is fraught with methodological problems (Polenske 1978). Erickson's case study (1975) of the interregional financial and employment impacts of the Boeing Company illustrates some of these problems. Boeing purchased approximately 10 per cent of its total processing sector inputs from local Puget Sound region suppliers. But the strongest ties with suppliers occurred in New Jersey, Connecticut, and California, specifically Hartford and Los Angeles–Long Beach with minor links to suppliers in Phoenix, Dallas, Rockford, Ill., Detroit, and Cleveland. Clearly such a complex national purchasing or linkage pattern for only one company is indicative of the measurement problems. In a similar but larger study, Pred (1977) found that for a sample of companies with headquarters in eight metropolitan areas in the western US 'the aggregate strength of nonlocal intra-organizational linkages created by these multi-locational business organizations is considerable . . . and is highlighted by ties with other large metropolitan complexes.' Data on intra-organizational linkages are particularly hard to come by, however, given that companies only have to report total earnings to the Securities and Exchange Commission regardless of location.

In another study on the purchasing and marketing linkages of manufacturing companies in the Dallas/Fort Worth area, one of the nation's fastest growing urban-industrial complexes in the 1970s, it was found that 68 per cent of materials purchased came from outside the metropolitan area and 60 per cent from outside the West South Central census region which includes Texas, Louisiana, Oklahoma, and Arkansas (Rees 1978). Over 30 per cent of inputs in fact came from the Manufacturing Belt, showing once again a higher degree of interregional interdependence with the Manufacturing Belt. Furthermore, when the backward linkage (purchasing) patterns of one large firm, a defense contractor, were examined over time, large temporal fluctuations were evident. In this particular case procurement from California increased from 13 to 42 per cent in two years and that from Connecticut declined from 28 to 5 per cent on total purchases between $237 and $393 million, involving numerous job changes.

These studies together highlight the interregional integration implicit in the American industrial sector, a pattern that can change significantly over time and add to the complexities of monitoring money flows and employment changes associated with such changes. Therefore, before the impacts of Federal and other government spending policies can be monitored over space and through time, more effort has to be devoted to basic research issues involving data sources and approaches used in analysis and evaluation.

6.3.3 Direct impacts of government policy

Certain government policies have an explicit, direct impact on industrial location. These include taxation policies at the State and local level which affect production costs, and defense procurement policy which affects the economic health of many manufacturers in various parts of the country, particularly of those wholly or partially dependent on government contracts. Policies that have a direct impact on industry also include the efforts of the Economic Development Administration, specifically established to aid distressed areas (see ch. 2.6.3), and policies of the Environmental Protection Agency (see ch. 4) which can have a major impact on the production costs of certain manufacturing sectors in specific regions. Other government policies have an implicit or an indirect impact on industrial location and regional change, and by definition these impacts are more difficult to trace. In this section assessments are made of the kind of policies that can have a direct impact on industrial location.

a. *Taxation policy and industrial location.* Most research on industrial location over the past 15 years has found little evidence that manufacturing industry's locational choices in the US are influenced to any significant degree by taxation policy, either Federal, State, or local. In a major synthesizing work on industrial location, David Smith states: 'studies that have attempted to measure the correlation between state and local taxes on the one hand, and industrial growth rates on the other conclude that tax levels are not important determinants of industrial location ... variations in tax costs are roughly one-tenth of the variations in the cost of labor, marketing and transportation' (1971, 53). On another view 'the relative importance of the tax differential factor in industrial location decisions appears to increase as the location process narrows down to a particular jurisdiction within a general region' (ACIR 1967, 78).

Yet when one looks around the country, State and local governments seem to suggest that they can influence industrial location development in their regions.

This is evidenced by the fact that 45 states offer tax-free state and local revenue bond financing to industry; 29 states offer other types of low interest loans; 25 states do not collect sales tax on newly purchased industrial equipment; 38 do not levy inventory taxes on goods in transit; virtually all states have industrial development agencies; and many state and local governments offer tax credits, abatements, and rapid depreciation to encourage new investment in plant and equipment. (Weinstein and Firestine 1978, 134)

One therefore has to question why such incentives are offered. The primary reason appears to be that local policy makers still *perceive* the taxation issue to be an integral part of their overall image to industry, their 'business climate' (see ch. 7, p. 274).

A recent study of interstate competition for industry (ACIR 1978) throws further light on the issue:

i. They found that State enactment of industrial incentives increased sharply in the 1960s and remained at a high level in the 1970s.

ii. While much of the publicity over competition for industry focusses on the Snowbelt versus the Sunbelt, States within the Snowbelt frequently compete with each other.

iii. Births of single-plant firms occurred more frequently between 1969 and 1976 in States with low taxes than in States with high taxes. But the Northeastern States are far from stagnant in terms of manufacturing 'births', so causality cannot be inferred from the association between taxes and manufacturing births.

iv. States without a personal income tax enjoyed better economic health than did States with personal income tax. Again causality cannot be established, but the data suggest that high personal taxes in Northern States force up salary scales for executive and managerial personnel, the kind of people most influential in making industrial location decisions. From this ACIR conclude that while the impact of business taxes on industrial location got the most attention in past studies, State personal income tax appears to be gaining in importance as a factor influencing industrial location decisions. Thus they pose a controversial question for consideration: 'should the federal government abandon its present policy of neutrality and adopt in its stead a pro-state personal income tax approach that would call for a federal incentive to encourage non-income tax states to join the income tax ranks?' They provide succinct arguments

234 United States Public Policy

both for and against the issue, but given the mood of fiscal conservatism in the country presently, tax enactment would hardly be given serious consideration.

The relative importance of personal income and corporate taxes as a factor in industrial location decision-making has been given further credibility in a comprehensive study of new firm location by Carlton (1978). Using national Dun & Bradstreet data on firm births around the country between 1967 and 1975, Carlton's econometric analyses do not support the view that State income and corporate taxes are important negative deterrents for new business location; neither do the findings show taxes to be a significant determinant of new births. Wages and agglomeration economies were still seen as two of the most important factors influencing industrial location, while no evidence was found that 'favorable business climates' alone could stimulate new locational activity. These recent studies do show taxation policies to be relatively unimportant as determinants of industrial location, though they seem to occupy a relatively more important position than they used to, particularly in the case of personal income taxes.

b. *Economic Development Assistance.* Another way by which government policy can influence industrial location is through economic development assistance to a specific geographical area (see ch. 2.6.3). Historically, however, the US government has assigned fairly low priority to the issue, particularly in comparison with other western countries (Hanson 1974). It is necessary to comment on approaches adopted as they affect or do not affect the location of industry in different parts of the US.

Despite the flirtation of the US government with regional development legislation, such as the TVA of the 1930s and the efforts of Senator Douglas in the 1950s, real interest in aiding depressed areas was not shown at the Federal level until the early 1960s. The Area Redevelopment Act (1961) and the Accelerated Public Works Act (1962) provided piecemeal assistance for industrial development and public facilities in stagnating communities. The major regional development legislation was not passed until 1965, with the Appalachian Regional Development Act and the Public Works and Economic Development Act. The former set up the Appalachian Regional Commission to coordinate joint Federal–State development efforts in parts of 13 States. The Economic Development Administration was also created at this time, as well as a number of other Regional Commissions (see ch. 2).

Within Appalachia, as later on within EDA itself, most investment funds went to dominant 'growth centers', each an area or city of sufficient size and potential to foster the economic growth activities necessary to alleviate the distress of redevelopment areas within the district. It should have sufficient population resources, public facilities, industry, and commercial services to ensure that its development can become relatively self-sustaining. This growth-center policy faced many difficulties and thus found many critics. One major difficulty was choosing acceptable criteria to define 'growth potential', so that local political pressure resulted in a plethora of growth centers (over 260 by 1975, according to Estall 1977). Another focal part of the debate included the size of center that could influence its hinterland through Myrdal-style 'spread' effects. Furthermore 'the dilemma of where best to allocate funds was made no easier by lack of a clear understanding of what best to spend the money on' (Estall 1977, 347).

Emphasis on encouraging industrial development in such growth centers was lost somewhere in the midst of the debate between investment in infrastructure and developing human resources. As Miernyk (1978, 4) reminded us: 'It is much safer to go the public works route where a complete failure is difficult to define . . . If public works stimulate economic development; well and good. If they don't, local residents still have the benefits of improved amenities . . .'. On the other hand if investment is made in industrial development and the entire venture collapses, the failure becomes much more conspicuous. As a result there has always been *a bias against direct incentives to industry* in the US in contrast to regional development policy in other western countries where such policies have been more elaborate, included more direct investment incentives to industry and generally experienced more beneficial results. A 1972 evaluation of EDA projects sums up the issue: 'traditional projects which aim at directly creating jobs through the location of industry cannot fully meet the development needs of some communities' (EDA 1972, 66). The provision of a theater, a cultural center, or a parking facility could, it was argued, produce new business enterprise far more quickly than 'traditional' public works projects! As a result, only 13 per cent of EDA's development budget as of 31 March 1978 was used to make business development loans.

The objective of the EDA Act then was to invest in public works in particular, business loans and planning assistance generally, while major human resource programs like labor training, health, education, welfare, were the prerogative of other Federal agencies. The broad objective of the EDA was to take work to the workers, as had been European regional policy for 30 years. The provision of infrastructure would, it was hoped, encourage needed investment by the private sector. That had also been the objective of the Autostrada Del Sole, linking southern Italy to the north, which resulted in very little decentralization of industry to the south. The assumption that investment in roads, water, and sewer systems and the like, or in public works generally, would ensure industrial development had been found to be a dangerous and fallacious one in many countries.

Without delving any deeper into the pros and cons of EDA, regional scholars generally concur that: 'The record of achievement under the 1965 Act has clearly been mixed and experience has led to no certainty that programmes of these kinds can achieve a great deal in a country such as the United States' (Estall 1977, 36). Despite the 'New Regionalism' of the 1970s, the same low priority was assigned to economic development assistance in the US in the 1970s. 'In terms of current 1972 dollars, the 1966 appropriation was slightly over $433 million, by 1975 appropriations had dropped to $341 million in real terms. In that year appropriations amounted to approximately one-fiftieth of one percent of the GNP . . . a little over 1/10 of one percent of total federal outlays' (Jusenius and Ledebur 1977, 48). Under the 'New Federalism' of the 1980s, economic development assistance will get even lower priority.

It is true that regional problems may only be manifestations of larger national problems, but unless these problems are monitored and alleviated at the regional level, there will always be a 'regional problem'. Certain people in certain places will continue to be at a disadvantage in the US.

c. *Defense procurement policy.* One of the major topics of contention in the recent debate on regional change in the US is the differential impact of Federal procurement policy, specifically involving national defense. Defense procurement, it has been alleged, is biassed against the Northeastern part of the country. According to the Coalition of Northeastern Governors and Northeast Midwest Research Institute, the 16 States of the Northeast and Midwest have lost a disproportionate share of the defense dollar since the 1950s and now receive a lower level of military expenditure than any other area of the country. This pattern of declining defense expenditures is seen to increase unemployment in the 16 State region covered by the Coalition, exacerbating their economic problems. The shift of expenditures to other areas on the other hand is seen to fuel an economic boom there.

This is not the first time that the impact of defense purchases on regional industrial growth has been the subject of academic debate in the US (Tiebout and Peterson 1964; Leontief *et al.* 1965; Bolton 1966; Karaska 1966, 1967). Leontief used his now famous input–output approach to simulate the direct and indirect effects of a defense cutback in various parts of the US. His results showed that certain Western States, Colorado, New Mexico, and California in particular, would be hard hit, together with States on the East Coast. More recently, Bezdek (1975) carried out a similar study of the regional and occupational shifts in defense spending by the year 1980. He found that for the nation as a whole decreases in defense spending would likely increase aggregated employment, but again regional variations would be great. Using an admittedly rigid input–output model where he assumed changes in national output would be distributed proportionately across all industries without any allowance for regional multiplier effects, he shows that defense spending (assuming it was transferred to domestic programs) would tend to increase total employment within the traditional Manufacturing Belt. The Western States on the other hand, including California and Texas, would suffer the greatest employment decreases, though New England and the South generally would not be very sensitive to changes in defense spending. These types of study are important from a policy perspective because they can highlight the dependence of certain regions on defense spending and provide policy-makers with a preview of the impacts of policy changes on specific regions.

Other studies that have played a role in the current debate on regional defense expenditures have lacked methodological rigor and even proper concern for data before making their recommendations'. The major data problem in many of these studies, particularly those using Federal Outlays, is the assumption that States receiving prime contracts are also the locations where all the work was performed. Back in the early 1960s Tiebout and others had shown that roughly 50 per cent of a defense prime contract was subcontracted, in many cases out-of-State. One source of information on subcontracting that has not been used by the studies reviewed here is the Bureau of Census's annual survey of defense-oriented manufacturing companies (Current Industrial Reports: Shipment of Defense Oriented Industries). State data have been reported since 1965 on sub- as well as prime-contract work. A comparison of these data by Holmer (1978) with those gathered by CSA for Federal Outlays indicated that the CSA data 'understate the fraction of direct federal expenditures from military procurement going to states in the Northeast, North Central, and West Census regions and substantially overestimate the fraction of military procurements going to states in the Southern Census region.' In order to confirm or contradict this finding, data on the shipments of defense-oriented industries by sub- as well as prime-contractor were examined for selected years. The findings are shown in Tables 6.3–5 and Fig. 6.3.

The years chosen for study were 1965 when the data were first available, 1969 the height of the Vietnam War, 1973 when the defense budget had been cut as a proportion of GNP, and 1977 with the latest available data. The data from the 1960s, therefore, include an era when defense spending was at its highest, while the data from the 1970s reflect defense cutbacks that may have had a regional impact. The data are based on a large sample of companies in 94 industries that undertake government contracts and account for 80 to 90 per cent of all Federal procurement. The results are aggregated at the census region level, with the three census divisions making up the Manufacturing Belt (the Northeast, Mid-Atlantic, and East North Central divisions). The definition of the periphery used initially in this study has been disaggregated here to isolate the impact of the Pacific region, particularly California, on the national pattern of defense spending. The areally vast, but relatively unimportant, defense-oriented Mountain region has also been excluded so that the periphery corresponds with the South and the West North Central Census divisions only.

One would expect the Manufacturing Belt to receive a larger absolute amount of government contract work than the periphery when one considers the absolute amount of production going on in that region. There is a greater absolute level of manufacturing activity in the three regions of the Manufacturing Belt than in the four regions of the periphery as defined here. The value of shipments of government contracts, mostly to DOD, but also NASA, ERDA, and other agencies, is broken down by region for selected years in Table 6.3. It shows that in 1965 nearly 42 per cent of all government contracting was carried out in the Manufacturing Belt, 27 per cent in the four census regions of the periphery, and 29 per cent in the Pacific census region alone. By 1977 the proportion of government contracting in the Manufacturing Belt was down to 35 per cent, while the periphery contributed 30 per cent and the Pacific region stayed at the high rate of 32 per cent. The image of the Pacific region, particularly California as the largest government contractor in the nation, is clearly evident. The Manufacturing Belt, as expected, received a greater proportion of government contracts than the periphery throughout the 1960s and 1970s.

Tables 6.4 and 5 show the proportion of government shipments allocated to prime and subcontracts by region, 1965 to 1977. The Manufacturing Belt compared to the periphery, was a larger receiver of prime-contract awards in

TABLE 6.3 *Government contracts by value of shipment per region, 1965–1977*
($ millions)

REGION	1965		1973		1977	
	Amount	Percentage of US	Amount	Percentage of US	Amount	Percentage of US
Manufacturing Belt		41.7		37.4		34.8
New England	2,985.2	10.4	3,258.6	10.8	5,529.5	11.0
Middle Atlantic	5,488.4	19.1	4,284.0	14.2	6,354.4	12.7
East North Central	3,504.1	12.2	3,740.7	12.4	5,576.2	11.1
Periphery		26.5		29.1		29.8
West North Central	2,102.2	7.4	2,361.0	7.9	3,990.1	7.9
South Atlantic	2,642.3	9.2	3,032.5	10.1	5,456.8	10.9
East South Central	841.8	2.9	1,274.5	4.2	2,030.1	4.1
West South Central	1,997.9	7.0	2,083.6	6.9	3,468.1	6.9
Other						
Mountain	892.6	3.1	1,132.4	3.8	1,702.6	3.4
Pacific	8,306.4	28.9	8,911.6	29.6	15,972.7	31.9
US	28,748.9	100.0	30,079.0	100.0	50,080	99.9

Source: Current Industrial Reports: Shipments of defense-oriented Industries, various years

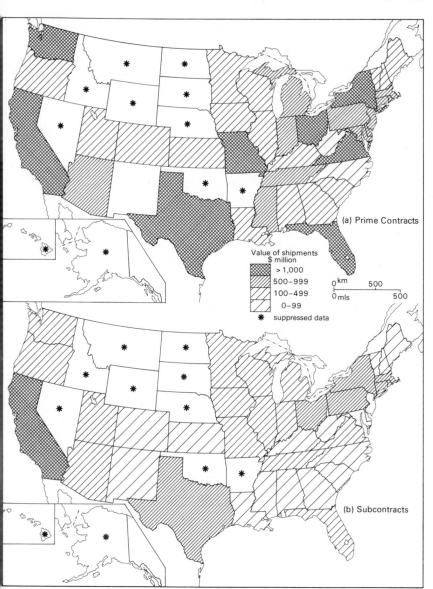

Value of shipments
$ million
> 1,000
500–999
100–499
0–99
✱ suppressed data

(a) Prime Contracts

(b) Subcontracts

6.3   Defense spending, 1977: (a) prime contracts; (b) subcontracts.

both 1965 and 1973, though in 1977 the periphery received 1.4 per cent more. The largest single receiver of prime contracts throughout the period was the Pacific census division once again. Table 6.5 shows the *consistent dominance of the Manufacturing Belt relative to the periphery as the location of subcontracting work carried out for the prime contractors.* The Manufac-

TABLE 6.4 *Regional share of prime contract awards 1965–1977*
($ millions)

REGION	1965 Amount	1965 Percentage of US	1973 Amount	1973 Percentage of US	1977 Amount	1977 Percentage of US
Manufacturing Belt		38.4		34.9		31.7
New England	2,113.0	9.9	2,438.2	10.5	4,001.3	10.9
Middle Atlantic	3,900.1	18.2	2,987.1	12.8	4,247.9	11.5
East North Central	2,192.1	10.3	2,700.6	11.6	3,428.4	9.3
Periphery		29.1		31.3		33.1
West North Central	1,681.6	7.9	2,082.5	9.0	3,264.9	8.8
South Atlantic	2,196.7	10.3	2,343.2	10.1	4,514.7	12.3
East South Central	661.7	3.1	1,090.8	4.7	1,684.9	4.6
West South Central	1,676.7	7.8	1,737.8	7.5	2,712.3	7.4
Other						
Mountain	639.7	3.0	794.2	3.4	1,111.0	3.0
Pacific	6,325.1	29.6	7,097.1	30.5	11,883.1	32.2
US	21,386.7	100.0	23,271.3	100.0	36,848.5	100.0

Source: Current Industrial Reports.

TABLE 6.5 *Regional share of subcontracts, 1965–1977*
($ millions)

REGION	1965		1973		1977	
	Amount	Percentage of US	Amount	Percentage of US	Amount	Percentage of US
Manufacturing Belt		*51.1*		*46.5*		*43.6*
New England	872.2	11.8	820.5	12.1	1,528.2	11.5
Middle Atlantic	1,588.3	21.5	1,296.9	19.1	2,106.5	15.9
East North Central	1,312.0	17.8	1,040.1	15.3	2,147.8	16.2
Periphery		*18.5*		*22.0*		*20.9*
West North Central	438.6	6.0	278.5	4.1	725.2	5.5
South Atlantic	445.6	6.0	689.3	10.1	942.1	7.1
East South Central	180.1	2.4	183.7	2.7	345.2	2.6
West South Central	301.2	4.1	345.8	5.1	755.8	5.7
Other						
Mountain	252.9	3.4	338.2	5.0	591.6	4.5
Pacific	1,982.3	26.9	1,814.5	26.7	4,089.6	30.9
US	7,373.8	100.0	6,807.5	100.0	13,232.0	99.9

Source: Current Industrial Reports.

turing Belt produced over 50 per cent of subcontracts in 1965, though this had fallen to 44 per cent in 1977. The periphery only accounted for 18 to 22 per cent of subcontracting work over the period 1965–77, an amount substantially less than that carried out in the Pacific region. The inference that can be made from Table 6.5 is that many of the prime contracts let in the periphery are subcontracted to the companies in the Manufacturing Belt. It tends to confirm the pattern of interregional industrial linkages between key growth centers of the Southwest and the more established manufacturing areas of the country, as suggested by other work (Rees 1978B; Malecki 1981). It also confirms the fallacy of assuming that the location of prime-contract work is also the location of subcontracts for the Federal government.

Figure 6.3 shows the State by State distribution of prime contracts and subcontracts for 1977. As expected from a lesser degree of aggregation, large variations are seen between States even within the census divisions discussed earlier. California stands out significantly as the largest receiver of both prime and subcontract work, with nearly $10 billion of prime and over $3 billion of subcontracting taking place in 1977. New York, Connecticut, Missouri, and Texas are way behind California as recipients of prime contracts, with $2 billion each.

The Northeast and Midwestern States stand out in Figure 6.3a as the largest receivers of prime contracts, with 11 States receiving over $500 million in prime contract awards in 1977. Apart from California and Texas, only 6 other States in the Union received over $500 million in prime awards, namely Washington and Arizona in the West, and Florida, Mississippi, Tennessee, and Virginia in the South.

From Figure 6.3b, the dominance of the Northeastern and Midwestern States in the subcontracting process is clearly visible. Out of 20 States in the Northeast and Midwest 15 received over $100 million worth of subcontracts in 1977, the exceptions being Maine, New Hampshire, Vermont, West Virginia, and Kentucky.

The data source used in this section allows more spatial disaggregation down to the SMSA level, and defense dependency varies even more at the urban scale, reflecting the different industrial structure of these areas. Differences at the urban scale have been discussed elsewhere (Bolton 1980; Malecki 1981).

d. *The impact of environmental protection policy.* The passing of the National Environmental Policy Act (1969) and the establishment of the Environmental Protection Agency (see ch. 4.1) epitomizes the new kind of 'social' legislation that has borne the brunt of the attack on government regulation in the US in recent years. Environmental protection also indicates a form of reactive policy-making or 'government by crises' when the brakes have to be applied harshly after a century of seemingly reckless driving. Yet in many respects it also demonstrates the kind of monitoring and impact analysis needed in other areas of policy. The Bureau of Economic Analysis, the Bureau of Census, as well as the EPA itself, are agencies that already monitor the structural and regional impact of environmental protection requirements, though data bases were only recently developed.

Such careful monitoring is a necessity, however, since EPA policy has the potential of a greater direct impact on the location of industry in the US than many other forms of policy. When Weidenbaum and DeFina (1978) estimated the total cost of administering and complying with Federal regulations at $66 billion in 1976, regulations pertaining to energy and the environment were the largest cost sector, at $8.4 billion, after industry-specific regulations. Total administrative and compliance costs of EPA itself were $8.2 billion or 12 per cent of the total national estimates. The ratio of compliance to administrative costs for government regulation as a whole was 19.7, while the EPA ratio was 18.7. Therefore, EPA compliance cost estimates of $7.8 billion were not out of proportion with other compliance estimates. Yet $7.8 billion is a large amount of capital investment in what many still regard as unproductive capacity, considering that most of these compliance costs were for plant and equipment necessary to meet Federal mandated standards and that total new capital expenditure by manufacturers in 1976 was only $40.5 billion. Clearly many policy-makers are concerned that the cost of complying with environmental regulations will result in inflationary price increases, particularly in a number of basic industries. Yet it has to be borne in mind that this is one area where costs are easier to define than benefits.

In his review of environmental controls Allen (1978) reminds us that one of the limitations of studies on the costs of environmental regulation is that they are based on computing the sums added to existing manufacturing costs, and do not take into account how such regulations may change the way in which the manufacturing process itself is conducted or how manufacturers adapt to other forms of production. In addition, Leone and Jackson (1978) suggest that major shifts in the competitive advantage of various industries may result from added costs. Short-run costs may put small firms out of business and thus make an industry more oligopolistic in the long run, which in turn has implications for the anti-trust policies of the FTC. Leone further suggests that the costs of EPA may not have been accurately perceived when the legislation was passed. 'If it is easy for legislators to pass regulations, it is far from easy to accommodate adequately the complex and indirect effects of these regulations in the policy making process' (Leone and Jackson 1978, 63). But given the unstable environment of the early 1970s this is hardly surprising.

One area of particular concern over the impact of environmental protection policy is its effect on plant closures and job losses. This topic has already received some attention, the most comprehensive study being undertaken by the National Bureau of Economic Research for the National Commission on Water Quality (NBER 1975). Their study sorts out the myths from the realities of plant closures, showing that companies can make other adjustments bar closure that can affect job potential:

Jobs can be lost even if a plant is not closed; pollution controls can force only its dirtiest units to be shut down. Conversely, the closure of some plants will intensify the operation of others and the resultant job creation would at least partially offset losses in the closed plants. Some jobs which would normally have been lost may actually be preserved for a time because of pollution controls ... It is entirely possible that pollution controls, when compared to other stresses and strains influencing job prospects may be only a minor concern. (p. 1)

While most industries can probably absorb the closure problem, particular sectors will be hard hit, like the textile industry (with specific regional impacts in New York, Massachusetts, Connecticut, New Hampshire, Georgia, and North Carolina), also paper mills and smaller iron and steel plants. Small plants are particularly vulnerable to closures. The NBER study showed that the closure rate in single-plant firms was between three and nine times higher than that for branch plants, which means that the larger multilocational companies have a comparative advantage over small firms. This in turn has implications for the competitive structures of certain industries. The NBER study also verified the popular notion that older industries in the Northeast are more susceptible to closures, with the region accounting for 25 per cent of jobs lost in Pennsylvania, New York, and Massachusetts. But plant closures in that region tend to be higher for other reasons apart from pollution abatement costs as reported in the Business Failure Records of the Dun & Bradstreet Company.

Contrasting views do exist, however on the possible effects of environmental controls on patterns of industrial location in the US. Stafford (1977) argued that these regulations may reinforce the natural tendency among manufacturers towards in-site expansion because it is probably easier to get permission to expand production in an area where firms already operate and any additional pollution would represent a marginally small increase in pollution levels than at a new site: 'It appears probable that the most stringent standards and restrictions will be placed on locales and regions at the ends of the economic development spectrum' (p. 745). Pollution controls may be difficult in areas already heavily polluted, whereas the cleanest areas have little room for industrial development, because of the requirement that no significant deterioration of the quality of the environment be permitted.

Some researchers have also suggested that the stringent environmental laws in the US may cause further loss or decentralization of manufacturing plants to foreign locations. The arguments suggest that investment will be driven out of nations with high environmental standards that result in high costs and will be attracted to countries having low standards with low costs. Gladwin and Welles (1976) suggest that the importance of such 'pollution havens' have been grossly exaggerated, given that pollution-abatement costs may only be a small fraction of the total operating costs of many multinational manufacturers, that marketing factors may be the major push for foreign direct investment, and that many pollution havens in developing countries have a greater political-risk factor. They conclude that 'there is little solid evidence of international locational spillover activity, with exceptions in the cases of certain copper smelters and petroleum refiners in the U.S., chemical plants in certain European countries, and heavy industry in Japan as part of its program of industrial decentralization' (p. 197). Also recent investments in the US by large European multinationals such as BP, BASF, ICI, Ciba, Geigy, and others show that marketing factors were sufficiently important for these companies to decide in favor of a country with stringent pollution control standards. However, if environmental as well as other regulations increase as a cost factor in the future, we may well see the increased export of hazardous and polluting plants, particularly to less-developed countries.

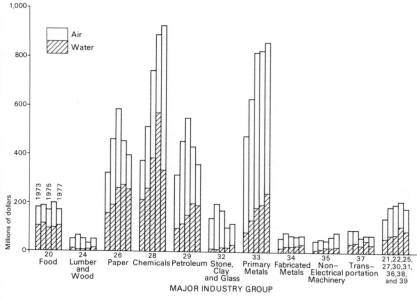

6.4   Manufacturers' air and water pollution abatement capital expenditures, by major industry group, 1973–7

To clarify further any differential impact that environmental controls may have on the changing regional industrial pattern within the US, Bureau of Census data on pollution abatement costs and expenditures were examined. These data have been collected only since 1973, so a comparison of pre- and post-EPA policies cannot be made. Figure 6.4 shows how pollution abatement capital expenditures hit certain manufacturing sectors severely compared to others. Over 70 per cent of new capital expenditures for pollution abatement were made by plants in four major industrial groups in 1977: chemicals, primary metals, paper products, and petroleum. Within these two-digit SIC groups specific manufacturers were sharply hit: blast furnaces and steel mills, petroleum refining, organic chemicals, and paper mills.

When regional shares of pollution abatement capital expenditures and operating costs are examined (Tables 6.6–7), differential regional impacts are evident. Table 6.6 shows that companies in the Manufacturing Belt consistently spent less in absolute terms on pollution abatement than those in the periphery over the period 1973–7. Whereas the Manufacturing Belt's share of these expenditures fluctuated between 35 and 42 per cent of the national total, the proportion spent by industries in the periphery increased from 42 per cent in 1973 to 49 per cent in 1976. Within these two macroregions industries in the East North Central and West South Central divisions spent the most on pollution abatement. Regional shares of pollution abatement *operating costs* on the other hand (Table 6.7) show a slightly different

TABLE 6.6 *Regional share of pollution abatement capital expenditures,*
1973–1977

REGION	1973	1974	1975	1976	1977
	(%)	(%)	(%)	(%)	(%)
Manufacturing Belt	*36.6*	*35.0*	*36.2*	*37.2*	*40.8*
New England	3.0	3.1	3.1	3.4	2.8
Middle Atlantic	13.5	14.3	12.4	13.4	16.0
East North Central	20.1	17.6	20.7	20.4	22.0
Periphery	*41.6*	*46.5*	*48.8*	*48.6*	*44.0*
West North Central	4.8	5.7	4.7	5.4	4.1
South Atlantic	14.8	14.9	15.5	12.9	12.5
East South Central	8.8	9.9	11.2	9.2	8.3
West South Central	13.2	16.0	17.0	21.1	19.1
Other					
Mountain	7.7	5.7	5.3	2.7[a]	2.4
Pacific	14.0	12.7	10.1	8.3[b]	9.7
US	100.0	100.0	100.0	100.0	96.9

[a] Excludes Utah.
[b] Excludes Alaska.

Source: Current Industrial Reports.

TABLE 6.7 *Regional share of pollution abatement operating costs,*
1973–1977

REGION	1973	1974	1975	1976	1977
	(%)	(%)	(%)	(%)	(%)
Manufacturing Belt	*47.2*	*46.3*	*45.5*	*44.3*	*42.5*
New England	3.7	3.7	3.3	3.1	2.6
Middle Atlantic	17.7	18.0	17.6	16.7	16.1
East North Central	25.8	24.6	24.6	24.5	23.8
Periphery	*36.6*	*38.5*	*39.1*	*40.5*	*42.9*
West North Central	4.3	4.8	4.5	4.5	4.1
South Atlantic	12.1	13.2	12.8	13.2	12.9
East South Central	6.6	6.9	7.4	7.1	7.4
West South Central	13.5	13.6	14.4	15.7	18.5
Other					
Mountain	2.8	2.9	3.0	2.9	3.2
Pacific	13.5	12.4	12.4	12.1	11.3
US	100.0	100.0	100.0	100.0	99.9

Source: Current Industrial Reports.

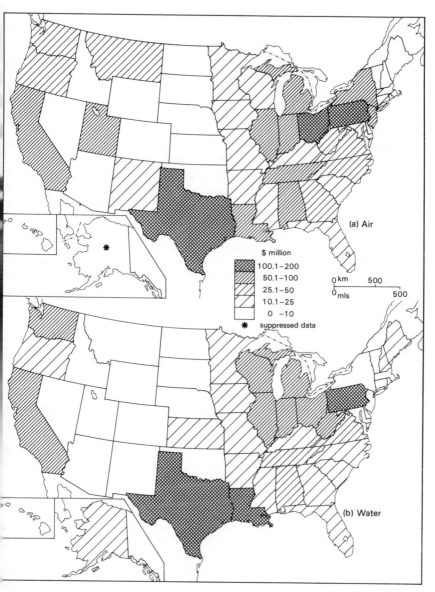

6.5   Manufacturers' capital expenditure on pollution control, 1977:
(a) air; (b) water

pattern. The Manufacturing Belt showed the largest share of the costs until
1977. Industries in the periphery experienced fewer operating costs, but in
increasing increments between 1973 and 1977 the hardest hit area in the
Manufacturing Belt was again the East North Central, while the hardest hit in
the periphery was the West South Central division.

State by State differentials in manufacturers' air and water pollution capital expenditures (1977) are clearly visible from Figure 6.5. While States in the Northeast and Midwest generally show higher expenditures for both air and water pollution abatement (specifically Illinois, Indiana, Michigan, Ohio, Pennsylvania, and New York State), the growth States of the Southwest show some of the highest expenditures *in absolute terms*, particularly Texas and Louisiana. The explanation for this lies largely in the States' industrial structure and the growth of the Gulf Coast petro-chemical complex.

Because the data shown in Figure 6.5 reflect absolute spending levels per State on pollution abatement, it is important to standardize for size of State. In Table 6.8 pollution abatement spending is shown as a proportion of total new capital expenditures in manufacturing by region and State. Table 6.8 shows that for 1973 and 1977, manufacturing companies in the growth States of the periphery (particularly the East South Central division) spend relatively more on pollution abatement than those in the older industrial States of the Manufacturing Belt. State by State differences in the ratio of antipollution spending to total new capital expenditures, on the other hand, show a high degree of variation for 1977. Alabama, West Virginia, and Montana are the only three States in which the ratio exceeds 20 per cent. The Northern New England States of Maine and New Hampshire and the North-western States of Washington, Idaho, and North Dakota all show ratios over 10 per cent, but all these States have a relatively small manufacturing base. Most of the growth States of the Southern Census region show pollution spending to be above 5 per cent of total capital expenditures, but so do most of the States of the Northeast and East North Central regions, the States that form the core of the Manufacturing Belt. From the State data alone, therefore, one cannot find major differences in the way companies spend on pollution abatement in proportion to their total capital investment between the growing Southern States and the relatively stagnant Northern States. Clearly more research is needed here on pollution abatement that takes into account differences in industrial structure and corporate organization at the urban scale. Such research is needed in particular before exact evaluations can be made on the microspatial impact of pollution control legislation. Without such research, however, policy-makers will continue to work without knowledge of the differential impact of environmental protection laws.

This section has so far reviewed US government policies which were perceived to have a *direct* impact on industrial location trends. Taxation policies were seen only to have a minor effect. Economic development assistance for the more distressed parts of the country has been given a low funding priority, resulting in very little impact on the industrial geography of the US. The fact that many manufacturing companies are dependent on government contracts for most of their sales means that certain regions and their workers are dependent on Federal purchasing policies, but little evidence has been found to date that this contributed in any major way to the decentralization of industry from the Northeast to the Southwest. Environmental protection policy was found to have potentially the greatest impact on the evolving US industrial location pattern. Here again there is little evidence

TABLE 6.8 *Pollution abatement spending as a proportion of new capital expenditures by region, 1973 and 1977*
($ millions)

REGION	1977			1973		
	Pollution abatement capital expenditure	Total new capital expenditure	Percentage	Pollution abatement capital expenditure	Total new capital expenditure	Percentage
Manufacturing Belt			6.8			6.4
New England	99.8	2,142.3	4.6	70.2	1,370	5.1
Mid-Atlantic	557.2	6,203.9	8.9	318.1	4,168	7.6
East North Central	767.9	12,412.6	6.2	473.8	7,449	6.4
Periphery			7.9			9.5
West North Central	143.6	2,645.3	5.4	112.4	1,526	7.4
South Atlantic	436.1	6,950.0	7.2	349.5	4,140	8.4
East South Central	288.0	2,466.7	11.7	207.2	1,898	10.9
West South Central	666.0	8,223.4	8.1	310.9	2,724	11.4
Other						
Mountain	185.8	995.9	18.6	181.3	830	21.8
Pacific	339.3	5,032.4	6.7	330.2	2,776	11.9

Source: Bureau of Census, Pollution Abatement Costs and Expenditures 1977; Census of Manufactures 1977.

that such policies are more detrimental to the declining regions than they are to the growth regions. In retrospect, therefore, these forms of government policy are seen to have only minimal impact on changing industrial location patterns within the US. Yet all forms of government policy eventually have some form of geographical manifestation, even if in the most indirect ways.

6.3.4 Indirect impacts of government policy

A host of government actions have had an indirect impact on US industrial location trends. Some have argued that the American 'love of newness' has meant that tax credits on investment in new plant and equipment have helped to 'subsidize' the growth of suburban areas as well as the new industrial regions of the South and West. Others would argue that higher Federal spending on R & D in the 1960s and the R & D tax credits introduced recently by the Reagan administration act as subsidies to growth sectors such as aerospace and electronics and hence contributed to the growth in Southern and Western States. It stands to reason that measurement problems multiply when indirect and induced effects of policies have to be evaluated.

One can also argue that reporting requirements and classification systems used by the Federal government are a deterrent to proper assessment of the impact of public policy. The Securities and Exchange Commission (SEC), for example, makes it very difficult to monitor industrial change from an intra-organizational perspective because companies generally have to disclose financial records in the aggregate, and not by location. This makes the behavior of the most dominant actor on the industrial scene, the multiplant firm, very difficult to monitor. With regard to classification systems, the categorization of acquisitions and mergers by the Federal Trade Commission has been called into question by industrial economists (Reid 1976). Reid suggests that many horizontal mergers in recent times (the kind of merger the FTC is supposed to monitor most of all) were camouflaged under the 'conglomerate' category and as a result the ownership of American industry became far more centralized. Reid's argument suggests that such misclassifications have resulted in the increasing external control of industry in many parts of the US. Yet, if it had not been for the conglomerate boom of the 1960s that allowed companies to grow internally in the US via product diversification, alternative growth strategies via geographical diversification might have sent many more companies abroad.

These problems of financial reporting, classification schemes, and methodology all make anticipatory policy analysis an important area of concern in the future if a more complete understanding of the intricacies of the American industrial system are to be understood. Because the regional allocation of capital is perceived to be more important during periods of slow national economic growth, it seems feasible that greater priority be given to improving data bases and analytical procedures to enable policy-makers to anticipate any indirect regional impacts of public policy. It has been suggested elsewhere (Rees 1980) that regional-impact analysis be a mandatory part of economic impact statements that accompany legislation at the Federal level. The kind of urban-impact analyses proposed under the Carter administration seem to have disappeared under the New Federalism of the Reagan administration.

6.4 FUTURE POLICY ISSUES

In addition to the dramatic changes in the political economy of the US in the last 20 years, other policy changes on the horizon may also have major effects on the evolving industrial patterns within the US. In this final section, two interrelated sets of issues are discussed: policy options for facilitating capital formation in various regions, and policy options relating to national economic recovery.

6.4.1 Capital formation

Historically, the mobilization of capital to support economic development in emerging regions of the US has not been a problem as long as sufficient external demand existed for the resources, products, and services provided by that region..Capital has flowed interregionally, and even internationally, to finance development whenever capitalists and industrialists perceived investment opportunities offering competitive long-term returns. In practice, the 'invisible hand' of the marketplace has been the principal mobilizer of capital.

Though occasional efforts at mobilizing private capital for specific purposes can be documented, these attempts have been largely unsuccessful. For example, proponents of an industrialized 'new South' made a concerted attempt to mobilize investment capital for industrial development shortly after the Civil War. Regional leaders such as Henry Grady called upon Southerners to become industrial entrepreneurs and urged capitalists from the North to send their money to the South (Danhof 1964). Indeed, industrialization became a veritable crusade during the 1880s and 1890s. Underlying market realities and technology, however, were not favorable to southern economic development until 60 years later, and the South continued to stagnate.

In the case of another growth region, the Mountain census division in the 1980s, the underlying market forces and technology will certainly be favorable to economic growth and diversification, and considerable entrepreneurial activity can be anticipated in the years ahead. Nonetheless, the popular press frequently assert that *the nation and its growth regions face an imminent capital shortage*. Home-builders bemoan the lack of mortgage funds for housing construction; small business and local governments often claim they are 'crowded out' of credit markets because of huge borrowings by the Federal government and large corporations; and these corporations, at least until quite recently, argued that capital was unavailable for retooling American industry because the national tax system encouraged consumption over saving and investment.

Similar claims are often voiced at the regional level. For example, the Council for Northeast Economic Action has argued for some time that the South and West face a severe capital shortage as more funds remain in the Northeast to support renewal of that region's industrial base. The revival of economic activity in the Northeast, the nation's major source of investment capital, may eventually lead to a smaller stock of capital for investments elsewhere.

The tax and budget cuts enacted under the Reagan administration have also generated a wave of anxiety about the ability of State and local governments to fulfil their traditional roles as providers of basic public infrastructure such as bridges, roads, sewerage, and water. A special report (*Business Week* 26 Oct. 1981) estimated that State and local governments needed to raise upward of $700 billion over the next decade to build new infrastructure and repair the old.

Without doubt, the new growth regions of the South and West will require huge infusions of capital over the next several decades, for both private and public purposes. Given the regions' relatively small population and underdeveloped financial institutions, they will remain net 'importers' of capital for the foreseeable future. In this sense, the South and West are capital-short regions, but dependency on exogenous funding should not be viewed with alarm. Indeed, it is better viewed as a barometer of the region's economic vitality. Over time, indigenous capital markets will develop and the relative dependency on external sources of funds will decline.

State and local governments across the US have attempted to influence the level of economic activity in their regions by offering a variety of inducements to private companies: i.e. tax-free industrial development bonds, low-interest loans, rapid depreciation to encourage new investment in plant and equipment, and the like. Because virtually all States provide similar industrial inducement packages, it can be argued that they have become superfluous in the industrial location calculus (ACIR 1978). Taken as a whole, therefore, *State and local incentives probably constitute a serious misallocation of resources.* In the main, government is subsidizing firms for performing activities they would have undertaken in any case. Furthermore, when one considers that any incentive designed to reduce a company's State tax bill or borrowing costs will increase that firm's Federal tax liability, owing to the deductibility of State taxes and interest in computing Federal net taxable income, the superfluity of State incentives becomes even more apparent.

6.4.2 *The State role in mobilizing and allocating capital*

Mobilizing capital to finance industrial development in the US in the future will require better use of existing mechanisms as well as the creation of new financing approaches. Some *direct* governmental intervention at the State and local level may be required. But Governors and local officials should recognize that their options are limited and that evidence shows public policies and interventions to be less powerful than basic market forces affecting the allocation of capital (ACIR 1978).

a. *Generating public capital.* Despite the New Federalism, Federal support for local public works projects will diminish substantially over the next several years. This retrenchment will hit especially hard at the fast-growing regions who have relied on Federal aid to finance nearly one-half of all public facilities construction in recent years (Choate and Walter 1981).

Tax-exempt general obligation bonds, issued and guaranteed by States and localities, have been the mainstay of capital facilities financing for decades (Bahl 1980). But rising interest rates are shutting out many State and local governments from the long-term bond market, even those with high credit ratings. Because competition for funds in the tax-exempt market is increasing, the spread between tax-exempt and taxable bonds is narrowing rapidly. At present, tax-exempt rates paid by State and local borrowers exceed 80 per cent of the cost of comparably rated taxable corporate bonds, far higher than the 65 per cent historical standard. This narrowing of the spread is likely to continue as personal tax rates on unearned income drop in the years ahead and institutional investors desert the market for higher returns elsewhere. In short, *the historical subsidy for State and municipal financing is eroding rapidly through inflation, tax rate changes, and the new competition in financial markets*. Probably the only way to recapture this lost subsidy would be to give States and cities the option of issuing taxable bonds, with the Federal government directly subsidizing the difference in interest rates of such bonds and tax-exempt debt.

Individual States should also consider greater application of user charges for public works-related services. Because of a dedicated, guaranteed flow of revenues, user fees to finance public service can improve access to capital markets. Furthermore, user fees generally result in a more realistic pricing of public services—i.e. equating costs with the value of benefits received. Hospitals, sewerage, parks, housing, airports, highways, and parking facilities are some of the areas where considerable unexploited potential exists for the imposition of fees.

Another way for State and local governments to reduce capital and operating costs, particularly under a leaner New Federalism, would be to relegate additional public services to the private sector. Although 'privatization' is not an option in all circumstances, it can be applied to the construction and operation of many kinds of public facilities. Many cities are already using private firms for waste collection and disposal because private firms can secure necessary capital funds irrespective of local expenditure limits. Privatization has the additional virtue of moving government toward a system in which public facilities and services receive priorities that reflect market realities.

b. *Generating private capital.* To date, most State programs to attract and retain *private* capital for economic development and diversification have concentrated on specific institutions and mechanisms. For example, State-chartered Business Development Corporations (BDCs) were extremely popular during the 1950s and 1960s as mechanisms for allocating funds to small and medium-sized firms which could not raise capital in conventional markets (Litvak and Daniels 1979; Daniels 1981). Funds were raised for BDCs by selling stock to public utilities, businesses, commercial banks, and individual investors, but for a number of reasons BDCs were not successful. In practice they were too thinly capitalized to support significant levels of lending, and the private-sector individuals who managed BDCs tended to be averse to risk.

Tax-exempt industrial development bonds (IDBs) have now replaced BDCs as the most popular financing device. Between 1975 and 1980, sales of IDBs increased from approximately $1.3 billion to a record high of more than $8 billion. Currently 47 states issue IDBs, and more than half of them put no restrictions on the use of the proceeds. A decade ago IDBs were used exclusively for manufacturing and related facilities. Today they finance all manner of ventures, from shopping centers to grocery stores to private sports clubs (see also ch. 7, p. 273).

Tax credits, exemptions, and abatements have also been employed by many State and local governments to bring about 'desirable' private investment; but here again there is little or no evidence to support the efficacy of these incentives. Unlike the Northeastern and Midwestern States, the Southern and Western States have by and large stayed away from tax credits. In view of recent cuts in Federal aid, States and localities across the country can ill afford to erode their tax bases.

In the 1980s States should begin to view problems of private capital formation in a broader context than conventional institutions and inducements. The world of finance, both domestic and international, is changing daily. During the decade ahead, financial markets and institutions across the country will be substantially deregulated. Already Federal interest-rate ceilings have been raised, and the prohibition against paying interest on consumer demand deposits has been repealed. Different types of depository institutions, such as savings and loans, savings banks, commercial banks, credit unions, and brokerage firms, are being granted broader powers to compete with each other, and the distinction between investment banking and commercial banking may soon be meaningless.

Another radical change looms on the horizon. In all likelihood, interstate banking will be a reality by the end of the decade. Indeed, it can be argued that a removal of geographic constraints is imperative if commercial banks are to compete in the new financial environment of the 1980s. *Interstate banking, though currently prohibited by law, is already a fact in the marketplace.* Corporate banking operates across State lines through the use of telephone and electronic funds transfer technology. Account officers travel outside their home State to conduct interstate corporate banking business, stopping short only of physically affecting the resulting transactions in the States visited. Loan production offices and representative offices have enabled major banks to locate their lending and servicing officers near business customers. For instance, Citicorp of New York currently has 482 offices in 40 States and the District of Columbia. Under the International Banking Act (1978) Edge Act subsidiaries of money-center banks are allowed to conduct international business across State lines (BankAmerica International has offices in 12 non-California cities) and 37 foreign-owned banks operate depository offices in more than one State (Weinstein 1980).

Against this background of radical and rapid change in banking and finance, some conventional financial institutions may find themselves at a competitive disadvantage in the future. For example, prohibitions on branch banking and multibank-holding companies in at least five States inhibit mobilization of *indigenous financial potential* and make it difficult for local banks to compete with money-center banks and other financial institutions. Some might argue that the multibank-holding company serves as a satisfactory alternative to statewide branching, but available empirical evidence indicates that branching permits economies of scale that can lead to lower operating costs (Horvitz 1981). The elimination of existing intrastate restrictions can also lower barriers to entry and extend the force of potential competition to all banking markets in the State.

As a precursor to interstate banking, many States should give serious consideration to the development of reciprocal banking agreements. Under existing Federal law, Colorado, as an example, could permit banks from Arizona to acquire Colorado banks as long as Arizona allowed Colorado banks to do likewise. Such legislation is being considered at time of writing in North Carolina, Florida, California, and New York. Reciprocity would allow banks within a multistate region to extend their service areas and could also facilitate the eventual development of regional multibank-holding companies. Most observers believe that interstate banking will come about in stages, with regional expansion as a first step. The formation of regional holding companies can help to ensure the survival of the region's financial institutions when the brave new world of interstate competition becomes a legal, as well as a *de facto*, reality. The real issue here then is not the future of banking *per se* but the fostering of new and larger financial institutions that can attract and retain developmental capital for the future needs of American industry in various parts of the country.

   c. *Capital policies for industrial diversification.* Most of the growth States of the West are rich in mineral resources. Large deposits of oil, gas, coal, uranium, copper, molybdenum, gold, and other minerals are found across this vast region. The development of mineral and energy resources affords a unique opportunity for increasing revenue flows to the States, especially through the use of severance, *ad valorem*, and *in situ* mineral taxes.

   At a time of decreasing Federal resources, all States with mineral endowments should give serious thought to developing mechanisms for translating this *mineral* wealth into *economic* wealth—i.e. using mineral taxes to facilitate industrial development and diversification. Some States already dedicate a portion of their mineral tax revenues for impact assistance to local governments. For example, 17.5 per cent of Montana's coal severance tax receipts are returned to localities to assist them in providing services and facilities needed as a direct result of coal development (Weinstein 1981; see also ch. 5.6.3). New Mexico has set up a severance tax permanent fund against which revenue bonds are sold to finance infrastructure improvements in areas experiencing rapid development due to energy or mineral extraction. The establishment of permanent funds deriving revenues from mineral taxes should be high on the agenda of all States with indigenous mineral resources.

   The earmarking of a portion of mineral taxes *for venture capital* to small and/or risky businesses is also worthy of consideration. A prototype already exists in Alaska where the Alaska Renewable Resources Corporation uses 5 per cent of oil tax revenues to invest in the start-up and expansion of renewable resource enterprises such as fisheries, forestry, agriculture, aquaculture, and power generation. In other States it would probably make more sense to target investments towards manufacturing, research, and experimentation activities. A variety of approaches could be used—grants, loans, or equity investments. A portion of State pension fund earnings could be combined with permanent fund earnings to provide venture capital for *the mobilization of indigenous entrepreneurial potential*, a factor that seems destined to play a vital role in the regeneration of American industry.

6.4.3 The regional role in reindustrialization

The changing environment for development finance may prove to be the most crucial area for concern to policy-makers who see American Reindustrialization (the dictum of the Carter administration) or Economic Recovery (the label of the Reagan administration) as their foremost priority for the 1980s. The links between invention, innovation, and real economic growth cannot be complete without appropriate financial flows. The reindustrialization issue, however, has a number of other dimensions of concern to policy-makers, including a regional one.

One basic issue is conceptual in nature and concerns the definition of reindustrialization and its relationship to industrial policy. The concept is best defined by what Joseph Schumpeter (1942) called 'the process of creative destruction', where new economic structures bypass existing ones that become obsolete at a time when obsolescence seems to occur more quickly over time. In an economic system as large as that of the US, reindustrialization or economic recovery *at the national level* can take place by market forces interacting at the *State or local level*, with capital migrating from regions of lower returns to regions of higher returns. Interregional factor mobility is, therefore, an integral part of the reindustrialization process at the national level, particularly when it is cheaper to build industrial plants on new green-field sites as opposed to reconstruction at existing sites. Reindustrialization is, therefore, implicit in the newer growth centers of the American South and West (Phoenix, Dallas, Houston, and the like) where profits are being ploughed back in the form of new investment in growth industries that are able to generate innovation and, therefore, new rounds of capital formation and real economic growth.

This aspect of reindustrialization, however, should be differentiated from what is conventionally seen as industry policy. Industry policy, which has also gone under the label of sectoral or industrial adaptation policy in various countries, involves cooperative efforts between the private and public sectors, and, in many countries, direct government assistance to industry (OECD 1980). Though the US has not applied the kind of industry policy used in Western Europe and Japan, there can be little doubt that American industry has benefitted greatly from Federal spending. Military contracts, including research and development as well as direct procurement in the private sector, can be viewed as a *de facto* form of industry policy, as can certain tax incentives and other indirect forms of financial assistance. Given the recent interest in a more explicit form of industry policy in the US (Choate and Schwartz 1980), there remains a need to examine the goals, instruments, and possible impacts of such policy before the adoption of any particular form of industry or sectoral policy can be advocated.

One of the sure pitfalls of any industry policy involves the selection of winners and losers. Lessons in this regard can be gleaned from a study carried out by the Bureau of Industrial Economics (BIE 1980) in which they identified sectoral winners and losers over a 20-year period from a variety of indicators that included output growth, inflation, earnings, profitability, import penetration, and export performance. Most of the 'winners' are fairly predictable, with a couple of exceptions. The top six sectors were: chemicals, scientific instruments, electrical and electronic machinery, and nonelectrical machinery, along with motor vehicles and tobacco. The American automobile industry was performing well nationally until 1973, while the tobacco sector is a large export sector, though limited geographically to very specific production areas. The BIE report itself sounds a cautionary note. 'Some readers may find it surprising that motor vehicles are in the list of winners in view of recent reports of declining sales, rising imports and low profitability' (BIE 1980, 21). Had this analysis been undertaken some 50 years ago, no doubt steel also would have been in the list of winners, as opposed to being in the list of the most likely losers. Still we know very little to date as to how variations in regional industrial performance would influence such an analysis.

Another caveat that needs to be made before advocating a more explicit form of industrial policy in the US is the link with other policies: fiscal, monetary, trade policy, regulatory policy, as well as urban and regional policy. The intersectoral and interregional impacts of current changes in monetary policy, for example, are very poorly understood. Furthermore, given the geographical concentration of American industry, any industrial policy which is not integrated with urban and regional policy would seem counterproductive. For example, an industry policy targeted towards subsidizing sunset industries such as steel would largely restrict itself in impact to the Great Lakes States and to cities like Pittsburgh, Youngstown, Gary, and Buffalo. On the other hand, an industry policy aimed at a sunrise industry such as electronics, an industry perceived to be footloose but still highly clustered spatially, would have to take account of the initial seedbed in New England (the Boston area in particular) which has since lost out to California (particularly Silicon Valley) and other growth centers like Dallas and Phoenix in the southern rim.

Yet the experience of other countries does show that sectoral and regional policies can be integrated with some success. France has experienced limited successes with DATAR in coordinating industrial and regional development policy (Hansen 1974; House 1978). Ewers and Wettman (1980) have advocated an *innovation-based regional policy* for West Germany where elements of national science policy, sectoral policy, and regional policy should be more tightly integrated. There 'innovation-based regional policy' and 'regionalized innovation policy' amount to the same thing. They point out the operational options open to governments, including the subsidy of new product/process developments in particular regions and targeting national research and development initiatives towards small and medium-sized firms in peripheral areas. Some of these concepts implicit in the links between national science policy, industrial policy, and regional policy seem to be worthy of serious consideration in the US context (Rees 1982). To date, however, many questions relating to geographical differences in innovation generation and diffusion, and to the causal linkages between financial markets, labor markets, and regional innovation potential are in need of examination before appropriate instruments of regional industrial policy can be advocated with a focus on innovation in the US.

6.5 CONCLUSION

The first part of this chapter reviewed a number of structural and locational changes in American industry since 1945. Major changes were found to have taken place at the interregional level, with links to other decentralization forces at the urban scale. Some powerful market mechanisms were seen to be behind these changes, particularly changes in technology which influenced the structure of industry and its locational requirements and the perpetual search for greater profitability by companies responding to cheaper production factors, regional growth in demand, and the image of greater efficiency in new areas.

The impact of government policies on these geographical changes in industry was specifically addressed in section 6.3, with emphasis on the role of taxation policy at the State and local level, the impact of economic development assistance in particular regions and of military industrial spending, and the role of environmental protection policy. Taxation policy was seen as a production factor that only marginally affected industrial location decisions. The lack of direct incentives to industry and the low priority given to economic development programs from Washington has caused government policy in this area to be of minimal influence. Certain industries in specific regions are seen to be heavily dependent on government procurement contracts, but the studies and data analyzed show little evidence that any major geographical bias linked such contracts to regional industrial change in the US. The stringent environmental protection policies that have evolved in the US since the early 1970s were seen to have a large potential impact on industrial development, but no overriding argument can be made that such policies have a more detrimental impact on the States of earliest industrialization than on the growth States of recent times. Since all governmental policies affecting industry have an indirect locational impact, this was found to be an important area for policy analysis and evaluation where geographers could have a major role to play in the 1980s.

The third part of this chapter (6.4) focussed attention on two topics which economic geographers need to explore further to gain a better understanding of the impact of government policy on US industrial location, at a time when the future of the American industrial system itself may be in danger. The link between development finance and industrial location, and the changing geography of industrial innovation are two issues of critical importance to understanding the future evolution of the American industrial system. In this vein the work of geographers could play an important role in anticipating appropriate instruments in the policy-making arena.

References

ADVISORY COMMISSION ON INTERGOVERNMENTAL RELATIONS (1967) *State–Local taxation and industrial location* (Washington, DC).
—— (1978) *Regional growth study*, prelim. rep. (Washington, DC).
—— (1978) *Study of interstate competition for industry*, prelim. rep. (Washington, DC).

ALLEN, J. W. (1978) *Costs and benefits of federal regulation: an overview* (Washington, DC: Congress Res. Ser.).

ALONSO, W. (1978) 'Metropolis without growth', *Public Interest*, 53 68–86.

ARPAN, J. and RICKS, D. (1975) *Directory of foreign manufacturers in the United States* (Atlanta, Ga.: Georgia State Univ.).

BAHL, R. (1980) 'State and Local Government finances and the changing national economy', *Special study on economic change*, Vol. 7, *Joint Economic Committee of the United States* (Washington, DC), 1–127.

BAHL, R. W. and WARFORD, J. J. (1971) 'Interstate distribution of benefits from the Federal budgetary process', *Nat. Tax J.* 24 169–86.

BAIN, J. S. (1968) *Industrial organisation*, 2nd edn. (New York: Wiley).

BEALE, C. L. (1976) 'A further look at non-metropolitan population growth since 1970', *Am. J. Agric. Econ.* 58 953–8.

BERRY, B. J. L (1973) *Growth centers in the American urban system* (Cambridge, Mass.: Ballinger).

BEZDEK, R. H. (1975) 'The 1980 economic impact—regional and occupational—of compensated shifts in defense spending', *J. Reg. Sci.* 15 183–98.

BOLTON, R. (1966) *Defense purchases and regional growth* (Washington, DC: Brookings Instn.).

—— (1980) 'Impacts of defense spending on urban areas', in GLICKMAN, N. (ed.), *The urban impacts of Federal policies* (Baltimore, Md.: Johns Hopkins Univ. Press).

BRIGGS, R. and REES, J. (1982) 'Control Factors in the Economic Development of Nonmetropolitan America', *Environ. and Plann. A* (forthcoming).

BROWNING, C. E. and GESSLER, W. (1979) 'The Sunbelt–Snowbelt: a case of sloppy regionalizing', *Prof. Geogr.* 31 1, 66–74.

BUREAU OF CENSUS (1965–76) 'Shipments of defense-oriented industries', *Curr. Ind. Rep.* (Washington, DC).

—— (1973–6) 'Pollution abatement costs and expenditures', *Curr. Ind. Rep.* (Washington, DC).

BUREAU OF INDUSTRIAL ECONOMICS (1980) 'Evaluating the Economic Performance of U.S. Manufacturing Industries', *Ind. Econ. Rev.* 6–19.

CAMERON, G. C. (1968) 'The regional problem in the United States: Some reflections on a viable Federal strategy', *Reg. Stud.*, 2 207–20.

CARLTON, D. W. (1978) 'Why new firms locate where they do', paper presented to *Comm. on. Urb. Publ. Econ.* (Baltimore, Md.).

CHOATE, P. and SCHWARTZ, G. (1980) *Revitalizing the U.S. economy: A brief for national sectoral policies* (Washington, DC: Acad. for Contemporary Probl.).

CHOATE, P. and WALTER, S. (1981) *The wearing out of America* (Washington, DC: Coun. of State Plann. Agencies).

CUMERBLAND, J. H. (1971) *Regional development: experiences and prospects in the United States of America* (Paris and The Hague: Mouton).

DANHOF, C. H. (1964) 'Four Decades of Thought on the South's Economic Problems' in GREENHUT, M. L. and WHITMAN, W. T. (eds). *Essays in Southern Economic Development* (Chapel Hill, NC: Univ. N. Carolina Press).

DANIELS, B. (1981) *Four Corners capital market study* (Cambridge, Mass.: Coun. for Community Devel.).

DENISON, E. F. (1978) 'Effects of selected changes in the institutional and human environment upon output per unit of input', *Surv. Curr. Busin.* 58 1, 21–43.

DICKEN, P. (1976) 'The multi-plant business enterprise and geographical space: some issues in the study of external control and regional development,' *Reg. Stud.* 10 401–12.

ECONOMIC DEVELOPMENT ADMINISTRATION (1972) *EDA Res. Rev.* (Washington, DC: USGPO).

260 *United States Public Policy*

ERICKSON, R. A. (1975) 'The spatial pattern of income generation in lead firm, growth area linkage systems', *Econ. Geogr.* 51 17–26.

—— and LEINBACH, T. R. (1978) 'The filtering-down process: characteristics and contribution of industrial activitis attracted to nonmetropolitan areas', Paper presented to Ass. Am. Geogr., New Orleans.

ESTALL, R. (1977) 'Regional planning in the United States', *Tn. Plann. Rev.* 48 341–64.

EWERS, H. J. and WETTMAN, R. W. (1980) 'Innovation-oriented regional policy', *Reg. Stud.* 14 161–80.

FRANKO, L. G. (1978) 'Multinationals: the end of U.S. dominance', *Harv. Busin. Rev.* Nov.–Dec. 91–101.

GLADWIN, T. N. and WELLES, J. G. (1976) 'Environmental policy and multinational corporate strategy', in WALTER, I. (ed.), *Studies in international environmental economics* (New York: Wiley).

GLICKMAN, N. (1980) *The urban impacts of Federal policies* (Baltimore, Md.: Johns Hopkins Univ. Press).

HANSEN, N. M. (1974) *Public policy and regional economic development: the experience of nine western countries* (Cambridge, Mass.: Ballinger).

HINES, F. K. and REID, J. N. (1977) 'Using Federal outlays data to measure program equity: opportunities and limitations', *Am. J. Agric. Econ.* 59 1013–19.

HOLMER, M. (1978) 'Preliminary analysis of the regional economic effects of Federal procurement', Paper presented to Comm. on Urb. Publ. Econ., Baltimore.

HORVITZ, P. M. (1981) 'Geographic restrictions on financial institutions', The future of the financial services industry, Working paper (Atlanta, Ga.: Fed. Reserve Bank of Atlanta).

HOUSE, J. W. (1978) *France: an applied geography* (London: Methuen).

JUSENIUS, C. L. and LEDEBUR, L. C. (1976) *A myth in the making: the southern economic challenge and northern economic decline* (Washington, DC: Office Econ. Res., Econ. Devel. Admin.).

—— and —— (1977) 'The Northern tier and the Sunbelt: conflict or cooperation', *Challenge*, March, 44–9.

KARASKA, A. J. (1966) 'Interregional flows of defense-space awards: The role of subcontracting in an impact analysis of changes in the levels of defense awards upon the Philadelphia economy', *Pap. Peace Res. Soc.* 5 45–62.

—— (1967) 'The spatial impacts of defense-space procurement: an analysis of sub-contracting patterns in the United States', *Pap. Peace Res. Soc.* 8 109–22.

KEEBLE, D. (1976) *Industrial location and planning in the United Kingdom* (London: Methuen).

KOCH, J. V. (1974) *Industrial organisation and prices* (London: Prentice-Hall).

LEONE, R. A. and JACKSON, J. E. (1978) 'The political economy of Federal regulatory activity', Res. Paper Harv. Univ.

LEONTIEF, W., MORGAN, A., BOLENSKE, K., SIMPSON, D. and TOWER, E. (1965) 'The economic impact industrial and regional, of an arms cut', *Rev. Econ. Stat.* 47 217–34.

LITVAK, L. and DANIELS, B. (1979) *Innovations in development finance* (Washington, DC: Coun. State Plann. Agencies).

LONSDALE, R. E. and SEYLER, H. L. (1979) *Nonmetropolitan industrialisation* (Washington, DC: V. H. Winston).

MALECKI, E. (1979) 'Locational trends in R & D by large US corporations', *Econ. Geogr.* 55 309–23.

—— (1981) 'Government-funded R & D: some regional implications', *Prof. Geogr.* 33 72–82.

MANSFIELD, E. *et al.* (1977) *The production and application of new industry tech-*

nology (New York: W. W. Norton).

MARKUSEN, A. R. and FASTRUP, J. (1978) 'The regional war for Federal aid', *Public Interest*, 53 87–99.

MCCARTHY, K. F. and MORRISON, P. A. (1978) 'The changing demographic and economic structure of nonmetropolitan areas in the 1970s', *Rand Pap.* 6062 (Santa Monica, Cal.: Rand Corpn.).

MIERNYK, W. H. (1976) *The changing structure of the Southern economy*, Conf. Paper (Sth. Growth Policies Board).

—— (1978) 'The tools of regional development policy: an evaluation', Paper presented to Reg. Sci. Ass., Chicago.

MORIARTY, B. M. (1976) 'The distributed lag between metropolitan-area employment and population growth', *J. Reg. Sci.* 16 195–212.

NATIONAL BUREAU OF ECONOMIC RESEARCH (1975) 'Water Pollution Control Act of 1972: economic impacts—plant closures' (Washington, DC: NTIS).

NATIONAL SCIENCE BOARD (1977) *Science indicators 1976* (Washington, DC: USGPO).

NORTON, R. D. and REES, J. (1979) 'The product cycle and the spatial decentralisation of American manufacturing', *Reg. Stud.* 13 141–51.

OECD (1980) *Regional policies in the United States* (Paris: OECD).

OKUN, A. (1978) *Capitalism and democracy*, McGraw Hill lecture, Columbia Univ. (New York).

PERLOFF, H. and WINGO, L. (1961) 'Natural resource endowment and regional economic growth', in SPENGLER, J. J. (ed.), *Natural resources and economic growth*, (Washington, DC: Res. for the Future).

PETERSON, G. E. and MULLER, T. (1977) 'The regional impact of Federal tax and spending policies', Conf. Paper *Alternatives to Confrontation, a national policy towards regional change*, Austin, Texas.

POLENSKE, K. R. (1978) 'Regional methods of analysis for stagnating regions', Paper presented at Internat. Inst. Reg. Sci. (Siegen, Germany).

PRED, A. (1977) *City systems in advanced economies* (New York: Wiley).

REES, J. (1978A) 'Manufacturing headquarters in a post-industrial urban context', *Econ. Geogr.* 54 337–54.

—— (1978B) 'Manufacturing change, internal control and government spending in a growth region of the USA', in HAMILTON, F. E. I. (ed.), *Industrial change: international experience and public policy* (London: Longman), 155–74.

—— (1979A) 'Technological change and regional shifts in American manufacturing', *Prof. Geogr.* 31 45–54.

—— (1979B) 'Regional industrial shifts in the U.S. and the internal generation of manufacturing in growth centers of the Southwest', in WHEATON, W. (ed.), *Interregional movements and regional growth*, *Pap. in Public Econ.* 2 51–73 (Washington, DC: The Urb. Inst.).

—— (1980) 'Government policy and industrial location in the United States', *Special study on economic change*, Vol. 7 *Joint Economic Committee of the United States* (Washington, DC: USGPO), 128–79.

—— HEWINGS, G. J. D. and STAFFORD, H. A. (eds.) (1981) *Industrial location and regional systems* (New York: Bergin).

REID, S. R. (1976) *The new industrial order: concentration, regulation and public policy* (New York: McGraw Hill).

SCHUMPETER, J. A. (1942) *Capitalism, socialism and democracy* (New York: Harper & Row).

SMITH, D. M. (1971) *Industrial location* (London: Wiley).

STAFFORD, H. A. (1977) 'Environmental regulations and the location of U.S. manufacturing', *Geoforum*, 8 243–48.

STERNLIEB, G. and HUGHES, J. W. (1977) 'New regional and metropolitan realities of America', *J. Am. Inst. Plann.* 43 227–41.
STERNLIEB, G. and HUGHES, J. W. (1978) *Revitalizing the Northeast* (Rutgers, NJ: Center for Urb. Policy Res.).
STRUYK, R. S. and JAMES, F. J. (1975) *Intrametropolitan industrial location* (Lexington, Mass.: D. C. Heath).
THOMAS, M. D. and LE HERON, R. B. (1975) 'Perspectives on technological change and the process of diffusion in the manufacturing sector', *Econ. Geogr.* 51 231–51.
TIEBOUT, C. M. and PETERSON, R. S. (1964) 'Measuring the impact of regional defense-space expenditures', *Rev. Econ. Stat.* 46 421–8.
VAUGHAN, R. S. (1977) *The urban impacts of Federal policies: Vol 2. Econ. Devel.* (Santa Monica, Cal.: Rand Corp. Rep.).
WEIDENBAUM, M. L. and DE FINA, R. (1978) 'The cost of Federal regulation of economic activity', *Am. Enterprise Inst. Reprint* 88.
WEINSTEIN, B. L. (1980) 'State energy taxation—produces state issues', *Proc. 73rd Nat. Tax Ass. Conf.*, 35–8.
—— (1981) *Report of the task force on the Southern economy* (Research Triangle Park, NC: Sth. Growth Policies Board).
—— and FIRESTINE, R. E. (1978) *Regional growth and decline in the United States* (New York: Praeger).
WHEATON, W. C. (1978) 'Area wages, unemployment and inter-regional factor mobility', Paper presented to Comm. Urb. Publ. Econ., Baltimore, Md.
—— (1979) (ed.) *Interregional movements and regional growth*, COUPE 2 (Washington, DC: Urb. Inst.).
WHITING, A. (1975) *The economics of industrial subsidies* (London: HMSO).

7. The Imprint of Federal Policy on Evolving Urban Form

CHRISTOPHER S. DAVIES
(*University of Texas at Austin*)

7.1 THE PARTITION OF A NATION: A GEOGRAPHICAL INQUIRY

This chapter discusses the role of Federal urban policies in accommodating individual preferences for a low-density living style, thereby helping to fashion geographic change in metropolitan America. The relative spatial distributions of people and their activities in US cities are examined with a prime focus on Federal aid programs which have encouraged the most dramatic changes in the social and physical pattern of the American city. Some Federal policies, such as inner-city poverty programs, are geographically targeted, others are spatial only in impact, as for example Federal tax deductions on the process of suburbanization. Federal policies are evaluated in their effects, positive or negative, on the continuing polarization of the US city into two nations: the inner-city poor and the suburban rich. As the term 'urban policy' was rarely used by Federal officials until the Kennedy–Johnson years (1962–9), this inquiry predominantly spans policies since the early 1960s.

A feature endemic to US SMSAs (Standard Metropolitan Statistical Areas) is the impoverishment of the inner city by the territorial withdrawal to suburbia of the more affluent residents (Berry 1980, 3). Although, on the one hand, the dominant trend in the ecological structure of the city is towards dispersion, increasing concentrations of low-income groups are to be found in the central city. Inner-city areas have a preponderance of under-privileged minorities, located in racially segregated housing areas. The process of internal territorial shifting shows how the upwardly mobile counteract Federal statutes that reinforced the locational rights of minorities (Harvey 1972, 2).

The two-nation split is now as much an urban planning problem as a class or racial one (Sternlieb and Hughes 1980, 177–80). To the extent this spatial distribution is the geographic expression of prevailing economic pursuits and lifestyle preferences, the Federal government is reluctant to interfere. While Federal policy has not deliberately created the drift of the US city into two nations, neither has it attempted seriously to prevent it. Rather, policy-makers have encouraged dispersion while proffering stopgap measures to prevent chaos and collapse in the inner city.

Until the 1960s there was no conscious development of a national urban policy. Policy was enacted to help city government achieve local employment, income, and housing objectives. The Truman administration's (1946–53) only significant domestic urban legislation was the Taft–Ellinger–Wagner Act (1949), authorizing the building of public housing to replace slums.

Emphasis on urban renewal also characterized the Eisenhower years (1953–61), although under a Republican administration the program shifted its main objective from the provision of public housing to renovation of commercial areas in city centers.

It was during and following the Kennedy–Johnson era (1962–9) that a plethora of legislative programs dealing with urban issues was passed by Congress. These included the Civil Rights Act (1964), the Economic Opportunity Act (1964), the Urban Mass Transportation Acts (1964 and 1966), the Model Cities Act (1966), and the Fair Housing Act (1968). Several of these programs were discontinued by the Nixon–Ford administration (1970–6), which engineered the revenue-sharing and block-grant programs. Under their provisions, cities were given greater discretion on how to spend this funding. The Carter administration (1977–80) substantially increased Federal aid to cities while reintroducing some of the restrictions of the Johnson administration on the freedom of local governments to spend Federal aid money.

By the late 1970s the political power of the new conservative right had overcome the influence of the liberal left in both the US and the UK; the shift to Fabian socialism and New Deal liberalism has waned. Progressive inflation, increased bureaucratic intrusion, and the failure of the New Society programs of Kennedy and Johnson led to the Reagan administration, whose main source of economic inspiration is Milton Friedman and Friedrich Hayek of the 'Chicago School of Economics' with their concept of individual choice through competitive capitalism and limited government trespass (Friedman 1962; Hayek 1964). The liberal revisionism of the Democratic New Society programs is being systematically dismantled.

The key Federal policies that shaped immediate postwar (1945–60) urban America were those affecting housing and the Federal tax structure; transportation programs and land-use regulation were later influences. Policy priorities changed dramatically: in the 1960s, in response to the emerging issues of poverty, crime, and minority unrest; in the 1970s, in answer to rising environmental, energy, and fiscal concerns; and in the 1980s, as the Reagan administration attacked inflation and unemployment, echoing the refrain that urban problems are the product of 'big government'.

Evaluating the impact of Federal policies is difficult. The spatial structures of people and activities interact with the policies that influence them. For instance, alleviating traffic congestion through a policy of freeway expansion also encourages urban sprawl. Concern over urban sprawl then generates tax assessment policies that favor the retention of farmland on the urban fringe. Usually, problem symptoms of this two-nation drift, inner-city poverty, crime, or traffic congestion, attract a policy response. Such policies generally avoid defining quantitative targets and this type of forecasting may in any case be superfluous, for external conditions function independently of policy and outside its limits. In urban renewal, for example, the housing problems of the poor were intensified rather than relieved, since forces external, or even contrary to the designs of policy-makers, caused trends largely in contradiction to policy intents. Geographical analysis can assess and predict the impacts of Federal policy on the inner city, suburbia, and exurbia and evaluate policy roles in either amplifying or attenuating the inequities wrought by the present distribution of people and opportunities (Adams 1979).

7.2 CONTEMPORARY US URBAN CHARACTERISTICS

7.2.1 A spatial sketch and historical evolution

Originally directed towards slum clearance and CBD revitalization, Federal urban policy reflected the rising national conscience concerning the antiquated and immovable features of the nineteenth-century city. During the Industrial Revolution in the US, major advances in production took place in cities, the new principal loci of wealth generation. Large-scale industrialization required and achieved the redeployments of people from farms to urban factories. Because of primitive nineteenth-century intra-urban transportation, factories developed as tightly clustered districts, adjacent to the equally compact, high-density residential communities that housed the working classes. These outdated factories, warehouses, and housing have decayed, largely in proportion to diffusion of economic prosperity to the urban periphery.

The split of Federal policy to include programs for stimulating centrifugal growth began in the last decades of the nineteenth century. Tightly focussed, core-dominated cities began to disintegrate, as steam, and later electric power, came in, and the railroad linked home and workplace. Transport innovations help to explain the timing of residential development and the subsequent cellular urban ring pattern.

As intra-urban transportation continued to improve, with the subsequent widespread adoption of the automobile, manufacturing establishments began to disperse from central-city locations. The new, more productive technology of horizontally extensive, assembly-line production required cheap land and was ill-suited to the congestion of urban cores. At the same time large numbers of central-city residents joined the movement to the suburbs to escape the dirt and noise of inner-city crowding. They moved to single-family buildings with private yards, on the relatively cheap land of the urban periphery. The centrifugal movement of industry and population in turn induced the movement of commerce and other services, to establish a clear trend of urban decentralization that continues to the present.

Oscar Handlin's phrase 'immigrants are America' (Handlin 1951) captures the essence of the social evolution of cities. Foreign-born citizens now constitute only a small proportion of ethnic groups, for recurring explosions of indigenous feelings around the turn of the century led to restrictive Federal immigration policies. These culminated in the Johnson–Reid Act (1924) that curtailed the ethnic geography of US cities (Thernstrom 1981). Today a rising sense of ethnicity may supersede the significance of class in urban social analysis. This reflects a declining confidence in national identity, the imprecise 'melting pot' metaphor, and the concept of increased exogamy (Cohen 1974). There is now strong support for ethnicity, since it eases the way in which a life increasingly controlled by large bureaucracies denies an individual sense of identity (Greeley 1977). Ethnic groups survive in neighborhood niches because organized groups reap political benefits, a concept not lost on black civil rights movements of the 1960s. The struggle of these immigrant groups for resources promoted ethnic hegemony, allegiance, and exclusiveness (Kornblum 1974, 138–60).

7.2.2. From metropolitan growth and suburban dominance to urban decentralization

Metropolitan growth burgeoned during the 1950s when migratory movements accelerated the long-run decline of isolated rural areas, leaving an aging population, substandard incomes, and declining industries in its wake (Palm 1981, 158–82). Rural to urban migration, including black migration, contracted by the early 1950s, to be replaced by migration up the urban hierarchy from small towns to large cities. As a result, SMSAs acquired over 5 million residents and grew at an annual rate of 3.8 per cent for the decade, compared with an average rate of 0.5 per cent for nonmetropolitan areas.

A similar pattern was recorded in the era of suburban dominance in the 1960s. Metropolitan areas continued to grow, but at a slower annual rate of 1.5 per cent, compared to 0.7 per cent for nonmetropolitan areas (Fig. 7.1). The total population in central cities grew by only 5 millions, largely through territorial expansion, compared to the suburban growth of nearly 20 millions for the decade. The falling growth rate of the central cities, averaging only 0.6 per cent annually, occurred despite the widespread annexation of former suburban land and population. Central-city decline was reflected in a new outmigration of 3.5 million people, while the suburbs experienced a net inmigration of some 9 millions during the same period.

Unbridled metropolitan growth subsided in the 1970s. A migration reversal began, in the form of growth in exurban and isolated rural areas, a reversal in harmony with the lifestyle preferences of America for increasing real income, leisure, and mobility. The long history of US metropolitan growth and concentration is on the wane. While national population grew 1.08 per cent per annum, 1970–80, to 226 millions, nonmetropolitan areas grew at an annual rate of 1.5 per cent, compared to only 0.9 per cent in the metropolises, as people migrated down the urban hierarchy. Central-city populations fell by 0.6 per cent per annum, 1970–8, while suburban population continued to grow, though at a slower rate of 1.8 per cent per annum. This trend to metropolitan stability is similar to those already experienced in other post-industrial societies and suggests that metropolitan areas are no longer the dominant national growth poles (Sternlieb and Hughes 1980, 58).

The nation's largest SMSAs were most affected by the slowdown in metropolitan growth in the 1970s (Fig. 7.2). Of SMSAs with over 3 million people only Washington had an annual growth rate of more than 1 per cent. Total SMSA population declined in Pittsburgh as it had in the 1960s, and decline also affected New York, Chicago, Los Angeles, Detroit, Seattle, Cleveland, and St. Louis among other SMSAs. In SMSAs of 1 to 3 million people the trends varied by region: in the Northeast and North Central regions little or no growth, and in the South and West small or moderate, but declining growth rates. SMSAs with fewer than 1 million people grew more rapidly.

Regionally there were contrasts (Fig. 7.3; see also chs. 2, pp. 44–5; 3, pp. 101–2; and 6, pp. 217–26). In the Northeast and North Central Regions

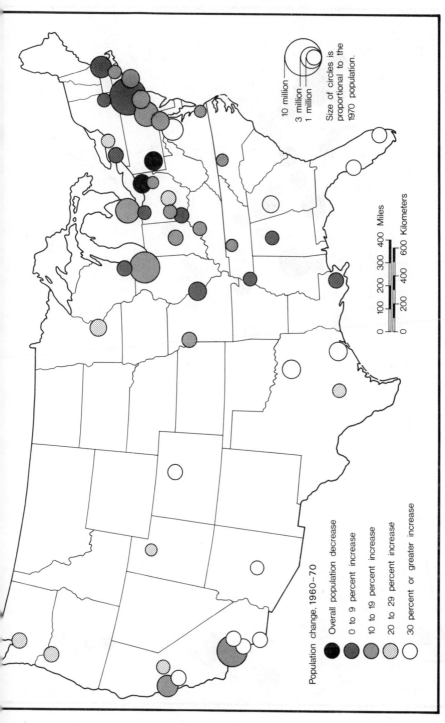

Population change, 1960–70

- Overall population decrease
- 0 to 9 percent increase
- 10 to 19 percent increase
- 20 to 29 percent increase
- 30 percent or greater increase

10 million
3 million
1 million

Size of circles is proportional to the 1970 population.

0   100   200   300   400 Miles
0   200   400   600 Kilometers

7.1   Population change, 1960–70, 50 largest SMSAs

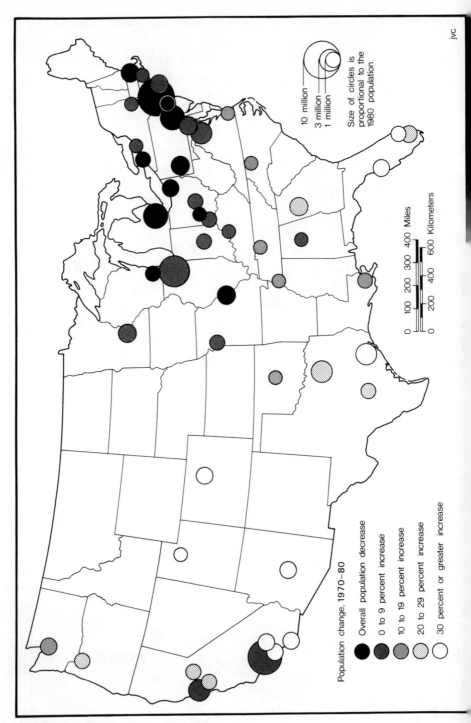

Population change, 1970–80

Size of circles is proportional to the 1980 population.

10 million
3 million
1 million

Overall population decrease
0 to 9 percent increase
10 to 19 percent increase
20 to 29 percent increase
30 percent or greater increase

Miles   0   100   200   300   400
Kilometers   0   200   400   600

jvc

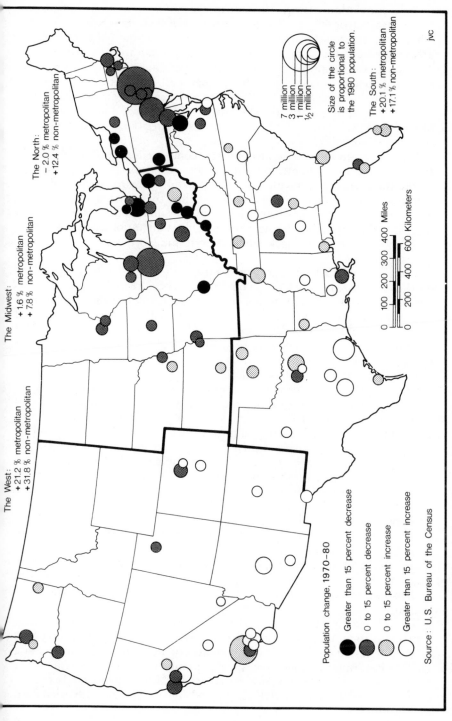

The North:
− 2.0 % metropolitan
+12.4 % non-metropolitan

The Midwest:
+1.6 % metropolitan
+7.8 % non-metropolitan

The West:
+21.2 % metropolitan
+31.8 % non-metropolitan

The South:
+20.1 % metropolitan
+17.1 % non-metropolitan

7 million
3 million
1 million
½ million

Size of the circle
is proportional to
the 1980 population.

jvc

0   100   200   300   400 Miles

0   200   400   600 Kilometers

Population change, 1970–80

Greater than 15 percent decrease

0 to 15 percent decrease

0 to 15 percent increase

Greater than 15 percent increase

Source: U.S. Bureau of the Census

7.3   The rise and fall of America's 100 largest cities, 1970–80 overall population growth slowed; in the South and West it increased. Northeast metropolitan areas lost 2 per cent of their population, 1970–80, while nonmetropolitan areas gained 12.4 per cent. In the West metropolitan areas increased by 21.2 per cent and nonmetropolitan areas by 31.8 per cent. The South was the only region where metropolitan growth of 20.1 per cent exceeded nonmetropolitan growth (17.1 per cent), though there were marked intraregional divergences, e.g. Florida 50.8 per cent nonmetropolitan, 39.2 per cent metropolitan growth. The Middle West showed a mere 1.8 per cent metropolitan increase and 7.8 per cent in nonmetropolitan areas (US Bureau of Census 1981).

Migration continued to be an important component of population change. In the 1970s, for example, net outmigration from the Northeast grew, to reduce the effect of natural increase on population growth. The racial composition of migrants changed markedly: in the 1960s net outmigration of 900,000 whites was more than offset by the inmigration of 1.6 million blacks; in the 1970s the national pattern of black migration came to resemble that for whites and net black inmigration to the Northeast from the South virtually ceased.

The reversal of national growth trends also relates to a declining rate of natural increase. Nationally, the birthrate has been reduced from 25 births per 1,000 people in 1955, to less than 15 per 1,000 in 1980. The average annual rate of natural increase by the 1970s was only 0.9 per cent, compared with 1.3 per cent a year in the 1960s. With a fairly constant mortality rate and a fertility rate projected to range between 2.1 and 1.4 children per female in the 1980s and 1990s, migration change has become the principal determinant of an area's growth or decline.

Given stable to lower demographic rates, migration trends now provide the most sensitive indicator of economic realities. Migration gain reflects economic vitality, whereas migration loss is a prelude to, or evidence of, economic stagnation. Rural migrants from the hollows of Appalachia and the flats of the Mississippi delta drifted to cities following the depression of the 1930s. A powerful *de facto* urban policy implicit in Federal agricultural programs stimulated this shift (Wingo 1975, 5). The demise of this movement by the 1960s reflects on the wage bribe no longer compensating for the negative aspects of life in large cities. The transportation advantages these cities once enjoyed are being eroded by innovations which allow 'footloose' electronic industries, no longer dependent on extractive resource locations to seek out the smaller economies of scale of exurban and nonmetropolitan locations. Freeway expansion permits their work force access to the advantages of neighboring cities. In a 'graying nation' social security payments, earlier retirements, and improved benefits permit this Spenglerian search for the rural ideal.

This idealization of the rural past manifests itself in the form of exurbia, retirement communities, weekend recreational and mobile homes, and 5-acre farms purchased on the profits accumulated in a Chicago, a Baltimore, or a Dallas. Returning to their 'rootstock', urbanites are shunting aside their country cousins in areas as varied as the Ozarks, New England, the Texas Hill country, North Georgia, and the Cajun and Gullah country of Louisiana and the Carolinas.

7.2.3. Inequalities of wealth and well-being

The most important single trend in American metropolitan development since the 1960s is the decline of central cities. Shifts of private investment to suburbs and the encouragement given to suburbanization by Federal aid for construction of new highways and middle- and upper-income housing have eroded the economic and fiscal base of central cities since World War II. In 1977 the greatest urban problem was seen as the maintenance and upgrading of public infrastructure and the reversing of the current downward trend in capital expenditure in central cities.

Decentralization, as an adjustment of urban form to changes in technology and automobile usage, has drastically undermined the economy and society of the central cities, reducing population there in relative or absolute terms, and increasing spatial inequalities of wealth and well-being in metropolitan America. Since the nineteenth century central cities have received a steady stream of poor, rural workers, many from the South, displaced by mechanization and other technological changes in agriculture. The movement of population to the suburbs, however, has worked to reduce central-city population, and the movement has been carefully selective, involving industry, commerce, and wealthier households, but excluding the poor.

This exclusion reflects the efforts of the growing numbers of the wealthy in suburbia to detach themselves from the welfare services' burden of inner cities by organizing suburban territory into local jurisdictions separate from the central cities. This jurisdictional independence is used to erect a formidable array of exclusionary zoning regulations, the most powerful planning tool in American cities. The city is a balkanization of segregated income, ethnic, and minority concentration, with the real-estate industry tacitly applying restrictive housing covenants to maintain this pattern (Wingo 1975, 5; Berry and Kasarda 1977, 369). The fragmentation of metropolitan government and the erosion of the central-city tax base through defections has reduced central-city revenues at a time when expenditures are inflated by the growing welfare burden of its poor.

The intensifying economic disparity between central cities and suburbs is seen in a comparison of average family income. In 1975 average central-city household income as a percentage of suburban household income was only 79 per cent in the Northeast, 85 per cent in the Midwest, 93 per cent in the West, and 96 per cent in the South. Of central city residents 15 per cent reported earnings below the Federally defined poverty level in 1980, compared to only 7 per cent of the suburban population. The overall black population in US cities grew from 18 per cent in 1950 to over 30 per cent in 1980, yet less than 10 per cent of the suburban population in 1980 was black. The major outcome of a *de facto* national growth policy has been to produce a segregated urban society with its opprobrious racial confrontations (Wingo 1975, 5–7).

7.2.4 Central-city tax-base erosion and rising costs of services

The combination of tax-base erosion and rising costs of city services has created a condition of fiscal disadvantage in central cities. Cities with the greatest population loss were those with the highest tax rates and per capita service costs, whereas growing cities exhibited the reverse. The median value of central-city, owner-occupied housing is some 15 per cent lower than in suburban areas, of particular significance since about 80 per cent of local tax yields come from property taxes. In some high-cost cities, the welfare burden and the effects of union-determined salaries are aggravated by obsolete service programs and a tendency to borrow against short-term insolvency. The reckless borrowing that catapulted New York City into fiscal disarray highlighted the dangers of excessive public spending, and curtailed service provision.

The crisis in New York City led to innovative finance proposals for cities even when there had been no lack of fiscal responsibility (Muller 1975B, 201–16). These proposals include the Federalisation of Welfare and Medicaid programs, currently funded between local, State, and Federal authorities; State responsibility for traditional local functions such as education and criminal justice; and the regionalization of taxes in metropolitan areas. The first two proposals would reduce costs faced by local governments, with limited borrowing capacity, by reassigning financial responsibility for expensive city programs to higher levels of government, with their greater fiscal capacity (Danielson 1971, 247–52). The third proposal would increase the central-city share of tax revenues generated by economic activity in metropolitan areas. President Reagan's withdrawal of Federal revenue for inner-city programs intensifies the cry for an areawide taxing base. If this does not transpire, then city budgets must also cover suburban growth since service levels in suburbia are well below expectation, resulting in suburbanites exploiting central-city services.

To accommodate these demands, there is a relatively higher employment ratio, workers per capita population, in central cities than in suburbs. Until the recession of the mid-1970s, the employment expansion in central-city services had exceeded the growth rate of urban population. The rising cost of these workers led to high and rising tax levies on central-city residents, who pay more of their incomes in State and local taxes than those residing in the suburbs (Muller 1975A). The generally higher tax burden in the central cities has been increasing, accompanied by the retrenchment of services (Berry and Kasarda 1977, 225–7).

Urban problems were aggravated by the Arab Oil Embargo of 1973–4 which thrust the economy into 'stagflation', a national recession accompanied by high inflation. With strong voter resistance to tax increases, city officials struggle even to maintain existing levels of service. The urban-policy debate has shifted from ameliorating conditions and creating new amenities and services to improving urban conditions within existing service levels.

Between 1955 and 1980, Federal aid as a proportion of local revenues rose from 1.1 per cent to 16.6 per cent for counties, 1.9 per cent to 22.8 per cent for cities, and 20.9 per cent to 38.0 per cent for States (*U.S. News and World Report*, Feb. 1982, 28). President Reagan's 1983 budget indicated a desire to divest the Federal government of this responsibility. This development will have an uneven impact on cities, with those in the energy rich States such as Texas, with a State surplus of $200 million in 1981, able to absorb change more readily than high unemployment and slow growth cities in States such as Michigan, with a $400 million deficit in 1981. Cities in energy-poor States want a Federal ceiling on severance taxes levied by coal-rich states such as Montana (ch. 5.4.2). A positive balance in State-operating funds is the key to fiscal health now that Federal contributions are plummeting. Cities challenged by the recession and increasing local taxes already face cutbacks as Federal grants to cities fell 15 per cent over 1981 figures, the first decrease since 1964.

The Federal cutbacks will force cities to continue trimming municipal jobs, welfare rolls, subsidized housing, and sewer and mass-transit service. It was vainly hoped that Federal income-tax reductions would offset State and local tax increases by stimulating private investment and thus increase State and city revenues. Consequently, in a high-interest property market, commuter, and payroll taxes are on the increase, as are service fees.

Already prudent because of Proposition 13 in California, cities are forced to do more with less. Limited help is expected from States, historically unsympathetic to cities, and now themselves to be burdened with welfare programs under President Reagan's New Federalism. Increased competition between cities and suburbs for limited State resources and increased inter-urban competition for new industry accentuates the divide between prosperous and declining cities. Between 1971 and 1981, the net increase in industrial revenue (development) bonds issued by States and cities as business recruitment funds for new factory and office construction, has risen from $0.1 to $5.0 billion (Federal Reserve Board 1981). Harnessing these funds to 'Shannon Ireland' development techniques, cities are wooing foreign businesses with free property tax, infrastructure incentives, and relaxed zoning codes (see also ch. 5, pp. 232–4).

7.2.5 National urban realignment

The cities of the Northeastern Manufacturing Belt experienced their zenith some decades back. Federal welfare disbursements to soothe potential unrest and to buttress those left behind in the inner cities do little to resuscitate their economies and only worsen their plight. As dependency on welfare grows (Yeates and Garner 1980, 430), it creates a climate alien to that desired by emerging quaternary industries, computer-based, electronics, telecommunications, and aerospace, of post-industrial economies (Gottmann 1970).

Loss of jobs started in the failure to capture a share of national prosperity during the 1950s and 1960s. Although industrial jobs continued to grow, the Manufacturing Belt's relative share fell from 70 (1950) to 56 per cent (mid-1960s) (Berry 1980, 3). A lessening of the current national recession will aggravate their plight as firms, people, and capital exit for the South and West. Exhibiting a declining ability to compete in international markets, Northeastern cities are unwilling partners to a 'fittest city shall survive' syndrome, a type of urban Darwinism resulting from a natural process of economic realignment (Perry and Watkins 1977, 13–17).

This geographical realignment of industry and the growing territorial imbalance in job opportunities between cities of the Northeast and those in the South and West has fostered the unfortunate view that the South's alarming urban growth, specifically that in Florida and Texas, is at the expense of declining Northeastern cities. The struggle is between such declining cities of the North as Detroit, Cleveland, or Pittsburgh, and growing cities in the South like Tulsa, Phoenix, or Austin. Since Federal largesse is based on census returns, Pittsburgh, down 5.8 per cent in population since 1970, perceives its abandonment as a threat to economic vitality.

The reversal of decades of northern urbanization is the subject of considerable debate (Downs 1983). It disguises complex migratory processes at work within the urban hierarchy (Hansen 1981, 47), exemplified in a comparison between Cleveland and New Orleans. Both are cities which have experienced population loss for different reasons. In the former, the number of households is declining in a shrinking metropolitan area, whereas the latter, although stagnant, is stagnant in a buoyant and growing metropolitan complex, a distinction that solicits different public policy responses. Because the Sunbelt and exurban movements are cumulative, a city like Austin, Texas, an SMSA that leaped from 56th to 41st largest city in the US following a 35.4 per cent growth, 1970–80, experiences overburdened services and increased taxation caused by arriving migrants.

The Sunbelt–Snowbelt controversy, which lies behind these regional differences in city growth and prospects is discussed in chapter 2.2.1; the industrial basis is considered in chapter 6.3.1. Attention here is confined to urban aspects of Federal government policy. Federal allocation and purchasing policies clearly have had differential regional and urban effects (Fossett and Osborn 1980, 76; Johnston 1980, 79–82). Though Federal purchases of goods and services have grown steadily, Federal agency responsibility has been increasingly contracted out of the private sector, in grants-in-aid to State and local governments, or as direct transfer payments to private industry (Perry and Watkins 1977). Both direct Federal urban policies, those of HUD or HEW, for example, and indirect policies, including defense (Bolton 1980), have differential impacts on towns and cities. The increased defense spending of the 1983 Budget will favor cities of the South and West.

The pro-business climate, with little unionization and 'right to work' laws favor Sunbelt cities, though corporations give little weight to individual inducements in location decisions (Vaughan 1979, 95–112). The climate may benefit the South, but cheap labor or costs of living are dubious assets, even if true. Perhaps the greatest inducements are lower State and local taxes as a percentage of State personal income (Genetski and Chin 1978; Adams 1981, 47), though this view is contested (see ch. 5, pp. 232–4). A lower than average increase in Southern States in this tax burden in the 1970s contributed to rapid urban growth there. Unfortunately, reduced tax burdens can adversely affect a city like New Orleans, burdened with higher welfare costs but limited in its tax ceiling (Adams 1981, 48).

7.3 FEDERAL TAX AND HOUSING POLICIES

Federal tax policies until the 1960s encouraged decentralization at the expense of inner-city well-being and supported the widespread middle-class preference for low-density home ownership. Private sector developers could provide this more cheaply on the urban periphery. The belief was that owner-occupied housing contributed to a sense of community stability and identity, encouraging families to build their own economic security by investing in an asset of significant value. In creating household wealth through home ownership, housing policy promoted not only urban sprawl but a new dimension, 'counter-urbanisation' (Berry and Dahmann 1977). Inner-city housing has not enjoyed the stabilizing influence of favorable mortgaging.

7.3.1 Subsidies favorable to fringe development

Home mortgage insurance and low-interest loans Attempts to promote home ownership and the unintended encouragement to decentralization date from the Great Depression of the early 1930s (Alsop 1982). The earliest creation (1932) of the Federal Home Loan Bank Board provided for refinancing mortgages held by financially distressed homebuyers. To attract more investment in the housing industry the National Housing Act (1934) committed the government to insure mortgages for families in middle-income housing and also provided low-interest mortgage financing over extended repayment periods. The Serviceman's Readjustment Act (1944) guaranteed insurance of GI loans for veterans engaged in home purchase or renovation. Four years later, the Truman administration liberalized the terms of mortgages eligible for Federal insurance. In subsequent years FHA (Federal Housing Authority) insurance programs have been finely tuned by successive Democratic and Republican administrations.

Income tax deductions for home ownership The provision of mortgage insurance and low-interest loans with extended repayment periods have not been the only Federal inducements to home ownership. An additional subsidy derived from the revamped income-tax code of the 1930s. To reduce or escape tax liability, home-owners have been allowed to deduct mortgage interest and property-tax payments from their taxable income, entailing a cost to the government in the revenue that is forgone. Because these deductions are not profitable for the taxpayer unless the amounts involved exceed the standard deduction, the tax laws on home ownership work to the benefit of middle- and upper-income households. This took on particular significance after World War II when Federal tax demands increased dramatically. As this tax subsidy is proportional to the owner's tax bracket, its value increases with rising household income levels (Berry 1980, 13). Since the subsidy increases with the cost of a house and the tax bracket of the owner, spaciousness and luxuriousness have been encouraged, leading to more large lot development and reinforcing the link between home ownership and suburban extension.

The tax subsidy for renting is about uniform over income levels, so the average taxpayer has more to gain from home ownership than paying rent (Tolley and Diamond 1977). Since World War II, with household income growth, the proportion of owner-occupied housing stock has risen from 48 to 64 per cent, principally in single-family suburban homes (Peterson 1977). About one-quarter of this growth stems from the tax system's favorable treatment of mortgage interest and property-tax deductions (Rosen and Rosen 1980), which since 1945 reduced the cost of home purchase by 14 per cent, increasing housing consumption by 20 per cent (Aaron 1970, 803).

Accelerated depreciation and inner-city abandonment   The suburban expansion has been reinforced by the effect of other tax provisions, specifically those favoring new construction over rehabilitation, which accelerates the rate at which buildings are replaced. The locational effect is to favor new suburban construction over central-city rehabilitation. The introduction of the 200 per cent declining balance method within the accelerated depreciation provisions of the Tax Reform Act (1954) permitted landlords to reduce taxes on new investment properties. As of 1976, the effect of this new tax code was to increase the after-tax return on investment in new construction, while reducing the return for an existing building (Peterson 1977).

Another important effect of accelerated depreciation is to concentrate the greatest tax benefits in the early years of property ownership, which emphasizes how policies serve the interest of material production and consumption rather than human accommodation. As the allowable deductions fall off, a building is sold, usually within 10 years (Brueggeman 1977). Investors contemplating such short holding periods often skimp on quality materials which explains, in part, the large and increasing areas of poor-quality buildings in cities. Moreover, when the tax benefits from depreciation taper off, and the benefits fall below what the landlord requires for proper building maintenance, deterioration and abandonment follow. A slum is the consequence of a rational investor decision (Davis 1970).

A variable crucial to the pace of housing abandonment is the magnitude of this replacement supply. New housing construction has exceeded household growth since the 1960s, with more than one-third of new, predominantly suburban housing-starts replacing, as opposed to augmenting, housing supply. The value and maintenance of older, inner-city housing stock has thus been undermined, leading to abandonments, subsequent depopulation, and peripheral urban expansion (Berry 1980, 16–17). Sunbelt and non-metropolitan migration has concentrated this abandonment in the older northeastern cities. In rapidly growing southern cities abandonment is less, with large numbers of housing-starts and a matching of household growth with housing construction.

Pursuing this rather wasteful policy, the Housing Act (1968) led to reduced private demand for existing inner-city housing stock. As this Act increased Federal subsidies for central-city repair, it undermined private investment from inner-city homeowners, resulting in further deteriorations and abandonments. Inner-city abandonment in response to housing policies and new lifestyles affects the homes of one-fourth of the nation's poorest citizens and is wasteful in the neglect of existing buildings and facilities.

Urban encroachment and differential tax assessment   Other tax laws have assisted the conversion of rural land to suburbs in expanding metropolitan areas. In many States, taxes subsidize infrastructure expansion on the urban fringe (Hart 1976). In Florida, for instance, private developers are permitted to pay for infrastructure costs outside the area of existing capital facilities by creating municipal utility districts authorized to issue tax-exempt bonds (US Congress, House 1977). Favorable tax treatment has also been accorded to corporate income generated from land speculation. Such income is considered a capital gain and taxed at one-half the rate of ordinary income.

This provision has increased the amount of land purchased by corporations for development. Businesses investing in suburban sites often buy far more land than is required for their operations, and later sell off the excess land as it appreciates in value. The gains from these sales are then taxed as capital gains, not at the higher corporate tax rates (Plaut 1980).

7.3.2 The failure of tax advantages favoring the inner city

Mortgage insurance and rent subsidies   Recent attempts to twist these tax advantages to favor the inner city have proven ineffectual; as a result, the polarization within society continues unabated. Until the late 1960s, Congress had restricted the provision of Federal mortgage insurance to 'economically sound' areas, and, following the lead of private-sector financial institutions, FHA staff had adopted neighborhood and borrowing standards that excluded declining or racially changing areas. The result was a bias against central cities in general, and nonwhite minorities in particular. In the aftermath of major urban riots by blacks, Congress advised FHA in 1966 to relax its normal requirements for mortgage insurance and to provide Federal loan subsidies.

The Housing and Urban Development Act (1968) created the two major programs dominating Federal housing policy to 1973. Under Section 235 of the 1968 Act, it was possible to obtain a Federally insured mortgage for a new or rehabilitated, moderate-income home with a small downpayment. Under Section 236 the Federal government paid subsidies to private developers of low- or moderate-income housing. This subsidy reduced their interest costs and extended the optional holding period, thereby encouraging better construction and maintenance.

In addition, until 1976 owners of rental housing could deduct construction period interest and taxes from their taxable income. The sum total of these tax benefits is thought to have reduced rental costs during the 1960s and early 1970s by about 17 per cent. It should be noted, however, that although owners of rental housing are accorded tax subsidies by the Federal government, the magnitude of the subsidy is lower than for home ownership (Tolley and Diamond 1977).

Unfortunately, both housing programs, 235 and 236, were to be destroyed by a series of scandals involving fraud by private developers and FHA officials. For example, Federal housing inspectors had been bribed to approve shoddy construction in insured housing, or to attest to 'rehabilitation' that was never undertaken. FHA appraisers were paid by developers to overvalue housing; and private banks offered insured mortgages to households that could not afford them. The result was that many of the poor, in attempting home ownership under Section 235, came to live in poorly constructed dwellings with obligations to meet mortgage repayments they could not afford, and ultimately they abandoned their dwellings. Abandonment typically involved little personal loss to these households because they had built up little equity in the properties they occupied. Private banks then passed the property on to the Federal government.

As a result of a rapid rise in the rate of foreclosures, the Nixon administration suspended Sections 235 and 236. Developers under these programs tended to build expensive projects, because their rate of return increased with project cost. Many project sponsors sold out to investors interested only in the tax shelter benefits. Since these benefits had a life of only 10 years, there was little incentive to maintain projects properly, and rapid deterioration of building quality occurred.

The Nixon administration changed from a strategy of directly subsidizing the building of low-income housing to one of increasing the income of low-income households through rent supplements to enable them to afford standard housing. The strategy shift was partly designed to reduce the need for a large bureaucracy and also to reduce the many financial institutions upon which development depended. Under Section 8 of the Community Development Act (1974) landlords of existing housing who agreed to participate in the program were paid the difference between a fair market rent and 25 per cent of a low-income household's earnings.

Real-estate boards have given only the most grudging support to this type of program, however, and Section 8 has been most widely used in recent years in conjunction with public housing projects. Rasmussen (1980) showed that the Section 8 program helped to move poor households out of the worst slum neighborhoods. Participating landlords in Phoenix and Pittsburgh made larger investments in repairs than did owners outside the program (pp. 249–53). The major criticism of this rent-supplement program had been its expense and its socialistic overtones.

Tax reforms　　Recognition of the perverse effect of the tax laws on the urban fabric of central cities focussed national attention on major tax reforms in the late 1960s. Although the Tax Reform Act (1964) had phased out 'recapture' provisions (taxation of excess depreciation, based on resale value, as ordinary income) for commercial buildings held longer than 10 years, a provision marginally favorable to central cities, the Tax Reform Act (1969) began to reduce the tax advantages enjoyed by suburbs. Passed in the first year of the Nixon presidency, but really championed by a Democratic Congress, the Act introduced a five-year write-off of rehabilitation expenses on rental housing, and permitted escape from capital gains taxes for property owners reselling residential structures to low-income individuals or groups. The five-year amortization on rehabilitation expenses, currently in force, is the most favorable depreciation schedule allowed by the Internal Revenue Service. As most low-rent properties generate insignificant incomes, landlords rely for profits on reduced tax liability from depreciation.

Additional tax-reform legislation again passed in 1976 when Congress elected to reduce the subsidy advantages to all real-estate properties, except low-income housing. The Tax Reform Act (1976) thus substantially increased the tax penalties on new, generally suburban, construction. Taxation of gains realized by accelerated depreciation was reintroduced for all buildings except low-income rental housing held by an owner for more than $16^{2}/_{3}$ years. Construction period interest and taxes, formerly immediately deductible, now had to be capitalized and written off over a 10-year period. The limited partnerships commonly formed to undertake new construction in the suburbs could now only allow members to take tax losses for amounts they actually invested in the partnership, not including borrowed money which had previously been counted.

Nevertheless, the disparity remains between the most favorable depreciation schedules for new housing, 200 per cent declining method, and for used housing, 125 per cent straightline depreciation. The Carter administration sought, unsuccessfully: first to abolish this differential favoring the suburbs by depreciating all real estate except low-income and new multifamily housing by the straightline method; and secondly to introduce a differential 5 per cent tax credit for investment in distressed urban areas. The slackening of tax trends favoring central cities continues, as is indicated by the tax provision of 1978 which reduces capital gains on new construction.

Federal tax policies have clearly served to accommodate the locational preferences of affluent Americans for suburban environments. In facilitating the development of homogenous, value-reinforcing suburbia, it was believed a sense of urban stability would evolve. This has not been the case, since income-distribution effects and housing discrimination prevent certain segments of society from participating in this process of decentralization. The result has been the development of two urban geographies: islands of inner-city housing deterioration and social deprivation collared by affluent suburbia.

Federal response has been to increase aid expenditures to central-city governments and households, particularly under Democratic control of the White House, while preserving older programs which continue to undermine central-city revitalization. The Democratic administration's efforts were erased by the New Federalism of the Republican party, following the charge that urban conditions were worse than ever. The massive flow of aid to these areas of inner-city deprivation intensified the dependence of urban governments upon Federal largesse, a situation to be remedied under the Reagan administration. However, given the sensitivity of elected officials to the opinions of those who vote, lobby, and contribute to elections—and election results show inner-city residents to be notoriously ill informed and remiss in exercising their voting privileges—it follows that Federal response will continue to favor the more affluent.

The new crisis   The three key demographic trends since World War II, the baby boom, its bust, and growth of the elderly, are pertinent to housing-demand changes. Whereas demand for suburban single-family homes was high after World War II, because of increased household formation, purchasing power, and rural–urban migration, the pattern is decidedly different today. With a slowdown in national population growth, large households are disappearing. Contrary to expectation, shrinkage in household size, constant over the US (3.37 persons in 1950 as opposed to 2.8 in 1980), has been much more significant as a housing-demand generator than absolute growth of the population. Changing household formation is now challenging the traditional hegemony of single-family suburbia. Although progeny of the baby boom remain a target for single-family suburban homes, the fastest growth sectors emanate from less common household groups: single persons, or two related or unrelated couples (Sternlieb and Hughes 1980, 1–92).

The emphasis on the middle-income suburban housing market is shown in the annual obligations for repayment, taxes, insurance, and maintenance of $3,500 on a median-cost FHA-insured house of $24,000 in 1971. As the US Bureau of the Census reported that only 25 per cent of overall earnings were expended on housing, this implies a family income of $14,000, a middle-income level for that period. Today a greater share of income has to be surrendered to meet basic housing costs. The belief that price and interest hikes in the early 1970s would return the more affluent to the rental market did not transpire, for couples viewed ownership as their only buffer against inflation. When new housing construction is buoyant, repair of existing stock lags; the reverse is true in a time period of inflation. In 1982, with an explosion in interest rates and house prices, new crises face first-time buyers, with the possibility of political unrest (Sternlieb and Hughes 1980, 153). Mortgage repayments are beyond those individuals on a median income of $22,000, driving them unwillingly back to the rental market. Any return to the central city is in default of other opportunities.

7.3.3 Federal aid programs

Public housing and urban-renewal programs grew under Democratic administrations in the 1930s and 1940s, but inner-city housing problems were neglected under the Republicans in the 1950s. In 1954 emphasis shifted to a less capital-intensive program of housing rehabilitation and neighborhood preservation, though Section 202 of the 1959 Housing Act authorized low-interest loans to private, nonprofit sponsors of rental accommodation for the elderly or handicapped.

The attempt of the Kennedy administration (1961) to create a Cabinet-level housing department was defeated in the Congress by a coalition of Republicans and Southern Democrats, supported by suburban real-estate interests. In 1965 President Johnson, with a landslide victory and a large Democratic majority in the Congress, created the Department of Housing and Urban Development (HUD). Within the administration's theme of a 'war on poverty' HUD stressed neighborhood independence and preservation.

Categorical aid program 1: public housing   The first Federal aid program to have a major impact on central-city housing blight was contained in the Housing Act (1937). The Federal government provided the financial backing for organized housing authorities to float tax-exempt bonds for financing the construction of multifamily housing units for needy families. Because of the social stigma attached to these housing projects, affluent suburban neighborhoods erected numerous barriers to ensure the continuing concentration of project sites in the central cities. It was not until the 1970s that a Supreme Court ruling required the placement of projects in suburban locations, a shift which has been negligible.

In the early years of the program, public housing agencies were expected to charge rents sufficient to meet operating costs. Later, it became clear that in many cases these costs were greater than the tenants could afford. The Federal government had to choose between allowing buildings to deteriorate from lack of proper maintenance and providing additional subsidies to operating costs. The growing subsidy burden of the public-housing program has been one reason for its unpopularity throughout the last two decades. Operating subsidies alone cost the Federal government $727 million in 1979. The reputation of most project sites as high crime areas, plagued by the destructive effects of vandalism, has magnified maintenance expenditures and soured public goodwill toward the program. Urban experts have criticized the primitive, unadorned style of project buildings, and their high-rise, high-density character which fosters distaste for such development.

Despite considerable public hostility to the program, public housing construction was rapidly expanded in the late 1960s, a reflection of the special efforts for the poor undertaken by the Johnson administration. The peak year was 1970 when 104,410 housing units were started or underwent rehabilitation. Yet three years later, the Supreme Court requirement that projects be built for the racially integrated clientele outside the central cities helped Republican administrations to curtail the program. By 1977 only 6,321 units were provided, compared to between 20,000 and 40,000 a year in the early 1960s. To revive the program the Carter administration raised construction and rehabilitation starts to 11,835 units in 1978. In the early 1980s, however, the total stock of public housing amounted to only about 1.2 million units, approximately 2 per cent of the nation's housing.

In an attempt to decentralize ghetto concentrations, public housing projects were to be racially balanced through quota systems. In planning an integrated spatial area based on quotas, was the Federal government discriminating, especially when some projects remained empty because demand came from the wrong color group? It was thought that the overall societal advantage of integrated housing warranted overriding the qualifications of those who in the absence of such quotas would have secured a position.

However, a recent contrary opinion, by the Supreme Court in the *Regents of California* vs. *Bakke*, rejected reverse discrimination and essentially nullified the use of quotas as a way of changing the balance in the distribution of minorities. Attempts to retract housing-ordinance freedoms from individuals who do not conform to stereotype societal norms is a constantly recurring and serious political issue in urban areas, and is not merely related to race. Anita Bryant's campaign against homosexuals in Dade County, Florida, in 1977, under the banner of 'Save our Children' led to the removal of housing ordinance freedoms for this group. A national campaign resulted in similar repressive ordinances appearing in such cities as Eugene, Oregon, and Wichita, Kansas (White 1980); and another, the focus of national attention in 1982, was soundly defeated in Austin, Texas. Such attacks generate responses in the form of politically potent 'gay power' caucuses, as witness their influence on the San Francisco mayoral election (Batchelor 1980).

Categorical aid program 2: urban renewal   The second Federal aid program with a primarily central-city impact was the urban-renewal program, mandated by the Housing Act (1949) to bring about the redevelopment of land in blighted urban neighborhoods. Through use of its eminent domain powers, the government was to consolidate designated areas under a single authority, demolish its buildings, upgrade its infrastructure with roads, street lights, and similar facilities, and then resell the cleared and improved land to private firms for the building of new industrial, commercial, or residential structures. By 1971 the Federal government had authorized $10.7 billion for renewal activities, with central cities receiving two to four times the outlays provided for suburban jurisdictions.

However, like public housing, this program ran into considerable criticism. It was attacked for being too expensive and for involving the wholesale demolition of neighborhoods that might have been revived by careful rehabilitation. Commitment to a demolition strategy, it was argued, was a mistake because it led to the large-scale destruction without replacement of the substandard housing used by the poor. As a result, there was widespread displacement of poor households, inadequately compensated for the disruption of their lives and the destruction of their neighborhoods. The replacement of low-income housing, largely by middle- and upper-income units, commercial, or industrial properties, helped to create local shortages of housing for the poor and raised its price in renewal areas, thereby generating significant financial hardship for the most impoverished classes. While the program was a bonanza for some businessmen who were getting preassembled tracts of cleared and improved land for about one-third of the private market cost, it forced the termination or relocation of many small businesses such as neighborhood groceries, restaurants, and personal-service establishments, with little compensation. Most of these firms, as well as evicted households, relocated in the immediate vicinity of the renewal areas, where they were required to pay higher rents.

Whatever negligible contribution urban renewal made to renovation of the central city's fiscal base, by the provision of facilities for new firms and more affluent households, its negative impact on the poor led to numerous attempts by the Congress to modify the early demolition strategy. In 1961 Congress authorized grants for demonstration projects in housing conservation and rehabilitation, and created the Section 221 (d) (3) program FHA insurance for long-term loans, undertaken by nonprofit organizations, to finance construction of low-income housing. Congress also authorized the Federal National Mortgage Association to purchase these mortgages. By 1968 Congress had established a $150 million fund for providing subsidized loans at 3 per cent interest for rehabilitation in renewal areas.

In a more direct attempt to safeguard the supply of low-income housing the Housing Act (1966) required renewal projects to include a 'substantial' supply of such housing, and in 1968 this requirement compelled a majority of all housing in renewal areas to be allocated for low-income families. Finally, one year later, the one-for-one replacement of any low-income residences destroyed in the renewal process was made compulsory. With the reduced emphasis on demolition and because of the contribution made to the interests of developers and central-city businessmen, urban renewal was maintained as the single largest Federal urban-aid program through the 1960s and early 1970s, with annual appropriations typically exceeding $1 billion.

7.3.4 The New Federalism: community-development programs

Disillusioned with the prevailing programs, the 'New Federalism' of the

Nixon administration sought more flexibility for local jurisdictions, allowing them a much greater role in deciding how their Federal aid money should be spent. In 1972 the phasing out of urban renewal and several other categorical aid programs was proposed and their replacement by a single Federal aid package, or 'block grant'. This was to be used by each recipient jurisdiction either to continue projects of the type funded by the categorical programs, or to develop new priorities which might or might not involve assistance to the poor. Under the Community Development Act (1974) seven major categorical programs of urban aid (Urban Renewal, Model Cities, Water and Sewer Facilities, Open Space, Neighborhood Facilities, and Public Facilities Loans) were replaced by the Community Development Block Grant (CDBG) Program. This program did not involve a competitive application process. Eligible localities were cities with populations of over 50,000, central cities of SMSA's and metropolitan areas of over 200,000 people. The original allocation formula was based on the city's population size and degree of overcrowding and poverty.

Congress changed the Nixon proposal by assigning to the Department of Housing and Urban Development responsibility for the award of block grants, to ensure that aid money would continue for the most part to be spent on assistance to low-income households or areas, rather than for alternative projects supported by more affluent households. Because of the nature of the programs it replaced, CDBG funds were primarily used for housing and other hardware programs. There was a reduced emphasis on urban renewal and a shift of resources to housing rehabilitation.

Although the CDBG appropriation actually was 15 per cent greater than the combined funding for all seven programs it replaced, the inclusion of the population criterion in the new aid formula had a spreading effect on the distribution of the aid, increasing the number of beneficiary localities, with the inclusion for the first time of a large number of small cities. The eventual effect of this was to reduce the share of aid going to central cities and to increase that going to the suburbs. Regionally, the spread effect involved a shift of aid resources away from the Northeast and the Midwest towards the West and South.

In 1977 the Carter Administration changed the allocation formula to mitigate this distributional change, and increased the aid amounts appropriated. The allocation change was achieved by adopting an additional formula based on population, poverty, and age of housing, rather than overcrowding, and entitling localities to claim the larger of the aid amounts dictated by a comparison of formulas. This dual formula approach increased the central-city share from 42 per cent to 55 per cent, but this remained well below the 70 per cent received under the superseded categorical programs.

The Department of HUD had left the level of CDBG targeting to local officials, and the local response was increasingly to shift spending from poverty programs and areas to recreational and residential projects in more affluent districts. The CDBG legislation (1974) required the program to 'give maximum feasible priority to activities which will benefit low or moderate-income families or aid in the prevention or elimination of slums or blight'. By 1976 it was clear that a substantial and increasing proportion of CDBG benefits was not going to lower income groups. Under President Carter determined efforts were made to increase the targeting of CDBG funds to poor households, as well as poor areas. HUD proposed regulations requiring at least 75 per cent of each annual installment of CDBG funds to go to projects that principally benefitted low and moderate-income families. Opposition forced amendments that made it difficult for HUD to refuse a locality's grant allocation because of inadequate emphasis on assistance to low-income households. Since 1976 urban renewal has been phasing out, but in a protracted manner.

One major success of the Carter administration was to secure $400 million annual funding for the Urban Development Action Grant (UDAG) Program, a program widely hailed as a success in helping cities prevent the defection of expanding businesses to suburbs. It met part of the cost of clearing land or providing public improvements, such as streets, utilities or other subsidies through infrastructure provision to private industry. Because UDAG funds are targeted to cities on the basis of need criteria, age and condition of housing, income levels, degree of tax base erosion, residential abandonment, and population loss to suburbs, central cities received 75 per cent of UDAG funds in 1978, compared with 12.5 per cent each for suburbs and non-metropolitan areas. Furthermore, the program has been successful in leveraging private money (Jacobs and Roistacher 1980, 348). Another major success came with the rapid expansion in the Section 312 rehabilitation program, which primarily assists households in central cities. Finally, the Carter administration expanded the funding and operations of the Economic Development Administration (EDA) in central cities.

The switch from the Categoric and Model Cities block grants of the 1960s to the Special Revenue Sharing Programs of the 1970s essentially redirected the emphasis on poverty reduction. Rather than concentrate on the Northeastern central cities, funds were allocated to all major US cities and to all areas within those cities. Based on this revamped and much criticized allocation formula, funding supplemented a city's social services program. By favoring Sunbelt States over Northeastern States this switch can be considered perverse in its redistributive character since the major social problems occur in the Northeast (Morris 1978; Fossett and Osborn 1980, 78).

As a city's wealth is related to the quality of its housing stock, the liability built into an aging housing inventory is of major concern. This liability exhibits striking interurban variations as cities of the Manufacturing Belt find their housing-stock replenishment from new construction and rehabilitation reduced by demographic shifts, and exhorbitant maintenance costs arising from an aging housing stock. Although at present there is a balance between households and housing units, resulting in few vacancies, there is a higher level of scrapping in older rental units. The sagging replenishment rates in cities of the Manufacturing Belt is matched by the modernity of housing in the South and West.

7.3.5 *Federal housing policies and private-sector investment*

The policy of the Federal Housing Administration (FHA) has been to provide home-ownership financing to middle-income groups and to push for urban-renewal programs for the poor. Over the years Congress aimed to increase the supply of housing for a variety of low-income groups. Housing Acts authorized below-market interest loans to a variety of public and private agencies sponsoring the construction or rehabilitation of rental housing for the elderly; provided grants to home-owners in distressed areas for rehabilitation of their property; and a rent-supplement program gave the government the authority to pay part of the rents due to landlords sponsoring new or rehabilitated housing for low-income households. The Federal urban-renewal program, the oldest and one of the largest Federal grant aid programs to urban areas, helped to refurbish central-city areas and to build modestly priced housing.

Unfortunately, the overall effect of all this legislation has been disappointing, largely because most housing programs have been underfunded or, as happened during the Nixon administration, dismantled altogether. In 1968 the Douglas Commission set a 10-year goal of 6 million subsidized housing units, but only about one-third have been built. The proportion of publicly subsidized housing relative to the total housing stock is only 5 per cent or less in nearly all US cities. These policies also failed because they were targeted to areas being abandoned through the forces of change.

Except for the hopelessly poor—AFDC recipients—the Federal urban-renewal program did little to help the poor and was chiefly of aid to middle- and upper-income groups. This program destroyed more lower-income homes than it built, and caused the disruption of many lower-income households. Apart from providing little in the way of new or rehabilitated housing in urban areas, the Federal government may have helped to inflate the price of housing for all consumers through tax laws which encouraged land speculation and inappropriate environmental regulation and building codes.

The complexity of the housing problem, the lack of finance, and the fragmentary nature of the decision-making process make a specific housing solution such as urban renewal or new towns within towns untenable (Wingo 1975, 8). Rehabilitation of existing inner-city housing stock has also proven costly and ineffective because of hidden structural and maintenance costs and poor management. Further, the method of improving one's housing through the 'filtering process' whereby better-quality older housing becomes available as new suburban dwellings develop, is less effective because of few suburban housing starts in this recessional period and the huge surge in home repair. The policy of urban renewal, by leaving desolate vacant spaces in juxtaposition with slums, has done little to renovate the inner city.

Declining house values and rising city taxes, the key indicators of a depressed housing market, suggest that presently there is little profit to be made by private investors in central-city housing. This unattractive investment climate also results in part from changing tastes, alternative housing choices, the age of the housing stock, and the preponderance of minorities.

Banks, loan institutions, and the FHA are reluctant to provide home-owner finance to poor central-city families because they are viewed as credit risks (redlining). This redlining of inner-city areas by the withdrawal of mortgage capital has accelerated housing decay and caused those families adjacent to encroaching blight to sell their housing at depressed prices. It has also denied home ownership to those desiring it and raised the living costs of renters who miss the tax benefits of such ownership (Darden 1980, 99).

As 80 per cent of US blacks reside in metropolitan areas, and 70 per cent of these live in the inner cities, blacks are particularly outraged over this red-lining or selective distribution of credit. The profit an investor realizes from the acquisition of property from fleeing whites at below market values and resale to blacks at above market value and inflated rates of interest, is a gain embittered blacks refer to as the 'black tax'. Yet, while the housing market is depressed, rents are not, as they are raised to match increasing maintenance costs and city taxes. Poverty consequently does not necessarily explain the existence of slum housing, as inner-city residents, nonwhites especially, find themselves paying rents comparable to the nonpoor located in better housing areas in other parts of the city (Sternlieb *et al.* 1982, 485–8).

Private-sector investment   Another suggested remedy for inner-city housing blight is to attract private-sector investment to support home owner-ship, thus reducing Federal investment in housing (Hayek *et al.* 1972). Home ownership can reduce housing decay and help to release rising tensions in US ghettos. Such ownership reduces transience, develops responsibility and respect for private property, and improves political awareness. By recharging the inner-city housing market with mortgage credit, protected by a national risk insurance program, both supply and demand for housing can be satisfied. The image of the inner-city landlords as ogres, earning extensive profits and plunging the poor into increasing indebtedness, is a myth. They should be championed as a cause rather than denigrated as pariahs. The so-called 'slum landlord' manages inner-city housing more efficiently and, contrary to pre-vailing opinion, provides better-quality housing at a more reasonable price than government housing policies (Stegman 1970; Sternlieb and Burchell 1973). Those who advocate punishing the landlord by 'taxing the profits out of slums' through tighter Federal laws fail to point out that there exist in the inner city declining housing prices, rising city taxes, insurance and main-tenance costs, and a paucity of buyers for the property. Further, civil dis-orders have made the security of private property in the inner city tenuous (Kerner Report 1968, 115). City officials can also administer penalties and take property from landlords not meeting increasingly stringent fire, health, and safety codes.

With husband and wife both working, the rental sector in the early 1970s was being skimmed of those most capable of absorbing escalating rent increases due to inflation and rising maintenance costs. This left a residue of the poorest, whose income deficiencies added to their problems. The fallacy that rental housing is central-city bound focussed Federal housing programs, but today rental housing is more dispersed, with less than one-third domiciled in central cities. Unless the investment climate is improved, the housing of the poor will become increasingly institutionalized.

The three dominant geographic contours in the spatial redistribution of the population—accelerated regional shifts, metro–nonmetropolitan dispersion, and increasing intraurban differences—reflect variations in housing demand. With decentralization in the ascendant, cities no longer serve as national growth poles. Whereas in 1960 central cities had most of the nation's housing stock, now suburban and exurban areas are dominant. This generalization masks interurban variations, since the largest proportion of the Manufacturing Belt's housing stock is still within central cities, whereas in the South, as a reflection of its rural past and present modernity, it is outside SMSAs. Housing inventory expansion in the 1970s dwarfed that of any other decade with home ownership for whites and blacks each rising some 26 percentage points between 1940 and 1980, from 1940 bases of 44 and 24 per cent, respectively. Recently, investment in real estate as opposed to industry has been the preferred conduit for wealth generation. In the postindustrial society, housing is much more important as an investment rather than as a shelter.

Federal investment in central-city housing has been considerable without producing significant change in either the geographic concentration of blight or the social evils housed there. Public housing constitutes a negligible percentage of low-income dwellings. Projects are notorious for vandalism which detracts from their aesthetic and social contribution to upgrading the immediate locality. These projects are more than a one-time capital investment as they also require maintenance and operating costs. The sum total of this expense seems unreasonable to the public, given the program's miniscule achievements.

In the attempt physically to erase poverty, urban renewal programs have perhaps simply compounded blight by increasing the concentration of households unable to filter into other urban areas. The profits of urban renewal, like those of Federally insured mortgages, largely fell to banks and developers, at the expense of central-city neighborhoods. The CDBG program has worked since 1974 to disperse funds previously concentrated on central cities, and reduce the amounts going to the distressed Northeast. Federal monies have been shared on a broader national scale and within a wider range of smaller cities and suburban locales. This geographical dilution of northeastern central city funds has become an alarming feature of the US urban system (Berry 1980).

Post-World War II housing had two constituents to satisfy: the latent demands for home-ownership of an emerging middle class and the demands of an increasingly visible urban poor. The former was to be satisfied by creative financing and the latter by Federal housing assistance. Today 90 per cent of Americans are satisfied with their housing, a view that holds across racial lines and for both owners and renters, although less vociferously among the latter. Consequently, the political clout of the dissatisfied central-city renters is limited in an era when sustained prosperity is no longer assured. Further, improved housing is not a high priority item among the poor. How then can a bureaucracy like HUD continue when its task has been set aside (Sternlieb and Hughes 1980, 543–55)?

7.4 PHYSICAL HARDWARE POLICIES: TRANSPORTATION AND ENVIRONMENTAL PROGRAMS

Few measures have had so dramatic an impact on metropolitan patterns of land development as the interstate highway system. Federal policy greatly enhanced the suburbanization process with a complex network of freeways, encouraging the development of intraurban linkages and thus facilitating ever greater extensions of commuter distance. The transportation concern of the 1950s and 1960s centered on highway congestion, mass transit decline, and the disruptive influence of expressway construction on low-income neighborhoods. Since the mid-1960s these issues have been muted and replaced by concern for air and noise pollution, auto safety, equity issues, the economic and national security concerns surrounding energy supply, and mass transit revival (Altshuler 1979, 26–42).

7.4.1   *The highway era*

In 1956 Congress enacted the world's largest domestic works project, the National System of Interstate and Defense Highways, designed primarily to improve interurban linkages for reasons of defense and commerce. This Act was supported by a powerful consortium of interest groups—auto, oil, steel, rubber, and labor unions—which rallied public support for this venture as a solution to the issue of congestion. The Highway Act (1956) established a Highway Trust Fund which distributed the taxes imposed on highway users to pay for the 90 per cent Federal share of the Interstate system costs. In 1956, combined Federal and State expenditure for highway construction was a lean $718 million, but by 1962 it had risen to $2.07 billion. Needs of the mass transit rider were virtually ignored and mass transit patronage declined in spectacular fashion.

The spatial impact of the Interstate system on urban form was twofold. At the interurban level it increased accessibility between cities, and locally it promoted suburbanization within cities. On the national scale, expressways increased interaction outside the Northeast, facilitating the access of commerce and people to the South and West and, by so doing, allowed national prosperity to diffuse into regions previously excluded (Vaughan 1977; for a contrary view see ch. 5, pp. 225–6). Surpassing rail as the nation's main inter-city transport mode for goods, the truck connected small, previously isolated manufacturing plants. By cracking the geographic isolation of cities beyond the traditional loci of industry and commerce, the Interstate Program provided the catalyst for the more rapid development of the national urban system. On the intraurban level, the path of the Interstate system attracted internal linkages and thus promoted central-city decline by facilitating the outward movement of commercial districts and residences. This freer movement of people was obtained at the expense of inner-city neighborhood integrity, as capacious paths of land were engulfed for Interstate rights of way.

For politicians the Interstate Highway Program was less controversial than a housing program, since most construction occurred between cities and the displeasure induced by internal disruption within cities was muffled by the 90 per cent Federal grant. Before this program, which did not influence city form until the 1960s, the most important Federal policy affecting city shape had been the Urban Renewal Program (1949). It was the first project to obtain vast swaths of private property through right of eminent domain. Within cities the Interstate was driven through renter-occupied minority areas where opposition to its encroachment was usually weak, late, and ill organized. This allowed planners, the errand boys of the politically influential, to use freeways to demarcate minority living space, and thus to wall off minority concentrations as effectively as any river or other natural barrier (Caro 1974).

The involuted effects of Federal policy on urban land use is well illustrated by central-city freeway construction. By delimiting ghetto areas, its immediate effect was to increase minority densities, already growing from the influx of rural migrants. Population and economic pressures resulted in the social unrest of the 1960s. Through 'block busting' ghetto residents fulfilled their need for housing, first by obtaining one or two homes in an adjacent white neighborhood. This perceived threat to real-estate values stimulated 'white flight' to the suburbs and delivered the remaining neighborhood residences to blacks at above-market prices. Freeway construction contributed to the crisis of the ghetto, stimulating the Great Society software policies of Democratic administration in the 1960s.

7.4.2 The rise of mass-transit support

The decisive policy reversal away from expressway construction began with urban Democrats under the Kennedy and Johnson administration. Anti-highway sentiment gave birth to a mass-transit revival with strong public pressure for providing cities with ample mass-transit operating and capital costs. However, even greater funding was provided by the conservative Republican administrations of Nixon and Ford. With the National Highway Acts (1973 and 1976) the Senate accommodated mass-transit revival and added it to their existing jurisdiction. To avoid the pro-black, big-city welfare issues championed by the Democrats, the mass-transit program provided a vehicle for the Republicans to embrace at arm's length many of the racial, welfare, and poverty issues of urban society, without becoming entwined with these seemingly intractable concerns. The main drawback of this approach was that it was confined to a few major cities. Sixty-one per cent of all capital funding was targeted for 5 urban regions between 1964 and 1975, and 10 urban regions received 80 per cent in 1975 (Altshuler 1979, 37).

Habitual traffic congestion continued to galvanize interest in urban mass transit. Traditionally, solutions were through capital-intensive methods: new highway capacity, cloverleaf, underpass, and bridge construction. There arose widespread criticism of congestion relief through increased highway capacity, especially in large cities where opposition to expressway disruption is most intense. Under Title III of the Federal Aid Highway Act (1973) cities could opt for using the Highway Trust Fund for mass transit rather than highway development, although in States like Texas, which contains a powerful highway lobby, few cities exercised this option. This Act also permitted cities to acquire highway rights-of-way for transit (e.g. the Shirley Freeway in Washington, DC), special bus lanes, and parking space. The National Mass Transit Act (1974) also permitted Federal grants to finance operating deficits of mass transit, a major effort by the Federal government to reduce the subsidy imbalance between highway and transit investment.

The debate over mass-transit revival sharpened in intensity and focus when attention was drawn to the enormous energy appetite of the auto, its high private cost, its landscape disruption, and its contribution to pollution. The early 1970s were a watershed for the once powerful environmental lobby which attacked the disruptive influence of the auto and its companion, the expressway. The specific turning-point in favor of a mass-transit resurgence was the Arab Oil Embargo of 1973–4 which first alerted the US to its precarious dependency on oil (ch. 5.1.2). As a result, the focus of the urban-transportation problem has changed. Excessive energy consumption, air pollution, equity issues, congestion, and land use are the current urban-transportation problems seeking solutions.

City officials have been attracted to costly, rapid rail systems because the Federal government contributes most of the capital investment. City officials may believe that their communities' images are enhanced by this exotic technology, but the impact on transportation flows and urban form has been the opposite of that envisioned. Not only have they failed to reduce auto trips in cities, but they tend to accelerate suburban dispersal rather than to enhance inner-city revitalization. The experience of the Bay Area Rapid Transit (BART), San Francisco, also shows that they require large Federal operating subsidies, and are prone to underutilization and early obsolescence. Even with knowledge of the interrelationships between physical and transportation planning, BART was conceived as a narrow technical pallia-tive to what proved to be a broader and less tractable policy problem (Webber 1976). Since politicians have to maximize their vote, they are vulnerable to pressure groups such as the advocates of BART. Hall explains this planning disaster on the vote-maximization theory and suggests that how a problem is perceived is considerably more important than how it is measured (Hall 1981).

In subsidizing exotic rail facilities such as BART and MARTA (Metro-politan Atlanta Rapid Transit Authority), and that in Washington, DC, the government has, in a sense, contributed to CBD revitalization, but only as far as increasing commercial rents by easing the access of suburban office-workers. Central-city residents have not gained significant mobility in resi-dence or job locations—one reason for the civil disorders in Los Angeles and Detroit in the late 1960s (Davies 1972). As the poor use buses for 89 per cent of transit trips, rapid transit for only 11 per cent, and commuter rail not at all, the Federal capital-cost subsidy barely reaches them. Operating subsidies, from which they do benefit, are being phased out (Altshuler 1979, 279–84). The transit subsidy can be considered redistributive in favor of the inner-city disadvantaged, not because they receive a disproportionate share of its bene-fits, but because they pay lower than average taxes. On the other hand, through the 1970s, most of Urban Mass Transit Authority (UMTA) capital costs were allocated to fixed rail facilities, a mode that favors the affluent and not the poor; an unwise investment, given the limitations and narrow appli-cations of a railroad system.

In the 1970s the trend had been a sharp increase in Federal and State contributions to the transit-subsidy burden (Altshuler 1979, 291). Federal mass-transit capital and operating assistance to cities would have continued up to 1985 if President Carter's mass transit bill had not been defeated in the

Senate. In accord with his policy of drastically reducing Federal expenditures and transferring Federal initiative to State and local authorities, President Reagan pruned Federal capital grants and intends to phase out Federal operating subsidies completely by the late 1980s.

This politicizing of transit policy comes as no surprise and reflects the differences in Democratic and Republican viewpoints. President Reagan will continue to provide matching Federal capital costs—80 per cent Federal and 20 per cent local, of which the States pay 65 per cent of the local share—because the administration favors fixed light rail and associated land development in suburbia. The curtailment of operating costs will reduce, if not end, bus transit in most cities, and consequently, increase the immobility of those in the inner city.

Rapid rail systems appeal to suburbia and big business and will continue to reinforce the dispersal of urban land use, in spite of the withdrawal of Federal funds. Since city-owned bus systems accommodate only a small percentage of work trips, primarily of the less affluent, the general public is not likely to support increased local taxes to counter the withdrawal of Federal operating subsidies. President Reagan's 1983 budget proposed a 38 per cent cutback in operating assistance to local bus systems. Reasonable fare-box increases will hardly offset this. Consequently, cities such as Austin and El Paso have received special legislative approval to present a public referendum, like that of Houston in 1978, for a sales-tax increase. This system of financing adversely affects the poor, while funds earmarked to support and make financially independent a local Regional Transit Authority favor rapid rail.

7.4.3 Environmental policy and urban form

While the Federal highway program exercised unprecedented influence on urban form, Federal attempts to control environmental quality, and thus, land use, have been systematically eroded (ch. 4). The environmental movement from the late 1960s was viewed as a *cause célèbre* that would negate growing US factionalism (Jones 1975, 25–35). Improved ambient air-quality standards became part of the environmental euphoria that culminated in the National Environmental Policy Act (1970) and the Clean Air Act (1970) with its amendments of 1977. For the first time, these amendments allowed the Federal government to withhold funds from States or local governments reluctant to comply with air-pollution standards and to enforce stringent regulations on stationary and mobile sources of pollution (Manners and Rudzitis 1981, 481).

These amendments suggested a trend toward a larger Federal role in the volatile issue of land use regulation. The Environmental Protection Agency's (EPA) two most controversial programs concerned the prevention of significant air-quality deterioration in clean-air areas and an emissions program for nonattainment areas (Raffle 1979). In the strictest sense, these programs prohibit both the expansion of existing and the location of new industry in areas that do not attain primary air-quality standards (ch. 5, pp. 243–4). However, with 'too much government' and 'too many Federal regulations' the prevailing rhetoric, and under repeated legal challenges from industry and State and local governments, this air-pollution regulation was softened by an 'emission offsetting policy'. This allowed local industrial expansion to occur only if the increased pollution was 'offset' by similar pollution reductions from existing sources elsewhere in the area (Manners and Rudzitis 1981, 484–500).

The spatial implications of these policies are that firms unable to secure the necessary offsets are required to locate elsewhere. In theory, firms wishing to locate in nonattainment areas would have to buy or exchange offsets through some air-exchange broker (Baumol and Oates 1975). To prevent 'clean' cities poaching from 'dirty' cities, the EPA introduced national offset standards. This did not mean that existing clean-air areas could attract industries by lowering their air-quality standards to the national norm (Disselhorst 1975). Following criticism, the EPA allowed cities to 'bank offsets' not required by a firm such as a computer industry, creating a type of 'allowance pool' from which polluting industries could draw (Federal Register 1976). The offset policy constitutes a victory for continued urban growth, since it is a tactical retreat from the original intent of the Clean Air Act (Manners and Rudzitis 1981, 50).

These laws of constraint were introduced after a decade of rapid economic growth, little unemployment, stable prices, and cheaper energy, and through contracted and expensive Federal litigation. The Arab Oil Embargo of 1973–4, however, led to the worst period of peacetime inflation in the US (Altshuler 1979, 187). In its concern over energy dependency and national security, Congress encouraged the auto industry to provide smaller cars, but it relaxed enforcement of air quality. Industries argued that they could not meet the deadlines set by the 1975–7 amendment (Grad *et al.* 1975) and threatened greater unemployment if the EPA insisted on compliance. In removing deadlines for compliance, Congress in 1975 shifted responsibility to State and local governments to demonstrate that 'reasonable air quality progress' was being made.

By preventing industrial growth in urban areas that fail to attain air-quality standards, these environmental laws illustrate the intention of Federal legislation with regard to land use. There is little evidence that the EPA is controlling industrial growth (Federal Register 1978); in fact the EPA has frequently accommodated industries by issuing PSDs in sensitive areas (Manners and Rudzitis 1981, 496–7). The EPA denies that the Clean Air Act has had any impact on unemployment levels or on the Sunbelt shift, and argues that plant age and technological obsolescence are more germane to northeastern plant closures than environmental regulation (Co. Environmental Quality 1979, 431–2).

Nevertheless, this crippled regulation continues to engender political resistance not only from cities in the Manufacturing Belt, but in jobless 'clean' rural areas where the poorest of the poor reside. The prevailing view of industry is that the program prevents or restricts growth. This opposition argues that present analytical procedures are inadequate to determine the impact of individual sources on air-pollutioin concentrations or to determine how environmental costs and benefits are distributed by income, class, and geographic location (Dorfman and Snow 1975, 101–15). Preliminary work suggests that the spatial distribution of net benefits is highly skewed in favor of the dirtiest cities of the Manufacturing Belt, while costs are borne by the entire population, and the poor in particular (Peskin 1978, 145–63).

According to the EPA, the failure of the Clean Air Act to accomplish many of its goals should not lead one to believe that clean air is unattainable, since EPA data show that city pollution has waned (Co. Environmental Quality 1979, 418–21). Deferral of the 1977 air-quality deadlines seemed to leave the EPA with only a symbolic commitment to enforcing its goals (Walker and Storper 1978, 189–257). Yet the EPA had made industry and communities cognizant of their environmental conditions and the growing potential for Federal involvement in land use and industrial location decisions.

In any complex environmental system an action designed to remedy one difficulty may create aberrations elsewhere in the system. Given our uncertain knowledge of biochemical reactions to pollution, incremental policy-making by Federal agencies such as the EPA, an agency not firmly steeped in scientific expertise nor independent of political and judicial supervision, can produce unanticipated repercussions (Ackerman and Hassler 1982).

The creation of a more equal society requires constraints on individual enterprise. The equality that results from this paradox increases society's amount of real freedom (Nelson 1981). However, in relaxing Federal emission constraints, the Reagan government believes that competitive industries can handle any unwanted 'spillovers' and that an extension of property rights will prevent the abuse of scarce resources. Such freedom depends on a nonexistent moral climate and a benign technology which modern industry does not possess. The reduction in individual choice arising from spillovers is identical to a similar reduction in individual rights arising from increased government involvement (Mishan 1980, 965).

In general, the impact of these programs on land-use regulation and concomitant urban form has been inconsequential. Reconciling air-quality objectives with urban growth and land-use regulation is too complex and the issues too intractable. In this post-oil-embargo climate, the environmental lobby, standing for compliance with air-quality standards, finds its support sharply diminished. It has proven impossible to enforce the goals of the Clean Air Acts because the consequences are economically unacceptable. The implementation of the stringent controls and siting policies required by the amendments did not occur. Consequently, the Clean Air Act amendments of 1977, forcing States to meet ambient air standards, have been deferred indefinitely, if not muted permanently. The Clean Air Act is an example of 'policy escalation' or 'policy beyond capacity' (Jones 1975).

7.5 SOCIAL SOFTWARE POLICIES: WELFARE AND UNEMPLOYMENT

Since Marx, one speaks of the progressive character of capitalism, its accompanying social change, and its creation, urbanism. The sheer scale of Los Angeles, Chicago, or Houston provokes the sense of a new human dimension, a city of impersonal forces, void of a collective conscience, within which acquisitiveness is the motivating force (Slater 1970, 81). Those dispossessed and unable to survive in this ceaseless hive of activity are dumped unceremoniously in the cities' poverty pockets where they are more directly observed and controlled.

Engels offered the thesis that the process of urbanization with its consequent exposures would lead to revolution and socialism (Williams 1973, 303). The socialist theme was taken up by utopian thinkers such as Robert Owen who set up New Harmony, Indiana, and still finds adherents today in communes and the 'beguiling simplicity' of New Towns as a national policy to redress urban ills (Alonso 1970, 37; Wingo 1975, 8). Revolution did not result, but urban violence on a massive scale is not uncommon to US cities (Kerner Report 1968, 35–108).

Population explosion, implosion, and racial transformation since World War II, and the emergence of post-industrial urbanization and a mass-media society have undermined traditional authority and created conditions for organized groups to broaden the definition of individual rights. The individual rights of minorities, the dependent, the deviant, and the impaired, previously ignored by public policy, have been reasserted by well-organized lobbies. Such challenges devolve into Federal policies that force institutions and transportation systems to accommodate the physically impaired. The concept of a neighborhood has been destroyed by bussing (Taeuber 1979), and less traditional attitudes toward sexual preferences have liberated housing ordinances (Batchelor 1981). These challenges, however, are not without their opponents (White 1980).

7.5.1   Ghettoization

The inner-city housing market is dominated by racially segregated residential quarters (Berry and Kasarda 1977, 52). Ghettoization of blacks is the persistent geographic expression of America's racial dilemma and the city's most enduring feature. Whether racially segregated housing areas exhibit a tightening or a relaxing of ghetto boundaries since the initiation of Federal civil-rights amendments in 1964 is a focus of current academic debate. Some scholars argue that even with reductions in the urban black population through migration, along with increased policing of overt housing discrimination, and a purported dissipation in racial prejudice, segregated housing patterns exhibit little change (Saltman 1979). Southern cities which historically displayed racially mixed housing areas now experience the more segregated concentrations familiar to northern cities. Other researchers suggest that a decline in the intensity of ghettoization is the prevailing trend in all regions today (Sorensen *et al.* 1975). It is too early to tell whether Federally enforced school desegregation has increased ghettoization by accelerating white flight to suburbia, or whether it has facilitated the racial mixing of areas (US Office of Education 1966).

Another variant on this theme centers upon whether the gradual separation of America into two societies—the suburban rich and the inner-city poor—is class, as opposed to race based. Because of housing discrimination, middle-class blacks have found it difficult to disengage themselves physically from low-income blacks. However, like their white contemporaries, they too are beginning to abandon the inner city (Nelson 1979). Although from low initial numbers, blacks are the fastest-growing sector of the suburban population (Sternlieb and Hughes 1980, 58). Whether they find themselves living in racially mixed neighborhoods or suburban black enclaves is not clear. Spanish-speaking Americans are in a similar situation, although they are less hermetically sealed in the inner city and can now be found in all areas of the community (Massey 1979).

7.5.2 Geographical implications

The era 1945–70 was a period of unmatched growth and stability, punctuated by only minor recessions. In the Truman–Eisenhower years little social legislation was passed, and President Kennedy too experienced a lack of legislative success. It was not until the Johnson presidency, with Johnson's shrewder control of Congress, that major welfare legislation was passed concerning Medicare, civil rights, and education.

After the creation of HUD (1964), urban policy underwent a significant change of direction. The major urban-aid programs inherited (public housing and urban renewal) were programs geographically targeted to remove or renovate the physical blight of slums. There was little provision, however, for social services in the fields of welfare, education, health, and psychological counseling, which might attempt to rehabilitate the individual who lived in poverty (see ch. 3.2.1). It was felt by a growing number of urban experts that to provide new or better housing for the poor was only a very limited response. If the people were poor, it was not only because they were demoralized by the physical decay of their surroundings, but also because low wages and chronic unemployment sapped motivation, bred despair and alienation, and, ultimately, led to antisocial behaviour (Moynihan 1965, 758–68).

Public awareness of areas of relative deprivation emerged as a result of the drift of urban society into two nations. The symptoms, unemployment and crime, stimulated policies spatially targeted to combat these problems. What was needed was a comprehensive program to combat the multiple causes of poverty (see ch. 3.2.1), to include job training, job counseling, welfare, day care, and other services, geographically targeted to supplement existing programs of slum clearance and housing provision. The major legislation embodying this more comprehensive approach to the poverty problem was the Demonstration Cities and Metropolitan Development Act (1966), the Model Cities program, skillfully pushed through Congress by the Johnson administration over the vigorous protests of conservative legislators.

The Model Cities program was initially conceived as a demonstration project to test a variety of approaches for reducing urban poverty in three cities. To build reluctant Congressional support for the large appropriations needed, its spatial coverage was massively extended to include 145 cities, but the effect was to reduce drastically the amount of money for any one city. Yet the concentration of appropriations in small areas was essential for success. A further problem arose because the Model Cities program was designed to reinforce support for the creation of Community Action agencies under the Economic Opportunity Act (1964). A year later, more than 500 agencies had been formed, to mobilize poor households and to generate ideas for the solution of local problems. The direct flow of Federal aid to poor neighborhoods and the stimulation this gave to neighborhood leadership and organization alarmed many municipal governments. They feared loss of political control over their poverty areas, and complained noisily to the White House and to Congress.

Unfortunately, the program took until 1969 to become operational, and by then its principal champion, the Johnson White House, had become a victim of the Vietnam War. Model Cities was eventually funded for about $2.5 billion, most of the money being spent in the early 1970s. Although phased out by an unsympathetic Nixon administration (1974), it had boosted by about one-third the amount larger cities were spending on public services, and had developed a number of specific antipoverty ideas that were to outlive the program itself. Among these were the creation of the Job Corps and the Neighborhood Youth Corps, to provide vocational education and other job training skills and work experience to inner-city youth; funding of an Adult Basic Education program; and provision of loans and technical assistance to minority businessmen under the Economic Opportunity Loan Program.

The decentralization ethic of Nixon's New Federalism shifted authority for manpower programs to local agencies and consolidated categorical programs of job training (Reagan and Sanzone 1981, 131–9). Passage of the Comprehensive Employment and Training Act (CETA) of 1973 made local governments responsible for initiating their own programs with minimal Federal supervision. CETA became a major vehicle of Federal aid to central cities, particularly larger ones, because of their high unemployment rates. Like other decentralization efforts, this too led to reduced attention to the neediest groups. Most CETA programs provided jobs for experienced workers rather than for the hard-core unemployed. In 1976 this tendency was addressed through Title VI funds which linked job vacancies with the chronically unemployed.

Economic recession in the US during the mid-1970s was sufficiently severe to give rise to a new program of Federal grants-in-aid. Democratic members of Congress overrode a veto by President Ford (1976) to establish an Anti-Recession Fiscal Assistance (ARFA) program, authorizing payments to States and local governments with unemployment rates exceeding 4½ per cent. The program was modified and expanded considerably in 1977, the first year of the Carter administration, with a shift in emphasis from countercyclical aid to fiscal relief, targeted to local governments in financial distress. The ARFA program, terminated in 1978, was well targeted to high unemployment areas, with two-thirds of its funds going to local governments and one-third to the States; the larger cities were important beneficiaries. Despite concentration of Federal construction investment in the suburbs, aggregate Federal expenditure benefitted central cities more than the suburbs (Vaughan 1977; Vernez 1980).

Attempts by the Carter administration to increase aid to the central cities met with only modest success. The President's 1978 urban-policy proposals included the provision of public- and private-sector jobs through public-works programs and tax and wage subsidies; a differential 5 per cent investment-tax credit for business moving to distressed cities; establishment of a National Development Bank authorized to extend loans to cities with high unemployment, slow employment, or slow income growth; revitalization in the form of funding for land assembly, infrastructure improvements, or other plans designed to prevent erosion of the tax base in distressed cities; and aid to New York City in the form of loan guarantees. Finally, it was proposed to reduce urban sprawl by cutting Federal subsidies to waste-water treatment plants and to amend the tax code to eliminate investment-tax credits favoring new construction on the urban fringe over rehabilitation of existing inner-city buildings. Few of these proposals of Carter's to correct Federal urban policy failures in the post-war period were passed by Congress.

President Carter was acutely aware that such aid programs should be geographically targeted and more carefully monitored. As a result, in 1978 he ordered the creation of a Community Impact Analysis by which all Federal agencies were required to judge any proposed legislation. This action addressed a major complaint among urban experts: that Federal policy impacts on urban economics were often indirect and inadvertent, and that the effects of deliberate policies, such as housing aid to declining central cities, might well be cancelled out by unintended consequences of other Federal programs unless their urban impacts could be constantly monitored (Clark 1980). The policy analysis recommended that the Federal government be willing to amend, or even abolish, programs in order to encourage 'energy efficient and environmentally sound' settlement patterns, essentially by mending the rift between the inner city and suburbia (Kain 1978).

The Federal government has created for itself a caretaker role in inner-city areas which private enterprise no longer views as profitable. In this sense, it functions as a national conscience, supporting declining services, cleaning up industrial wastes, and coping with the social distress of a depleted population.

7.5.3 *The New Federalism and urban enterprise zones*

President Reagan wished to end this Federal caretaker role with its 'jungle of welfare' programs by creating a New Federalism, realigning responsibilities to State and local governments. This is a major change from the Carter years when Federal programs were targeted directly to declining areas of cities. President Reagan's return to Federalism has two main features. The first calls for the Federal government to take over the health program for the poor, Medicaid, and for the States to assume the costs of the major welfare program, food stamps and Aid to Families with Dependent Children (AFDC). The second element proposes to turn back to the States some 43 major grant-in-aid programs. During this swapping period, a Federal Trust Fund financed by revenues from existing Federal taxes on alcohol, tobacco, and telephones, plus 2 cents of the gasoline tax and a portion of the windfall-profits tax will be made available to States and cities. Between 1987 and 1991 this trust fund would dissipate, and States and cities, if they wished to continue any of the programs, would have to support them from their own resources. The transfer of responsibility has several implications for cities. Cities would be at the mercy of their States, since only States can exercise the tax hikes necessary to support the new responsibilities. Migration will be triggered between cities in States that can afford welfare programs (Texas), from those that cannot (Mississippi). Further, civil rights groups argue that critical social concerns will be in the hands of 50 State governments with variable resources and uncertain sensitivities towards equity for the disadvantaged.

This is the intent of the plan. With its reduction in aid for the poor in housing, welfare, employment, and mass transit, and its increase in defense spending, the 1983 budget reflected this intent. However, its full implementation is extremely doubtful, not because of the difficulty in rescinding the programs, but because States, although desiring increased decision-making, are reluctant to accept the concept since it cancels an attractive source of Federal funds. Two major statistics make success problematical: the 1982 $100 billion deficit, which will prevent interest rates from falling; and the reluctance of Congress to agree to the deep cuts proposed in the social welfare programs.

An attractive feature of the Reagan administration's grand design is the Urban Enterprise Zone Bill, a tax-incentive plan for the rebirth of blighted urban areas such as the South Bronx and East St. Louis, which presently produce little tax revenue. Similar to that initiated in Puerto Rico, this plan should stimulate private investment in industrial parks, preferably for small businesses. Some of the tax incentives would eliminate capital gains tax on investment, exclude from taxation half of all income earned by zone enterprises, and provide a tax credit of up to $1,500 a year for each hard-core unemployed worker hired. Relaxation of safety and air-emission standards, and of the minimum wage, is also proposed. Like the post-World War II experiment around Shannon Airport, Ireland, these zones should attract foreign investors or American companies currently hiring cheap labor in areas, such as Mexico, under the twin-plant Border program.

The sponsors of this bill can expect difficulties: jealousy over the subsidy from nonenterprise zone industries, the renovation of one blighted area creating another as firms leave their original locales for the zones; the difficulty of finding sufficient vacant land and ensuring that private land in zones is developed or not held for real-estate speculation. The assurance that this plan will counter racial violence stemming from the Federal cutbacks in housing, jobs, and welfare assistance, or guarantee CETA candidates employment, or raise local property taxes, or stimulate private investment, which the tax cuts failed to do, is still speculative.

The rising minimum wage now under review by the Reagan administration is thought likely to increase unemployment among the inner-city poor by raising the price of unskilled work compared with skilled. This encourages firms to shift to high-skill production methods and precipitates their move to the suburbs where skilled workers are concentrated. Central-city manufacturing employment declined between 1963 and 1980 by some 10 per cent, but grew in suburban areas of SMSAs by over 20 per cent. In the same period, decreases in manufacturing were most severe in the Northeast where central-city employment in manufacturing declined by over 20 per cent while suburban growth was only 7 per cent. As the impact of recession is most pronounced in central cities, especially those with economies based on the manufacture of durable goods, the Reagan administration proposes to continue CETA. However, in urban enterprise zones, the minimum wage stoutly defended by organized labor will be suspended for those under 19 years of age.

Are these inner-city programs merely temporary palliatives in an era of automatic poverty (Kerner Report 1968, 483)? Unemployment and falling wages occur if automation saves labor costs rather than expands output. What Ricardo perceived as a short-term problem from innovations in the previous century is for youth and the unskilled laborer today an intractable dilemma. The central city is now the nation's whipping boy, the recipient of moralistic pronouncements about violence and decay. The recent metaphors to match this atmosphere of collapse and disintegration, 'a ticking timebomb, brewing rage', apply to black teenagers aged 16 to 19 whose jobless rate in the fourth quarter of 1981 was twice that of white teenagers, and almost five times the rate of all workers. CETA at its zenith provided 4.7 million jobs for the disadvantaged in 1981; this was cut to 2.6 million. One pays either through CETA or through the social costs of unemployment—crime, drugs, and higher welfare and unemployment compensation. The automatic poverty they experience can be countered by a greater sharing of the work load through a reduced working week, the resulting drop in income to be balanced by an increase in the social wage, leisure. The erosion of jobs by innovation, however, begets skepticism. Whether the reduced work force will be prepared to support the increasing numbers of retirees and the never employed, without resorting to repression, is debatable (Graeber 1981).

7.5.4 The failure of Federal software policies

Software policy is essentially a product of the last two decades, possibly enacted on the realization that urban renewal did little to resolve slum problems. Federal antipoverty policy has been funded at varying levels of intensity and disjointedly imposed by successive administrations. At times, policy has presumed to eradicate poverty—for example Johnson's 'War on Poverty' or the vision of Kennedy's 'Camelot'. Nevertheless, more people today are seeking some form of welfare than in 1964 at the onset of the Great Society programs. At other times, and largely during Republican administrations, the attempt simply amounts to devising ways of dealing with the hopelessly poor, in the belief that the causes of poverty may be impossible to isolate, if not treat. There is little merit in evaluating such fluctuating policy, which because of delayed timing, political maneuvering, altered funding, or outright mismanagement, could not be expected to fulfill the original objectives. What does seem clear is that poverty lay heavily on the national conscience during the riotous 1960s, given the degree of Federal investment.

Crisis, in the form of social violence, often motivates Federal policy, as local resources may be insufficient to deal with the problem. Local failure is implied by Federal intervention. Inner-city crime, for instance, has proven consistently intractable to Federal formulas. One social-science theory of the 1960s posed crime, with its distinct pattern of inner-city genesis and ecology, as a function of poverty. While antipoverty programs made some reduction in the poverty population—36.1 million in 1964 as opposed to 29.3 million in 1981—the crime rate burgeoned. Similar miscarriages have soured government officials to the utility of such theories as the basis of policy. This is unduly harsh since failure may be more a question of lax timing and inadequate Federal commitment.

The Federal government has been successful with software policy only to the extent that it has defused social pressures in order to maintain a tenuous urban calm. Inner-city poverty has been bandaged when it threatened to become a running sore and infect other parts of the society. This type of policy naturally breeds cynicism among ghetto residents who view such institutions as job-training centers as middle-class tokenism of uncertain duration and limited commitment. The humanist geographers touch on the crux of Federal policy failure when they object to dealing with software issues in sterile dimensions (Tuan 1974, 207–9; Harrington 1963, 10). Their approach rejects statistical studies and the skeletal representation apparent in factorial studies which discount subjective elements verified only in an imprecise and unschooled manner (Entriken 1976, 615; Steiner 1979, 133–4). Such methods of formal analysis are insufficient, since although one can assess the poverty population by measuring its numbers and location (Smith 1973, 77) without knowledge of what it is like to be domiciled in deprived conditions, quantitatively derived programs will have limited success (Gans 1962, 104).

Nevertheless, insensitivity to poverty is not just a failure of public policy, but an integral part of it. Poverty is generally accepted now as a constant in US society, and the proportion of the Federal budget allocated for software programs is a suggestive guide to prevailing public tolerance levels. When poverty conditions threaten the economically advantaged (e.g. by rising crime rates), expenditures are increased. Unfortunately, the stimulant is anarchic behavior.

7.6 CONCLUDING REMARKS

In assessing the impact of these hardware/software policies on urban form, it is important to ask whether the dispersal to suburbia is a negative feature of urbanism and whether any Federal legislation can, or should, alter this movement. As to the first point, antidispersal advocates focus their arguments for decreased decentralization and increased inner-city revitalization on: lost agricultural land, energy wastage, service-extension costs, an accentuation of class/race differences, and increased job-access problems for inner-city residents. Much of this criticism vanishes under close examination. Obviously, agricultural land is valuable. Yet less than 5 per cent of the US mainland is in urban use. More land and larger crop yields are now available as a result of the withdrawal of Federal farming subsidies, improved fertilizers, and farming methods (Berry 1978, 2–8). On the question of fuel wastage, the substitution of smaller for larger cars has allowed dispersal to continue unabated (Altshuler 1979, 385). Access to suburbia already exists, and suburban highways are used below capacity. Since 90 per cent of urban transportation expenditure is controlled by the private sector, it, rather than the Federal government's relatively meager contribution, manipulates urban form (Altshuler 1979, 19). As for higher service costs from extensions, one can offer counter evidence that the social pathologies, such as crime, associated with high-density living, incur even larger service expenditure (Muller 1975, 21–4). To the argument that increased physical distance increases social distance, and that this accentuates class or racial differences, the response is that regardless of liberal rhetoric, the affluent will not reside next to the poor. Evidence that divergences in real income arise from employment and service-access difficulties remains inconclusive. Most dispersal today is occurring in the low-density cities already existing in the South and West. These cities are now no different in terms of per capita income and industrial composition of the work force than cities of the non-South. The experience of simultaneous industrial and postindustrial growth has given rise to urban environments substantially different from those in older cities of the Manufacturing Belt (Clarke 1981, 242–4).

As for the second point, at no Federal, State, or local government level is there consensus concerning optimal urban size or ideal city shape, or that dispersal is a negative feature of urbanism (Altshuler 1979, 374). No level of government supports increased urban density or central-city rehabilitation as a planning goal because of its complexity and enmeshment with social syndromes, especially crime (Gordon 1968). The 1971 law requiring Presidents to comment on urban policy has produced observations which suggest that they favor the promotion of suburbanization by private market forces with only limited Federal involvement (*Congressional Record* 1971, 52503–7). In their allocation of funds, for every dollar spent under the Special Revenue Sharing Program for inner cities, 10 were expended to continue the process of suburbanization (Wingo 1975, 4). Cities grow on the basis of a myriad of individual decisions, increasingly affected by corporate oligarchies with planning institutions the conduit for these decisions, and the Federal government a weak overseer. The pursuit of a national policy for more compact cities in a complex pluralistic society such as the US, predicated on its tradition of privatism, seems both impossible and aimless (Warner 1978, 4).

Certainly, some increased inner-city density, through commercial renovation and revitalization of the central city, is occurring (Lipton 1977, 138), but this is more than offset by policies supportive of dispersal. There is some evidence since the 1970s of private market renovation of selective inner-city neighborhoods in cities with the lowest rates of housing replacement (Cybriwsky 1980, 26). A slowdown in housing construction, higher prices, and changing personal preferences have led to a demand by 'empty nesters' for high-density, space-conserving condominiums and townhouses juxtaposed to downtown retail and recreational amenities. This has led to acrimonious class struggles between low-income residents and newcomers among whites in attractive older neighborhoods. Whether 'gentrification' will constitute a new form of displacement of blacks is yet to be seen (Laska and Spain 1980). This small, albeit selective, revitalization of the central city will not increase substantially, given the demise of the baby-boom generation, and the location of massive concentrations of racial minorities afflicted with seemingly intractable unemployment and social problems (Sternlieb and Hughes 1980, 179).

For its captive residents, the central city is no longer a vibrant source of employment, as deliberately focussed inner-city housing projects have located them tangentially next to jobs they are least capable of filling (Davies and Huff 1972). Much funding is spent on the symptoms of their distress—teenage pregnancy, drug addiction, and crime—but the educational system and environment fail to prepare them for successful entry into an increasingly competitive job market, the cause of their distress (Berry 1980, 27). Cost of living, both real and perceived, is higher in northeastern inner cities whose tainted luster no longer attracts postindustrial enterprises (Berry 1980, 5). It is difficult to conceive that Federal policies or private market forces can do much to redress the emergent welfare belt of the US heartland.

In seeking to comprehend the imprint of Federal policy on urban form, it is essential to understand the basic tenet of the US political system, which is the search for broad support and system stability. Thus the Federal government is an accompanying force in shaping urban form. Politicians approach change with circumspection, and strive to minimize conflict by blurring tensions. Policy is characterized by cautious accretion and is often precipitated only by crisis. The ideal policy adjusts to public desires rather than attempts to control them. The least acceptable policy is one that attempts to constrain prevailing individual preferences and lifestyles (Altshuler 1979, 12).

The American city is a remarkably successful venture in urban living. It illustrates an unprecedented ability of private market forces to accommodate the housing and movement of millions of people at a price acceptable to most (Altshuler 1979, 468). The immense capital investment in the present pattern of land tenure and building stock prohibits any dramatic shift in the form of the US city. The present spatial distribution of the city's urban fabric is the geographic expression of the economic pursuits and lifestyle preferences of the American public. Individual preferences will inexorably continue to define its shape. If any dramatic structural changes are to occur, they will stem from some metaphysical change in individual values.

7.6.1 Urban futures

The pace of innovation in transportation and communication technology has altered the time–distance relationship between cities (Janelle 1969). Distance is less significant today, leading to the progressive convergence of communities and affecting relative locations within the constellation of US cities. This erosion of the constraints to geographic space has also dissolved the agglomeration advantages of cities, making nonmetropolitan living possible.

The traditional view of a city as an entity organized around a central core is antiquated. Briefly, the present US settlement pattern can be characterized as clusters of densely populated metropolitan areas, their intermetropolitan peripheries, and thinly populated rural sectors (Berry and Horton 1970, 29–59). The coalescence of northeastern cities into one dense urban corridor is a regional feature in contrast to the more isolated SMSAs found in other areas. The city now forms a large urban field of varying population densities in which demarcation of the rural–urban fringe is increasingly difficult.

The 1982 Federal antitrust rulings against AT&T and IBM have had more profound implications for urban form than most spatially targeted Federal housing or transportation programs. As a condition of divestiture of regional telephone companies, AT&T can compete with IBM in the emerging 'telecommunication' industry—visuals, computers, information—touted to be the third major transportation revolution in history following those of the rail and auto. No longer inhibited by the publisher's arguments that the firm that owns the telephone wire should not provide the information flowing over it, companies can compete to feed information to terminals in every firm and home. The subsequent repercussions of 'communicating to work' for our perception of time and distance will be reflected in the form of the urban cadaster (Brooker-Gross 1980, 157). The implication is for accelerated metropolitan sprawl and the intensified growth of smaller cities. This revolution recalls the words of H. G. Wells in 1902 following the arrival of the automobile: 'These coming cities will not be, in the old sense, cities at all, they will present a new and entirely different phase of human distribution.' This vision, proven so correct, is not new; Somerville (1848), writing on the coming of the railways, suggested: 'each new subjugator of time and geographic distance, be it steam ... or electricity ... each is a subjugator of enmities and social distances' (p. 182). Given the many giants in the circuit of urban futures, the texts of Wells or the movie *Metropolis* of F. Lang, Germany, 1926, it requires a conviction of visionary proportions to envision the impact of this third major transportation revolution on city structure.

References

AARON, H. (1970) 'Income taxes and housing', *Am. Econ. Rev.* 60 789–806.
—— (1972) *Shelter and subsidies* (Washington, DC: Brookings Instn.).
ACKERMAN, B. A. and HASSLER, W. T. (1982) *Clean coal/dirty air* (New Haven, Conn.: Yale Univ. Press).
ADAMS, J. R. (1981) 'The Sunbelt', *Dixie dateline: the south in an age of change*, Seminar, New Orleans: Tulane University, *Tulanian*, 52 5, 45–49.
ADAMS, J. S. (1976) *Urban policymaking and metropolitan dynamics* (Cambridge, Mass.: Ballinger).
—— (1979) 'A geographical basis for urban public policy', *Prof. Geogr.* 31 2, 135–45.
ADVISORY COMMISSION ON INTER-GOVERNMENTAL RELATIONS (1977) *The Intergovernmental grant system as seen by local, state and federal officials* (Washington, DC).
ALONSO, W. (1970) 'What are new towns for?', *Urb. Stud.* 7 37–55.
ALSOP, J. (1982) *FDR, a century remembrance* (London: Thames & Hudson).
ALTSHULER, A. (1979) *The urban transportation system* (Cambridge, Mass.: MIT Press).
ANDERSON, M. (1964) *The federal bulldozer* (New York: McGraw-Hill).
BAHL, R. (ed.) (1978) *The fiscal outlook for cities: implications of a national urban policy* (Syracuse, NY: Syracuse Univ. Press).
BATCHELOR, E. (1981) *Homosexuality and ethics* (New York: Pilgrim Press).
BAUMOL, W. J. and OATES, W. E. (1975) *The theory of environmental policy* (Englewood Cliffs, NJ: Prentice-Hall).
BERRY, B. J. L. (1973) *The human consequences of urbanisation* (New York: St. Martin's Press).
—— (1980) 'Inner city futures: an American dilemma revisited', *Trans. Inst. Brit. Geogr.* NS 5 1, 1–28.
—— and DAHMANN, D. (1977) 'Population redistribution in the United States in the 1970's', *Pop. and Dev. Rev.* 3 443–71.
—— and HORTON, F. E. (1970) *Geographic perspectives on urban systems* (Englewood Cliffs, NJ: Prentice-Hall).
—— and KASARDA, J. D. (1977) *Contemporary urban ecology* (New York: Macmillan).

BERRY, D. (1978) 'Effects of urbanisation on agricultural activities', *Growth and Change,* 9 2–8.

BOLTON, R. (1980) 'Impacts of defense spending in urban areas', in GLICKMAN (ed.) *The urban impacts of federal policies,* 151–74.

BORCHERT, J. R. (1972) 'America's changing metropolitan regions', *Ann. Ass. Am. Geogr.* 62 352–73.

—— (1978) 'Major control points in American economic geography', *Ann. Ass. Am. Geogr.* 68 214–32.

BRITTAN, S. (1973) *Capitalism and the permissive society* (London: Macmillan).

BROOKER-GROSS, S. R. (1980) 'Usages of communication technology and urban growth', in BRUNN and WHEELER, 145–61.

BRUEGGEMAN, W. D. (16 June 1977) 'Tax reform, tax incentives, and investment returns on rental housing', *U.S. Congress, House, Hearings before Subcommittee on the city, of the Committee on banking, finance and urban affairs,* 95th Congr., 1st Sess., 196–292 (Washington, DC: USGPO).

BRUNN, S. D. and WHEELER, J. O. (eds.) (1980) *The American metropolitan system* (New York: V. H. Winston).

CAMPBELL, A. K. *et al.* (1976) *Urban options* (Columbus, Ohio: Acad. for Contemporary Problems).

CARO, R. (1974) *Robert Moses the power broker* (New York: Alfred Knopf).

CLARK, C. (1940) *The conditions of economic progress* (London: Macmillan).

CLARK, G. L. (1980) 'Urban impact analysis: a new tool for monitoring the geographical effects of Federal policies', *Prof. Geogr.* 32 1, 82–5.

CLARKE, S. B. (1981) 'A political perspective on population change in the South', in POSTON, D. L. and WELLER, R. H. (eds) *The population of the South* (Austin, Tex.: Univ. of Texas Press), 227–68.

COHEN, A. (1974) *Urban ethnicity* (London: Tavistock Press).

COLMAN, W. G. (1975) *Cities, suburbs and states* (New York: Free Press).

Congressional Record (1971) 92nd Congr., 1st Sess., *117* 29, S2503–S2507 (Washington, DC: USGPO).

COUNCIL ON ENVIRONMENTAL POLICY (1979) *Environmental quality 1978. The Ninth Annual Rept.* (Washington, DC: US Council on Environ. Pol.).

CYBRIWSKY, R. A. (1980) 'Revitalisation trends in downtown-areas neighborhoods', in BRUNN and WHEELER, 21–37.

DANIELSON, M. N. (1971) *Metropolitan politics* (Boston, Mass.: Little, Brown).

DARDEN, J. T. (1980) 'Lending practices and policies affecting the American metropolitan system', in BRUNN and WHEELER, 93–111.

DAVIES, C. J. and DAVIES, B. (1975) *The politics of pollution* (Indianapolis: Ind.: Bobbs-Merrill).

DAVIES, P. and NERE, B. (eds) (1981) *Cinema, politics and society in America* (Manchester: Manchester Univ. Press).

DAVIES S. (1972) 'The reverse commuter transit problem in Indianapolis', *Persp. in Geogr.* Vol. 2 (DeKalb, Ill.: Nthn. Illinois Univ. Press), 169–97.

—— and HUFF, D. L. (1972) 'Impact of ghettoization on black employment', *Econ. Geogr.* 48 4, 421–27.

DAVIS, O. A. (1970) 'Economics and urban renewal: market intervention', in CRECINE, J. P. (ed.) *Financing the metropolis.* (Beverly Hills, Cal.: Sage).

DISSELHORST, T. M. (1975) 'Sierra Club v. Ruckelshaus—on a clean day', *Ecol. Law. Q.* 4 730–80.

DORFMAN, N. S. and SNOW, A. (1975) 'Who will pay for pollution control?', *Natl. Tax Journ.* 28 101–15.

DOWNS, A. (1973) *Federal housing subsidies: how are they working?* (Toronto: D. C. Heath).

—— *Urban decline and the future of the American city*, forthcoming (Washington, DC: Brookings Instn.).

ENTRIKIN, J. N. (1976) 'Contemporary humanism in geography', *Ann. Ass. Am. Geogr.* **66** 615–32.

Federal Register (1976) **41** 3280.

—— (1978) **43** 4772.

Federal Reserve Board Statistics 1981–2 (1981) (New York: Salomon Bros.).

FISHER, A. G. B. (1935) *The clash of economic progress* (London: Macmillan).

FOSSETT, W. F. and OSBORN, C. C. (1980) 'Federal grants in large Sunbelt and Frostbelt cities', *Texas Busin. Rev.* **54** 2, 74–9.

FRIEDEN, B. and KAPLAN, M. (1975) *The politics of neglect: urban aid from model cities to revenue sharing* (Cambridge, Mass: MIT Press).

FRIEDMAN, M. (1962) *Capitalism and freedom* (Chicago: Univ. Chicago Press).

—— and FRIEDMAN, R. (1980) *Free to choose: a personal statement* (New York: Secker & Warburg).

GALLE, O. *et al.* (1970) 'Population density and pathology: what are the relations for man?', *Science*, **176** 23–30.

GANS, H. (1962) *The urban villages* (New York: Free Press).

GENETSKI, R. J. and CHIN, Y. D. (1978) *The impact of state and local taxes on economic growth*, Harris Econ. Res. Office Service (Chicago, Ill.: Harris Trust & Savings Bank).

GLICKMAN, N. J. (ed.) (1980) *The urban impacts of Federal policies* (Baltimore, Md.: Johns Hopkins Univ. Press).

GORDON, K. (ed.) (1968) *Agenda for the nation* (Washington, DC: Brookings Instn.).

GOTTMANN, J. (1970) 'Urban centrality and the interweaving of quaternary functions', *Ekistics*, **29** 332–41.

GRAD, F. P. *et al.* (1975) *The automobile and the regulation of its impact on the environment* (Norman, Okla.: Univ. Oklahoma Press).

GRAEBER, W. (1981) *A history of retirement: the meaning and function of an American institution* (New Haven, Conn.: Yale Univ. Press).

GREELEY, A. (1977) *The American Catholic: a social portrait* (New York: Basic Books).

GREER, S. (1973) *The urban view* (New York: Oxford Univ. Press).

HALL, E. K. (1963) 'A system for the notation of proxemic behavior', *Amer. Anthropologist*, **65** 6, 1003.

HALL, P. (1981) *Great planning disasters* (London: Weidenfeld & Nicolson).

HANDLIN, O. (1951) *The uprooted: the epic story of the great migration that made the American people* (New York: Little, Brown).

HANSEN, N. (1981) 'Subnational regional policies in the United States', in HOFFMAN (ed.) *Federalism and regional development*, 41–68.

HARRINGTON, J. (1963) *The other America* (New York: Macmillan).

HART, J. F. (1976) 'Urban encroachment on rural areas', *Geogrl. Rev.* **66** 1–17.

HARVEY, D. (1972) 'Society, the city, and the space economy of urbanism' *Ass. Am. Geogr. Res. Pap. Ser.* **18** 2.

HAYEK, F. (1964) *The road to serfdom* (Chicago, Ill.: Univ. Chicago Press).

—— *et al.* (1972) 'Verdict on rent control' (Inst. Econ. Aff.), *Readings* 7.

HOFFMAN, G. W. (ed.) (1981) *Federalism and regional development* (Austin, Tex.: Univ. Texas Press).

JACOBS, S. C. and ROISTACHER, E. A. (1980) 'The urban impacts of HUD's Urban Development Action Grant Program', in GLICKMAN (ed.) *The urban impacts of Federal policies*, 335–62.

JANELLE, D. G. (1969) 'Spatial reorganisation: a model and concept', *Ann. Ass. Am. Geogr.* **59** 2, 348–64.

JOHNSON, J. H. and BRUNN, S. D. (1980) 'Spatial and behavioral aspects of counterstream migration of blacks to the South', in BRUNN and WHEELER, 59–76.

JOHNSTON, R. J. (1980) The geography of federal spending in the USA, *Res. Stud. Ser.* (New York: Wiley).

JONES, C. O. (1975) *Clean air: the policies and politics of pollution control* (Pittsburgh, Penn.: Univ Pittsburgh Press).

KAIN, J. F. (1978) 'Failure in diagnosis: a critique of Carter's national urban policy', *Policy Note P. 78–2*, Dept. of City and Reg. Plann. (Cambridge, Mass.: Harvard Univ. Press).

—— and PERSKY, J. J. (1968) 'The north's stake in southern rural poverty', *Rural poverty in the United States*, National Advisory Commn. on Rural Poverty (Washington, DC: USGPO).

KERNER, O. (Chairman) (1968) *Report of the National Advisory Commission on Civil Disorders* (Kerner Report) (New York: Bantam Books).

KING, L. J. and GOLLEDGE, R. G. (1978) *Cities, space, and behavior: the elements of urban geography* (Englewood Cliffs, NJ: Prentice-Hall).

KORNBLUM, W. (1974) *Blue collar community* (Chicago, Ill.: Univ. Chicago Press), 138–60.

KRAMER, D. (1974) 'Protecting the urban environment from the federal government', *Urb. Aff. Q.* 9 359–68.

LAIDLER, D. (1969) 'Income tax incentives for owner-occupied housing', in HARBERGER, A. C. and BAILEY, M. J. (eds) *The taxation of income from capital* (Washington, DC: Brookings Instn.), 50–76.

LASKA, S. and SPAIN, D. (eds) (1980) *Back to the city: issues in neighbourhood revitalisation* (New York: Pergamon).

LIPTON, S. G. (1977) 'Evidence of central city revival', *J. of the Am. Inst. Planners*, **43** 136–47.

MANNERS, I. R. and RUDZITIS, G. (1981) 'Federal air quality legislation: implications for land use', in HOFFMAN (ed.) *Federalism and regional development*, 479–527.

MASSEY, D. S. (1979) 'Residential segregation of Spanish Americans in United States urban areas', *Demography*, **16** 553–63.

MEINIG, D. W. (1971) 'Environmental appreciation: localities as a humane art', *West. Human. rev.* **25** 1 Winter, 1–11.

MERCER, J. and HULTQUIST, J. (1976) 'National progress toward housing and urban renewal goals', in ADAMS (ed.) *Urban policymaking and metropolitan dynamics*, 101–62.

MEYER, J. D., KAIN, J. F. and WOHL, M. (1966) *The urban transportation problem* (Cambridge, Mass.: Harvard Univ. Press).

MILGRAM, S. (1970) 'The experience of living in cities: a psychological analysis', *Science*, **167** 1461–68.

MISHAN, E. J. (1980) *Times Literary Supplement*, 5 Sept., 965–66.

MORRIS, R. S. (1978) *Bumrap on American cities* (Englewood Cliffs, NJ: Prentice-Hall).

MOYNIHAN, D. P. (1965) 'Employment, income, and the ordeal of the Negro family', *Daedalus, J. Acad. Arts and Sciences*, **94** 4, 758–68.

MULLER, T. (1975A) *Growing and declining urban areas: a fiscal comparison* (Washington, DC: Urban Press).

—— (1975B) 'The declining and growing metropolis—a fiscal comparison', in STERNLIEB, G. H. and HUGHES, G. and J. W. (eds) *Post-industrial America: metropolitan decline and inter-regional job shifts* (New Brunswick, NJ: Rutgers, Univ. New Jersey), 197–220.

NELSON, K. P. (1979) *Recent suburbanisation of blacks: how much, who, and where?*

(Washington, DC: Office of Policy Devel. and Res., US Dept. Housing and Urban Development).

NELSON, W. D. (1981) *On justifying democracy* (New York: Routledge & Kegan Paul).

NETZER, D. (1968) *Impact of the property tax: its economic implications for urban problems* (Washington, DC: USGPO).

New York Times (1977) 'Economic gains in South linked to under use of its taxing potential', 11 March.

PALM, R. (1981) *The geography of American cities* (New York: Oxford Univ. Press).

PECHMAN, J. A. (1977) *The 1978 budget: setting national priorities* (Washington, DC: Brookings Instn.).

PERRY, D. C. and WATKINS, A. J. (eds) (1977) *The rise of the Sunbelt cities* (Beverly Hills, Cal.: Sage).

PESKIN, H. M. (1978) 'Environmental policy and the distribution of benefits and costs', in PORTNEY, P. R. (ed.) *Current issues in US Environmental Policy* (Baltimore, Md.: Johns Hopkins Univ. Press), 145–63.

PETERSON, G. E. (16 June, 1977) 'Federal tax policy and urban development', *US Congress, House, Hearings before Subcommittee on the City of the Committee of Banking, Finance and Urban Affairs*, 95th Congr. 1st Sess., 10–34 (Washington, DC: USGPO).

—— and MULLER, T. (1978) 'The regional impact of federal tax spending policies', paper presented at the conference 'A national policy toward regional change' (Austin: LBJ School of Pub. Aff., Univ. Texas) September 1978.

PIKARSKY, M. and CHRISTENSEN, D. (1976) *Urban transportation policy and management* (Lexington, Mass.: D. C. Heath).

RASMUSSEN, D. W. (1980) 'The urban impacts of the section 8 Existing Housing Assistance Program', in GLICKMAN, N. J. (ed.) *The urban impacts of federal policies* (Baltimore, Md.: Johns Hopkins Univ. Press).

REAGAN, M. D. and SANZONE, J. G. (1981) *The New Federalism*, 2nd edn. (New York: Oxford Univ. Press).

SALKMAN, J. (1979) 'Housing discrimination: policy research, methods, and results', *Ann. Ass. of the Am. Aca. of Pol. and Soc. Sci.*, 441, 186–96.

SARGENT, C. S. (1976) 'Land speculation and urban morphology', in ADAMS (ed.) *Urban policymaking and metropolitan dynamics*, 21–58.

SINCLAIR, U. (1906) *The jungle* (New York, Doubleday, Page).

SINGLEMAN, J. (1981) 'Southern industrialisation', in BOSTON, D. L. and WELLER R. H. (eds) *The population of the South* (Austin: Univ. Texas Press), 175–98.

SLATER, P. (1970) *The pursuit of loneliness* (Boston: Beacon Press).

SMERK, G. M. (1974) *Urban mass transportation: a dozen years of Federal policy* (Bloomington, Ind.: Indiana Univ. Press).

SMITH, D. M. (1973) *The geography of social well-being* (New York: McGraw-Hill).

—— (1974) *Human geography: a welfare approach* (London: Arnold).

SOMERVILLE, A. (1848) *Autobiography of a working man* (London: C. Gilpin).

SOMMER, R. and ROSS, H. F. (1967) 'Sociofugal space', *An. J. of Soc.* 72 654.

SORENSEN, A. *et al.* (1975) 'Indexes of racial residential segregation for 109 cities in the United States, 1940 to 1970', *Soc. Focus*, 8 125–42.

STEGMAN, M. (1970) 'The myth of the Slum-land', *Am. Inst. Architects J.* 53 45–9.

STEINER, G. (1979) *Martin Heidegger* (New York: Viking Press).

STERNLIEB, G. and BURCHELL, R. W. (1973) *Residential abandonment: the tenement slum landlord* (New Brunswick, NJ: Rutgers, St. Univ. New Jersey Press).

——, ——, HUGHES, J. W. and JAMES, F. J. (1982) 'Housing abandonment in the urban core', in BOURNE, L. E. (ed.) *Internal structure of the city* (New York: Oxford

Univ. Press), 472–90.
—— and HUGHES, J. W. (1980) 'The "Two-cities" phenomenon', in STERNLIEB and HUGHES, *America's housing*, 177–85.
—— and —— *et al.* (1980) *America's housing* (New Brunswick, NJ: Rutgers, St. Univ. New Jersey Press).
——, ROISTACHER, E. A. and HUGHES, J. W. (1976) *Tax subsidies and housing investment: a fiscal impact analysis* (New Brunswick, NJ: Center for Urb. Pol. Res., Rutgers University).
STRUYK, R. J. (1976) *Urban homeownership: the economic determinants* (Lexington, Mass.: D. C. Heath).
SUNDQUIST, J. (1972) 'The problem of coordination in a changing federalism', in FOX, D. (ed.) *The new urban politics* (Pacific Palisades, Cal.: Goodyear).
TAEUBER, K. E. (1979) 'Housing, schools, and incremental segregation effects', *Ann. Am. Acad. Pol. and Soc. Sci.* **441** 87–96.
THERNSTROM, S. (ed.) (1981) *Harvard encyclopedia of American ethnic groups* (Cambridge, Mass.: Harvard Univ. Press).
THOMAS, M. D. and LE HERON, R. B. (1975) 'Perspectives on technology and change and the process of diffusion in the manufacturing sector', *Econ. Geogr.* **51** 231–57.
TOLLEY, G. amd DIAMOND, D. B. (16 June, 1977) 'Homeownership, rental housing and tax incentives', *US Congress hearings before Subcommittee on the City of the Committee on Banking, Finance and Urban Affairs*, 95th Congr., 1st Sess., 114–95.
TUAN, YI-FU (1974) *A study of environmental perceptions, attitudes, and values* (Englewood Cliffs, NJ: Prentice-Hall).
—— (1979) *Landscapes of fear* (New York: Pantheon Books).
US BUREAU OF CENSUS (1981) *Preliminary population reports* (Washington, DC: USGPO).
US CONGRESS, HOUSE, Committee on Banking, Currency and Housing (1976) *The rebirth of the American city, hearings*, 94th Congr. 2nd Sess. Part 1 (Washington, DC: USGPO).
——, Committee on Banking, Finance and Urban Affairs (16 June, 1977) *Federal tax policy and urban development*, Hearings before the Subcommittee on the City, 95th Congr., 1st Sess. (Washington, DC: USGPO).
—— Committee on Ways and Means (1976) *Summary of the conference agreement on the Tax Reform Act of 1976* (Washington, DC: USGPO).
US CONGRESS, JOINT COMMITTEE ON TAXATION (1978) *Summary of the President's 1978 tax reduction and reform proposals* (Washington, DC: USGPO).
US DEPT. HEALTH, EDUCATION AND WELFARE (1976) *Poverty studies task force* (Washington, DC: USGPO).
US DEPT. HOUSING AND URBAN DEVELOPMENT (1978) *A new partnership to conserve America's communities* (Washington, DC: USGPO).
US NEWS & WORLD REPORT (February 1982), Basic data: Advisory Committee on Intergovernmental Relations, **28**.
US OFFICE OF EDUCATION (1966) *Equality of educational opportunity*, The Coleman Report (Washington, DC: USGPO), chs. 1–3.
VANCE, J. E. (1977) *This scene of man: the role and structure of the city in the geography of western civilisation* (New York: Harper's College Press).
VAN VALEY, T. L. *et al.* (1977) 'Trends in residential segregation: 1960–1970' *Am. J. of Soc.* **82** 826–44.
VAUGHAN, R. J. (April 1977) *The urban impacts of federal policies:* vol. 2, *Economic development* (Washington, DC: Co. State Planning Agencies).
VERNEZ, G. (1980) 'Overview of the spatial dimensions of the Federal budget', in GLICKMAN (ed.) *The urban impacts of federal policies*, 67–102.

——, VAUGHAN, R. J. and YIN, R. K. (April 1979) *Federal activities in urban economic development* (Santa Monica, Cal.: Rand Corpn.)

WALKER, R. and STORPER, M. (1978) 'Erosion of the Clean Air Act of 1970: a study in the failure of government regulation and planning', *Boston Coll. Environmental Aff. Rev.*

WARD, D. (1971) *Cities and immigrants: a geography of change in the nineteenth century* (New York: Oxford Univ. Press).

WARNER, S. B., Jr. (1978) *Streetcar suburbs: the process of growth in Boston, 1870–1900*, 2nd edn. (Cambridge, Mass.: Harvard Univ. Press).

WASSER, R. L. (1971) 'The sociology of knowledge and the problems of the inner city', *Soc. Sci. Q.* **52** 3, 474.

WATSON, J. W. (1979) *Social geography of the United States* (New York: Longmans).

WEBBER, M. M. (1976) 'The BART experience—what have we learned?', *The Public interest*, Fall, 78–108.

WEBER, M. (1976) *The Protestant ethic and the spirit of capitalism*, trans. Talcott Parsons, 2nd. edn. (London: Allen & Unwin).

WEICHER, J. (1972) *Urban renewal: national program for local problems* (Washington, DC: American Enterprise for Pub. Pol. Res.).

WHITE, E. (1980) *States of desire: travels in gay America* (New York: A. Deutsch).

WHITE, M. J. and WHITE, L. J. (1977) 'The tax subsidy to owner-occupied housing: who benefits?' *J. Public Econ.* **3** 111–26.

WILLIAMS, R. (1973) *The country and the city* (Cambridge: Cambridge Univ. Press).

WINGO, L. (1975) 'Issues in a national urban development strategy for the United States', *Urb. Stud.* **9** 1, 3–28.

WOLPERT, J. *et al.* (1972) 'Metropolitan neighborhoods: participation and conflict over change', Washington, DC: *Am. Assn. of Geogr. Resource Pap.*, Ser. 16.

YEATES, M. and GARNER, B. (1980) *The North American city*, 3rd edn. (San Francisco, Cal.: Harper & Row).

ZELINSKY, W. (1977) 'The Pennsylvania town: an overdue geographical account', *Geogrl. Rev.* **67** 127–47.

8. In Conclusion

In their critique of a selection of public policies with strong spatial implications the authors have shared a common interest in and concern for the process of policy-making. The principal intention has been to increase the understanding and interpretation of policies, in the belief that geographers, among other social scientists, have a distinctive contribution to make to that task. In the absence of widespread teaching of applied geography in the USA geographers need first to be trained in its principles before being introduced to the policy process. Policy-makers and the public in their turn need to be persuaded that a geographical contribution, among others, can be both helpful and worthwhile.

Though sharing in a common purpose, the structure and thrust of each chapter have been distinctive and varied. The study of regional and area development policies (ch. 2) showed a consistent lack of firm commitment to differential spatial aid, by any level of government at any time in the US. The fragmentary, piecemeal, incremental outcome, in spite of some occasionally impressive institutions, was as much a tribute to American values and political culture, in particular, as it was perhaps an inevitable reflection of the innate and variegated geography of the US national space-economy. Policies related to social problems (ch. 3) more directly concerned people, focussing on deprived groups and the variable and changing delivery of social services throughout American society. A problem-oriented study of social processes highlighted a range of problems, setting these against the impact of legislation designed to promote and diffuse a modicum of welfare to needy, often ethnic minority, groups. The second-tier or State governments had long had an influential role in this, but in spite of a diversity of Federal interventions much remains to be done. Under the Reagan administration further withdrawal by the Federal government from the welfare arena is under way.

Of all the chapters, that on environmental issues (ch. 4) most directly addressed specific policies, in a range of legacies from Federal land-use legislation. Particular Federal Acts were analyzed and their impact on States and communities assessed. Legal aspects of the policy process were touched in and there was a feel for a turbulent conflict of interest in the political arena. Public pressure groups and the environmental lobbies confronted powerful corporate interests and their political backers, with the Federal government an uncertain referee holding the ring.

Chapter 5, on energy problems and policies, was concerned with perhaps the most serious and complex of all the policy problems under review. Energy questions have always been a sensitive political issue in the US, the source of many of the 'religious wars in American politics'. Widespread and deep-seated tensions plague actors in the energy game, in which powerful and politically influential corporations in energy production have traditionally limited competition and organized the market. Governments have long been involved in the energy arena, in defense of the public interest, but the complexities of intervention in matters such as pricing have often defeated their very purpose. Foreign influence, direct and indirect, is an inescapable and little-controllable force conditioning and constraining US government efforts in the energy field. In all this, the public has all too often been the residual loser.

Of all American activities manufacturing has been the greatest beneficiary of the free enterprise or market system. Transformation of the industrial economy, even partial deindustrialization of the US in recent times (ch. 6), led to serious structural and spatial problems with a record 11 million, or 10 per cent of the workforce unemployed in the Fall of 1982. Neither taxation nor any direct form of US government policy on industry has even had more than a minimal effect, and indeed, there have been altogether few such policies in any case. Government procurement policies have not, on balance, had unfair regional impacts, though the tracing of indirect implications of policies is a largely untapped field, one of the major roles for geographers in the 1980s. The process and impact of industrial innovation and the spatial significance of development finance are two further themes for priority research commitment.

Federal policies for the American city (ch. 7) have, perhaps, been more numerous than for any other purpose, but as problems became more severe and policies proliferated their impact somewhat paradoxically diminished. The two-nation concept in the city, the suburban affluent and the inner-city poor and deprived, underlines a basic ambivalence in Federal policies. The trend to urban dispersal and suburbanization is probably the most powerful social force in American lifestyle preferences. Though the social problems of deprivation and decay lie in the inner city, the net effect of Federal intervention in the city, in either hardware or software policies, has granted greater benefits to the suburbs. In any case the Federal government has characteristically acted as a 'weak overseer' of the life and death of the American city, accommodating to change, belatedly, incrementally, and usually inadequately.

8.2 WHAT HAS POLICY BEEN ABOUT?

To define policy other than in the categorical legislative terms of particular Acts is to give a false identity to what, by its very nature is ambiguous, complex, and controversial. The central problems underlying the policies considered in preceding chapters are inequality and uneven, at times unfair, allocation of resources or prospects among human groups or across space. The questioning then became: what should, should not, can or cannot be done to improve the situation, by whom, where, and for whom, at what time, and by what means?

Around such questions are formulated organizational choices among alternatives, with the accompanying design, implementation, and measurement of the effects of policy. The formal structure of the policy process (Fig. 1.1) proved to be a rather imperfect guide to the realities of the policy arena once particular legislation was examined. Almost all policies were seen to be the compromise outcome of countervailing forces, the end-product of competing ideas and values (Nagel 1975). In most cases the competition lay between those advocating safe, conservative, minimal incremental change and those intending radical transformations. Since all policy-making takes place in a political climate, any critique must first relate to overall views on society, as well as being based upon what is politically feasible or even in the ultimate ethical. One extreme view (Castells 1980; Harvey 1982) sees the present crisis as an inevitable outcome of the late stage of capitalism in the global economy. 'The powerful mechanisms of social control and economic regulation prevent major transformations of the capitalist system as long as political factors remain unmodified' (Castells 1980). The unacceptable purpose of State intervention under capitalism is to 'facilitate the accumulation of capital and legitimise the social order' (p. 175) in a situation in which the dynamics of inequality are less a function of internal arrangements than 'the result of transforming the internal composition of the GNP and general trends of the system' (p. 199).

Even if such a diagnosis of current American ills is acceptable, any changes will have to be moderated through the existing political system, and for the foreseeable future. In the US policy arena (ch. 1) processes were seen to be so fragmented, complex, incremental, and *ad hoc* that tracing the course of political change or evaluating its impacts proved exceptionally elusive. As Berry (1978, 205) aptly put it, 'Policy-making [in the US] must contend with differing and changing goals of competing interest groups in a society that values democratic pluralism as an end in itself.'

Decentralized, cooperative federalism provided the framework in which there has always been broad support for system stability (ch. 7, pp. 302–3). Neither individual preferences nor lifestyles should be constrained in a society strong in local initiatives and community participation, flexible in its adaptation to change, and totally disinclined either to stimulate or to restrain free enterprise within a market economy. In many of the policies considered a 'policy triangle' proved influential, with middle-level bureaucrats, selected members of the Congress, and powerful outside interests the moving forces (Edwards and Sharkansky 1978). Most characteristically, government proved weak in policy implementation under challenge, political stances in the ultimate triumphed over technocratic advice, and variegated economy, society, and policy of the US diffused any attempts at uniformity of policy prescription or implementation.

8.3 THE SOCIAL SCIENCE CONTRIBUTION

Chapter 1 (pp. 6–15) outlined a general critique of social science involvements in policy-studies. The conflicting purposes, structures, peer-group evaluation, and reward systems in the political arena and in social science were emphasized as a constraint on more meaningful cooperation. Such a limitation has features of permanency, for 'the social scientist cannot be expected to provide technical solutions to political dilemmas, nor can some unique or clever policy-managing research generate such a "social science fix"" (Zysman 1980, 158). Trust in gathering information, good judgment in selecting information, and sufficient access to bring influence to bear on policy-making will enhance the prospects of social science successs (Leach and Stewart 1982, 119), but in the light of past experience and the skeptical political climate, expectations on both sides are likely to remain modest.

Social science analysis 'can help further operational efficiency, resource allocation (including the geographical input of "where"), program evaluation and planning alternatives' (Quade 1975), provided that the questions are asked by policy-makers in a form to which social scientists can reasonably respond. It remains true that any resultant policy adjustments will be small and at the margin, and that past conditions will continue to be a major restraint on possible change. However, even marginal adjustments can be signficant and can make a great difference in outcomes (Quade 1975, 242). Furthermore, the momentum of policies may continue even after the legislation lapses, giving rise to an important research field on longer-term impacts as a result.

Political science   By contrast with geographers, political scientists have made more progress in the policy-studies arena (Dye 1981). The complexity of reality is ordered through the formulation, testing, and application of model frameworks, though no single model is ever adequate. In theory, the great divide between rational models for policy-making and incremental models for policy-implementing holds good, but the verdict of authors in this book is that incremental, even indirect policies have had the greatest effect. The source of power in the policy process is a prime focus in research, using group or elite theories and institutional frameworks for the study of political activity. Policy analysis is systems-based, using techniques such as linear programming on queuing theory, or game theory in competitive–conflictual situations. All too often values are allocated to only segments of a problem.

Geography   Opportunities for geographers in the policy field are strengthened by two recent trends, even though 'geographic distribution of national growth should not be determined through a centralised policy process' (White House Conf. 1978). First, there has been a shift from concern with the causes of public policy to what public policy causes, to which geographers might add 'and where'? Secondly, there is wider recognition that there are 'spatial effects as governments and major corporations attempt to adjust to economic problems . . . social science failed to anticipate these shifts and their institutional and political aspects' (Clavel *et al.* 1980, 13). The opportunity is thus clearly open for geographers, primarily concerned with spatial considerations, though necessarily aware that space, though important and neglected, may continue to be a decision variable of limited significance.

In chapter 5 (p. 214) the geographical task in policy analysis is seen as the study of 'the interaction between economic structure, the policy-making process and the country's regional (spatial) fabric'. This broad but focussed definition of man–environment relationships sets the terms of reference for the application of geographical skills. Within those bundles of skills both general and specialist attributes are important and need to be used in combination.

Generalist skills relate to seeing problems 'in the round', using predominantly qualitative data to analyse and synthesize from the complex reality which is geographically differentiated space (Berry 1980). Prime focus is upon distributional effects, though these palpably are not only geographical in character (Leach and Stewart 1982, 50). Generalist attributes are breadth of coverage, connectivity, and flexibility across space and time, in a multidimensional study of man–environment relationships.

Analysis of distributional effects differentiates: the unique from the general, the basis for either selective or comprehensive policies; nationwide uniformity from more localized policy initiatives or responses; the resources base, transactional flows, and trends of spatial change and interaction. The interrelationship of human geography and politics 'in the round' as in general decision theory, relates particularly to 'problem formulation, the building of model frameworks and preference evaluations' (Quade 1975, 184). The most appropriate models to interpret and simplify complex spatial realities are geometrical, ecological, or regional in character.

Specialist inputs by geographers to the policy process are far more characteristic at the survey and analysis stages. The present study does not examine the degree of success or the shortcomings of past case studies by geographers. Some are mentioned under the references for each chapter. Other, more general assessments are made in Coppock and Sewell (1976) and more specifically for the US by Frazier (1982). The specialist geographical skills are drawn from the relevant branches of the discipline, with theories, methodologies, and techniques appropriate to more specific problems. The data base is characteristically quantitative and the treatment often statistical. There is also general convergence of practice with that of other social sciences. Given the diversity today in geographical perspectives, from the technocratic positivist to the experiential interpretation by humanists or the ideology of Marxists, there is an equally variegated spectrum of specialist applications to the study of environment, society, economy, and polity.

8.4 IMPLICATIONS FOR GEOGRAPHICAL TRAINING

The half-truth that all geographical learning is potentially capable of application holds good, but with additional purposeful training this could be more clearly and widely evident. The essentials of an applied approach include preparation for meeting the operational needs of a diversity of clients, focussing on problem orientation in which the problem is often defined by others. Deliberate concern for alternative futures and ability to assess the impact of alternative courses of action are explicit and a convergent track with other social sciences is imperative. Training in applied geography must depart from a sound overall preparation in general geography including the human, physical, regional, and practical aspects of the subject. The *additional* preparation should be based upon:

(i) Orientation towards third-party problem solving, through case-study analysis based on policy–relevant experience, at different spatial scale-levels. Evidence should cover the resources, environmental, social, urban, and regional fields.

(ii) Systematic study of the policy process, including methodology and techniques of policy studies, political organization, planning, and management studies.

(iii) Regional science, theory, methodology, and techniques; the use of simulation and gaming methods to model and test policy-relevant situations and the space-economy.

In this manner the training of geographers might become more directly relevant to the needs of policy-makers and decision-takers (House 1973). The urgent problems of the times are many and deep-seated: unemployment and the need to escape from recession (ch. 1); the issues of individual human rights and social justice for places (ch. 2) as well as human groups (ch. 3); environmental integrity (ch. 4); national energy security and the nuclear dilemma (ch. 5); reindustrialization (ch. 6); and the life and death of the American city (ch. 7). On all these problems a commentary and critique has been offered here. The purpose of the book then, has been to persuade geographers to think more coherently and relevantly about policy-making to meet the needs of environment, society, economy, and polity. In so doing there remains implicit the kind of contribution that applied geography might offer to the debate on the utility of social science in the service of government or, no less importantly, that of the governed.

References

BERRY, B. J. L. (1978) 'Notes on an expedition to Planland' in BURCHELL, R. W. and STERNLIEB, G. (eds) *Planning theory in the 1980s* (New Brunswick, NJ: Center for Urb. Pol. Res.), 201–8.
—— (1980) 'Creating future geographies', *Ann. Ass. Am. Geogr.* 70 449–58.
CASTELLS, M. (1980) *The economic crisis and American society* (Oxford: Basil Blackwell).
CLAVEL, P., FORESTER, J. and GOLDSMITH, W. W. (1980) *Urban and regional planning in an age of austerity* (New York: Pergamon).
COPPOCK, J. T. and SEWELL, W. R. D. (eds) (1976) *Spatial dimensions in public policy* (Oxford: Pergamon).
DYE, T. R. (1981) *Understanding public policy* (Englewood Cliffs, NJ: Prentice-Hall).
EDWARDS, G. C. III and SHARKANSKY, I. (1978) *The policy predicament* (San Francisco, Cal.: Freeman).
FRAZIER, J. W. (ed.) (1982) *Applied geography: selected perspectives* (Englewood Cliffs, NJ: Prentice-Hall).
HARVEY, D. (1982) *The limits to capital* (Oxford: Basil Blackwell).
HOUSE, J. W. (1973) 'Geographers, decision-takers and policy-makers', ch. 8 in CHISHOLM, M. D. I. and RODGERS, H. B. (eds) *Studies in human geography* (London: Heinemann), 272–305.
LEACH, S. and STEWART, J. (1982) *Approaches in public policy* (London: Allen & Unwin).
NAGEL, S. (1975) *Policy studies in America and elsewhere* (Lexington, Mass.: D. C. Heath).
QUADE, E. S. (1975) *Analysis for public decisions* (New York: American Elsevier).
WHITE HOUSE CONFERENCE (1978) *Growth and balance: the States' view* (Washington, DC).
ZYSMAN, J. (1980) 'Research, politics and policy: regional planning in America', ch. 4 in OECD *The utilisation of the social sciences in policy-making in the USA* (Paris: OECD), 121–58.

INDEX

ital. refers to Figures in the text